KARL MARX:
SOCIALISM AS SECULAR THEOLOGY
A Philosophic Study

KARL MARX:
SOCIALISM AS SECULAR THEOLOGY
A Philosophic Study

by
Catherine Riegger Harris, Ph.D.

WARREN H. GREEN, INC.
St. Louis, Missouri, U.S.A.

Published by

WARREN H. GREEN, INC.
8356 Olive Boulevard
St. Louis, Missouri 63132, U.S.A.

ISBN No. 0-87527-469-2

Printed in the United States of America

Introduction

As a socialist, and as a sociologist, I have been concerned with major problems included in Marx's theory of socialism and of history. It has seemed to me that the nature of these problems could be clarified if his system were to be approached as a secular theology. I have proceeded here along these lines. The critical interpretation which follows reflects my interest in religion and philosophy and in the history of religion. I regard Marx's socialist world view as an important development within that history. As such, it is interesting and valuable in its own right. It merits and repays careful attention.

For the past several decades, a number of theologians and social philosophers have called attention to the "prophetic" aspects of original Marxism. James Luther Adams, in an essay on "Socialist Humanism and Religion," has expressed a widely held view when he states that ". . . the similarities and dissimilarities between Christianity and Marxism have been given cryptic formulation in the familiar assertion that Marxism is a Christian heresy . . . Marx himself promoted a humanism that had some of its roots in previous Judeo-Christian outlooks" (1). For the most part, however, neo-Marxists and other commentators on Marx's systematic theory have minimized or disregarded its theological content, taking him at his own evaluation, as a post-religious thinker.

The validity of the word "theology" as applied to Marx is open to question. In the definition of the word I am adopting here, philosophical doctrines are theological when they relate humanity and society to a cosmic order thought to have a morally significant connection with human life. It can be demonstrated, from textual evidence, that Marx's philosophy comes within this definition.

Marx believed that he had discarded metaphysics, and that he had successfully inverted Hegel's philosophy, so as to exclude the objectionable mystifying elements. Yet his own world view contains a number of obscure symbolic constructions. It incorporates premises and ways of thinking and perceiving that go considerably beyond the limits of "common sense."

1. Essay written in 1967, republished in *On Being Human Religiously.* Selected essays by Adams on religion and society, Beacon Press, Boston, 1976.

Marx had a confidence in the future that could not have been derived from historical "facts." It must be remembered, however, that his socialism was culturally linked to other forms of progress philosophy which had risen to prominence in the eighteenth century. The optimistic outlook of progress philosophy has persisted well into our own twentieth century. It has included the belief that Western and world civilization would continue to advance indefinitely, with no end in sight. Such a secular faith is not so easy to come by today.

Marx did, in fact, forecast increasing misery and a deteriorating global situation, which capitalist society would be unable to halt or to reverse. But the fate of humanity was not in doubt. Cosmic resources of time, space and nature guaranteed the security of the future. The victory of socialism over capitalism was said to be historically inevitable, although the process of struggle and of change might be a prolonged one. Socialism would establish society and human life on a new and higher foundation, putting an end to the irrationalism, the conflicts, and the forms of anarchy and of evil which characterized the society of the present.

Marx's inevitability thesis includes hopes that cannot be ruled out as absurd. The peoples of the world might become united, eventually, into a peaceful, cooperative world community, bound together by a spirit of equality and brotherhood. This was an essential part of Marx's vision. It is obvious, however, that such an outcome cannot be proclaimed as certain, unless it be on explicitly theological grounds convincing only to those who share in a particular belief system.

Marx's tie to Hegel, underlined by Marx himself, has been widely recognized. His relation to Kant was also important. Kant, as a philosopher of progress, had been especially concerned about the problem of war. He doubted that political humanity, in its presently immature state of moral development, possessed the power, i.e., the necessary rational will and desire, to establish a peaceful world order.

Kant maintained an optimistic faith in the ultimate outcome by discounting, theologically, the negative aspects of the political present. He suggested the possibility that history was being guided, in unknown ways, by an imminent (and transcendent) Providential power. God, as an unknowable cosmic reality operating through nature, might be ensuring the eventual fulfillment of humanity's higher rational and moral potentialities.

Kant turned back toward the teleological philosophy of Aristotle. Thomas Aquinas, in the thirteenth century, had adapted Aristotle's cosmology and nature philosophy so as to provide a philosophical support for Church doctrines. In the age of modern science, Kant, starting from a Protestant background, thought that Aristotle's teleological nature philosophy, when applied to human "natural history," might provide a supra-scientific but philosophically defensible support for his own religious and moral hopes.

Hegel had followed with a post-Kantian teleology of history. He linked humanity – an immortal species – to an historical realizing process which was supported by a cosmic abstract mind, existing as Idea, outside of physical space and nature, but working through nature. Marx eliminated the Idea in his post-Hegelian philosophy, but he retained the dialectical core of Hegel's cosmic security system. History, as he saw it, was ordered according to dialectical, organic laws operating above the level of contingency. Contingent events might impede the advance toward socialism, but it could not be halted.

Marx tried as far as possible to represent history as a field completely open to rational scientific understanding. Human history was a part of natural history. A science of history was, therefore, a form of natural science. In going beyond Hegel, he believed that he was also going beyond metaphysics. But in spite of what he thought about his own work, no form of "materialism," and no coherent, intellectually impressive interpretation of history, is more conspicuously metaphysical than that which Marx developed as the underpinning of his own philosophy of nature, society, and man. He superimposed a framework of his own upon the field of history, in such a way that he seemed to be perceiving directly, as through a clear glass, the form of the future that was taking shape in the time of the present.

Capitalism, in Marx's view, was organically linked to the future. The conditions for the emergence of a higher form of society were being created in the capitalist economy and society. For Marx, the society that was coming-to-be was more fully *actual,* more fully imbued with life, than the transitional capitalist form. He perceived the future as immanent, and as evident, in the reality of the present.

Marx incorporated two ideal-moral concepts of Kant into his philosophy of socialism:

1. Kant's belief that the destiny of humanity on earth could not be fulfilled until civilization had eliminated the practice and the moral evils of international warfare. Marx, however, focussed primarily on the class war between capital and labor. The socialist movement was, by definition, an international, world-unifying movement.

2. Kant's interpersonal "kingdom of ends" morality. Kant had said that all persons ought to be treated by others with the respect due to them as spiritually equal members of the human species. They should also show this respect to others. This categorical imperative was "admittedly an ideal." Kant could suggest no ways in which it could become universal practice. Marx expected that a "kingdom of ends" condition could be realized, effortlessly and naturally, in a socially harmonious way of life after the society of capitalism, and the period of class struggle, had been left behind.

Marx regarded the socialist transformation of society as a morally redemptive process, affecting society as a whole, and individuals as part of society. The proletarians of modern industry, uniting against capital in heroic struggles, constituted the indispensable human, social force required to overcome morally intolerable conditions of the present. They were the bearers of a world-redemptive and world-emancipating historical mission.

He insisted that his concept of socialism was not utopian, i.e., that he was not expecting or demanding the impossible. Under socialism, individuals would be freed from forms of oppression and enslavement that were not only objective and institutional, but also subjective and psychological. Nevertheless, he was taking account of certain "natural limitations of the human will" which could never be overcome. The nature-given limitations of humanity were to be offset, in post-capitalist time, by the acquisition of a degree and kind of "mastery over nature" that could not be forthcoming under capitalism.

Marx made considerable use of the work of non-Germanic thinkers. His relation to Hobbes is being discussed at some length in this study. Hobbes had said that a condition of "scarcity" was the ultimate cause of the "war of all against all." Marx expected that communism would be the means of abolishing scarcity and its attendant evils. Through working class victory, humanity would be able to progress beyond the present condition of universal social and economic competition, finally achieving a universal peace that would apply equally to relations within each separate nation, and to relations among the nations. Hobbes had said that such a condition could not be established *within* history, but only at the end of history, at the time of the Second Coming of Christ. In Marx's philosophy, the successful completion of the proletarian mission serves as an equivalent of the Christian *parousia.* It was not history, however, but only "pre-history," which was to come to an end.

Scarcity, as conceived by Hobbes and by Marx, was not merely economic and material, but also supra-material, the symptom of a rational and moral deficiency. Scarcity in socialist society would be overcome through social production activities which would convert external nature into an inexhaustible resource for humanity. This could come about only when production was managed according to norms of socialist rationality and socialist morality. Capitalism, for the sake of short run gain, was undermining the resources of nature on which humanity must forever depend. Under socialism, these resources would be preserved and enriched in the process of being put to human use. Material poverty would be eliminated, but at the same time the resources required for the use of future generations would be conserved and expanded.

The limitations of terrestrial space did not enter into Marx's highly abstract, cosmological projection of a future socialist economy. Earth population could apparently increase indefinitely, without running into material resource limitations. The need of people for physical living space was left out of account. He expected that an unlimited process of material expansion would not only be possible, but also inevitable. The social necessity of perpetual economic development, and especially of unceasing technological innovation, was built into his dialectical theory. His secular theology is integrally related to his concept of future social necessity as well as to other aspects of his moral and political outlook which are discussed in the chapters which follow.

Marx's earlier socialist writings contain the primary philosophical foundation of his theory. Nevertheless, his outlook on history and society underwent further development. In his later works his perspectives broadened, and he introduced some important modifications. I am taking account of these changes. I am also referring to works which date from the pre-socialist period of Marx's career. These shed light on the later system he constructed.

Marx's thought is often difficult and complex. He sometimes loads several major propositions into a single paragraph. Certain key passages have to be discussed in more than one context. In most of the later chapters, the presentation is based on the exposition given in preceding chapters. I have tried, as far as possible, to support my interpretation of Marx by the evidence of his writings, i.e., by quoting from his various texts.

I am greatly indebted to Thelma Z. Lavine, Professor of Philosophy at George Mason University, for her unfailing help and encouragement. I also thank my son Stephen E. Harris for reading certain portions of the manuscript, and for his useful advice.

Contents

KARL MARX:
SOCIALISM AS SECULAR THEOLOGY
A Philosophic Study

1

From Christianity To Communism

This chapter centers on the complicated relation of Marx's socialism to Christianity. It includes a good deal of material that seems to have little to do with Christianity as such, and a great deal to do with Marx's philosophy. His socialism included a philosophy of knowledge and of science as well as his expectations concerning a future life condition, personal and communal, that would be beyond the evils of the present time. He developed a form of scientific absolutism and idealism which had originated in philosophy, and had been adapted from the absolutism and the idealism of Hegel. Both forms of absolutism, the Hegelian and the Marxist, were related to Christianity in ways that were indirect and by no means obvious.

As a communist and a materialist, Marx represented socialism as a wholly secular movement, growing out of the unprecedented conditions that had developed in the era of capitalism, and in the age of modern science and industry. The movement was to result in the establishment of a morally higher and freer from of community life, and was to realize some of the aims of early Christianity, as Marx defined these aims. Nevertheless, the eventual world wide victory of communism would install a society and a culture which had severed its religious ties to the past. Only that portion of past historical development which had contributed to the emergence of the modern scientific world view, and to the achievements of modern technology, would remain meaningful for the generations of the future. He insisted, also, that the society of communism would be beyond the need for philosophy.

I will be concentrating in this chapter chiefly on writings that date from the pre-socialist period of Marx's life. Certain of the premises and aims of his later outlook as a communist were carried over from the earlier period. His doctoral dissertation (completed in 1841) is especially important for the understanding of Marx as a philosopher. Much of this chapter will be devoted to an exposition of certain parts of this difficult work.

In the dissertation Marx had already formed an opinion of Hegel as a philosopher which endured throughout his later life. He regarded Hegel's philosophy as the culmination of the general movement of modern Western philosophy. It was an intellectually constructed system which presaged the end of all such future systems. No equally outstanding synthesis of comparable scope could appear in the future. Indirectly, Marx was predicting the demise of modern philosophical theology. Hegel's philosophy had been such a theology, developed as a Protestant replacement for earlier Catholic forms of philosophical theology. Hegel had claimed that his own system involved no conflict with Christianity, but he himself had defined Christianity in such a way as to eliminate the possibility of conflict. His philosophy was compatible with the secularized "religion of nationalism" that had appeared in all the major Western countries in the Protestant era, and which had been sanctioned by the established Christian churches. Hegel's "religion of the State" was in some ways exceptional. The relation of the moral individual – the philosopher – to the State was described as a form of total personal and moral commitment that displaced an earlier, monastic commitment to the Catholic Church. The post-Catholic, non-monastic way of life was said to be vastly preferable. In the modern age, the moral person derived no spiritual benefit from remaining apart from marriage and family life. Furthermore, he was expected to stay within the normal sphere of middle class economic life. It was only by becoming fully a part of the secular life activity of his society that he could also be qualified to participate in "the divine life." In his work in the world, he was engaging in a form of service which enjoined absolute moral obedience to a divinely sanctioned institutional political power, the institution of the State:

> Instead of the vow of chastity, *marriage* now ranks as the ethical relation; and, therefore, as the highest on this side of humanity stands the family. Instead of the vow of poverty (muddled up into a contradiction assigning merit to whosoever gives away goods to the poor, i.e., whosoever enriches them) is the precept of action to acquire goods through one's own intelligence and industry – of honesty in commercial dealing, and in the use of property – in short, moral life in the socio-economic sphere. And instead of the vow of obedience, true religion sanctions obedience to the law and the legal arrangements of the state – an obedience which is itself the true freedom, because the state is a self-possessed, self-realizing reason – in short, moral life in the state . . . . The divine spirit must interpenetrate the entire secular life. . . . (1)

There is no indication that Marx ever identified Hegel's philosophy and moral outlook with the religion of Christianity. He seems to have regarded it as essentially post-Christian. Psychological and moral membership in Hegel's ideal political society of the State was not contingent on membership in any Christian church, nor on the acceptance of any specifically Christian theological doctrine. Persons of any religion, or of no religion *other* than the religion of the state, were qualified to participate in the "moral life in the State." As

---

1. *Hegel's Philosophy of Mind* (1830), part III of The Enclyclopedia of the Philosophical Science, Oxford University Press, 1971, Section 551, page 286.

a communist, however, Marx repudiated Hegel's philosophy of the State. In going beyond Hegel, he was anticipating the emergence of a post-Christian society. In that society, the "social spirit," rather than the Hegelian "divine spirit," would interpenetrate the entire way of life.

In recent decades, Marx's tie to Hegel has been recognized by many commentators. There has been a less general recognition of his tie to Christianity. A number of writers, however, have called attention to the partial continuity of Marx's communism with Judaism and with Christianity. His socialism has been linked with the pre-modern "prophetic tradition." Erich Fromm, for example, has concluded that:

> Marx's philosophy was, in secular, non-theistic language, a new and radical step forward in the tradition of prophetic messianism . . . . Marx's aim, socialism, based on his theory of man, is essentially prophetic Messianism in the language of the nineteenth century (2).

The German philosopher Karl Löwith has devoted an entire chapter to Marx in his book on *Meaning in History*. He describes him as ". . . a man of Old Testament stature, though an emancipated Jew of the nineteenth century who felt strongly anti-religious and even anti-semitic. It is the old Jewish messianism and prophetism . . . and Jewish insistence on absolute righteousness which explains the idealistic basis of Marx's materialism." Marx's modern class war conception ". . . corresponds to the Jewish-Christian belief in a final fight between Christ and Antichrist in the last epoch of history," while ". . . the task of the proletarian corresponds to the world-historical mission of the chosen people . . . the redemptive and universal function of the most degraded class is conceived on the religious pattern of the Cross and the Resurrection . . ." Furthermore, ". . . the whole process of history as outlined in *The Communist Manifesto* corresponds to the general scheme of the Jewish-Christian interpretation of history as a providential advance toward a final goal which is meaningful" (3).

References to Marx as a latter day prophet can be misleading, even though they are also illuminating and do point to important characteristics of his socialism. His tie to modern philosophy is apt to be overlooked in such statements, which imply that there is a direct link between Marx's neo-Hegelian moral outlook and that of the ancient prophets.

The Italian priest and scholar, Guilio Girardi, in his book on *Marxism and Christianity,* has concluded that there are profound differences and equally profound similarities between the philosophy of communism and Christianity as the latter is generally conceived by the Christian churches. Marxism, he says, presumes the existence of a radical antagonism between socialism and Christianity, one which is posed

---

2. *Marx's Concept of Man,* Frederick Ungar, N.Y., 1961, chapter 1, pp. 3-5.
3. University of Chicago Press, 1949.

> . . . in terms of a rivalry between the secular and the religious spheres, or between earth and heaven. The Marxist chooses earth. On earth he will build his paradise. In opposition to heavenly messianism he sets up a terrestrial messianism; in opposition to the fruitless expectations of the heavenly city he proposes an effective effort to construct an earthly city (4).

Marx himself stated on more than one occasion that his communism was to be a replacement for Christiantiy. The modern revolutionary working class movement was comparable to the social movement of primitive Christianity, even though there was no direct cultural link between them. Christianity had taken hold in the beginning as a popular social movement because it held out hope to victims of oppression. The content of religious hope, and the meaning of what Marx called "religious suffering" was a response to conditions that it was within the power of communism to remedy. In his Introduction to *A Critique of Hegel's Philosophy of Right* (1843) he declared that

> *Religious* suffering is at the same time the *expression* of real suffering and the *protest* against real suffering. Religion is a sigh of the oppressed creature, the heart of a heartless world, as it is the spirit of spiritless conditions. It is the *opium* of the people (5).

Marx did not regard popular folk Christianity as a threat to the proletarian movement. He assumed, rather, that the majority of the workers were already disillusioned. They now no longer believed in the "illusory heaven" that had been promised, nor were they inclined to be impressed by the authority of the clergy. While many of them were still passive politically, it was not adherence to Christianity as such that was to blame for this condition. Christian aspirations and hopes had been, at the beginning, potentially revolutionary. In a speech delivered at the Hague Congress of the First International (September 8, 1872) he went so far as to suggest that the early Christians, participants in the persecuted sectarian movement that existed before Christianity had passed into its churchly, institutional Catholic phase, might have achieved their aims then and there had they been properly political and militant in their attitude toward the existing social and political order:

> The workers will have to seize political power one day in order to construct the new organisation of labour; they will have to overthrow the old politics which bolster up the old institutions, unless they want to share the fate of the early Christians, who lost their chance of heaven on earth because they rejected and neglected such action (6).

---

4. The MacMillan CoL., N.Y., 1968 translated by Kevin Traynor, chapter 1, p. 36.
5. Translated by Easton and Guddat, in *Writings of the Young Marx on Philosophy and Society* Doubleday and Co., N.Y. 1967.
6. Reprinted in *Karl Marx: Political Writings,* Volume III, edited and introduced by David Fernbach, The Marx Library, Random House, N.Y. 1974.

Several years later, in a letter to Domela-Neuwenhuis in the Hague (February 22, 1881) Marx noted what he believed were certain psychological parallels between the situation of the early Christians who believed that the end of the world was approaching, and the struggles of the working class, who had a scientifically warranted confidence that the capitalist system could not endure:

> The dream that the end of the world was near inspired the early Christians in their struggle with the Roman Empire and gave them confidence in victory. Scientific insight into the inevitable disintegration of the dominant order of society continually proceeding before our eyes and the ever-growing fury into which the masses are lashed by the old ghostly governments, while at the same time the positive development of the means of production advances with gigantic strides – all this is sufficient to guarantee that the moment a real proletarian revolution breaks out the conditions (though these are certain not to be idyllic) of its immediately next *modus operandi* will be in existence . . . (7).

Marx had also identified the working class struggle and the socialist cause with the story of the historical Jesus, as recorded in the New Testament. Eleanor Marx recalled, in "A Few Stray Notes" about her father:

> . . . how I remember his telling me the story – I do not think it could ever have been so told before or since – of the carpenter whom the rich men killed, and many and many a time saying, "After all we can forgive Christianity much, because it taught us the worship of the child" (8).

While Marx compared the struggles of the early Christians against Roman oppression with the working class struggle against capital, he made more than one kind of historical analogy in his dramatization of the working class struggle. In his address on *The Civil War in France* (1871) in commemoration of the defeated Communards of Paris, the defense of the city was seen as the defense of an emerging higher civilization against barbarian reaction. It was comparable to the heroic struggle of Roman citizens against foreign barbaric invasion in the declining days of the Roman Empire:

> . . . the real women of Paris showed again at the surface – heroic, noble, and devoted, like the women of antiquity. Working, thinking, fighting, bleeding Paris – almost forgetful, in its incubation of a new society, of the cannibals at its gates – radiant in the enthusiasm of its historic initiative! (9)

---

7. *Marx and Engels: Selected Correspondence.* Progress Publishers, Moscow, 1965.
8. Reprinted in Fromm, *op. cit.*
9. *Marx and Engels: Selected Works,* Volume II, Progress Publishers, Moscow, 1969. I have cited here only one of several passages in this address in which Marx compares the events of the Paris Commune with events which had taken place in Roman antiquity.

There was Biblical symbolism in Marx's philosophy of communism, but it occurred in combination with elements derived from Greek mythology. The idea of a radical opposition between heaven and earth first appeared in a dramatic form in his doctoral dissertation, and seemed to have no direct connection with Christianity. It was represented as the heroic struggle of the Titan Prometheus against the arbitrary decrees of the tyrant Zeus, the supreme God of the Greek pantheon. Marx was not then a communist. Later on, the working class was identified with the Bound Prometheus, the struggle against capital becoming a Promethean struggle for collective self-liberation. The working class could succeed, where the isolated hero and victim had failed. The proletarian movement was a collective, social counter-power strong enough to overthrow the oppressive earthly powers.

Marx's philosophy of communism had also been linked, in its inception, with the romantic movement in German literary culture of the early nineteenth century. The movement looked back to classical antiquity, retrospectively idealized. Greek mythology and religion was being preferred to Biblical mythology and religion. The movement was antithetical to Judaic and Christian forms of moral and cosmological dualism.

THE ADOLESCENT WRITINGS

Marx's interpretation of early Christianity as an aborted social and political movement which had failed to direct its energies to the task of overthrowing the oppressive worldly powers, provides no insight into the meaning that Christianity had held for him during an important period of his early life, long before he became a communist.

The most direct evidence of Marx's personal tie to Christianity is contained in certain of his adolescent writings. He had been influenced in his adolescent years by the philosophical and religious education he received at the Lutheran academy which he had attended. The theological instruction given at the academy was an adaptation of Kant's philosophical theology. The two essays which Marx wrote in fulfillment of senior year high school requirements are of special interest. His essay on religion seems to have expressed his own personal reaction and was not merely a recapitulation of the instructor's interpretation of a particular text. The essay is entitled "The Union of the Faithful with Christ, John 15:1-14, Exhibited in its Ground and Essence, in its Absolute Necessity and its Effect" (10). Marx depicts the Creator God as a

---

10. It is impossible to determine on the basis of present information whether Marx selected this particular passage himself, or whether it was assigned to him by his examiner, Parson Kupper, a friend of Heinrich Marx [the father of Karl] who was the religious instructor at the academy. Kupper wrote the following comment on Marx's essay: "It is profound in thought, brilliantly and forcefully written, deserving of praise, although the topic – the essence of union – is not elucidated, its cause is dealt with only one-sidedly, its necessity is not proved adequately." Cited by David McClellan in *Marx before Marxism,* Harper and Row, 1970.

judging, standard-setting, condemning authority whose high expectations of humanity have so far been disappointed. The redemptive Christ – the religious teacher – is identified with the "forgiving Father" aspect of God ". . . who had earlier appeared as an offended Sovereign, now as a forgiving Father, as a kind teacher." The communicant experiences a special religious love for Christ. "Since we are permeated with the highest love for him we turn our hearts at the same time to our brothers, who he has bound more closely to us, for whom also he sacrificed himself." The duality of human nature is emphasized. Man's position in nature is unique but also insecure on that account. The struggle within the self becomes acute when sexual maturity is reached:

> . . . the flame of desire chokes the sparks of the Eternal, the alluring voice of sin drowns out the enthusiasm for virtue; a low striving after worldly goods displaces a striving after knowledge, and a longing for truth is extinguished by the sweet-flattering power of falsehood, and so there stands man, the only being in nature which does not accomplish its aim, the only member in the whole of creation which is not worthy of God who created it.

Unworthiness can be overcome in commitment to the higher way of life, but only through first experiencing the special union with Christ:

> This is the great cleft which separates Christlike virtue from every other and raises it above every other, this is one of the greatest effects which the union with Christ begets in man. . .
>
> Who would not gladly endure sorrows when he knows that through his persevering in Christ, through his works, God himself is honored.
>
> So the union with Christ bestows an inner exaltation, comfort in sorrow, a quiet confidence and a heart which is opened to the love of man, to all honor, all sublimity, not out of ambition, not out of glory-seeking, but only on account of Christ. . .(11).

The second essay, written for another examiner, the headmaster, who taught history and philosophy, was entitled "Reflections of a Young Man on the Choice of an Occupation." Here the sacrificial Christ of the gospel of John is transformed into an "idea:" "Religion itself teaches us that the idea for which we are all striving sacrificed itself (sic) for humanity, and who would dare destroy such a statement." The emphasis is on the singular greatness of man's life as compared with the more limited life of the animals, who do not have to strive toward a transcendent goal:

---

11. Translated by Robert B. Fulton in *Original Marxism: Estranged Offspring:* A Study of Points of Contact and of Conflict Between Original Marxism and Christianity, Christopher Publishing House, 1960. Another translation is available in *The Collected Works of Marx and Engels,* Volume I, International Publishers, 1975.

> Nature has assigned to the animal the sphere of its activity, and the animal acts calmly within it, not striving beyond, not even surmising that there is another. To man, too, the Deity gave a general goal, to improve mankind and himself, but left it up to him to choose the position which is most appropriate and from which he can best elevate both himself and society.

The whole of the vocational life is to be directed toward overcoming the gap between the special perfection that is attainable by humanity and the initial human and social condition which must be transcended. The individual who is free to do so should undertake a vocation which will enable him to improve himself and the society to which he belongs. Some persons, through no fault of their own, are not able to choose such a vocation: "Our social relations, to some extent, have already begun to form before we are in a position to determine them." The young man who is able to set his feet on the appropriate path that is right for him personally has a chance to acquire special distinction, moral merit, and posthumous if not immediate social acclaim:

> When we have weighed everything, and when our relations in life permit us to choose any given position, we may take that one which guarantees us the greatest dignity, which is based on ideas of whose truth we are completely convinced, which offers the largest field to work for mankind and approach the universal goal for which every position is only a means; perfection . . . .
>
> The main principle . . . which must guide us in the selection of a vocation is the welfare of humanity, our own perfection. One should not think that these two interests combat each other, that the one must destroy the other. Rather, man's nature makes it possible for him to reach his fulfillment only by working for the perfection and welfare of his society. . . . (12).

When he became a university student, Marx decided to concentrate on the study of philosophy and of law. He was attracted to Hegel's philosophy, but he believed that German idealism had set up a false opposition between "physical" and "mental" nature which was unfavorable to the self-perfecting endeavor. He was fired with a desire to undertake a new philosophic venture that would go beyond what Hegel had accomplished. In a long letter which the nineteen-year-old Marx wrote to his father after having completed two years of study at the University of Berlin, he said that:

> Setting out from idealism – which, let me say in passing, I had compared to and nourished with that of Kant and Fichte – I hit upon seeking the Idea in the real itself. If formerly the gods had dwelt above the world, they had now become its center.

12. Translated by Easton and Guddat, *op cit.* Other translations available in Fulton, *op. cit.* and in *The Collected Works of Marx and Engels, op. cit.*

Marx had been influenced by Hegel's statements on the unity of the Ideal and the Real. He seems to have thought that Hegel was positing a Cartesian kind of body-mind dualism, in which "physical nature" was completely separated from "mental nature" on the biological and personal level. He proposed to disprove this dualism:

> I had read fragments of Hegel's philosophy and found its grotesque craggy melody unpleasing. I wished to dive into the ocean once again but with the definite intention of discovering our mental nature to be just as determined, concrete, and firmly established as our physical nature – no longer to practice the art of fencing but to bring pure pearls into the sunlight (13).

Marx had been concerned, two years earlier, in his high school essay on choosing an occupation, about an opposition between the "physical" and the "intellectual" principle. The opposition must be resolved, so that the young man setting out on his chosen path can be securely integrated, able to devote himself single-mindedly to the process of self and social perfecting. In the effort to pursue one's appropriate vocation

> Even our physical nature often threateningly opposes us, and no one dare mock its rights!
>
> To be sure, we can lift ourselves above it, but then we fall all the faster. We then venture to construct a building on rotten foundations, and our entire life is an unfortunate struggle between the intellectual and physical principle. When one cannot calm the elements fighting in himself, how can he stand up against life's tempestuous urge, how is he to act calmly?

THE DOCTORAL DISSERTATION

For two years, from 1839-1841, Marx was engaged at the university in working on his doctoral dissertation. The dissertation was entitled "The Difference between the Democritean and Epicurean Philosophy of Nature." He selected this theme, according to his own account, because such a study could aid in the understanding of the situation of philosophy in the present era. In addition to the dissertation itself, there were voluminous preparatory notebooks. These shed further light on his concept of the powers, functions and problems of philosophy, as well as on his views about its relation to Christianity. It should be noted here that a number of passages in the notebooks, and also in the dissertation itself, are difficult. Some are impossible to understand. A good deal of interpretation is needed in an attempt to give a partial

---

13. *Ibid.*

exposition of the content of these works (14). It is evident, however, that Marx was conceiving of philosophy as a Promethean, liberating power. Philosophy was able to emancipate the community from the superstitions of popular religion. The philosopher as an individual was also able to achieve a kind of personal autonomy that was in contrast to the condition of religious dependency which Marx associated with Christianity. It was evident that in the dissertation and in the notebooks Marx was already separating himself from the other radical, anti-religious "young Hegelians" who had been his associates at the University of Berlin. These Hegelians of the left had rejected Hegel's theology and had declared themselves to be post-Christian atheists. They had concluded that the Hegelian God concept was merely a representation of human functions and powers, falsely projected on to supersensible, cosmological plane. There was, in fact, no noumenal reality in back of the Hegelian God of Idea. Marx accepted this neo-Hegelian critique of Hegel. The necessary revision had not detracted from the greatness of Hegel. He regarded Hegel as the greatest of modern philosophers, deserving to be ranked along side of Aristotle. Years later, in *Capital,* he called Aristotle "the greatest thinker of antiquity" (15).

Marx rejected the Hegelian supersensible Idea, but he retained an Hegelian style conception of the historical presence and power of a universal World Spirit that was carrying history forward dialectically through successive developing phases of Western culture and civilization. He saw philosophical thought as reflecting the working through a "world purpose" that encompassed the whole of history. Philosophy served to advance this purpose, although it was only one aspect of a general movement. The movement proceeded through phases of growth and decline, with each new phase being more advanced than the preceding one.

In his philosophy of knowledge, the powers of Marx attributed to philosophy were just as absolute as those Hegel had assigned to philosophical Reason. According to Hegel, that reason, in its most highly developed Germanic phase, was capable of penetrating directly into the noumenal realm of ultimate reality. The mind of philosophy was in a position to understand reality as a whole, including the meaning of God in nature and in history. No mysteries in nature or in universe were impenetrable to philosophical reason. Marx elevated philosophy in a similar way. Enlightened, rational, critical philosophy had direct access to absolute knowledge.

---

14. The Dutch philosopher, Arend Th. Van Leeuwen, delivered a series of Gifford lectures in 1970 and 1972 centered on Marx's philosophy in relation to Christianity. The first volume (the 1970 lectures), *Critique of Heaven* (Charles Scribner's Sons, 1972) is devoted to a detailed exposition of the text of Marx's doctoral dissertation and of the preliminary Notebooks. Van Leeuwen notes the problems confronting the interpreter: ". . . I have tried carefully to follow the main argument of Marx's dissertation and of the preparatory studies. It has not always been a simple matter to understand his intentions, sometimes because of the extreme conciseness of his style and sometimes owing to the abstruseness of his style of thought."

15. International Publishers, N.Y., 1967, Volume I, chapter 15, p. 408.

In his dissertation Marx concentrated on those functions of philosophy that had been connected, by Hegel, with theology, and that were related also to his philosophy of the State. Marx was not attacking the Hegelian system. Criticism had already done its work. He was involved, rather, in an attempt to demonstrate, in another way, what Hegel had already demonstrated in his idealism, namely that nature was neither a transcendental power nor a locus of Spirit. Only by repudiating the reality of external powers of a threatening, supra-human kind, either in nature or beyond nature, could the philosopher achieve a condition of personal oneness and freedom from disturbance which had made the practice of philosophy an adequate substitute for religion.

It was not until some time later, after he had become a communist and had developed his materialist conception of history, that Marx articulated a synthesis of his own that seemed to dethrone the supreme Hegelian science of philosophy. This synthesis was narrower in range than the Hegelian one. The philosophical sciences were eliminated. There were no special cultural sciences. The Hegelian sciences of spirit were absorbed into a post-Hegelian dialectical science of history, which was declared to be a natural, presumably post-philosophical science. The marked philosophical interest that Hegel had shown in the natural sciences was absent, since Marx centered almost exclusively on human historical events. A considerable narrowing of focus was already indicated in his doctoral dissertation.

EPICUREAN PHILOSOPHY AS PRACTICAL SCIENCE

In his doctoral dissertation, Marx selected Epicurus as the philosopher whose views were most congenial to his own. He set out to demonstrate why, and in what respects, the post-Aristotelian atomism and cosmology of Epicurus (341-270 B.C.) was different from and superior to the pre-Aristotelian atomism of his predecessor, Democritus (born about 460 B.C.). He classed both Democritus and Epicurus as scientists, but it was only Epicurus whose approach to science was philosophical. The two atomists are said to differ in their ". . . theoretical judgments . . . concerning the certainty of science and the truth of its objects," and this difference ". . . *manifests* itself in the *disparate scientific energy* and *practice* of these men." Epicurus turns his back on the search for truth through the methods of natural science. He turns toward the practical science of philosophy:

> *Epicurus has nothing but contempt for the positive sciences,* since in his opinion they contribute nothing to *true perfection.* He is called an *enemy of science,* a scorner of grammar. He is even accused of ignorance (16).

16. *Collected Works of Marx and Engels,* Volume I, The Doctoral Dissertation, p. 40.

Through his practice of philosophy, Epicurus had become, according to Marx, "*satisfied* and *blissful* in philosophy." He "takes refuge in philosophy" and is thus able to avoid personal disturbance, achieving a "true freedom" which he could not have obtained through the pursuit of natural scientific investigations. Marx quoted Epicurus:

> You must serve philosophy so that true freedom will be your lot. He who has subordinated and surrendered himself to it does not need to wait, he is emancipated at once. For to serve philosophy is freedom itself . . . and the man who says that the age for philosophy has either not yet come or has gone by is like the man who says that the age for happiness is not yet come to him, or has passed away (17).

Democritus, on the other hand, had pursued his quest for knowledge and truth in a futile way, and could not find this kind of freedom. He is

> . . . driven into *empirical observation.* Dissatisfied with philosophy, he throws himself into the arms of *positive knowledge.*

In spite of his scientific erudition, Democritus had become an eternal wanderer, seeking out knowledge in many lands and from many authorities: "On the one hand it is the *lust for knowledge* that leaves him no rest; but it is at the same time *dissatisfaction with true, i.e., philosophical, knowledge* that drives him far abroad."

Marx praised Epicurus in spite of, not because of, the latter's antagonism to the natural sciences. Philosophy in the post-Hegelian era had nothing to fear from science. Epicurus, however, had been compelled to oppose earlier, pre-modern forms of science, because science at that time had not yet been able to nullify the claims of religion. Epicurus had been able to free himself, to find his own true self-center, by turning his back on Greek astronomical and mathematical science. That science had been linked with a cosmological religion and with conceptions of the universe that represented the powers of humanity as subordinate to the powers of the non-human cosmic and natural order. This false cosmology had been rejected by Epicurus, although science had been temporarily sacrificed. He had been the one and only Greek philosopher to challenge the prevailing religious cosmology. He was ". . . the greatest representative of the Greek Enlightenment" (18), in spite of the fact that ". . . he fights not only against astrology, but also against astronomy itself, against the eternal law and rationality in the heavenly system" (19). He merits the high praise given to him by Lucretius (*De Rerum Naturum*) who had described him as a "man of Greece" who lived at a time "when human life lay grovelling in all men's sight, crushed to earth under the dead weight

17. *Ibid.*
18. *Ibid.*, p. 73.
19. *Ibid.*, p. 70.

of religion whose grim features loured upon mortals from the four quarters of the sky" (20).

Marx said that the cosmology of Epicurus was just as projective, and just as subjective, as the cosmology of his opponents. Epicurean subjectivism, however, was more acceptable. It could be harmonized more readily with the modern view approved by Marx. The atom of Epicurus, according to Marx, was not merely a physical atom. It was also a representation of the detached or "abstract" self-consciousness of the philosopher, Epicurus. His atomic theory took the form that it did because he was living at a time when the political culture and civilization of Greece was disintegrating. The socio-political unity of the Greek State, which was sanctioned by community religion, was falling apart. The Epicurean "free atom" represented pure "being-for-itself," in a condition of "absolute" existence, beyond the limitations of "relative" historical and communal existence as lived in any specific society. The freedom of this ego-atom brings with it the power to think and to pursue personal life aims in independence of other people. For Epicurus

> The purpose of action is to be found, therefore, in abstracting, swerving away from pain and confusion, in ataraxy. Hence, the good is the flight from evil, pleasure is the swerving away from suffering. Finally, where abstract individuality appears in its highest freedom and independence in its totality, there it follows, that the being which is swerved away from is *all being*. . . .(21).

Ataraxy means "serenity" or peace of mind, achieved through self-insulation from outer disturbances, i.e., through a capacity for psychic withdrawal. "Swerving away," the term used by Marx, seems to be in the case of Epicurus a withdrawal to a position outside of the non-self universe of history and nature, as well as a withdrawal from political life.

Modern philosophy, unlike the philosophy of the Greeks, will be able to abolish objectively, in social reality, those obstacles to the attainment of the Epicurean goal of "ataraxy" which Epicurus had been able to attain for himself through the private practice of philosophy. Like Epicurus, the modern philosopher must be prepared to repudiate the authority of external religious and social opinions and condemnations. In his foreword to his doctoral dissertation (March 1841) Marx wrote that

> As long as philosophy still has a drop of blood left in its world-conquering, absolutely free heart, it will not cease to call to its opponents with Epicurus: "Not the man who denies the gods worshipped by the multitude, but he who affirms of the gods what the multitude believes about them, is truly impious."

---

20. Lucretius, *The Nature of the Universe*, translated, with an introduction by R.E. Latham, Penguin Classics, 1951, p. 29.
21. Doctoral Dissertation, *op. cit.* p. 51.

Philosophy is one with the spirit of Prometheus, who had declared in the *Prometheus Bound* of Aeschylus: "In one short sentence, I hate all the gods." Prometheus the god-defier is elevated beyond all heavenly and earthly judgments, declared to be ". . . the noblest saint and martyr in the calendar of philosophy" (22). He quoted a passage from David Hume's *A Treatise of Human Nature* (Book I, Part IV, sec. V) in support of philosophy's Promethean claim to immunity from external judgments, adding italics not present in the English original:

> 'Tis certainly an indignity to philosophy, whose *sovereign authority* ought everywhere to be acknowledged, to oblige her on every occasion to make apologies for her conclusions and justify herself to every particular art and science that may be offended at her. *This puts one in mind of a king arraigned for high treason against his subjects.*

THE LIBERATION OF PHILOSOPHY FROM COMMUNAL JUDGMENTS

In the dissertation, Marx made no reference to Christianity, but was indicating his hostility to any form of cosmic religion. In the voluminous preparatory Notebooks of 1839-41, he did, however, refer to Christianity and its relation to philosophy. He disconnected the New Testament religion of Christianity from philosophy. He defined philosophy as a means for liberating the philosopher – and all individuals – from the need to depend on redemption through Christ. At the same time, he was also conceiving of philosophy as a means for eliminating any possible moral opposition between the single individual and the public society of which he was a member. He was going beyond the "ethical State" philosophy of Hegel, but was at the same time retaining certain aspects of the Hegelian moral outlook.

Marx associated the Promethean power of philosophy with a kind of salvation and emancipation that would eliminate the subordination of the individual to any form of religious authority, including also any norms of communal morality that carried some kind of religious sanction. The individual was to be joined with the spirit and mind of his own society in such a way that he could never be brought before the bar of public judgment, condemned for violations of publicly accepted norms, or for opposing in any way the commonly accepted opinions and norms. He maintained that Platonic philosophy, and indeed all philosophy, ancient or modern, *begins* where Christianity as a religion of salvation leaves off. The Christian believer starts with a consciousness of sin, which is followed by the redemptive experience

---

22. I have cited the translation of the Foreword given in the collection of essays entitled *Marx and Engels on Religion,* Moscow, 1957, reprinted by Shocken Books, 1964. A revised translation is available in *The Collected Works of Marx and Engels,* Volume I.

of grace. Salvation through Christ is possible because of the dependence of the individual on the religious teacher, Christ. Philosophers, on the other hand, begin by "freeing the soul from empirical limitations." They are engaged in a process of self-emancipation, one which excludes religious dependency and also a consciousness of sin (23).

The elimination of a Christian type of religious dependency and consciousness was a necessary, but not a sufficient condition of philosophical emancipation. The kind of functional and moral link that had tied pre-Epicurean philosophers to the community of their time had to be broken. Epicurus, who had withdrawn from participation in community religion, had been able to free himself in a way that had not been possible for Socrates. The willingness of Socrates to submit to the public judgment against him was an indication that he had not yet broken his own spiritual ties to community religion. He was the victim of his attachment to the laws and the religion of his people.

In the modern age, the individual who is the bearer of the "World Spirit" of philosophy is still not fully united with the total community of which he is a part. In the confused, obscurely worded concluding section of the dissertation, Marx expressed dissatisfaction with philosophy as presently carried on by neo-Hegelians. Hegel's philosophy was being reviewed and parts of his system were being rejected, but the break had not been radical enough. The neo-Hegelians were still being inspired by the thought-energy that originated in the Hegelian system which was already obsolete. They do not know just where they are going or what they are doing: ". . . they are themselves engaged merely in the act and immediate energy of development – and hence have not yet theoretically emerged from that [Hegelian] system. . ." To "emerge from the system" is to suspend all merely abstract philosophical activity. Marx suggested that just as the great age of philosophy, in Greek civilization, has been superseded by the post-philosophical, practical age of Roman civilization, so also, modern civilization was entering upon a post-philosophic, post-Hegelian era of practical, progressive activity.

In the Notebooks written in connection with his dissertation, Marx had sharply distinguished Christianity from philosophy. This distinction was not as clearly maintained when he became a communist. The necessity of a general moral transformation was emphasized in the writings of Marx's early communist period. The movement of world history was to realize certain aims of Christianity as well as certain aims of philosophy.

CHRISTIANITY AND THE TRANSITION TO COMMUNISM

Marx found his life work toward the end of 1843, when he joined forces with the revolutionary communist movement of his day. He started

23. *Collected Works of Marx and Engels,* Volume I, pp. 495–496.

out by proclaiming that philosophy had found its appropriate contemporary function. Both as theory and as practice, it could enter actively into the transforming process of history. Critical, neo-Hegelian philosophy had successfully demonstrated that religion was based on illusion. The "critique of heaven" must be followed by an equally stringent "critique of earth." In his Introduction to *A Critique of Hegel's Philosophy of Right* [law], written late in 1843, he had declared that

> . . . it is the task of history, once the otherworldly truth has disappeared, to establish the *truth of this world.* The immediate *task of philosophy,* which is in the service of history, is to unmask human self-alienation in its *unholy forms* now that it has been unmasked in its *holy form.* Thus the criticism of heaven turns into the criticism of the earth, the *criticism of religion* into *criticism of law,* and the *criticism of theology* into the criticism of politics (24).

When combined with the material power of the working class movement, philosophy can help expedite the aims of communism. One major section of the population – the working class – is living under conditions which make the individuals of that class especially ready and willing to carry through the radical, negative aims of critical philosophy: "As *philosophy* finds its *material* weapons in the proletariat, the *proletariat* finds its *material* weapons in philosophy." Eventually, philosophy will lose its identity and its reasons for remaining in existence. The proletariat will likewise disappear: "Philosophy cannot be actualized without the transcendence [Aufbehung] of the proletariat, the proletariat cannot be transcended without the actualization of philosophy."

Modern humanity was perceived to be in a condition analogous to the unredeemed condition of humanity before the appearance of Christ, in the Christian gospel of salvation. In an essay on "The Jewish Question," written in 1843, just before he had gone on to formulate his concept of the task of philosophy and his idea of the proletarian mission, he had described the present condition. Man, as he manifests himself in his social actions and in his relations with other men in modern economic society is

> . . . man in his uncivilized and unsocial aspect, in his fortuitous existence and just as he is, corrupted by the entire organization of our society, lost and alienated from himself, oppressed by inhuman relations and elements – in a word, man who is not yet an *actual* species being (25).

---

24. Translated by Easton and Guddat, *op. cit.*

25. From the first and longest of these two essays, translated by Easton and Guddat, *op. cit.*

Although the process of communism includes redemption from moral evil, it by-passes the Christian road to salvation. The concept of sin, confined to the religious frame of reference, does not apply. The nature of moral evil is differently conceived, and redemption takes place in a different way. The individuals who were to inhabit the redeemed society of communism were to be liberated from the need for any kind of morally significant law and from dependency on moral authority, as well as from any concern with problems of moral conduct. In this respect the secular terrestrial society of classless communism bears some resemblance to the concept of a spiritual community of transformed, redeemed believers, as projected in the gospels of Paul. It was to be beyond evil, just as the Pauline after-life community, beyond death, would be beyond sin. In the Pauline community, there would be no need for the external authority of law. Neither would there be any need for political government.

It appears that Marx had been influenced by Hegel's way of relating certain aspects of Christianity to the religion and morality of the political State. The Hegelian state had advanced beyond Christianity in some respects. It was more inclusive. The freedom obtainable through membership in the state was open to individuals irrespective of their religious affiliation. Hegel had opposed the exclusion of Jews and other religious minorities from full participation in the spiritual life of the state (26). In his Introduction to *The History of Philosophy* he said

> In Christianity the individual, personal mind for the first time becomes of real, infinite and absolute value; God wills that all men shall be saved. It was in the Christian religion that the doctrine was advanced that all men are equal before God, because Christ has set them free with the freedom of Christianity. These principles make freedom independent of any such things as birth, standing, or culture. The progress made through them is enormous, but they still come short of this, that to be free constitutes the very notion of man (27).

Marx accepted Hegel's view that Christianity was the most advanced and also the final stage of world religion. Communism was to be built on the "human foundations" of Christianity. Individuals in the future society would be social, but they would not be political. They would no longer be political citizens. They would be spiritually and socially equal members of a universal society. Hegel had merged the religious equalitarianism and universalism of Christianity with the form of the modern Protestant state. Marx merged Christian universalism with one particular form of the State, the political democratic form, as it had appeared in those societies which had proclaimed, by law, the separation of church and state. Christianity, as a religion of

26. *Hegel's Philosophy of Right,* translated by T.M. Knox, Clarendon Press, Oxford, 1952, Section 270.
27. *Hegel on Art, Religion and Philosophy*, Harper and Row, 1970, p. 255.

redemption, affirmed the spiritual equality of all persons and their equal human value, ignoring differences which divided people from one another in secular society. So also, the democratic state abolished, but on an ideal and formal level only, the distinctions that still prevailed in the civil economic society:

> The [democratic] state abolishes distinctions of *birth, rank, education* and *occupation* in its fashion when it proclaims that every member of the community *equally* participates in popular sovereignty without regard to these distinctions (28).

In the post-political society of communism, these distinctions would be abolished in the civil life, not merely in law. The society would have a perfection of structure corresponding to the equalitarian condition proclaimed by Christianity. This was to be an equality in sovereignty. The future members of that society need no longer be subordinate to any external, oppressive, or punitive power: "Political democracy is Christian in that it regards man – not merely one man but every man – as *sovereign* and supreme" (29). In this interpretation of the meaning of Christianity, Marx seems to be referring to an elevated and transformed condition of self-being attained by the individual believer through the saving action of Christ, which elevated humanity up to a "divine" level. The most highly evolved form of the state, the modern political democratic state, is "atheistic" because it elevates man as citizen "above religion." It is transitional to communism, but it must lose its identity as form, its ideality, if the human foundations of Christianity are to be realized in the community life:

> . . . the perfected Christian state is not the so-called *Christian* state acknowledging Christianity as its foundation in the state religion and excluding all others. It is, rather, the *atheistic* state, the *democratic* state, the state that relegates religion to the level of other elements of civil society. The state that is still theological and still officially prescribes belief in Christianity has not yet dared to declare itself to be a *state* and has not yet succeeded in expressing in *secular* and *human* form, in its *actuality* as a state, those *human* foundations of which Christianity is the sublime expression (30).

The transformation that was to come about through communism would transcend the sectarian limits of Christianity or of any other religion. There was no moral justification for the exclusion of Jews from rights accorded to other persons who professed Christianity, although this exclusion, decreed and enforced by the reactionary German government, was being defended by Bruno Bauer, one of the most prominent of the "young Hegelian" philoso-

28. First essay on "The Jewish Question," Easton and Guddat, *op cit.*
29. *Ibid.*
30. *Ibid.*

phers. All persons, Jews and Christians alike, were equally removed from the truly human condition of the future. But the changes to be brought about through communism would result in the establishment of a universal society that was linked more directly to Christianity than to Judaism. The attack on Judaism, which appeared in the second and shorter essay on "The Jewish Question," had been influenced by Hegel's negative comments on Judaism, as given in *The Phenomenology of Mind* (31) and also by Feuerbach's hostility to Judaism, expressed in *The Essence of Christianity* (1841). Marx wrote that pre-Christian Judaism has been the national religion of a society which possessed only ". . . unfounded superficial law," which was

> . . . only the religious caricature of unfounded, superficial morality and law in general, the caricature of merely *formal* ceremonies encompassing the world of self-interest.
>
> Here also the highest relation of man is the *legal* relation, the relation to laws which apply to him not because they are laws of his own will and nature but because they *dominate* him and because defection from them will be *avenged* (32).

There had once been an element of "sublime thought' in the religion of Judaism. This had been absorbed into Christianity, leaving Judaism devoid of sublimity: "Christianity is the sublime thought of Judaism." At present there was nothing left of Judaism but the "practical" every day Jew, who is represented by Marx as the ideal-type of the modern "economic man," plus a dead husk of formal, ritualized religion, represented by the "sabbath Jew." Christianity today was also a dead letter, nothing but Judaism under a different label: "Christianity arose out of Judaism. It has again dissolved into Judaism."

It was Christianity in its Protestant form that was associated by Marx with those defects of society which communism was to eliminate. Christianity had dissolved into Judaism in the Protestant era. The individualism of Protestant religion was identified with capitalist economic individualism. It was especially in the most advanced political democratic countries such as the United States that persons retained a tie to Protestant forms of Christianity. Each person was concerned only with his own private religious salvation, just as each was also concerned only with the pursuit of his own private economic self-interest:

---

31. Kant and Hegel had both rated Judaism lower than Christianity. Hegel's view of Judaism in his later writings was less negative than in his earlier works. This is true of Marx also. The anti-Judaism that appeared in his 1843 essays does not appear in his later writings. In *Capital* and elsewhere he makes some favorable references to Old Testament scriptures. Nathan Rotenstreich, in *The Recurring Pattern: Studies in Anti-Judaism in Modern Thought* (Horizon Press, N.Y., 1964) reviews the ideas of Kant and Hegel on this question.

32. Second essay, dealing with Bruno Bauer's article on "The Capacity of Present-day Jews and Christians to Become Free," translated by Easton and Guddat, *op. cit.*

> If we find even in a country with full political emancipation that religion not only *exists* but is *fresh* and *vital* we have proof that the existence of religion is not incompatible with the full development of the state. . . . .
>
> Man emancipates himself *politically* from religion by banishing it from the sphere of public law into private right. It is no longer the spirit of the *state* where man – although in a limited way, under a particular form, and in a particular sphere – associates in community with other men as a species-being. It has become the spirit of *civil society,* of the sphere of egoism, of the *bellum omnium contra omnes* . . . The splitting of man into *public* and *private,* the *displacement* of religion from the state to civil society, is not just a step in political emancipation but its completion. It as little abolishes man's *actual* religiosity as it seeks to abolish it (33).

The primary struggle against religion, in the modern era, was an internal, intra-psychic struggle against forms of religiosity that Marx associated with Protestant, Lutheran Christianity. He regarded medieval Catholisicism as a socio-political, communitarian religion which united individuals in a bond that cut across differences in economic and social status. All individuals in the "lay" community had been subordinated to external religious authority and to the external power of the priesthood. The battle against the Catholic church had been won in the Protestant era. The Lutheran revolt had discredited priestly authority, but the freedom it brought was only partial, the destruction of a merely "physical," i.e., socially imposed institutional power, which held the individuals in bondage to external authority. The anti-clerical upheaval had internalized the struggle against religion. The individual striving for optimum personal freedom was at war with a part of his own nature. In the Introduction to *A Critique of Hegel's Philosophy of Right,* Marx had said that

> *Luther,* to be sure, overcame bondage based on devotion [to the church] with bondage based on *conviction.* He shattered faith in authority by restoring the authority of faith. He turned priests into laymen by turning laymen into priests. He freed man from outward religiosity by making religiosity the inwardness of man. He emancipated the body from its chains by putting chains on the heart.
>
> But if Protestantism was not the true solution, it was the true formulation of the problem. The question was no longer the struggle of the layman against the priest external to him, but his struggle against his own *inner priest,* his *priestly nature* (34).

33. First essay on "The Jewish Question," *op. cit.*
34. Easton and Guddat, *op. cit.*

The authority of faith that Luther had restored was the authority of the Bible. The individual who is struggling against his own priestly nature has direct access to these materials, unmediated by clerical authority. Marx seems to have thought that Protestant believers were bound to accept the authority of the Bible in a total, uncritical, non-selective way. The religious faith component, the belief in the supernatural basis of Biblical religion, revelation, and prophecy, could not be dissociated from the social and moral teachings. Marx left his readers to assume that there is a general agreement among Christians as to what they ought to do if they are to prove their worth as Christians, their fidelity to the letter and the spirit of the Holy Scriptures. In his first essay on "The Jewish Question" he said that the so-called Protestant Christian state established in Germany was committing religious sacrilege when it claimed that its authority was founded on Christianity. No Protestant state could lay claim to being Christian. The state could do so only if it were Catholic, and if the political authorities acknowledged their subordination to Church authority:

> The separation of the "spirit of the Gospel" from the "letter of the Gospel" is an *irreligious* act. The state that permits the Gospel to speak in the letter of politics or in any other letter than that of the Holy Spirit commits a sacrilege if not in the eyes of men at least in the eyes of its own religion. The state that acknowledges Christianity as its highest rule and the *Bible* as its charter must be confronted with the *words* of the Holy Writ, for the Writ is holy in every word. This state as well as the *human rubbish* on which it is based finds itself involved in a painful contradiction, a contradiction insoluble from the standpoint of religious consciousness based on the teachings of the Gospel . . . in its own consciousness the official Christian state is an *ought* whose realization is impossible . . . the infamy of its *secular* purposes cloaked by religion irreconcilably conflicts with the integrity of its *religious* consciousness. . . . (35).

It appears that the Protestant Christian is religiously disqualified from participation in political life and especially in governing power. If he does participate in such power without renouncing his faith, he is involved in duplicity and hypocrisy. The evils of capitalism were intensified, in Marx's view, by the fact that the civilization of capitalism was nominally Christian. Protestant civilization had failed to justify its right to be called Christian. The socialist, working class movement has no religious pretension. It does not profess Christianity, and cannot be accused of profaning what is holy. In *The Communist Manifesto,* Marx declared that in capitalist civilization

> All fixed, fast-frozen relations, with their train of ancient and venerable prejudices and opinions, are swept away, all new-

35. *Ibid.*

> formed ones become antiquated before they can ossify. All that is solid melts into air, all that is holy is profaned, and man is at last compelled to face with sober senses his real conditions of life, and his relations with his kind.

Those Protestant believers who accepted the authority of faith were committed to a way of life incompatible with life as it was lived in the outer secular world. The believer was bound to accept the norms of conduct prescribed by the New Testament Gospels. His loyalty to his faith required a personal withdrawal into an inner world beyond society. This is what Marx's attitude seemed to imply. Christianity had to be discarded because it was unsuited to the realities of social and economic life.

Marx insisted upon disconnecting Protestantism, and religion in general, from communism. He did, however, also denounce the system of capital as if he were speaking from the standpoint of a believer in the religious morality of the Bible, especially as this applied to the economic life. In some of his later writings, including *Capital,* his condemnation of capitalism appeared to be partly in the nature of a religious interdiction. He used criteria of judgment which he could not have acquired except through his own tie to the religious and moral tradition which he was trying to reject in its entirety. His attitude toward Christianity was ambivalent, and his statements on the relation of communism to Christianity were ambiguous. He attacked the individualism of Prostestant Christianity in his essay on "The Jewish Question," but at the same time he also seemed to represent it as the only spiritual resource available to the alienated individuals who felt themselves cut off from a higher moral center in the Hobbesian economy and society of acquisitive, competitive individualism. It was because society was defective that a religion which negated that outer society by withdrawal was able to flourish. The proletarian communist movement offered an alternative spiritual resource, which thereafter became identified with those aspects of the Christian aspiration which Marx was able to accept as desirable and as realizable.

When he first developed his materialist conception of history in *The German Ideology* (1845-46) he declared that philosophy was to be displaced by science. This did not mean, however, that he was abandoning his opposition to the kind of scientific positivism which he had repudiated in his comments on Democritus. Nor did it mean that he had lost his earlier sympathy with the aims of Epicurean philosophical practice. The limitations of Epicurean individualism were to be overcome, and the value of science as a means for implementing these aims was being affirmed. The problems of society, humanity, and also of philosophy, were to be resolved through communism.

Philosophy, as practiced by neo-Hegelian critical theorists, produced nothing but mystifications and illusions. The science of history, as presented by the "practical materialist" who had accepted communism, disclosed the "empirical facts" beyond the "sensuous appearance:" "Actually, when we conceive things thus, as they really are and happened, every profound philosophical problem is resolved, as will be seen even more clearly later on, quite simply into an empirical fact" (36). The reality beyond appearance was "sensuous," i.e., knowable by the "senses." In a footnote preceding the passage just quoted, Marx had said that

> Feuerbach's failing is not that he subordinates the flatly obvious, the sensuous appearance, to the sensuous reality established by the more accurate investigation of the sensuous facts, but that he cannot in the last resort cope with the sensuous world except by looking at it with the "eyes," i.e., through the "spectacles" of the *philosopher.*

Marx was saying that philosophical spectacles are distortions of reality, or at best ways of evading it, but that the perception of the "practical materialist" who looks at "facts" is not distorting. It is a direct insight into the inner laws and processes, conferring on the knower a true understanding of history.

Marx's Promethean communism suffered from certain forms of over-subjectivism. The personal biographical aspects of this subjectivism were combined with a more general philosophical and cosmological subjectivism that appeared in Western culture in the modern age of physical science. Personal problems which could not have been resolved through institutional, economic and social change entered into the construction of his historical and social theory. The personal elements are especially evident in his early writings (37). The historical demise of Christianity as a religion was a necessary condition of the attainment by the future self of that state of "ataraxy" and freedom from disturbance which Epicurus, in the pre-Christian era, had been able to achieve through his practice of philosophy.

---

36. Volume I, Part I, p. 57, Progress Publishers, Moscow, 1964.

37. Robert C. Tucker, in his interesting discussion of *Philosophy and Myth in Karl Marx* (Cambridge University Press, 1961) has interpreted the symbolic and mythic elements in Marx's thought by applying ideas derived in part from the neo-Freudian theory of neurosis developed by Karen Horney. He also interprets certain tendencies in Kantian and Hegelian theology by applying this type of theory. My outlook on Marx and also on problems of human society and human conflict does not exclude a psychiatric frame of reference. However, there is much in Tucker's personal perspective and in his interpretation of Marx which I cannot accept. He introduces some major misconceptions. Furthermore, he comes close to overlooking the objective social, historical and cultural reality of the various supra-personal problems, political, moral, and intellectual, with which Marx was trying to cope and which he was trying to reduce to manageable dimensions. My own view of Marx does converge with that of Tucker to a limited degree. Marx projected certain inner difficulties of a personal nature onto the outer social and political situation. This projective tendency influenced his class struggle theory and also his expectations as to what could be achieved through communism.

2

The Cosmological Philosophies Of Hegel And Marx

This chapter will describe the way in which Marx developed his philosophy of communism in the process of criticizing and revising Hegel's philosophical theology. It will deal with a selected group of Marx's early writings, essays known as the "Paris manuscripts," or as "the philosophic and economic manuscripts of 1844." They include materials not found in the same form in his later writings. He was making use of Hegel's philosophical language and a good deal of what he said makes sense only when that language and the conceptual scheme to which it refers – the Hegelian system – has been deciphered. While I will discuss Hegel's cosmology at some length, the importance of Kant for both Hegel and Marx is also emphasized. Hegel and Marx were united in their acceptance of certain Kantian premises.

In his "Critique of Hegelian Dialectic and Philosophy in General" (1844), Marx said that he was going beyond Hegelian idealism, and also beyond previously developed forms of philosophical materialism, combining the strong points of both positions. He was thus achieving an understanding of "the act of world history:"

> We see here how a consistent naturalism or humanism is distinguished from both idealism and materialism as well, and at the same time is the unifying truth of both. We also see how only naturalism is able to comprehend the act of world history (1).

Hegel appeared to have an absolute confidence in philosophical reason and in his own ability to penetrate to a knowledge of God that had become possible only in the modern era. Marx inherited from Hegel this kind of cognitive confidence. Hegel had said that certain major contradictions, apprehended by the mind of philosophy, could be transcended in thought. Marx, rejecting this claim, was convinced that they could be eliminated in *reality*. In his essay on "Private Property and Communism" (1844) he wrote that

> . . . communism as completed naturalism is humanism, as completed humanism it is naturalism. It is the *genuine* resolution of

1. Translated by Easton and Guddat, in *Writings of the Young Marx on Philosophy and Society, op cit.*

> the antagonism between man and nature and between man and man; it is the true resolution of the conflict between existence and essence, objectification and self-affirmation, freedom and necessity, individual and species. It is the riddle of history solved and knows itself as this solution (2).

Marx identified humanism with atheism, but his particular kind of humanism was closely allied to the man-centered cosmological and theological systems of Kant and of Hegel. German transcendental philosophy carried over into the modern age certain aspects of Christian universalism. All individuals were members of one species. All shared the same spiritual, cosmological status. The species-status of every human being was inalienable, existing regardless of the individual's class position and status in society, and irrespective of differences in race or creed. All participated in those attributes that distinguished humanity from the animals and provided evidence of the superiority of human beings and of their preeminent value in the scheme of total creation.

The value of nature, apart from man, consisted in the way in which it functioned as the support of human life. In *The Groundwork of the Metaphysics of Morals* (1785), Kant had said that all human beings belonged to "the kingdom of ends." The reality of this kingdom was the basis for an ethic that was both personal and social:

> I understand by a *"kingdom"* a systematic union of different rational beings under common laws. . . . .
>
> For rational beings all stand under the *law* that each of them should treat himself and all others, never *merely as a means,* but *always at the same time as an end in himself.* But in so doing there arises a systematic union of rational beings under common objective laws – that is, a kingdom. Since these laws are precisely directed to the relation of such beings to one another as ends and means, the kingdom can be called a kingdom of ends (which is admittedly only an Ideal).
>
> A rational being belongs to the kingdom of ends as a *member.* . . . (3).

Kant divided the world of materially perceptible objects into "things" and "persons." Only persons had absolute, unconditional value. The value of humanly produced objects (labor products) was "conditioned," i.e., derived from the unconditional value of the human creative subject. The value of natural objects not produced by man – animals, plants, etc. – was only "relative," deriving from their utility as a means for supporting human life. Nature, like man, produces materially perceptible "things:"

---

2. *Ibid.*
3. Translated by H.J. Paton, Harper and Row, 1964 (first edition 1948), pp. 100-101.

> Thus the value of all objects that can *be produced* by our action is always conditioned. Beings whose existence depends, not on our will, but on nature, have none the less, if they are non-rational beings, only a relative value as means and are consequently called *things.* Rational beings, on the other hand, are called *persons* because their nature marks them out as ends in themselves. . . .(4).

Kant said that humanity, not nature, was the final end and aim of creation. No manifestation of nature, no matter how impressive to an observer, could account for the existence of nature, and of the process and power of creation manifest in nature. The final end of creation is Man: "Without men the whole creation would be a mere waste, in vain, and without final purpose" (5). This proposition was said to be "self-evident," a conclusion shared by all who give thought to the question.

Marx's curious phrase "completed naturalism" expresses the idea that nature itself will be brought up to a higher stage of development through the full realization of Man as species. The equally curious phrase "completed humanism" meant that neither nature nor man could be brought to completion, i.e., to fulfillment at the highest possible level, until human beings were no longer subjected to de-humanizing treatment at the hands of their fellow human beings. All persons in communist society would be treated as "ends in themselves," none were mere "objects" serving as means for others.

In presenting "naturalism" as the "unifying truth" of idealism and of materialism, Marx was saying 1) that natural processes in human history were overcoming the opposition between the philosophical Idea and the human and social actuality, which Kant and Hegel failed to eliminate; 2) that natural processes were inherently dynamic. Cosmological matter was not inert, set in motion merely through the application of external forces. "Materialism," insofar as it was identified with such a mechanical view of the physical cosmos, was just as defective as idealism.

HEGEL'S COSMOLOGICAL IDEALISM

Hegel's idealism combined certain aspects of Platonic and Aristotelian philosophy with an outlook that was distinctly modern. He declared that Christianity was a "revealed religion" which proclaimed the truth that human beings were above the sphere of merely organic, natural existence. All persons possessed "infinite value:" "Christianity, we know, teaches that God wishes all men to be saved. That teaching declares that subjectivity has an infinite

---

4. *Ibid.,* p. 96.
5. *Critique of Judgement* (1790), translated by H.H. Bernard, Hafner Publishing Co., N.Y. and London, 1968, sec. 86.

value" (6). "Subjectivity" here means human self-consciousness and a truth consciousness available only to human beings. Hegel may have been referring to the statement in Tim. 2:3-4: "God our Saviour . . . will have all men to be saved and to come unto the knowledge of the truth."

Hegel observed that nature is commonly treated as a mere means to the realization of self-interested human ends. To act in this way is a natural prerogative of man. Although various natural species other than man are equipped with self-defensive powers, these cannot prevent them from being consumed, used as mere means, by other species. Man is the only species incapable of being turned into a mere means. Man alone possesses Spirit, and is thereby removed from the mere means category:

> If, for example, we admire the wisdom of God in nature because we seek how animals are provided with weapons, partly to obtain their food and partly to protect them against enemies, yet it is presently seen in experience that these weapons are of no avail, and that those creatures which have been considered as ends are made use of by others as means (7).

No actions of Man in relation to the inferior realm of nature are to be considered "ungodly," To support his position Hegel cited a passage from the New Testament, saying that ". . . the admiration of God as revealed in natural things, as such, in trees, and animals" is "opposed to what is human:"

> It seems to be expressed by such a view that human action as regards nature is ungodly; that the operations of nature are divine operations. But the productions of human reason might, at least, be esteemed as much as nature. . . The pre-eminence of human thought must forthwith be avowed. Christ says on this subject (Matt. vi. 26-30) "Behold the fowls of the air" (in which we may also include the ibis and the Kokilas), "are ye not much better than they? Wherefore if God so clothe the grass of the field, which today is, and tomorrow is cast into the oven, shall He not much more clothe you?" The superiority of man, of the image of God, to animals and plants, is indeed implicitly and explicitly established. . . Spirit is infinitely high above nature, in it the divine spirit manifests itself more than in nature (8).

Hegel's philosophy of Spirit had much to do with death. He had lost the Christian belief in the resurrection of the dead, and in the literal immor-

6. *Hegel's Logic* (1830), Part I of the Encyclopedia of Philosophical Sciences, Translated by William Wallace, Clarendon Press, Oxford, 1975, sec. 147, p. 210.

7. *Hegel on Art, Religion, Philosophy, op. cit.* from "On Religion," Hegel's Introduction to The Philosophy of Religion, p. 138.

8. *Ibid.* from "On Philosophy," Hegel's Introduction to The History of Philosophy, pp. 271-272. A reader who turns back to the Biblical version of the passage quoted will note that Hegel omitted certain of the most famous sentences in the original, without acknowledging that he had done so.

tality of personal self-consciousness on a post-corporeal plane of existence. In spite of this, Hegel said that humanity was partly beyond the natural organic realm. He believed that persons are nullified as corporeal beings belonging to the world of Nature, but not as spiritual entities whose absolute subjectivity is linked with the infinite subjectivity of God or Idea. The personal consciousness of individuals dies with them. The supreme subjectivity of the Idea is indestructible. It appears that humanity as species is endowed with an immunity to death, corporeal as well as spiritual, that is not possessed by other species.

The Idea of Hegel was derived from Aristotle's concept of the Divine Nous, the supreme Intellect existing beyond materiality and outside of body. In Hegel's philosophy, the infinite Mind or Idea had not only created the entirety of the natural universe. It was also dynamic and self-expansive. It strives to actualize itself, to become something more than it was at the beginning. It begins by positing "matter," i.e., by producing matter (9). The Idea requires nature as a means to a self-actualization that is also beyond nature. The sciences of nature, disclosing the rationality inherent in processes of nature, demonstrate the self-actualizing power of the Idea. The science of physics is not a merely mechanical science, and the laws of physics are not reducible to mechanical laws (10).

Hegel rated the sciences of life above the inorganic sciences. His cosmology was not only mind-centered and man-centered. It was also, to a striking degree, life-centered and earth-centered. Life in all its forms was a higher manifestation of the power of God in nature than was to be found in the sub-organic level: "In fact, I do rate what is concrete higher than what is abstract, and an animality that develops into no more than a slime, higher than the starry hosts" (11). Physical matter is nature at its most "abstract," and therefore also at its lowest level. The physical bodies in outer space have significance only when they support life on earth. The solar system is a higher manifestation of the Idea than the remote, humanly irrelevant stars:

> We may suppose the stars in their interrelationships to exhibit a formal rationality, but they belong to the sphere of dead repulsion. . . We must certainly not set this system on the same level as the solar system, in which we first discern the system of Reason as a reality in the heaven. . . (12).

Animal organisms, as a broad category, are on a higher plane of being than plant life: "The plant is a subordinate organism whose destiny is to sacrifice itself to the higher organism and to be consumed by it. . . This animal

---

9. In Aristotle, abstract matter is eternal and uncreated, co-existing with the eternal and uncreated Nous. The two, combining, produce the entire universe of phenomenal nature, including human life.

10. *Hegel's Logic,* section 195.

11. *Hegel's Philosophy of Nature,* section 341, p. 297.

12. *Ibid.,* section 268, pp. 61-62.

process [of consumption] which is higher than that of the plant is its ruin" (13).

The mind of man is able to perceive and to identify various ascending stages of development in nature. On the deific level of Idea, Mind also creates these stages. There are qualitative "leaps" in the universe which nature, apart from mind, is too irrational and too chaotic to produce. Nature can produce only "repetitions." It cannot supply the *telos,* the movement toward realization, that runs through the hierarchies of nature:

> Nature is to be regarded as a *system of stages,* one arising necessarily from the other and being the proximate truth of the stage from which it results; but it is not generated *naturally* out of the other but only in the inner Idea which constitutes the ground of Nature (14).

Nature, on its own, produces a superabundant variety of organic forms, many of which are unnecessary or defective. These defects and irrationalities are excluded in the process of qualitative advance to the plane of Spirit.

The abstract consciousness of the divine Intellect, devoid of any content, is thought-activity. It is paralled on the human level by the consciousness of being an Ego, an "I," which is therefore also a consciousness of being an "object" for self, or perceiving the existing of oneself. It appears as though thought activity is the ground of the experience of Selfness. To perceive that one exists as Ego is "thinking:"

> Nature does not bring its *nous* into consciousness: it is man who first makes himself double so as to be a universal for a universal. This first happens when man knows that he is 'I.' I means myself, a single and altogether determinate person. And yet I really utter nothing peculiar to myself, for every one else is an 'I' or 'Ego' . . . In the 'Ego' we have thought before us in its utter purity. While the brute cannot say 'I,' man can, because it is his nature to think. . . Man, therefore, is always thinking, even in his perceptions. . . (15).

In this way, through their possession of self-consciousness, human beings are linked directly with the Idea, i.e., with thought activity that is *beyond* nature, and that is not produced *by* nature.

The cosmic Idea becomes conscious of its own world-creating powers when these powers are objectified in the works of creation. The Idea acquires this expanded and enriched "self-consciousness" through "externalization" and "objectification" in nature. The final end and aim of the self-objectifying process is described as a "return" to the original psychic center. The divine consciousness, at the stage of "return into Self," is indistinguishable from the

13. *Ibid.,* section 349, pp. 350-351.
14. *Ibid.,* section 249, p. 20.
15. *Hegel's Logic,* section 24, p. 38.

mind of philosophy as it has developed in historical culture. Each philosophically important stage of cultural advance serves as the ground for the next stage, a process parallel to the development occurring in nature. In the world of nature, the highest product is Man as an animal organism. This becomes the natural and necessary ground for the incarnation of the Nous element, the mind and spirit, and the absolute Ego or I. From the biological standpoint, Man as animal is a standard by which all other species can be measured, and in relation to which all others in general are undeveloped (16).

On the natural level, Man is a limited, finite being. As Spirit and self-conscious Ego, and as the possessor of Reason and Mind, he participates in the infinity and the freedom of the Idea. Biologically, humanity is a fit receptacle for the incarnation of the Divine. The Idea, then, produces and uses nature as a means to a self-actualizing "return" which is not a negation of nature, but a negation of the imperfections and irrationalities inhering in the materiality of nature. Nature itself, as the essential ground of life in all its forms, cannot be destroyed, since matter, the manifestation of the Idea that has been dragged down into the time process, is being continually created as well as annihilated. Nature, by the very fact that it exists, is a "degradation" of the Idea, a departure from the initial condition of Actuality (17).

The stage of "return to Self" via the necessary process of externalization in nature, is a return to the perfection of unity that was present at the beginning. That unity is now greatly enriched, the Self more than it was at the beginning. It is only when the Mind of Philosophy reaches a stage of comprehension that developed in what Hegel called "Teutonic civilization" that human Reason is able to attain the level of absolute self-knowledge. Teutonic philosophy is the third and final stage in the development of Western philosophy.

Philosophy is an "action of the Spirit," and the vehicle through which the Nous achieves absolute self-knowledge. The "return to Self" on the deific level is described as the overcoming of the alienated and divided condition which had begun with the creation of the natural universe. The external and internal obstacles that stand in the way of attaining the absolute condition of fully actualized self-consciousness are annihilated by the power of the Idea. Nature itself seems to acquire a self-destructive force which is psychic in origin, a manifestation of the drive of the Idea to "return to Self," free from the limitations and imperfections of material nature:

> The goal of Nature is to destroy itself and break through its husk of immediate, sensuous existence, to consume itself like the phoenix in order to come forth from this externality rejuvenated

---

16. *Hegel's Philosophy of Nature,* section 352, p. 357.
17. *Ibid.,* section 248, p. 17.

> as spirit. Nature has to become an other to itself in order to recognize itself again as Idea and to reconcile itself with itself (18).

It was hardly surprising that the neo-Hegelian successors and critics of Hegel perceived that the concept of God developed by Hegel was a projection of the mind of Hegel himself. They went on to reject the idea of God as self-consciousness.

MARX'S REVISION OF HEGEL'S COSMOLOGY

Turning now to Marx, what must be stressed first of all is that in the essays of 1844 he was writing and thinking on a level of abstraction that was commensurate with the level maintained in Hegel's *Logic,* in his *Phenomenology of Mind,* in his *Philosophy of Nature* and in other works in which nature is related to man and to Idea. Marx reacted against the nature-destroying aspects of Hegel's philosophy of Spirit:

> Man *lives* by nature. This means that nature is his *body* with which he must remain in perpetual process in order not to die. That the physical and spiritual life of man is tied up with nature is another way of saying that nature is linked with itself, for man is a part of nature (19).

Hegel had not actually said that human beings were independent of nature, nor that mind on the human level could actually exist without body. He had made this clear not only in *The Philosophy of Nature* but also in his *Logic:*

> Nature is far from being so fixed and complete as to subsist even without mind [i.e., without the constant presence and activity of the Divine Nous] ; in Mind it first, as it were, attains its goal and its truth. And similarly Mind on its part is not merely a world beyond Nature and nothing more; it is really, and with full proof, seen to be mind, only when it involves Nature as absorbed in itself (20).

In view of the evidence uncovered by geographical science, Hegel was ready to grant that Nature preceded the appearance of humanity; "Nature is the first in point of time, but the absolute prius is the Idea; this absolute prius is the last, the true beginning, Alpha is Omega" (21). The human mind, as self-consciousness and reason, develops in and through history. It does not

18. *Ibid.,* section 376, p. 444.
19. Easton and Guddat, *op. cit.,* "Alienated Labor" (1844).
20. *Hegel's Logic, op. cit.,* section 96, pp. 141-142.
21. *Hegel's Philosophy of Nature, op. cit.,* section 248, p. 19. See also *Hegel's Philosophy of Mind, op. cit.,* section 381, p. 14.

exist fully blown in the first, primitive stages of human society. But the essential species-mind powers are given, as potential, at the beginning, and are actualized through the power of the Spirit, operating through human cultures and civilizations.

Marx was grappling with the multiple ambiguities of Hegel's idealism and of his self-actualization philosophy. He introduced certain misrepresentations. He was objecting to Hegel's theological dualism, to the way in which the Nous (the supreme Intellect) and the abstract Ego are separated from matter and nature. But he also implied that Hegel was postulating a human self-consciousness and mind abstracted from dependence on body:

> Man is assumed [in Hegelian philosophy] as equivalent to self. But the self is only man conceived *abstractly*, derived through abstraction. Man is a *self*. His eye, his ear, etc. belong to *a self;* every one of his essential qualities has the quality of *selfhood.* But on that account it is quite false to say that *self-consciousness* has eyes, ears, essential capacities. Self-consciousness is rather a quality of human nature, of the human eye, etc.; human nature is not a quality of *self-consciousness* (22).

There is no such thing as an abstract Self beyond nature which produces corporeal man and nature. Hegel's concept of absolute knowledge, as a function of a ". . . self-comprehending or absolute, that is, superhuman, abstract mine [*Geist*] – is altogether nothing but the *expanded essence* of the philosophical mind, its self-objectification." Hegel is trying to get beyond man and nature: "Actual man and actual nature become merely predicates or symbols of this concealed, unreal man and nature." Hegel had been describing but also misrepresenting an actual process of alienation which had occurred in the course of history. Man, not an Absolute subject, was alienated and divided. Hegelian philosophy is a symptom of this general human condition, and cannot provide anything but a false solution to the problem of getting beyond that condition:

> The *philosopher* – himself an abstract form of alienated man – sets himself up as the *measuring rod* of the alienated world. The entire history of *externalization* and the *withdrawal* from externalization is therefore nothing but the *history of production* of abstract, that is, of absolute, logical, speculative thought.

In spite of Hegel's "vindication of the objective world for man," he ends by regarding all human expressions and productions as mental entities only, claiming that

> . . . *spirit* alone is the *genuine* essence of man and the true form of spirit is the thinking spirit, the logical, speculative mind. The

---

22. "Critique of Hegelian Dialectic and of Philosophy in General" (1844), translated by Easton and Guddat, *op. cit.*

> *human quality* of nature, of nature produced through history, and of man's products appears in their being products of abstract spirit and hence phases of *mind,* thought-entities.

Marx presented a counter-thesis which seemed to detract from the power of nature in a way which was more extreme than in the Hegelian system. Nature, as known to human perception and to science includes, in Hegel's philosophy, the element of Spirit or Idea which was supposedly derived from an initially external, abstract Mind power. In Marx's anthropocentric cosmology, on the other hand, human work activity transforms the material natural substratum in such a way that the element of "spirit," form, or essence in nature, is deprived of independent stability and cohesiveness (23). Man, not Idea, is identified as the active history-making agent, and also as the producer of the objects – the "things" – that form his external environment. These objects are not products of original nature. They have been altered through transforming labor activity. This labor is not the labor of abstract thought, which Hegel had seemed to value above all other forms of human activity. It is activity in which human mental and physical powers are combined. This labor makes use of material produced by nature, in such a way that nature is "humanized" and altered. The dividing line which Hegel had established between natural history, apart from Man, and human history, was obliterated in Marx's early writings as a philosopher of communism. In his "Critique of Hegelian Dialectic and Philosophy in General," Marx wrote that:

> . . . man is not only a natural being; he is a *human* natural being. That is, he is a being for himself and hence a *species-being;* as such he must confirm and express himself as such in his being as in his knowing. Accordingly, *human* objects are not natural objects as they immediately present themselves nor is *human* sense immediately and objectively *human* sensibility, human objectivity. Neither objective nor subjective nature is immediately present in a form adequate to the *human* being. And as everything natural must have its *genesis,* man too has his genetic act, *history,* which is for him, however, known and hence consciously self-transcending. History is the true natural history of mankind (24).

The true, fully empowered and realized nature of Man is not given, at the beginning, by nature apart from Man. The distinctively human qualities that remove humanity from the original natural condition are self-cultivated and self-developed in work upon objective materials produced by nature.

---

23. It is not possible, in this chapter, to discuss all the implications of Marx's transformational philosophy. Chapter 3 will continue the exposition begun in this chapter, and will refer also to statements Marx made in his later writings.

24. *Ibid.*

These essential, self-objectifying qualities of humanity are manifest in the transformed environment of human civilization, in productions that have been brought into existence by material labor. These productions demonstrate that humanity does not owe its existence to a God of Idea, a God of Philosophy, above nature, but to itself, i.e., to its own labor activity;

> Since for socialist man. . . the *entire so-called world history* is only the creation of man through human labor and the development of nature for man, he has evident and incontrovertible proof of his *self-creation,* his own formation process. Since the essential dependence of man in nature – man for man as the existence of nature and nature for man as the existence of man – has become practical, sensuous and perceptible, the question about an *alien* being beyond man and nature (a question which implies the unreality of nature and man) has become impossible in practice (25).

Although a proto-human man originally appeared on earth through creational processes of unconscious nature, the species does not enter the process of history until it separates itself from the unconscious natural substratum. In so doing, humanity does not sever its vital, organic link with the material, natural substratum.

As a cosmologist, Marx begins with nature, not with the Hegelian Idea. Nature exists, and must simply be accepted as having come into being. Speculation is futile. There is no need to think of a first cause beyond nature. In developing his critique of Hegelian philosophy, he retained Hegel's emphasis on the earth center and on life. He eliminated from his frame of reference most of what Hegel had said about the characteristics of inorganic, physical matter and the way in which they manifested the Idea, which had also been interiorized, in a more advanced way, in organic life forms. Marx was not, and never did become, a philosopher of nature, in the sense in which this term can be applied to Hegel. He was not concerned with defining the differences between life and non-life, nor with the problem of the variability and multiplicity of natural life forms. A vital, organic type of universal, reciprocal need seems to bind together, in an ascending hierarchy, all essential manifestations of nature that are prior to and necessary for the life of man. Man is bound to nature by virtue of his need for material sustenance. In the essays of 1844, the earth is said to have been "self-generated," and is identified with a vital creativity that inheres in material nature. No supra-terrestrial cosmic process needs to be assumed to account for the creation of the earth:

> The creation of the *earth* has been severely shaken by geognosy [rather, by geogeony], the science which presents the formation

25. "Private Property and Communism" (1844), translated by Easton and Guddat, *op. cit.*

> and development of the earth as a self-generative process. Generatio aequivoca is the only practical refutation of the theory of creation (26).

Marx's cosmology was restricted to the solar system, which is also simply *there.* The arguments which he uses to discredit the idea of initial creation were derived from Hegel's *Philosophy of Nature.* In the section called "organics," which begins with a study of "geological nature," Hegel refers to the earth as the ground for the emergence of life through a process called "generatio aequivoca," meaning many-sided generation, resulting in a diversity of primitive life forms. The earth, from one standpoint, was inorganic. From another standpoint it was part of a system of relations described as organic. The earth is an "inanimate organism" which is "fructified into vitality" after the set of conditions necessary for the emergence of organic life have appeared on its surface:

> . . . because the geological organism is only implicitly [*an sich*] vitality, the truly living organism is an other than the geological organism itself. . . The earth is fertile – fertile simply as the ground and basis [*Boden*] of the individual vitality upon it (27).

In Marx's system, it is organic "need" that seems to bind the sun, the earth, and life on earth together in a condition of reciprocal interdependency and interactivity. Needs developing on the organic level call out the dormant potentialities in the chief inorganic body, the sun, which fulfills its own nature in making life on earth possible, in objects outside of itself:

> *Hunger* is a natural *need;* it thus requires *nature* and an *object* outside itself to be satisfied and quieted. Hunger is the objective need of a body for an *object* existing outside itself, indispensible to its integration and the expression of its nature. The sun is the *object* of the plant, indispensable to it and confirming its nature, just as the plant is object for the sun, expressing its life-awakening, its *objective* and essential power.
>
> A being which does not have its nature outside itself is not a *natural* one and has no part in the system of nature (28).

Marx projected qualities of vital responsiveness into nature, blurring the distinction between inorganic and organic processes. Human need is the supreme, over-riding need. It is active, dynamic, driving forward to achieve the end condition of universal self-actualization:

> The whole of history is a preparation for *"man"* to become the object of *sensuous* awareness and for the needs of "man as man"

---

26. *Ibid.*
27. *Op. cit.,* section 341.
28. "Critique of Hegelian Dialectic and Philosophy in General," *op. cit.*

> to become sensuous need. History itself is an *actual* part of *natural history,* of nature's development into man. Natural science will in time include the science of man as the science of man will include natural science: there will be *one* science (29).

In his attitude toward sub-human nature, Marx, like Hegel, affirmed the superiority of man over the animals. A great deal of the essay on "Alienated Labor" (1844) was a discussion of the ways in which the productive, self-objectifying powers of human workers exceeded the productive powers of animals. Humanity is free *within* nature, although not free from material dependency on nature. The worker is free as a designer of materially objectified new forms, which are not merely utilitarian and may also be aesthetic. He has a need for such self-production and expression, quite apart from material need. Animals do not produce objective material structures through their own activity except by instinct, in order to survive and reproduce their kind. Their instincts, according to Marx, are purely biological:

> To be sure, animals also produce. They build themselves nests, dwelling places, like the bees, beavers, ants, etc. But the animal produces only what is immediately necessary for itself or its young. The animal produces under the domination of immediate physical need while man produces free of physical need and only genuinely so in freedom from such need. The animal only produces itself, while man reproduces the whole of nature. The animal's product belongs immediately to its physical body while man knows how to produce according to the standard of any species and at all times knows how to apply an intrinsic standard to the object. Thus, man creates also according to the laws of beauty (30).

It is only Man that has the ability to distance himself from the objective forms he has produced through his own activity, and to recognize the object as a product of self and of his own human powers:

> The animal is immediately one with its life activity, not distinct from it. The animal is *its life activity.* Man makes his life activity itself into an object of will and consciousness. He has conscious life activity. It is not a determination with which he immediately identifies. Conscious life activity distinguishes man immediately from the life activity of the animal (31).

Man is also the only species, according to Marx, that can have social relations, an ability to relate to other members of his own species, to perceive them as "objective," apart from himself, but in such a way as to recognize his

---

29. "Private Property and Communism," *op. cit.*
30. "Alienated Labor," Easton and Guddat, *op. cit.*
31. *Ibid.*

own identity as Man in this way, and his tie to others who are in the same species-identity group. Marx spelled this out in *The German Ideology* (1845-46) where he said that animals could have no "relations" of any kind:

> . . . an animal does not enter into any relation at all. For the animal, its relation to others does not exist as a relation. Consciousness is, therefore, from the very beginning a social product and remains so as long as men exist at all (32).

Humanity makes use of nature in many ways, not only to maintain itself in existence on the physical level, but also to maintain and develop the social and spiritual life, which is exclusively human. Humanity absorbs nature into itself by a process of total assimilation:

> . . . as man is more universal than the animal, the realm of inorganic nature by which he lives is more universal. As plants, animals, minerals, air, light, etc. in theory form a part of human consciousness, partly as objects of natural science, partly as objects of art – his spiritual inorganic nature which he first must prepare for enjoyment and assimilation, so they also form in practice a part of human life and human activity; they may appear in the form of food, heat, clothing, housing, etc. The universality of man appears in practice in the universality which makes the whole of nature his *inorganic* body. . . (33).

What Marx was describing was a unity of being and of consciousness that would be fully achieved only in the classless society of communism. That society, however, could develop only in modern Western civilization, which already possessed scientific and industrial power capable of changing all aspects of original nature. Only in that civilization had humanity acquired a type of self-consciousness that included a full awareness of being separate from and superior to the sub-spiritual, sub-social realm of nature.

In his earlier writings, Marx was especially concerned with eliminating from human self-consciousness attitudes toward nature which seemed antithetical to the recognition of Man as the supreme spiritual and natural entity in the cosmos.

Although the future society was to be post-Christian, the kind of species introversion that Hegel identified with Christianity was to be carried forward into the new age. Christianity, which elevated a human being above any manifestation of the natural world, was the highest stage of religion, vastly preferable to any form of "nature worship," ancient or modern. Like Hegel, and also like Kant, Marx was opposing tendencies developing in Germany, among some philosophers and writers, to upgrade nature religiously. He and Engels were antagonistic toward the nineteenth century animal pro-

32. Progress Publishers, Moscow, 1964, Volume I, Part I, p. 42.
33. "Alienated Labor," *op. cit.*

tection movement, identifying it with a regressive "nature religion." In a review article published in 1850, they ridiculed a type of nature philosophy being advocated by a German philosopher, G. Fr. Daumer, in a book called "The Religion of a New Age." Daumer had attacked the radical working class movement and the class struggle program as a form of barbarism, a threat to culture. One of his chief complaints against the movement was its lack of sympathy with the animal protection movement: ". . . . the frightful tortures that unfortunate beasts suffer at the tyrannous and cruel hand of man are for these barbarians 'rubbish' that nobody should bother about!" In their counterattack, Marx and Engels declared that Daumer was manifesting a "petty bourgeois vulgarity" that rejoices in the slaughter of proletarians by their class enemies at the same time that it is ". . . indignant at the raillery of which sentimental societies for the prevention of cruelty to animals are the object." The implication was that this raillery was justified. Furthermore, Daumer's "cult of nature" was a form of "effeminate resignation." He had ". . . managed to be reactionary even in comparison with Christianity. He tries to establish the old pre-Christian natural religion in modern form" (34). An equally sharp attack on "natural religion" appeared in other writings of Marx. He sometimes paraphrased Hegel's statements on nature worship, especially when referring to the religion of India, in journal articles written in 1853. The conquest of India by the British was culturally progressive. The agricultural village communities of India, destroyed by the British, had ". . . brought about a brutalizing worship of nature, exhibiting its degradation in the fact that man, the sovereign of nature, fell down on his knees in adoration of Kanuman, the monkey, and Sabbala, the cow" (35).

THE ALIENATION OF MAN IN MODERN SOCIETY

In his 1844 essays, Marx presented an alternative view of the self-alienating, externalizing, self-objectifying process described by Hegel in his philosophical theology. It is not the divine Nous that externalizes and "loses itself" by positing external nature, "returning to self" in consciousness through the mediating activity of the Mind of Philosophy. It is man as species who has externalized himself and become "lost to himself" in his objective historical creations.

Marx made use of Hegel's account of the feudalistic "Lordship and Bondage" relation, as given in *The Phenomenology of Mind* [Geist]. This was a symbolic, quasi-theological account of an economic and social relation of domination and subordination. It centered on a description of two kinds of

34. Reprinted in *Marx and Engels on Religion,* Moscow, 1857; Shocken Books edition, 1964.

35. "The British Rule in India," reprinted in *The Selected Works of Marx and Engels,* Volume I, Progress Publishers, Moscow, 1969; also in *The American Journalism of Marx and Engels,* edited by Henry M. Christman, New American Library, 1966.

"self-consciousness," one of which was attributed to the worker in nature, the other to the master or overlord who possessed superior power and could therefore lay claim to what was produced by the bound worker.

Marx displaced the activity of the Hegelian Idea in nature on to the activity of the human Worker in nature. He also anticipated that when the bondage of the proletarian and universal worker to the lords of capital had been eliminated, the "Lordship and Bondage" relation would be transcended, both in economic society and in consciousness, giving way to a universal species consciousness. Man the Worker would be subordinate to no human overlord but would participate in a socially shared consciousness of mastery in and over Nature. He wrote, in his "Critique of Hegelian Dialectic and Philosophy in General," that

> The great thing in Hegel's *Phenomenology* and its final result – the dialectic of negativity as the moving and productive principle – is simply that Hegel grasps the self-development of man as a process, objectification as loss of the object, as alienation and transcendence of this alienation; that he thus grasps the nature of *work* and comprehends objective man, authentic because actual, as a result of his *own work* (36).

Marx declared that the present day industrial worker, the enslaved proletarian, is in a condition of self-nullity and emptiness similar to that which Hegel had attributed to the worker when he had first become enslaved by the Master. Only when this condition of subordination is eliminated will the worker be able to recognize himself in the objective world created by human labor. When this occurs, the power of the Master – the capitalist – will be absorbed into the power of the worker. The functions of productive creation and destructive consumption will be combined. The type of universal self-consciousness resulting from this absorption and fusion will, however, be different from any form of worker consciousness or master consciousness that had previously developed in history. It will indicate also the moral transformation that has taken place when the individualism of the private property system, and the condition of universal competition, has been abolished. The alienation of the worker in capitalist industry is not only a nullification of his own personal existence. It is also a nullification of his inner social and moral tie to society and to other people (37).

Although Man as species had differentiated himself from the remainder of nature through work in nature, he had become self-alienated, self-divided, estranged from himself in this process. This alienation had been necessary to the evolutionary advance beyond the degraded condition of primitive unity and "natural religion" existing at the beginning. But the process of alienation had developed to its utmost extent of bourgeois society. No further historical

36. *Op. cit.*

37. The situation of the worker, as conceived by Marx in his early works, will be discussed further in Chapter 5 on "The Social Condition of the Modern Working Class."

function could be served by a perpetuation of the present condition. Relations between human beings in bourgeois society were merely external, utilitarian relations. This externalization will be eliminated through the revolutionary and evolutionary process of communism. Eventually all persons will regard themselves, and one another, as members of a universal kingdom of ends, i.e., as "ends in themselves." No person will be a mere "thing," a mere means to support the life of another. Nature, too, will no longer be regarded as a mere external utility. It will be used for human ends, i.e., for the benefit of all persons, not merely for the benefit of a dominant ruling class. Individuals will be able to enjoy life without thereby also denying enjoyment to others. They will be able to develop and use all of their capacities without denying such opportunities to any one else. The "senses" and aptitudes of all persons will be enhanced in some transcendental, partly aesthetic, and partly social way:

> The overcoming of private property means therefore the complete *emancipation* of all human senses and aptitudes [Eigenschaften], but it means this emancipation precisely because these senses and aptitudes have become *human,* both subjectively and objectively. . . Need and satisfaction have thus lost their *egoistic* nature, and nature has lost its mere *utility* by becoming *human* use. . . (38).

The process of "return to self" begins, in Marx's cosmology, with the abolition of the capitalist economy. The movement of communism, properly defined and understood ". . . knows itself as the redintegration or return of man to himself, as the overcoming of human self-alienation. . . (39).

When the process of return has been completed, the potentialities that inhered in the beginning of the process but which had to be historically developed, will have been realized:

> . . . Atheism and communism are no flight from, no abstraction from, no loss of the objective world created by man as his essential capacities objectified. They are no impoverished return to unnatural primitive simplicity. Rather, they are primarily the actual emergence and actual, developed realization of man's nature as something actual (40).

The "return to self" as experienced by the single person will also be a return to society, to a form of self-consciousness and to ways of knowing and perceiving a humanized cosmos which is shared by all persons and that could have developed only through social power, through life and labor in society. Society was the originating source of human mentality. The capacity of the individual for self-consciousness developed as a result of his interactive rela-

38. "Private Property and Communism," *op. cit.*
39. *Ibid.*
40. "Critique of Hegelian Dialectic and Philosophy in General," *op. cit.*

tions with other human beings, who were objects for him, outside of himself, not created by himself, but having corporeality. Language had developed in this way. Thought is "living" when it is linked with nature and society and is expressed as language. It is not an abstract, self-enclosed intra-psychic activity having no relation to the external world of nature and of other persons:

> The element of thought itself, the element of the life-expression of thought, *language,* is perceptible nature. The *social* actuality of nature and *human* natural science or the *natural science of man* are identical expressions (41).

The absolute Mind and Ego of Hegelian theology was a false, unrealizable projection of a unitary self-condition that would be experienced, in a different way, in the post-alienated society. In the future time, no individual will appear as alien or as hostile to any one else.

Society is a supra-individual combined power that has enabled humanity to become the producing source of the world of "objects" existing in a humanized form: Referring to a single individual, Marx wrote that

> His own sense perception only exists as human sense perception for himself through the *other* man. The object for man – man himself – is nature, sense perception; and the particular, perceptible and essential powers of man can attain self-knowledge only in natural science because they are objectively developed only in *natural* objects (42).

In the society of communism, humanity will have absorbed, assimilated and "humanized" nature without abolishing the vitality and materiality of the humanly untransformed residue. So also the individual as a mind and self-center will be united cognitively with others, sharing the same perceptions of the world, without eliminating the corporeal ground of the single self, and personally variable traits that arise on the individual-biological level. Alienated man has been deprived of both personal and social power, but these will be totally restored: "Human nature had to be reduced to this absolute poverty so that it could give birth to its inner wealth" (43).

> Only here [in the post-alienated society of communism] has the *natural* existence of man become his *human* existence. Thus society is the completed, essential unity of man with nature, the true resurrection of nature, the fulfilled naturalism of man and the humanism of nature (44).

---

41. "Private Property and Communism," *op. cit.*
42. *Ibid.*
43. *Ibid.*
44. *Ibid.*

Marx said that Hegel's concept of "return to self" was a movement of "thought externalized and hence *thought* abstracted from nature and actual men. It is *abstract* thinking" (45). When Man as species is realized, it will be through a movement going beyond abstraction. Abstraction indicates also the isolated ego condition. To be social is to be non-abstract, inwardly linked in a positive, self-enhancing way, with the society of other people. Intellectual activity carried on by an individual person in isolation from immediate association with others will be social nevertheless in the society of communism. The individual will be conscious of his dependence on society, and of his social nature:

> Even as I am *scientifically* active, etc. – an activity I can seldom practice in direct community with others – I am *socially* active because I am active as *man*. Not only is the material of my activity – such as the language in which the thinker is active – given to me as a social product, but my *own* existence is social activity; what I make from myself I make for society, conscious of my nature as social (46).

What the thinker produces or constructs will be continuous with the "living form" of community life.

> My *general* consciousness is only the *theoretical* form whose *living* form is the *real* community, the social essence, although at present *general* consciousness is an abstraction from actual life and antagonistically opposed to it (47).

He said also that

> . . . it is only when objective actuality generally becomes for man in society the actuality of essential human capacities, that all *objects* become for him the *objectification* of himself, become objects which confirm and realize his individuality as *his* objects, that is, *he himself* becomes the object.

He is referring here to materially perceptible objects apprehended through the various physical senses. The individual's own "senses," which he shares with all other human beings, and which also include what Marx called "mental senses," are embodied in the object which has been socially created:

> *How* they become this depends on the *nature* of the *object* and the nature of the *essential capacity* corresponding to it, for it is precisely the *determinateness* of this relationship which shapes the particular, *actual* mode of affirmation. For the *eye* an object is different than for the *ear*, and the object of the eye *is* another object than that of the *ear*. The peculiarity of each essential

45. "Critique of Hegelian Dialectic and Philosophy in General," *op. cit.*
46. "Private Property and Communism," *op. cit.*
47. *Ibid.*

> capacity is precisely its *characteristic essence,* and thus also the characteristic mode of its objectification, of its objectively *actual,* living *being.* Thus man is affirmed in the objective world not only in thought but with all his senses (48).

THE TRANSITION TO HISTORICAL MATERIALISM

In transitional writings that marked the beginning of what is known as his historical materialism, Marx tried to drop the Hegelian language used in the cosmological essays of 1844, although he was unable to do so completely. In *The Holy Family,* the first transitional work (1844), he defined communism as a form materialism. This seemed to be at odds with his earlier definition of communism as "naturalism" and as "humanism" which was ". . . distinguished from both idealism and materialism" but which was "at the same time the unifying truth of both." In these transitional works, however, there was no substantial alteration in the views on the interrelations between Man and Nature that he had developed in the essays of 1844.

The Theses of Feuerbach (1845), eleven in all, rank among the most obscure and difficult works ever to be penned by a German philosopher. Marx declared, in the first thesis, that the materially constituted objects which are known through human "sense perception" have themselves been produced by human "practical activity." Thus, there seems to be no discontinuity between the activity of the subject and the objective reality so produced, other than the capacity of Man as active agent to distance himself mentally from the created object, and so to recognize his own human essence in the object produced. He also called attention to the fact that his own kind of materialism was different from every other known variety of philosophical materialism:

> The main shortcoming of all materialism up to now (including that of Feuerbach) is that the object, the reality, sensibility, is conceived only in the form of the *object* or of the *perception* [Anschauung], but not as sensuous human activity, *practice* [Praxis], not subjectively. Hence, the *active* side was developed abstractly in opposition to materialism by idealism, which naturally does not know the real sensuous activity as such. Feuerbach urged the real distinction between sensuous activity and thought objects; but he does not conceive of human activity itself as an *objective* [gegenstandlich] activity. Hence he deals in the *Essence of Christianity,* only with the theoretical attitude, as genuinely human, while practice is conceived and determined only in its dirty-Jewish form of appearance. He therefore does not apprehend the significance of the "revolutionary," practical critical activity (49).

---

48. *Ibid.*

49. Translated by Nathan Rotenstreich, in *Basic Problems of Marx's Philosophy,* Bobbs-Merrill Co., Inc. 1966.

Here Marx seems to be saying that no problem of knowledge relating to a world of objects existing apart from the activity of the subject can exist, since there is no such objective world. What he is expressing is a complete disinterest in aspects of nature that seem to be resistant to human control, or which cannot be used for purposes of control. In *The German Ideology* (1845-46) he cast doubt on Feuerbach's assumption that the natural sciences can perceive and discover, through specialized procedures and techniques, certain hidden processes and "secrets" in nature. He argued that nature had already been so much altered by human practical productive activity that nothing is left of "original nature" in the biological environment surrounding man. Feuerbach had said that natural science can uncover the "true essence" of natural objects. Marx noted that this assumption was philosophical. According to Feuerbach, natural science, penetrating beyond the level of observation available to the non-scientific perceiver, discloses a natural cosmic harmony that is evident to the contemplative vision of philosophers. Marx said that this thesis, which included a belief in an inherently given harmonious relation between Man and Nature, is without foundation in reality. There is no pre-existing, ante-historical "natural harmony" of this kind, revealed in the productions of original nature:

> Feuerbach's "conception" of the sensuous world is confined on the one hand to mere contemplation of it, and on the other to mere feeling. . . he necessarily lights on things which disturb the harmony he presupposes, the harmony of all parts of the sensuous world and especially of man and nature. To remove this disturbance, he must take refuge in a double perception, a profane one which only perceived the "flatly obvious" and a higher philosophical one which perceived the "true essence" of things. He does not see how the sensuous world around him is, not a thing given directly from all eternity, remaining ever the same, but the product of industry and of the state of society; and, indeed, in the sense that it is an historical product, the result of a whole succession of generations. Even the objects of the simplest "sensuous certainty" are only given him through social development, industry and commercial intercourse. . . For that matter, nature, the nature that preceded human history, is not by any means the nature in which Feuerbach lives.

The structure of Feuerbach's perceived world, his own existence and the objects which he perceives, would disappear, if the human labor of material production and economic exchange were to cease:

> Feuerbach speaks in particular of the perceptions of natural science; he mentions secrets which are disclosed only to the eyes of the physicist and chemist: but where would natural science be without industry and commerce? Even this "pure" natural science is provided with an aim, as with its material, only through

> trade and industry, through the sensuous activity of man. So much is this activity, this unceasing sensuous labour and creation, this production, the basis of the whole sensuous world as it now exists, that, were it interrupted only for a year, Freuerbach would not only find an enormous change in the natural world, but would very soon find that the whole world of man and his own perceptive faculty, nay his own existence, were missing (50).

Marx was concerned exclusively with the establishment of an inner societal harmony and unity that had no connection with any pre-existing naturally given harmony. Nature, as originally existing, must be transformed in order that the inner social harmony can be established. It appears that the necessary transformations of external nature have already taken place. The function of revolutionary "practical-critical" activity is to establish internal social harmony, by demolishing those aspects of the social and institutional world which support and perpetuate the alienated self-condition of the present, and so prevent the "return of Man to himself," i.e., the reunification of Man with Man.

Marx had said that Feuerbach had a "great advantage" over "pure materialists" since "he realizes how man too is an 'object of the senses'." However, Feuerbach remains in the realm of theory because he does not also conceive of man as "sensuous activity," as the dyanmic, creative, history making transformer of nature. The power to transform nature is also the power to transform human nature, since nature and man are essentially one. In the society of communism, nothing in human nature will exist inwardly, in private self-existence, that is not compatible with what is objectified outwardly in society, to others, manifest to all. When he referred to object perception Marx was operating within a specially enclosed metaphysical frame of reference which can be called organic interactionism.

A major problem in Marx's cosmology arises in connection with his philosophy of mind, which relates also to his philosophy of knowledge and of science. Subjective mind, as a process and power of the individual psyche, is overly socialized, historicized, and objectivized. The inner, biologically given attributes of the psyche are subsumed under a general, historically mutable life process, and seem to share in the organic fluidity and mutability of those sub-social biological life forms that are below the human level. In *Capital* Marx referred to "The life process of society, which is based on the process of material production. . ." (51). His metaphysical materialism was combined with a *social* theory of human mind and self-origin which left the biological basis of the individual psyche, i.e., of conceptual and perceptual subjectivity, somewhat in doubt.

---

50. *Op. cit.*, Volume I, Part I, pp. 57-58.
51. Volume I, *op. cit.*, Chapter I, p. 80.

3

Historical Progress: The Increasing Domination Of Man Over Nature

In this chapter, I will be discussing Marx's theory of human evolution as this relates especially to the thesis that he first presented in the philosophical manuscripts of 1844, namely, the idea that ". . . the entire so-called world history is only the creation of man through human labor and the development of nature for man." This concept was modified in his later writings, but Marx never abandoned his belief that Nature was organically and morally linked with Man in such a way as to ensure the ultimate victory of the human spirit over the forces of death, decay, and spiritual impoverishment that were temporarily ascendant in capitalist society.

In the manuscripts of 1844, Marx had been describing a situation of the future in which the unity of Man and Nature was so complete that processes of nature were almost wholly absorbed into processes of human activity. Nature was simply the "inorganic body" of human society. In the later works, the fusion is not as complete, even though the organic link between Man and nature still holds firm. There is some kind of opposing material, produced by nature, that continually reappears, and which must be continually transformed by man. Man is said to be the "sovereign of nature," and this implies that some kind of dominating rule is being maintained over a subordinated natural realm.

As a philosopher of Man and Nature, Marx occupies a special place in Western intellectual history. He was sympathetic to the development of the science of evolutionary biology. He believed that the human species had been through a process of evolution which had taken place in the remote past, and which had resulted in a biological advance beyond an original condition of proto-human existence. He wrote in a letter of Engels (January 16, 1861) that

> . . . Darwin's book is very important and serves me as a natural-scientific basis for the class struggle in history. One has to put up with the crude English method of development, of course. Despite all deficiencies, not only is the death-blow dealt here

> for the first time to "teleology" in the natural sciences but its rational meaning is empirically explained (1).

He seems to be saying that the reasons for evolutionary development on the sub-human level are adequately explained by Darwinism, yet it is hard to see in just what way Darwin's theory provides "a natural scientific basis for the class struggle in history." Marx was not able to give a coherently "Darwinian" expression to a theory of human bio-evolutionary development. He suggested, in another letter to Engels (June 18, 1862) that Darwin's account of the competitive struggle for existence in nature was also a description of conditions prevailing in capitalist economic society:

> Darwin, whom I have looked upon again, amuses me when he says he is applying the "Malthusian" theory *also* to plants and animals, as if with Mr. Malthus the whole point were not that he does *not* apply the theory to plants and animals but only to human beings – and with geometrical progression – as opposed to plants and animals. It is remarkable how Darwin recognizes among beasts and plants his English society with its division of labour, competition, opening up of new markets, "inventions," and the Malthusian "struggle for existence." It is Hobbes's *bellum omnium contra omnes,* and one is reminded of Hegel's *Phenomenology,* where civil society is described as a "spiritual animal kingdom," while in Darwin the animal kingdom figures as civil society. . . (2).

Marx's own theory of human evolution underlined the uniqueness of Man and the impossibility of demonstrating that any kind of "class struggle" between human beings, corresponding to what supposedly takes place in the plant and animal kingdoms, had been instrumental to the acquisition of uniquely human species powers, including the power to dominate original nature.

The idea that Man, in the present age of science and technology, has acquired the power to "master" or dominate external terrestrial nature is a widespread belief by no means confined to Marxism. Hegel, too, had declared that humanity was equipped with such powers. Nature on earth could be safely exploited and destroyed by Man to serve economic ends. The superior mind of man could always contrive ways of beating nature at her own game:

> The practical approach to Nature is, in general, determined by appetite, which is self-seeking; need impels us to use Nature for our own advantage, to wear her out, to wear her down, in short, to annihilate her. . . The necessities and the wit of man have found an endless variety of ways of using and mastering Nature. . The cunning of his reason enables him to preserve and maintain

1. *Marx and Engels: Selected Correspondence,* Progress Publishers, Moscow, 1965.
2. *Ibid.*

> himself in the face of the forces of Nature, by sheltering behind other products of Nature, and letting these suffer her destructive attacks. Nature herself, however, in her universal aspect, he cannot overcome in this way, nor can he turn her to his own purposes (3).

Marx does not make the Hegelian distinction between nature in her "universal," cosmological and creational aspect, and those manifestations of nature that are within the economically usable human environment. The kind of power that Man acquires in and over nature, in the course of evolutionary development and historical progress, is not a fully "external" power, disconnected from nature. It has been developed only because material nature itself, in its universal aspect, has inner qualities that actively support the human enterprise.

In this discussion of Marx's evolutionary progress philosophy, I will consider 1) his concept of the situation of humanity in relation to nature in the economy of capitalism; 2) his views about the pre-capitalist stages of evolutionary development; and 3) his concept of the future socialist economy and the way in which that society will relate to nature.

THE PROGRESS OF MAN IN THE POST-FEUDAL AGE

Marx expected that the stage of evolutionary history leading from capitalism to ultimate communism would enable Man to achieve control over forces and tendencies in human nature that could not be controlled in capitalist society. He declared, in the Grundrisse (1857-58) that this kind of control would be achieved, eventually, but only in the society of ultimate communism, after "wealth" in the fullest sense of the word, had become available to humanity:

> . . . when the narrow bourgeois form has been peeled away, what is wealth, if not the universality of needs, capacities, enjoyments, productive powers, etc., of individuals, produced in universal exchange? What, if not the full development of human control over the forces of nature – those of his own nature as well as those of so-called "nature"? What, if not the absolute elaboration of his creative dispositions, without any preconditions other than antecedent historical evolution which makes the totality of this evolution – i.e., the evolution of all human powers as such, unmeasured by any *previously established* yardstick – an end in itself? What is this, if not a situation where man does not reproduce himself in any determined form, but produces his totality?

3. *Hegel's Philosophy of Nature,* Clarendon Press, Oxford, 1970, section 245, p. 5.

> Where he does not seek to remain something formed by the past, but is in the absolute movement of becoming (4)?

Capitalist civilization had prepared the ground for this future advance. In spite of the evils brought by capitalism, it had been a necessary phase of world history. He wrote, in Volume III of *Capital* that

> Development of the productive forces of social labour is the historical task and justification of capital. This is just the way in which it unconsciously creates the material requirements for a higher mode of production (5).

But in the present age there is a glaring paradox. Power over external nature is a power of material wealth production. But this power is offset by moral deterioration. In a remarkable speech, written in English and delivered on April 14, 1856 at an anniversary celebration of the founding of the "People's Paper," a Chartist publication, Marx said that

> In our days everything seems pregnant with its contrary. Machinery, gifted with the wonderful power of shortening and fructifying human labour, we behold starving and overworking it. The new-fangled sources of wealth, by some strange weird spell, are turned into sources of want. The victories of art seem bought by the loss of character. At the same pace that mankind masters nature, man seems to become enslaved to other men or to his own infamy. Even the pure light of science seems unable to shine but on the dark background of ignorance. All our invention and progress seem to result in endowing material forces with intellectual life, and in stultifying human life into a material force. This antagonism between modern industry and science on the one hand, modern misery and destitution on the other hand, this antagonism between the productive powers and the social relations of our epoch is a fact, palpable, overwhelming, and not to be controverted. Some parties may wail over it; others may wish to get rid of modern arts, in order to get rid of modern conflicts. Or they may imagine that so signal a progress in industry wants to be completed by as signal a regress in politics. On our part, we do not mistake the shape of the shrewd spirit that continues to mark all these contradictions. We know that to work well the new-fangled forces of society, they only want to be mastered by new-fangled men – and such are the working men. They are as much the invention of modern times as machinery itself. In the signs that bewilder the middle class, the aristocracy, and the poor prophets of regression, we do recognize our brave friend, Robin

4. *Pre-Capitalist Economic Formations* (Excerpts from the Grundrisse), International Publishers, New York, 1964, pp. 83 and 84.
5. Chapter 15, p. 259, International Publishers, N.Y., 1967.

> Goodfellow, the old mole that can work in the earth so fast, that worthy pioneer – the Revolution (6).

Marx here expresses an almost mystical confidence in the natural historical emergence of "new men" equipped with heroic powers that will prove equal to the greatness of the task which it is their mission to accomplish.

Marx expected that the society of socialism would carry forward all of the civilizational and cultural gains achieved over more than two thousand years of Western development. At first Man had been totally subordinated, materially and spiritually, to the forces of external nature. The early advances beyond this condition had occurred because the primitive men had been compelled to develop various means of using nature, and of defending themselves against nature, in order to survive. Civilization advanced as a result of economic, material expansion which was to a large extent made possible by cumulative improvement in material production techniques. The latest, most advanced stages of Western civilization began with the scientific enlightenment. The bourgeois revolution against feudalism and Catholicism was regarded by Marx as the victory of rational, scientific civilization over the reactionary civilization of the middle ages. The movement of socialism was culturally continuous with the modern bourgeois revolution in certain fundamental respects. In his political and historical writings of 1848 and 1849, Marx had identified bourgeois society as a "society of knowledge." In a speech before a Cologne jury (February 1849) he appealed to the jury in the name of the bourgeois enlightenment, in his attack on the reactionary feudalistic authority of the Prussian State:

> This was not a case of a political conflict between two parties standing on the ground of *one* society, it was a *conflict between two societies,* a *social* conflict which had taken on a political form, it was the struggle of modern bourgeois society with the old *feudal-bureaucratic society,* the struggle between the society of free competition and the society of guild organization, between the society of industry and the society of landownership, between the society of knowledge and the society of belief (7).

Marx called attention to what he regarded as recent, progressive changes in the relation of modern society and people to the land, and therefore also to the whole of nature. Capitalism had disrupted the traditional ties that had once bound workers and also landowners to the soil, and to particular localities. Land was now thoroughly commercialized in the more advanced capital-

---

6. *The Selected Works of Marx and Engels,* Progress Publishers, Moscow, 1969, Volume I.

7. *Karl Marx: The Revolutions of 1848,* Political Writings Volume I, The Marx Library, Random House, New York, 1974, edited and introduced by David Fernbach. Marx was here presenting a point of view which he had also incorporated into an article on "The Bourgeoisie and the Counter-Revolution," written in December 1848, reprinted in *The Selected Works of Marx and Engels,* Volume I, *op. cit.*

ist countries. Individuals, too, had been uprooted, detached, and displaced. This process was to be welcomed and even encouraged by socialists, as a transitional phase of social-economic transformation. Persons were no longer to be subordinated to an archaic way of life and to limited, restrictive attachments. He expected that the working class movement would "appropriate" the nature-mastering forces of production developed in the capitalist economy, together with the land and its resources. The old ties had to be dissolved before a higher universal community could be formed which would unite humanity to the universe of nature in a new way. In the cooperative economy of socialism, a rational, communitarian will and purpose could be superimposed on all of nature, including human society and human nature. The new order, however, would not be restrictive or oppressive. It was to be universal liberation from all past and present forms of oppression and subordination, in nature and in society.

HUMAN EVOLUTION THROUGH PRODUCTIVE ACTIVITY

Marx's theory of historical evolution included a belief that humanity had acquired new powers of an inner psychological kind by engaging in productive activities that resulted also in transformations of the social and economic environment, in the nature of relations between various human groups and individuals, and in the relation of humanity as species to external nature. Some of these new powers were acquired through the activation of nature-given genetic potentialities present in Man from the very beginning. Other powers seem to have been added to the original endowment.

His evolutionary outlook was the product of a period that preceded the development of Mendelian genetic science. His theory that Man evolves himself through productive activity was compatible, in a general way, with the Lamarckian assumptions concerning the inheritance of experientially acquired characteristics which were widely prevalent in the nineteenth century, among philosophers and scientists, including the British sociologist Herbert Spencer, as well as Darwin himself. In his book on *The Rise of Anthropological Theory,* Marvin Harris contrasts the modern biogenetic view with the earlier Lamarckian perspective, with special reference to Marx. In his chapter on dialectical materialism, he concludes that Russian Soviet culture had inherited Lamarckian conceptions from Marx and from Engels, and that this accounted for what Harris calls ". . . the twentieth century disaster of Soviet genetics," during the period when the work of Lysenko was given the stamp of official approval. Marx is said to have ". . . shared with Spencer the prevailing and erroneous notion of a Lamarckian feedback between behavior and heredity" (8). It was only with reference to Man, however, that Marx could be called a "Lamarckian." Humanity was an exceptional species, and the process of development he described had widened the qualitative gap that had always existed between Man and the rest of natural creation.

8. Thomas Y. Crowell, New York, 1968.

Humanity, Marx believed, had gone through a prehistoric period which shaded gradually into a primitive period that was more clearly historical. In the indefinitely protracted initial stages of development, individuals had acquired certain psychic characteristics that were not in evidence at the beginning. During the ages of post-primitive Western civilization, however, mankind had been in full possession of those essential powers that Marx associated with freedom from instinctual pre-determination, but also with culturally acquired changes in attitudes toward external nature.

In the prehistoric state, Nature seemed to be transcendent over Man, and was experienced by the proto-humans as an external force and threat of an overwhelming kind. In this situation, men were said to have had an "animal-like" natural religion, described as

> . . . consciousness of nature, which first appears to men as a completely alien, all-powerful, and unassailable force, with which men's relations are purely animal, and by which they are overawed like beasts; it is thus a purely animal consciousness of nature (natural religion) (9).

But this "animal consciousness" indicates that humans are different from animals, even at the beginning. Animals have no "consciousness" either of nature or of other members of their own species. They can have no religion of any kind. Marx observed that "Men can be distinguished from animals by consciousness, by religion, or anything else you like" (10). The mere possession of these uniquely human tendencies was not what enabled the species to advance, to raise itself out of the proto-human condition. History, and the subsequent progressive advance of humanity beyond the animal-like condition of immersion in Nature begins when Man starts to produce his material means of subsistence. Only then do human beings begin to acquire a sense that they are humans, and that they are different from sub-human animals:

> They themselves [men in general] begin to distinguish themselves from animals as soon as they begin to *produce* their means of subsistence, a step which is conditioned by their physical organization. By producing their means of subsistence men are indirectly producing their actual material life (11).

"Actual material life" includes the social and economic relations between human beings that develop in connection with production activity. The nature of individuals as manifested in any given economic system "coincides" with the nature of their material production activity:

> The way in which men produce their means of subsistence depends first of all on the nature of the actual means of subsistence they find in existence and have to reproduce. This mode of

9. *The German Ideology*, Volume I, Part I, p. 42, Progress Publishers, Moscow, 1965.
10. *Ibid.*, p. 31.
11. *Ibid.*, p. 31.

> production must not be considered simply as being the reproduction of the physical existence of the individual. Rather it is a definite form of activity of these individuals, a definite form of expressing their life, a definite *mode of life* on their part. As individuals express their life, so they are. What they are, therefore, coincides with their production, both with *what* they produce and with *how* they produce. The nature of individuals thus depends on the material conditions determining their production (12).

Production activity included not only the production of the material means of subsistence, but also reproductive activity, the biological reproduction of the human population. These primary activities result in changes that react back upon the human producers, thereby changing the mode of life, their relations with one another, and their relations with nature. All modes of life, however, are expressions of "human nature." The term "human nature" in this context refers to all manifest expressions and activities carried on by human beings in various historical societies. Human nature contains a vast number of divergent potentialities. The way in which these are developed and expressed depends a good deal on the particular social and cultural situation in which human beings find themselves. A great many innate aptitudes of individuals require exercise and cultivation, otherwise they exist only as undeveloped potentialities. When he wrote as a theorist of history, Marx included negative as well as positive expressions of manifestations of "human nature," i.e., those of which he himself might disapprove and condemn, as well as those which he wished to see perpetuated in a society of the future. The historical variability of human nature is an asset, not a liability. From the very first, humanity was endowed by nature with special capacities for change, and with a special kind of mutability and openness, a freedom from the kind of genetic pre-determination which limited the life of all other species. The non-human species could develop only to the extent of those powers whose outermost limits had been fixed in advance. Humanity, on the other hand, was open to the future; its end was not contained in a naturally pre-determined beginning.

In *The German Ideology* and in other writings that dealt with the passage of humanity beyond the initial primitive state, Marx described the way in which human consciousness developed out of a condition of preconscious existence. His theory was based on a number of mythic assumptions concerning the primordial condition, assumptions which antedated the rise of scientific anthropology. The appearance of mental powers was correlated with a process of psychic individuation, whereby persons acquired a consciousness of self that removed them from the "sheep-like" condition in which they had only a pre-personal collective consciousness. In *The German Ideology* Marx wrote that

12. *Ibid.*, pp. 31-32.

> The beginning is as animal as social life itself at this stage. It is mere herd-consciousness, and at this point man is only distinguished from sheep by the fact that with him consciousness takes the place of instinct or that his instinct is a conscious one (13).

Language capacities and a personal identity awareness develop in a process of social interchange which is both material and practical:

> . . . it is quite obvious from the start that there exists a materialistic connection of men with one another, which is determined by their needs and their mode of production, and which is as old as men themselves. This connection is ever taking on new forms, and thus presents a "history" independently of the existence of any political or religious nonsense which would especially hold men together. . . we find that man also possesses "consciousness," but, even so, no inherent, no "pure" consciousness. From the start the "spirit" is afflicted with the curse of being "burdened" with the matter, which here makes its appearance in the form of agitated layers of air, sounds, in short, of language. Language is as old as consciousness, language *is* practical consciousness that exists also for other men, and for that reason alone it really exists for me personally as well; language, like consciousness, only arises from the need, the necessity of intercourse with other men (14).

Marx here gives an inordinate weight to language as the material medium of communication. In denying the existence of an "inherent" or "pure" consciousness that pre-exists society and language, he is also depreciating those internal mental and conceptual powers and activities of consciousness in the individual that must co-exist with linguistic capacities. As a "practical materialist" Marx conveys the impression that what he calls "the language of real life" is not ideational or conceptual at all. He does admit that ideas are produced as functions of linguistic consciousness. Referring to the early stages of evolutionary development, he said that

> The production of ideas, of conceptions, of consciousness, is at first directly interwoven with the material activity and the material intercourse of men, the language of real life. Conceiving, thinking, the mental intercourse of men, appear at this stage as the direct efflux of their material behavior (15).

The situation in more advanced, post-primitive societies is much the same. Mental production is considerably expanded, but this expansion occurs as a by-product or a "direct efflux" of material expansion. Social behavior, the relations of individuals to one another, is always a "material activity." Individuals change personally, as social, psychological and mental beings,

13. *Ibid.*, p. 42.
14. *Ibid.*, pp. 42-43.
15. *Ibid.*, p. 37.

when the objective material and social processes and conditions of their life change. What they express on the ideological level is therefore always an expression, i.e., a "direct efflux," of a total, pervasive change that affects society as a whole, and themselves as individuals in that whole:

> The same applies to mental production as expressed in the language of politics, laws, morality, religion, metaphysics, etc. of a people. Men are the producers of their conceptions, ideas, etc. – real, active men, as they are conditioned by a definite development of their productive forces and of the intercourse corresponding to these, even up to its furthest forms. Consciousness can never be anything else than conscious existence, and the existence of men is their actual life-process (16).

Marx's perspective on human history included a vaguely formulated Lamarckian theory, a belief in the inheritance of acquired characteristics, which applied exclusively to the human species. Humanity had existed, to begin with, in a primordial, undeveloped, "instinctual" condition. Powers not originally given by nature had been acquired as a result of material work activity. The universal workers had achieved an ability to create independently in ways that surpassed the naturally given unconscious creative processes and powers of original nature. Through social communication and interchange arising in connection with practical work, they had also developed powers of speech. Somewhat later, they had acquired a self-consciousness, a sense of separate individuality, which superseded a pre-individualized tribal or collective consciousness.

In *Capital* Marx called attention to the way in which valuable moral capacities had been acquired by individual workers through a direct, socially unmediated interaction with external nature. These had been internalized biologically, passed on through inheritance to later generations. This, at least, is what Marx seemed to be saying, although he did not make a clearcut distinction between the activation of dormant faculties that had existed as potentialities before the workers became materially active, and the acquisition of humanly significant new powers. One process seems to have involved the other.

The stimulus of material, vital need had set in motion the process of evolutionary transformation which resulted in the development of the powers of the worker in nature up to the most fully advanced, human level. The worker had been able to acquire a personal mastery over the materials with which he worked, and also a mastery over himself. While mastery over nature had reached its highest level in the economy of capitalism

> . . . it by no means follows from this that the most fruitful soil is the most fitted for the growth of the capitalist mode of production. This mode is based on the dominion of man over Nature.

16. *Ibid.*

> Where nature is too lavish, she "keeps him in hand, like a child in leading-strings." She does not impose upon him any necessity to develop himself. It is not the tropics with their luxurient vegetation, but the temperate zone, that is the mother-country of capital (17).

The process of human evolution was now complete in the biological sense. It had come to an end at some time far in the past, long before the development of the capitalist mode of production. Humanity had progressed beyond the stage at which work had been merely instinctual, carried on in some preconscious way. In his chapter on "The Labor Process," Marx defined material labor as being

> . . . in the first place, a process in which both man and Nature participate, and in which man of his own accord starts, regulates, and controls the material reactions between himself and Nature. He opposes himself to Nature as one of her own forces, setting in motion arms and legs, head and hands, the natural forces of his body, in order to appropriate Nature's productions in a form adapted to his own wants. By thus acting on the external world and changing it, he at the same time changes his own nature. He develops his slumbering powers and compels them to act in obedience to his sway (18).

It appears that in the primordial condition, before the process of psychic individuation had taken place, and before linguistic capacities had developed, human labor had been "primitive" and also "instinctive:"

> We are not now dealing with those primitive instinctive forms of labour that remind us of the mere animal. An immeasurable interval of time separates the state of things in which a man brings his labour-power to market for sale as a commodity, from that state in which human labour was still in its first instinctive stage. We pre-suppose labour in a form that stamps it as exclusively human. A spider conducts operations that resemble those of a weaver, and a bee puts to shame many an architect in the construction of her cells. But what distinguishes the worst architect from the best of bees is this, that the architect raises his structure in imagination before he erects it in reality. At the end of every labour process, we get a result that already existed in the imagination of the labourer at its commencement (19).

Modern man has developed powers of conscious will, purpose and imagination which he brings to the labor process, powers which the early proto-humans did not have. The historically acquired ability to surpass the

---

17. Volume I, chapter 16, p. 513, International Publishers, N.Y., 1967.
18. *Ibid.*, chapter 7, p. 177.
19. *Ibid.*, p. 178.

level of "instinctive labor" is weighted with moral significance. In altering the objective materials of nature, the worker develops and demonstrates his capacity for self-discipline. He has a foresightful, constructive imagination and also a rational moral will. He can impose a law upon himself, for the sake of fulfilling a self-accepted purpose. "Willing" in this context implies an ability to refrain from yielding to counter-impulses which could result in an unfinished project. It is also an ability to tolerate unpleasantness and dissatisfaction over an extended period, a power to persist at a task which may be uncongenial and uninteresting, for the sake of achieving an ultimate objective. The worker

> . . . not only effects a change of form in the material on which he works, but he also realizes a purpose of his own that gives the law to his modus operandi, and to which he must subordinate his will. And this subordination is no mere momentary act. Besides the exertion of the bodily organs, the process demands that, during the whole operation, the workman's will be steadily in consonance with his purpose. This means close attention. The less he is attracted by the nature of the work, and the mode in which it is carried on, and the less, therefore, he enjoys it as something which gives play to his bodily and mental powers, the more close his attention is forced to be (20).

By inventing tools as an extension of his bodily organs, the worker is able to use the entirety of Nature as an "instrument of his own activity":

> He makes use of the mechanical, physical, and chemical properties of some substances in order to make other substances subservient to his aims. Leaving out of consideration such ready-made means of subsistence as fruits, in gathering which a man's own limbs serve as the instruments of his labour, the first thing of which the labourer possesses himself is not the subject of labour but its instrument. Thus Nature becomes one of the organs of his activity, one that he annexes to his own bodily organs, adding stature to himself in spite of the Bible. As the earth is his original larder, so too it is his original tool house (21).

In this account of the labour process and of the changes brought about by this means, Marx was adapting concepts originally developed by Aristotle, in his teleological philosophy of nature. Marx eliminated the anthropomorphic elements in Aristotle's description of the species creating and species-actualizing power immanent in Nature. To Man alone belongs the power of design, will and purpose which Aristotle had projected on to Nature. In the section of the *Metaphysics* which deals with the category of material cause, Aristotle had written: "Now we recognize four kinds of cause: i) the defini-

20. *Ibid.*, p. 178.
21. *Ibid.*, p. 179.

tion, essence, or essential nature of the thing, ii) its matter or substratum, iii) its source of motion, and iv) opposite to the third, the 'end' or 'good' which is the goal of all generation and movement." In *Capital* Marx was depicting Man the Worker as the formal, final and dynamic cause of transformations occurring in the material substratum. Man as the active agent of transformation, imposes his own will and purpose on nature.

Aristotle had attributed an almost human kind of rationality and intentionality to creational Nature. He writes, in *De Anima:* "Nature, like mind, always does whatever it does for the sake of something which is its end." In another work, *The Parts of Animals,* he writes:

> Plainly. . . that cause is the first which we call the final one. For this is the Reason, and the Reason forms the starting point, alike in works of art and in works of nature. For consider how the physician or the builder sets about his work. He starts by forming for himself a definite picture, in the one case perceptible to the mind, in the other to sense, of his end – the physician of health, the builder of a house – and this he holds forward as the reason and explanation of each subsequent step that he takes, and of his acting in this or that way as the case may be. Now in the works of nature the good end and the final cause is still more dominant than in works of art such as these. . . (22).

The reader of *Capital* is tempted to think that Marx may have been influenced by this passage when he projected his image of Man the Builder, the architect, whose product is the manifestation of mind acting upon nature-given materials which are re-arranged to accord with the human design. Marx makes no mention, however, of the physician, who in the execution of his aim must devote himself to the study of biological structures and processes occurring in nature. The labour process, as conceived by Marx, is always transformational. Man, as the highest manifestation of mind, will, and purpose in Nature, is the 'good end' and the 'final cause' of the historical nature-transforming process which he himself initiates.

Marx rejected Aristotle's anthropomorphism, which imputed some kind of purpose to nature as the creator of life forms. He also upgraded the cosmological status of matter. In Aristotle's cosmology, matter pre-exists nature, but has no causational powers at all, no part in being or becoming, except when it is combined with the higher vital and telic elements deriving from the divine Nous, the Prime Mover (23). Nature creates human life, mind and consciousness as well as all other life forms, because it has internalized the telic and vital powers. In Marx's system, matter is never merely potential. It always exists in nature. Natural materiality binds together all material phenomena, organic and inorganic, including Man as an organic being. Natural

---

22. *The Works of Aristotle,* Volume V, *op. cit.* Book I, i, 639b 15-20.
23. See also the discussion of Aristotle's cosmology in relation to Hegel's idealism, in chapter II, above.

materiality has vital form-creating potentialities and properties. It is an amorphous material substratum with inherent powers of creativity which are, however, limited powers. The higher will and rationality of Man, arising out of the unconscious natural substratum, becomes a supra-natural telic force, capable of transmuting the forms and structures that are products of natural unconscious creativity. As a field of human activity, the entirety of unconscious nature becomes primarily a passive, form receptive material substratum with little or no power to resist the transformations brought about by Man. Human nature itself, insofar as it rests on a psycho-organic natural foundation, has a passive, negative but also a vital and responsive capacity for becoming assimilated or adapted to a variety of historically developed social forms and social structures, new patterns of economic and social organization. These develop and change in response to changes initiated by the purposive activities of Man the producer, the worker in Nature.

Humanity, as a self-evolving species, is both *active* and *passive.* As a social transformer, Man, the Worker in nature, becomes the active external power that operates on the passive material substratum, supplanting the active power of the Divine Nous that Aristotle said was immanent in Nature. External, organic-inorganic nature responds to the needs of Man, provided active, conscious efforts are made to secure this result. Human nature, in so far as it is *social,* is also adaptable, malleable, sharing in the amorphousness and the form-receptive passivity of *matter.* Human beings are capable of manifesting different qualities in different historical epochs. By the same token, certain qualities that might otherwise appear in manifest form can be suppressed, or fail to develop, under certain conditions.

In his essays of 1844, Marx had stressed the organic continuity of external nature with the corporate body of humanity, conceived as a united social entity. Nature is the subject, passive but also vital and responsive, which is acted upon by the human transforming agent. Changes brought about by conscious human activity utilize the powers of the universal material substratum which binds humanity to the natural cosmos:

> The universality of man appears in practice as the universality which makes the whole of nature his *inorganic* body. . . Nature is the *inorganic* body of man, that is, nature insofar as it is not the human body. Man *lives* by nature. This means that nature is his *body,* with which he must remain in perpetual process in order not to die. That the physical and spiritual life of man is tied up with nature is another way of saying that nature is linked to itself, for man is a part of nature (24).

Marx referred to the historically developed technological powers that had become available to humanity in the age of capitalism as social instruments and organs, to be used by society, considered as a corporate, quasi-organic entity. In one of the lengthier footnotes in *Capital,* he wrote:

24. Easton and Guddat, *op. cit.* "Alienated Labor."

> A critical history of technology would show how little any of the inventions of the 18th century are the work of a single individual. Hitherto there is no such book. Darwin has interested us in the history of Nature's technology, i.e., in the formation of the organs of plants and animals which organs serve as instruments of production for sustaining life. Does not the history of the productive organs of man, of organs that are the material basis of all social organization, deserve equal attention? And would not such a history be easier to compile, since, as Vico says, human history differs from natural history in this, that we have made the former, but not the latter? Technology discloses man's mode of dealing with Nature, the process of production by which he sustains his life, and thereby also lays bare the mode by which he sustains his life, and thereby also lays bare the mode of formation of social relations, and of the mental conceptions that flow from them. Every history of religion even, that fails to take account of this material basis, is uncritical (25).

Marx emphasized the dependency of modern society on material nature. He expected that the power of social technology would be sufficient to supply all the material needs of humanity, once this power had been fully socialized and was used for the benefit of all. The wealth-creating powers of technology did not derive solely from the labor input, or from the instruments and techniques developed by Man, but also and equally from the way in which Nature responded to the needs of man, and to human initiatives. In *The Critique of the Gotha Programme* (1875) he objected to the German Social Democratic party statement that "Labour is the source of all wealth and all culture. . . " He declared, in opposition:

> Labour is *not the source* of all wealth. *Nature* is just as much the source of use values (and it is surely of such that material wealth consists!) as is labour, which itself is only the manifestation of a natural force, human labour power. That phrase is to be found in all children's primers and is correct only in so far as it is *implied* that labour proceeds with the appropriate subjects and instruments. But a socialist programme cannot allow such bourgeois phrases to cause the *conditions* to be ignored that alone give them meaning. And in so far as man from the beginning behaves toward nature, the primary source of all instruments and subjects of labour, as her owner, treats her as belonging to him, his labour becomes the source of use values, therefore also of wealth (26).

Man, as the owner of Nature, has transformed the entire earth into an "instrument of labour." Earth territory is both an instrument and a resource.

---

25. Volume I, chapter 15, p. 372.
26. International Publishers, N.Y., 1938.

The changes brought about by human productive activity then become earth resources, expanding the resources beyond the original level. Techniques and tools, including machines, are "conductors of [labour] activity:"

> In a wider sense we may include among the instruments of labour. . . all such objects as are necessary for carrying on the labour process. These do not enter directly into the process, but without them it is either impossible for it to take place at all, or possible only to a partial extent. Once more we find the earth to be a universal instrument of this sort, for it furnishes a locus standi to the labourer and a field of employment for his activity. Among instruments that are the result of previous labour and also belong to this class, we find workshops, canals, roads, and so forth (27).

The modern labor process involves first, the abstraction of natural raw materials from their initial rootedness in nature, and secondly, the manipulation, recombination, and further alteration of the materials thus abstracted:

> With the exception of the extractive industries, in which the material for labour is provided immediately by Nature, such as mining, hunting, fishing, and agriculture (so far as the latter is confined to breaking up virgin soil), all branches of industry manipulate raw material, objects already filtered through labour, already products of labour. Such is seed in agriculture. Animals and plants, which are accustomed to consider as products of Nature, are, in their present form, not only products of, say, last year's labour, but the result of a gradual transformation, continued through many generations, under man's superintendence, and by means of his labour (28).

The practical, nature-transforming modern sciences achieve their success because they have acquired knowledge of how nature works. The practitioners are able to *imitate* on a conscious level the unconscious creative processes going on in nature apart from Man. In the first chapter of *Capital,* Marx wrote that:

> The use-values, coat, linen, etc, i.e., the bodies of commodities, are combinations of two elements – matter and labour. If we take away the useful labour expended upon them, a material substratum is always left, which is furnished by Nature without the help of man. The latter can work only as nature works, that is by changing the form of matter. Nay more, in this work of changing the form he is constantly helped by natural forces. We see, then, that labour is not the only source of material wealth, of use-

---

27. *Capital,* Volume I, chapter 7, p. 180.
28. *Ibid.,* p. 181.

values produced by labour. As William Petty puts it, Labour is its father and the earth its mother (29).

Just how did Nature change the forms of matter? In a footnote to the phrase "changing the form of matter," Marx appended a quotation from an Italian economist, Pietro Verri, who had written in 1773:

> The phenomena of the universe, whether the production of man's hand or of the universal laws of physics, give one and all the idea, not of actual creation, but solely of a modification of matter. Bringing together and taking apart – these are the only elements which human intelligence can discover when it analyzes the idea of production, including the production of value or wealth – whether it be that of earth, air, and water are transformed into the fields of grain; or that by the hand of man the sticky secretion of an insect is changed into silks and velvets, or a few scraps of metal are made into a repeater watch.

Such a view implies that the organic-inorganic matter of nature has a power of self-motion and of cohesion. It separates into parts which combine accidentally to produce various complex forms. These can also disintegrate. The material can then combine itself in new ways. These processes suffice to account for the appearance of formations and transformations occurring independently of a human manipulator and designer.

MODERN TECHNOLOGY AS SOCIAL POWER

Marx regarded the historical evolution of nature-dominating instrumental powers as a social process and a social achievement. The accumulated knowledge that was of such great service to man was a social product, not only because of the obvious fact that many individuals had contributed to the advance of that knowledge, but also because such personal contributions could survive and could accumulate only through social communication and through transmission from one generation to the next. But Marx did also call attention to one particular kind of social productive power that had nothing to do with acquisition and development of practical knowledge as such. This was collective power, a form of physical and psychological energy arising in direct social cooperation, in situations where large numbers of individuals worked together, side by side, as equals, on a unifying work project. In *Capital,* he noted that impressive constructive and engineering projects had been accomplished in pre-industrial civilizations through the mobilization of masses of workers – usually slaves, serfs, or poor peasants – who were conscripted by a ruling monarch, and set to work to carry out his personal architectural and engineering designs. In the modern industrial era, collectivized

29. *Ibid.,* chapter 1, p. 43.

"mass labour" was becoming the predominant form of necessary material labour. Such labour constituted the material base of modern capitalist society. The added social power of mass labor, in combination with the power of machinery, had raised the material productivity of labor in capitalist society to an unprecedent level:

> . . . the sum total of the mechanical forces exerted by isolated workmen differs from the social force that is developed, when many hands take part simultaneously in one and the same undivided operation, such as raising a heavy weight, turning a winch, or removing an obstacle. In such cases the combined labour could either not be produced at all by isolated individual labour, or it could only be produced by a great expenditure of time, or on a very dwarfed scale. Not only have we here an increase in the productive power of the individual, but the creation of a new power, namely, the collective power of masses. . . . (30).

In this frame of reference "individuality" is said to be a "fetter." The individual acquires an added dimension of personal capability in cooperation with others which emerges in the collective social interaction processes:

> When the labourer cooperates systematically with others, he strips off the fetters of his individuality, and develops the capabilities of his species (31).

The phrase "social labour" as used both in *Capital* and in *The Communist Manifesto,* referred not only to the new scientific techniques but also to the added power of cooperative group labour. In the *Manifesto* Marx had written:

> The bourgeoisie, during its rule of scarce one hundred years, has created more massive and more colossal productive forces than have all preceding generations together. Subjection of Nature's forces to man, machinery, application of chemistry to industry and agriculture, steam-navigation, railways, electric telegraphs, clearing of whole continents for cultivation, canalization of rivers, whole populations conjured out of the ground. What earlier century had even a presentiment that such productive forces slumbered in the lap of social labour (32)?

The socialization which creates the power of "associated labour" has been made possible by the social uprooting which took place in Europe in the early period of capitalist development, and which is still going on. In the most advanced bourgeois countries the new labor system was being extended to the

---

30. *Ibid.,* chapter 13, p. 326.
31. *Ibid.,* p. 329.
32. Monthly Review Press, 1968 edition, Samuel Moore translation.

rural areas, to agricultural production, as well as to urban society and urban industry.

When Marx describes the increase in labor productivity which is due to the socialization of production he is referring to the economy of capitalism but also to the future socialist economy. In the extractive industries, production can be maximized by employing several shifts of workers, so that Man and Nature "work together" with no interruption:

> In the extractive industries, mines, etc. the raw materials form no part of the capital advanced. The subject of labour is in this case not a product of previous labour, but is furnished by Nature gratis, as in the case of metals, minerals, coal, stone, etc. In these cases the constant capital consists almost exclusively of instruments of labour, which can very well absorb an increased quantity of labour (day and night shifts of labourers, etc.). All other things being equal, the mass and value of the product will rise in direct proportion to the labour expended. As on the first day of production, the original produce-formers (now turned into the creators of the material elements of capital), man and Nature – still work together. Thanks to the elasticity of labour, the domain of accumulation has extended without any previous enlargement of constant capital [tools and machines] (33).

In the field of agriculture production, mechanization of agriculture and the collectivization of the work process are so closely associated that their combination is called ". . . a purely mechanical working of the soil:"

> In agriculture, the land under cultivation cannot be increased without the advance of more seed and manure. But this advance once made, the purely mechanical working of the soil produces a marvelous effect on the amount of the product. (34).

In the pre-capitalist mode of agricultural production, the worker had retained a direct, personal tie to nature and to the land on which he worked. In the mechanized, capitalist mode of production, he is related directly only to other workers who constitute a social environment by which he is surrounded, and to the socially devised machines and techniques which he employs. The earlier, non-mechanized procedures were "irrational," i.e., less efficient and less productive than the new methods:

> In the sphere of agriculture, modern industry has a more revolutionary effect than elsewhere, for this reason, that it annihilates the peasant, that bulwark of the old society, and replaces him by the wage-labourer. Thus the desire for social changes, and the class antagonism are brought to the same level in the country as

---

33. *Capital,* Volume I, chapter 24, p. 603.
34. *Ibid.*

> in the towns. The irrational, old-fashioned methods of agriculture are replaced by scientific ones. Capitalist production completely tears asunder the old bond of union which held together agriculture and manufacture in their infancy. But at the same time it creates the material conditions for a higher synthesis in the future, viz., the union of agriculture and industry on the basis of the more perfected forms they have each acquired during their temporary separation (35).

The earlier unity to which Marx referred was the unity of the single, independent worker with the materials of nature, to which he had direct access both as an agricultural producer and as a handicraft worker. In each of these activities, he was the director of his own projects, and the developer of his own tools and techniques. As a philosopher of labour and of human work in relation to nature, Marx operated with two distinct but complementary frames of reference. The personal activity of the independent, project-conceiving worker-producer in utilizing and transforming the original forms of Nature appears to account for the initial acquisition of supra-instinctual personal powers. But once this transformation has been completed, the emphasis shifts to collectivized cooperative group production, to projects which the single worker does not initiate or complete in accordance with his own personal design, will and purpose. Designs are then standardized and mass-produced. The entire society will be united in a collective production project when capitalism gives way to socialism. When he refers to the nature-transforming activities that will become the material basis of the future society, Marx represents the collective, mechanical mode of production as superior to the individualized, pre-mechanical mode.

In *Capital* Marx developed a dialectics of economic progress which applied only to the period leading from European feudalism to modern capitalism and socialism. The individualized, pre-mechanical mode of interaction with nature had to be developed as far as it could go, before it could be superseded by a collectivized, mechanical mode of interaction. In his discussion of "the historical tendency of capitalist accumulation," Marx said that capitalism in its early stages had brought with it the

> . . . the expropriation of the immediate producers, i.e., the dissolution of private property based on the labour of its owner. . . The private property of the labourer in his means of production is the foundation of petty industry, whether agricultural, manufacturing, or both; petty industry, again, is an essential condition for the development of social production and of the free individuality of the labourer himself. Of course, this petty mode of production exists also under slavery, serfdom, and other states of dependence. But it flourishes, it lets loose its whole energy, it attains its adequate classical form, only where the labourer is the

35. *Ibid.*, chapter 15, p. 505.

> private owner of his own means of labour set in action by himself; the peasant of the land which he cultivates, the artisan of the tools which he handles as a virtuoso. This mode of production pre-supposed parcelling of the soil, and scattering of the other means of production (36).

He then enumerates the various desirable features of large-scale production which have developed as a result of the destruction of the classical form of individualized production. The archaic mode had excluded "the concentration of the means of production." it also excludes

> . . . cooperation, division of labour within each separate process of production, the control over, and the productive application of the forces of Nature by society, and the free development of the social productive powers. It is compatible only with a system of production, and a society, moving within narrow and more or less primitive bounds. To perpetuate it would be, as Pecqueur rightly says 'to decree universal mediocrity.' At a certain stage of development, it brings forth the material agencies for its own dissolution. From that moment new forces and new passions spring up in the bosom of society; but the old social organization fetters them and keeps them down. It must be annihilated; it is annihilated. . . Self-earned private property that is based, so to say, on the fusing together of the isolated, independent labouring-individual with the conditions of his labour, is supplanted by capitalist private property, which rests on the exploitation of the nominally free labour of others, i.e., on wage-labour (37).

In the higher unity of socialism, there will be a "fusing together" of free labour, the labour of all producing members of society, with all the conditions of labour, including the earth itself, which will become a socially owned instrument and resource. The material and moral well-being of the future society can be maintained only when the united workers subordinate themselves, as individuals, to the requirements of a publicly essential productive task. Indeed, Marx seemed to expect that the admirable capacity of the individual worker for self-discipline and self-subordination to a task which he imposes on himself will carry over into the future age of social production, contributing to the solidarity and the viability of post-capitalist society.

MARX'S TREATMENT OF THE POPULATION QUESTION

Marx expected that the socialist world economy would be able to support the existing population at a material standard of living that would be suf-

36. *Ibid.*, chapter 32, p. 761.
37. *Ibid.*, p. 762.

ficient to abolish modern poverty. This meant also that conditions of work would be improved, and hours of labour shortened. He was strongly opposed to the view that working class poverty could never be overcome because population would inevitably grow at a rate that would outstrip the earth's natural resources. His position on the population question was related specifically to capitalism, and to arguments advanced by economists of capitalism. He said that any so-called population surplus arising in the bourgeois economy was artificial, relative to the nature of the economic system. Looking back on various economic systems of the past, he said that ". . . every special historic mode of production has its own special laws of population, historically valid within its limits alone. An abstract law of population exists for plants and animals only, and only insofar as man has not interfered with them" (38).

These historical laws describe what had been bound to happen inevitably in a particular historical situation, given the nature of the economy. The law of population which Marx noted as "peculiar to the capitalist mode of production" was one which makes inevitable the continuing and increasing misery of the modern working class. As capitalism evolves toward its most advanced, monopolistic, concentrated form the "organic composition of capital" changes. The use of labour-saving machinery (constant capital) expands relative to the total output. Capitalist industry is able to produce as much or more than before, while employing fewer wage labourers. From the very first, capitalism had been a stimulus to rapid population growth. Capitalist accumulation, however, is bound to produce an economically surplus population, i.e., a population in excess of the labour force requirements of capitalist industry:

> . . . it is capitalistic accumulation itself that constantly produces, and produces in the direct ratio of its own energy and extent, a relatively redundant population of labourers, i.e., a population of greater extent than suffices for the average needs of the self-expansion of capital, and therefore a surplus population. . . The labouring population therefore produces, along with the accumulation of capital produced by it, the means by which itself is made relatively superfluous, is turned into a relative surplus-population; and it does this to an always increasing extent (39).

In the economy of socialism, there will be no such relative, system-bound surplus population. No part of the population will become non-productive and economically redundant. The "industrial reserve army" of capitalism, made up of unemployed or underemployed workers, which is essential to the operation of the capitalist system, would disappear. All workers would then be needed and valued as social producers.

---

38. *Ibid.*, chapter 25, p. 632.
39. *Ibid.*, pp. 630 and 631.

The economic theorists who preceded Marx did not believe that capitalist economic expansion could continue indefinitely. They maintained that material expansion would eventually encounter limits that were to a considerable extent ecological. Marx rejected the conclusion of the "dismal science" of Malthusian and Ricardian economics. The poverty of the working class could not be abolished under capitalism, but this was one of the strongest of all possible arguments for socialism. He gave Malthus credit for objecting to the excessive lengthening of the hours of labor in industrial England, but he added that

> . . . the conservative interests, which Malthus served, prevented him from seeing that an unlimited prolongation of the working-day, combined with an extraordinary development of machinery, and the exploitation of women and children, must inevitably have made a great portion of the working class "supernumerary" . . . It was, of course, far more convenient, and much more in conformity with the ruling classes, whom Malthus adored like a true priest, to explain this "over-population" by the external laws of Nature, rather than by the historical laws of capitalist production (40).

Marx did not project any future "law of population" that would apply to the post-capitalist economy. He did seem to expect that the upsurge in population which had accompanied the expansion of production in the capitalist era would continue on into the age of socialism, as part of a general, indefinite process of "unconditional" social and economic expansion. He wrote, in Volume III of *Capital:*

> The *real barrier* of capitalist production is *capital itself.* It is that capital and its self-expansion appear as the starting and the closing point, the motive and the purpose of production; that production is only production for *capital* and not vice versa, the means of production are not mere means for a constant expansion of the living process of the *society* or producers. . . The means – unconditional development of the productive forces of society – comes continually into conflict with the limited purpose, the self-expansion of the existing capital (41).

It is impossible to arrive at any conclusion about Marx's views concerning future population expansion or its possible limits from this statement. But elsewhere, in a number of his works, he gives his readers the impression that he regards population increase as one indicator of the general progress of modern civilization. It is also a dramatic testimony to the immense "power over nature" inherent in modern scientifically rationalized, mechanized and collectivized production methods. He seems to expect that under socialism,

40. *Ibid.,* chapter 17, p. 529n.
41. Chapter 15, p. 250.

the economy will be managed so as to allow room for further population growth and also for the expansion of per capita material needs, with no foreseeable limit in sight.

There is substantial ground for thinking that when Marx referred to "abstract laws of population" that existed "for animals and plants only," he was saying that there were definite resource limitations for each of these life forms, because of the limited capacities of these forms. On this natural level, population could increase only to the point where an insufficiency of nutritional supplies would induce inter-individual competition, and thus the Malthusian, or Darwinian, struggle for existence, with the elimination of an absolute surplus of individuals. Socialism, as a system of economic and social cooperation, is the antithesis of socio-economic inter-individual competition as it occurs on the human level, in capitalist society. The future socialization of natural resources, and of the labor process, greatly enhances productive power, breaking through previously existing historical limitations, and also through all present and future planetary territorial limitations. This breakthrough closes off the possibility that pressure against resources will ever recur in such a way as to induce a relapse into the kind of competition that existed in capitalist society, and which Marx identified with Hobbes's "war of all against all."

Marx was not oriented to any kind of spatial, geographic limitation with respect to the nutritional and material support for human life and for modern civilization. He seemed also to think that other, non-economic undesirable social and psychological effects of over-crowding would be eliminated in socialist society by a more even geographic distribution of population which would do away with an excessive concentration in the urban centers.

ECOLOGICAL CONDITIONS IN SOCIALIST SOCIETY

In *Capital* Marx recognized certain negative effects of capitalist methods of land utilization. Yet it cannot be said that he was ecologically minded in the usual sense of that term. He expected that nature in the socialist economy would no longer be exploited as in the economy of capitalism. It would not be exhausted in the process of being used by Man. The capitalist economy was recklessly consuming and shortening the lives of the workers through exploitation of this vital human resource. The natural resources of the earth were being consumed in a similar way. Capitalism was not concerned with protecting the earth's resources, except as a private monoply preserve. As an institutional system, it was incapable of long range foresight, of concern about the future generations who would also have to depend on the resources of nature:

> Capital cares nothing for the length of life of labour-power. All that concerns it is simply and solely the maximum of labour-

> power that can be rendered fluent in the working-day. It attains this end by shortening the extent of the labourer's life, as a greedy farmer snatches increased produce from the soil by robbing it of its fertility. . . *Apres moi le deluge!* is the watch-word of every capitalist and of every capitalist nation. Hence Capital is reckless of the health or length of life of the labourer, unless under compulsion from society. To the out-cry as to the physical and mental degradation, the premature death, the torture of overwork, it answers: Ought these to trouble us since they increase our profits (42)?

Socialism would be the embodiment of the protective power of society, a power that even in the age of capitalism had some ability to impose external restraints on the practices of private capital. Under socialism, the destructive exploitation of natural resources will cease, along with the destructive exploitation of labour power.

Marx declared that the economic destruction of small independent farm and peasant holdings by the extension of capitalist methods of concentration and exploitation into agriculture, with the resulting proletarianization of workers on the land, was a necessity of social progress, to be welcomed and encouraged by socialists. But he also declared that both land and labour were being victimized in this process:

> . . . all progress in capitalistic agriculture is a progress in the art, not only of robbing the labourer, but of robbing the soil; all progress in increasing the fertility of the soil for a given time is a progress toward ruining the lasting sources of that fertility. The more a country starts its development on the foundation of modern industry, like the United States, for example, the more rapid is this process of destruction. Capitalistic production, therefore, develops technology, and the combining together of various processes into a social whole, only by sapping the original sources of all wealth – the soil and the labourer (43).

As Marx saw it, a good deal of the soil depletion that occurred in the capitalist economy was the result of the rupture of a previously existing "bond of union" between agriculture and manufacturing in the period immediately preceding the rise of industrial capitalism. This rupture will be repaired in the re-unified, organic, self-renewing economy of socialism. At the present time

> Capitalist production, by collecting the population in great centers, and causing an ever-increasing preponderance of town population, on the one hand concentrates the historical motive power of society; on the other hand, it disturbs the circulation of matter

42. Volume I, chapter 10, pp. 265 and 270.
43. *Ibid.*, chapter 15, pp. 506-507.

> between man and the soil, i.e., prevents the return to the soil of its elements consumed by man in the form of food and clothing; it therefore violates the conditions necessary to lasting fertility of the soil (44).

Marx implied that in the pre-capitalist handicraft and peasant economy of Europe, there had been an adequate replenishment, a return to the land of bio-degradable materials remaining after the process of production and consumption had been completed. He also implied that in the post-capitalist economy, population would be more evenly diffused than in the capitalist economy. Capitalism was responsible for the evils of excessive urbanization as well as for the destructive exploitation of the workers and of the land:

> . . . it destroys at the same time the health of the town labourer and the intellectual life of the rural labourer. But while upsetting the naturally developed conditions for the circulation of matter, it imperiously calls for its restoration as a system, as a regulating law of social production, and under a form appropriate to the full development of the human race (45).

His major theme, in *Capital,* is that socialism will be more rational than capitalism. Rationality is not merely technical, scientific or instrumental. It is also social and moral. There must be a concern for the welfare of present and future generations of workers, and therefore also for the preservation and the renewal of the earth's resources. He wrote, in Volume III of *Capital* that.

> The moral of history, also to be deduced from other observations concerning agriculture, is that the capitalist system works against a rational agriculture, or that a rational agriculture is incompatible with the capitalist system (although the latter promotes technical improvements in agriculture), and needs either the hand of the small farmer living by his own labour or the control of the associated producers (46).

The technical rationality of capitalism is correlated with the dissolution of the natural organic relations that had prevailed earlier. In the future economy of the associated producers, organic ties will be restored, in the form of a union of humanity with the entirety of Nature.

Marx anticipated the restoration of what he believed had been a once prevalent recycling process, a restoration of humanly extracted materials to the soil, in the future socialized economy. Under socialism, this would also be an expansion of nature's producing power. A simple replacement of the removed materials would not in itself mean that an indefinite increase in the material support derived by man from nature could be assured through organic restoration. Marx here interpolated a remarkable kind of eco-logic.

---

44. *Ibid.*, p. 505.
45. *Ibid.*, pp. 505–506.
46. Chapter 6, p. 121.

He established a transcendental connection between the development and enrichment of human life – the life of each individual in the society of the future – and the enrichment of nature. Development on the *social* level of personal and communal existence seems to react back upon material nature, which responds in such a way that the economic basis of the fully human life can never be threatened by material insufficiencies. Marx set up a higher category of "real wealth" which requires "material wealth" as its basis. Nature responds to the human, social and essential needs of man, by providing the material support. In the *Grundrisse* manuscripts of 1857-58, he said that the "full development of the individual" will "react back upon the productive power of labour as itself the greatest productive power" (47). In *The Critique of the Gotha Programme* (1875) he likewise expected that the "productive forces" will be increased because all the major contradictions of the capitalist era will have been eliminated. In what he called "the higher phase of communist society," the "productive forces [will] also have increased with the all-round development of the individual, and all the springs of cooperative wealth [will] flow more abundantly" (48). Economic planning, even in the first stages of socialism, within the territory of a single country, would take account of the needs of future generations. It would not be oriented, as was capitalist production, to obtaining maximum immediate returns, in the form of profit, to the capitalist owners of the material means of production. But neither would it be oriented exclusively to the meeting of collective social needs of a present generation that took no account of the well-being of generations that were to follow. Social production, under working class control, would be based on nationalization of the land. This nationalization, however, did not confer an absolute right of social ownership and of exploitation on any single generation. Exploitation of labor and of nature, which was depletion without replenishment, would come to an end in socialist societies where the future as well as the present would be at the center of public concern. Nationalization, so defined, was almost synonymous with universal social ownership that transcended the bounds of national territories. In *Capital* III, Marx declared that

> From the standpoint of a higher economic form of society, private ownership of the globe by single individuals will appear quite as absurd as private ownership of one man by another. Even a whole society, a nation, or even all simultaneously existing societies taken together, are not the owners of the globe. They are only its possessors, its usufructuraries, and, like *boni patres familias,* they must hand it down to succeeding generations in an improved condition (49).

---

47. Translated with introduction, by Martin Nicolaus, The Marx Library, Random House, N.Y., 1973, pp. 711-712.
48. *Op. cit.*
49. Chapter 46, p. 776.

THE PRIMACY OF THE SOCIAL ENVIRONMENT

The ecology of socialist society was being conceived by Marx as a nutritional process, through which humanity absorbs, utilizes and also transforms the essential natural ingredients on which it must remain forever dependent. Nature will be absorbed into man not only materially, but also spiritually. It will at the same time not only be preserved but enhanced, since humanity constitutes "nature" at its highest level of realization (50). External non-human nature, when properly used by humanity in post-capitalist time, will support the transformation of the inner social environment, enabling the individual to experience the surrounding society of other people as sustaining and non-threatening. The individual will also be able to use his human esthetic and creative faculties in ways that had not been possible earlier, in the alienated society of capitalism. What counts primarily, as far as the effect on the individual's spiritual life is concerned, is the transformation of the social environment. Marx was noticeably lacking in concern about the negative environmental effects of the "civilizing" changes in production methods that would be carried over from capitalism into socialism. He welcomed the prospect of a future population growth which would be the means whereby the human, social environment would encroach progressively on the natural environment, destroying and transforming original nature and cutting off the access of the future social individuals to aspects of nature that had not been "mastered," transformed, or massively invaded by man.

In the chapter on "The Labor Process" (*Capital* I), the worker in nature, as described by Marx, ". . . starts, regulates and controls the material relations between himself and Nature." In other words, he controls the reactions of Nature to his own activity in such a way as to avert damage to himself. This kind of regulation will be carried on also by the associated producers in the post-capitalist economy. Nature, once it has been subjected to such regulation, does not react against the regulating agency. Marx is concerned with establishing an inner social environment which will enclose and surround each individual, providing him with unfailing material and spiritual security. Nature, under such conditions, will be so much a part of the "body" of the future society that it can suffer from no separate affliction as long as the higher entity – Humanity – exists in a state of internal social harmony and internal freedom from divisive and oppressive conditions.

In *The German Ideology*, Marx had objected to a passage in Feuerbach's *Philosophy of the Future* in which the existence of most human beings was said to be "naturally" in harmony with their essence, and comparable to the natural harmony of non-human species with their life-supportive environment. Marx said that Feuerbach was mistaken on two counts. In the first place, existing life conditions for the majority of workers, and for the majority of human beings in capitalist society, were by no means the environ-

50. See the discussion of Marx's nature philosophy in chapter 2 of this book on "The Cosmological Philosophies of Hegel and Marx."

ment required from the realization of their human "essence." Feuerbach conceives of exceptions to the rule as due to

> . . . an unhappy chance, as an abnormality which cannot be altered. Thus, if millions of proletarians feel by no means contented with their living conditions, if their "existence" does not in the least correspond to their "essence," then, according to the passage quoted, this is an unavoidable misfortune, which must be borne quietly. The millions of proletarians and communists, however, think differently and will prove this in time, when they bring their "existence" into harmony with their "essence" in a practical way, by means of a revolution (51).

Feuerbach was also wrong in supposing that the natural ecological harmony that had once prevailed elsewhere in nature, in the relation of non-human species to their natural environment, was still in existence. Man in the modern era had disrupted the environment of the non-human species, and had even altered the species forms themselves. This meant that Man had learned to "subdue" nature to further his own ends:

> Feuerbach . . . always takes refuge in external nature, and moreover in *nature* that has not yet been subdued by men. But every new invention, every advance made by industry, detaches yet another piece from this domain, so that the ground which produces examples illustrating such Feuerbachian propositions is steadily shrinking. The "essence" of the fish is its "existence," water – to go no further than this one proposition. The "essence" of the freshwater fish is the water of a river. But the latter ceases to be the "essence" of the fish and is no longer a suitable medium of existence as soon as the river is made to serve industry, as soon as it is polluted by dyes and other waste products and navigated by steamboats, or as soon as its water is diverted into canals where simple drainage can deprive the fish of its medium of existence (52).

The human and social environment was to be altered through revolution in such a way that the human essence would be fully in harmony with the conditions of *social* existence.

Humanity is linked with nature, both spiritually and biologically, in a way that is extremely abstract and essentially mediated by the indispensible social powers of technological science and industry. These literally supra-natural productive powers, when socially operated for universal good, give humanity almost unlimited access to natural resources. At the same time, humanity is treated as if immune to the negative impact of man-induced environmental changes.

---

51. Volume I, Part I, pp. 54–55.
52. *Ibid.* See also the reference to Marx's critique of Feuerbach in chapter 2 of this book.

4

Marx's Dialectical Interpretation Of History

Marx believed that history was tending, inevitably, toward a condition of realization to be achieved through the supersession of capitalism by socialism and communism. His well-known inevitability thesis was a teleological doctrine derived from the historical teleology and dialectical method of Hegel. He adapted Hegel's dialectic in ways that served to support his own post-Hegelian dialectical science of history.

DIALECTICAL METHOD IN HEGELIAN AND MARXIST PHILOSOPHY

Hegel's dialectic, considered as theology, was a teleo-logic of immanence and transcendence which linked together his cosmology and his philosophy of history. The dialectical process guarantees the actualization of Reason and Spirit in history. This outcome was contained in the supra-historical beginning, in the Mind potentialities that were then actualized and manifested in historic time. Historical events were said to conform to a rationally intelligible, dynamic process of progressive development. This proceeds through stages which are naturally determined in the sense that they arise out of the nature of thought and of reality beyond thought. Each new stage involves some kind of contradiction with the preceding stage. The earlier stage is negated and transcended in ways that contribute to a general historical advance.

The dialectical method was a philosophy of knowledge as well as an account of the realizing process in history. It provided the knower with a grasp of a totality that was more than the sum total of its various parts or aspects. It was also a way of perceiving the past from the more advanced standpoint of the present. Some aspects of the past were excluded as irrelevant to the present, even though they had contributed to the advance. Other aspects had contributed nothing, and were, therefore, below the level of historical significance.

For both Hegel and Marx, the dialectic was a means of penetrating to an underlying level of reality and of truth that was not open to "common sense" perception. Marx, however, rejected Hegel's category of philosophical Reason. According to Hegel, the mind of philosophy, in its most highly developed Germanic phase, was in a position to understand reality as a whole, including the meaning of God in nature and history. Hegel had also elevated philosophy above the specialized non-philosophical sciences. It could provide an integrative view that related them to a fundamental ground of absolute knowledge.

Marx rejected Hegel's claim that reality had dimensions inaccessible to science. Dialectical science is able to abolish all mysteries, when it penetrates beyond superficial and misleading appearances. The belief that there were mysteries in nature, society and history that could not be fathomed by the human mind could persist only in cultures where science was insufficiently developed. In discussing problems of economic science, he said that a certain part of Adam Smith's analysis had been too superficial. He therefore ". . . contradicts the esoteric – really scientific – part of his own exposition" (1). Referring to the law of surplus value he observed that ". . . this law clearly contradicts all experiences based on appearance . . . Vulgar economics . . . here as everywhere sticks to appearances in opposition to the law which regulates and explains them" (2). In lectures on economics written in 1865 and delivered before a British working class audience he said that his theory of profits (surplus value)

> . . . seems paradox and contrary to everyday observation. It is also paradox that the earth moves round the sun, and that water consists of two inflammable gasses. Scientific truth is always paradox, if judged by everyday experience, which catches only the delusive appearance of things (3).

In Volume III of *Capital* he makes a still broader generalization: ". . . all science would be superfluous if the outward appearance and the essence of things directly coincided" (4).

When these statements are considered in relation to his historical theory, it becomes evident that Marx was establishing a remarkable post-Hegelian dualism which separates the particular sciences from his overall dialectical interpretation of history. The distinction between two levels of perception is being retained and emphasized in regard to scientific activity. This contrasts with the dialectical approach that he applies to social experience and social perception. The contradictions between superficial appearance and underlying truth that presently exist in this field are to be eliminated in future time. All mysteries in *society* will disappear as the contradic-

---

1. *Capital,* Volume II, chapter 10, p. 212.
2. *Capital,* Volume I, chapter 9, p. 307.
3. *Selected Works of Marx and Engels, op. cit.* Volume II.
4. Chapter 48, p. 797.

tions arising in present day economic and political life are eliminated in the post-capitalist era. After existing forms of alienation and disunity have been overcome, the inner and outer manifestations will no longer be contradictory. The transformations culminating in ultimate communism will nullify the conditions that presently stand in the way of this kind of absolute unification.

Marx emphasized the differences between his own use of dialectics and Hegel's system. In his preface to the second German edition of *Capital,* dated January 24, 1873, he identified his own outlook as dialectical. At the same time he described it as the "direct opposite" of the Hegelian method:

> . . . In Hegel's writings, dialectic stands on its head. You must turn it right way up again if you want to discover the rational kernel that is hidden away within the wrappings of mystification (5).

He was referring here to Hegel's cosmological idealism. He had, however, made conspicuous use of many aspects of the dialectical method in ways that could by no means be described as a complete reversal.

In the same preface, Marx had endorsed without qualification an account of his method which had been given by a Russian reviewer, who had said, in part, that

> Marx regards the social movement as a natural process, guided by laws which are not merely independent of the will, consciousness, and the purposes of men, but, conversely, determine their will, their purposes. . . The scientific value of such an investigation lies on the disclosure of the special laws that regulate the origin, existence, development and death of a given social organism, and its replacement by another and higher one. Such, in fact, is the value of Marx's book.

Marx had commented that

> What the writer describes so aptly, and (so far as my personal application of it goes) so generously, as the method I have actually used, what else is he describing but the dialectic method?

In this particular application of the dialectic, Marx had made use of Hegel's socio-organic logic. Hegel had referred to political economic societies as organic entities, emphasizing the cultural and socio-psychological elements uniting the members of the society into a supra-individual spiritual whole. Marx conceived of political-economic societies as organically integrated producing systems. Both believed that a replacement of earlier socio-organic forms by later systems was a progressive advance toward a higher stage of realization.

---

5. Translated by Eden and Cedar Paul, *Capital,* Volume I. New York: International Publishers, 1929. Alternate translation in 1967 International Publishers edition.

MATERIALISM AS THE RESTORATION OF REALIZING POWER

Marx's concept of dialectical, natural law operating in and through the process of historical development was not fully formed in his earlier works. In *The German Ideology* he was restoring the realizing force of Hegel's transcendental Reason, the power of the Idea operating in and through history. This had been extinguished in the writings of neo-Hegelian critical philosophers. At the same time, he was also demolishing the Idea. The force was "material." Hegel had written, in his introduction to *The Philosophy of History:*

> Reason . . . is *Substance,* as well as *Infinite Power*. . . It is the *Infinite Energy* of the Universe; since Reason is not so powerless as to be incapable of producing anything but a mere ideal, a mere intention – having its place outside of reality, nobody knows where; something separate and abstract, in the heads of certain human beings.

Marx complained that the German ideologists were elevating the power of human consciousness and thought activity in a way that obscured a recognition of the real process of history. They supported misleading beliefs about the historical importance of ideas and motives classed as "ideal:"

> For instance, if an epoch imagines itself to be actuated by purely "political" or "religious" motives, although "religion" and "politics" are only forms of its true motives, the historian accepts this opinion. The "idea," the "conception" of the people in question about their real practice, is transformed into the sole determining, active force, which controls and determines their practice (6).

According to Marx, these philosophers ignored the material, economic activities required to support human life. They treated human life as if it were totally independent of nature. They believed that they had achieved a "pure" detached philosophical consciousness which was uninfluenced by, and independent of, the primary material life-supporting activities. They criticized certain ideas and beliefs, but they did not perceive that such criticism was incapable of changing the conditions which give rise to these forms of consciousness. The only effective method of change was "practical materialism," which

> . . . does not explain practice from the idea but explain the formation of ideas from material practice; and accordingly it comes to the conclusion that all forms and products of consciousness cannot be dissolved by mental criticism. . . but only by the practical overthrow of the actual social relations which gave rise to this idealistic humbug; that not criticism but revolution is

6. *The German Ideology,* Volume I, Part I, p. 51.

the driving force of history, also of religion, of philosophy, and other types of theory (7).

The "idea" of communism which arises in consciousness has no independent force of its own. As idea, it is "absolutely immaterial," i.e., utterly impotent, when detached from the driving force that will make it effective:

> . . . as far as practical development is concerned, it is absolutely immaterial whether the *idea* of this revolution has been expressed a hundred times already, as the history of communism proves (8).

In *The German Ideology* Marx was retreating from the view he had expressed in his *Introduction to a Critique of Hegel's Philosophy of Right* (1843). There he had said that the realizing power of communism resulted from a fusion of the mind-power of philosophy with the material power of the revolutionary working class movement:

> As philosophy finds its *material* weapons in the proletariat, the proletariat finds its *intellectual* weapons in philosophy. And once the lightning of thought has deeply struck this unsophisticated soil of the people, the *Germans* will emancipate themselves to become men. . . the *head* of this emancipation is philosophy, its *heart* is the *proletariat* (9).

In *The German Ideology* Marx disconnects the thought-force of philosophy from the proletarian movement. The working class is a social force, a power that will defeat capitalism. The individuals constituting the class are able to acquire on their own a sufficient insight into the nature of present day reality as it affects their life situation. They are wholly disillusioned, and have no use for "theoretical notions":

> For the mass of men, i.e., the proletariat, these theoretical notions do not exist and hence do not require to be dissolved, and if this mass ever had any theoretical notions, e.g., religion, these have now long been dissolved by circumstances (10).

Thought activity which was in line with reality had been defined by Marx as "practical-critical" revolutionary activity in his *Theses on Feuerbach* (1845). This activity was included within the total movement of history. In the first of the *Theses* Marx complained that Feuerbach, although a materialist, had not gone beyond a merely abstract, static, philosophical way of perceiving the society of the present. "He therefore does not apprehend the significance of the 'revolutionary' practical-critical activity." In the second *Thesis* he went on to say that

---

7. *Ibid.,* p. 50.
8. *Ibid.,* pp. 50–51.
9. Translated by Easton and Guddat, *op. cit.*
10. *The German Ideology,* Volume I, Part I, p. 52.

> The question whether objective truth is to be assigned to human thinking is not a question of theory, but a practical question. In practice, man is bound to prove the truth, that is, the reality and force, the this-worldliness of this thinking. The dispute over the reality or non-reality of his thinking isolated from practice is a pure *scholastic* question (11).

Marx seems to be saying two things: 1) thinking is objective and therefore true when it corresponds to a reality that exists independently of the perceiver or knower; 2) this reality can be directly perceived by a knower whose personal consciousness functions as a "clear glass" which does not distort the object, and which does not mistake illusory mind-constructed objects for the reality. In this context, however, Marx is referring to a reality that is not yet fully objectified. Theory here functions projectively, bridging the time gap required for objectification and thus for verification. Revolutionaries undertake to prove the truth by working, practically and theoretically, toward the establishment of a social order that will eliminate the evils of the present.

Marx was substituting practical-critical activity for the task of philosophy as Hegel had presented it in his Introduction to *The History of Philosophy:*

> . . . It is the business of philosophy, as opposed to [one-sided, abstract] understanding, to show that the truth of the Idea does not consist in empty generalization, but in a universal, and that it is in itself the particular and the determined. If the truth is abstract, it must be untrue. Healthy human reason goes out toward what is concrete; the reflecting of the understanding comes first as abstract and untrue, correct in theory only, and amongst other things unpractical. Philosophy is what is most antagonistic to abstraction and it leads back to the concrete (12).

The task of philosophy is also to demonstrate that Reason is fully actualized in a concrete universal society. For Hegel, this is the society of the present to which he himself belonged. For Marx, it is the society of the future.

Hegel had said also that abstract moral and social ideas about what *ought to be* which go beyond the non-abstract life of the present society have no power to influence the future course of social and political history (13). Marx abides as far as possible within the limits of Hegel's determinism. The revolutionary movement is not seeking to superimpose on the course of future history an abstract-ideal moral framework. He delcared, in *The German Ideology,* that

---

11. Translated by Nathan Rotenstreich, in *Basic Problems of Marx's Philosophy.* Bobbs-Merrill Co., 1965.

12. Reprinted in *Hegel on Art, Religion, Philosophy.* Harper and Row, 1970, p. 232.

13. The best known statement of this view appears in the Preface to *The Philosophy of Right* [Law].

> Communism is for us not a *state of affairs* which is to be established, an ideal to which reality will have to adjust itself. We call communism the *real* movement which abolishes the present state of things (14).

In opposition to Hegel, Marx declares that society must pass beyond the time of the present, in order to arrive at a state of concrete actualization. Present society is an incomplete, abstract formation whose historical appearance has nevertheless been dialectically necessary. The future society that is in the process of emerging out of the present society is more vital and more "actual" than the existing form. The present society is already fading into the past, its strength and power being more apparent (illusory) than real.

Marx thought that his own way of understanding and perceiving the dialectal process of history did not require the use of a specialized language or logic going beyond the "non-abstract" language and ways of knowing and thinking that sufficed for the ordinary non-philosophical person (15). The proletarians were "ordinary men," not inclined to "abstract" ideological thinking.

Hegel had said that self-conscious philosophical reason had developed gradually, over the course of many generations. The materials with which the philosopher worked are made available by the labor of past generations. They are received by the mind of philosophy as a legacy from the past. The received material is then "metamorphosed" by the work of the oncoming generation of philosophers:

> . . . the universal mind does not remain stationary . . . for its activity is its life. This activity presupposes a material already present, on which it acts, and which it does not merely augment by the addition of new matter, but completely refashions and transforms. . . this legacy is reduced to a material which becomes metamorphosed by mind. In this moment that which is received is changed, and the material worked upon is both enriched and preserved at the same time (16).

Marx seems to have been adapting Hegel's statements on philosophical history when he wrote, in *The German Ideology,* that

> History is nothing but the succession of the separate generations, each of which exploits the materials, the forms of capital, the productive forces handed down to it by all the preceding ones, and thus on the one hand continues the traditional activity

---

14. Volume I, Part I, p. 47.

15. Marx dissociated his own outlook from "logic" and from "abstract thought" in his 1844 essay "Critique of the Hegelian Dialectic and Philosophy in General." This discussion was amplified in chapter 5 of *The Holy Family,* (1844). The theme was continued in a later, highly polemical philosophical work *The Poverty of Philosophy* (1846-47).

16. Introduction to *The History of Philosophy, op. cit.* p. 212.

> in completely changed circumstances, and, on the other, modifies the old circumstances with completely changed activity (17).

THE CONTRADICTION BETWEEN THE FORCES AND RELATIONS OF PRODUCTION

The Hegelian structure of Marx's interpretation of history is disclosed in the way he conceived of historical development as being impelled forward by the appearance of contradictions, which are resolved by a realizing power that works through all stages, up to and including a final stage of unity beyond alienation, conflict, and abstraction. Marx selected one primary contradiction as the logical center of his system, namely the contradiction between the forces of production and the relations of production. The forces of production include the nature-transforming energies of materially productive labor, and they are contained also in the historically developed instruments, materials, and techniques of production. Each stage of economic life beyond the initial pre-historic beginning point was said to have developed a contradiction between the forces and relations of production. The contradictions appearing at any given stage are resolved when the forces of production that have developed within the limits of that form, break through their confinement in a way that results in the establishment of a more advanced form. On this more advanced level, the same contradiction reappears, and is resolved in a similar way. The socialist revolution, however, will be a radical break with the past. Post-capitalist society will not pass through an organic cycle leading beyond maturity to decadence and death. The new form will not be destroyed by vital forces seeking to expand beyond its limiting confines. The relations and conditions of production will never become an obstacle to the further development and expansion of the material forces of social production. The dialectical contradiction will have been resolved, never to recur.

Marx summarized his central thesis in his Preface (1859) to *A Contribution to the Critique of Political Economy,* which read, in part

> At a certain stage of their development, the material forces of production in society come into conflict with the existing relations of production, or – what is but a legal expression for them – with the property relations within which they had been at work before. From forms of development of the forces of production these relations turn into their fetters. Then occurs the period of social revolution. With the change of the economic foundation the entire immense superstructure is more or less rapidly transformed. In considering such transformations, the distinction should always be made between the material transforma-

17. Volume I, Part I, p. 59.

> tion of the economic conditions of production which can be established with the precision of a natural science, and the legal, political, religious, aesthetic or philosophical – in short, ideological – forms in which men become conscious of this conflict and fight it out (18).

In this same Preface, he construed the dialectical movement of history as a problem-solving process when he said that

> No social order ever disappears before all the productive forces, for which there is room in it, have been developed; and new higher relations of production never appear before the material conditions of their existence have matured in the womb of the old society. Therefore, mankind always sets itself only such problems as it can solve; since, on closer examination, it will always be found that the problem itself arises only when the material conditions for its solution already exist or are at least in the process of formation.

Only those movements and changes that have been successful in helping to resolve an antagonism, a contradiction, between the forces and relations of production can be counted as part of the dialectical movement. Marx's problem-solving thesis is absurd, if we attempt to apply it to the class struggle doctrine he presented in *The Communist Manifesto,* where he declared that "The history of all hitherto existing society is the history of class struggles." It could not mean that individuals in revolting underclasses undertake rebellions against the opposing class only when they are assured in advance that they will succeed. Marx did not say or imply this in any of his works. It is not the class struggle as such that moves history forward. Rather, it is the recurring situation of contradiction and of resolution.

Relations of production include class and caste relations, relations of domination and subordination, all of which are property relations, relations between owners and non-owners of materially productive property. Such relations are essential constituents of the "mode of production" (19). They are part of the economic foundation, i.e., the real foundation, even though they may be reinforced by political processes which Marx had placed in the "superstructure" in the 1859 Preface:

> In the social production which men carry on they enter into definite relations that are indispensable and independent of their will; these relations of production correspond to a definite stage in the development of their material powers of production. The

---

18. This is the standard translation first published in Chicago by I.N. Stone in 1904, as slightly modified by T.B. Bottomore, in *Karl Marx: Selected Writings in Sociology and Social Philosophy,* and by John McMurtry, in *The Structure of Marx's World View,* Princeton University Press, 1978.

19. John McMurtry has noted that the phrase "mode of production" most often includes both the relations and forces of production. *Op. cit.,* p. 10n.

> totality of these relations of production constitutes the economic structure of society – the real foundation, on which rise legal and political superstructures and to which definite forms of social consciousness correspond. The mode of production in material life determines the social, political and spiritual processes of life in general. It is not the consciousness of men that determines their existence, but, on the contrary, their social existence determines their consciousness.

Marx is saying that "superstructural" elements develop naturally within any established system of production relations. They serve to unify the system across caste and class lines. In any such system, the socially effective "will" and consciousness available to persons in the politically dominant ruling groups cannot change the system in any fundamental way. This structural determinism is also an organic, metaphysical functionalism. An historical function is being served by the fact that people in various economic societies have been bound together in definite relations which are both economic and supra-economic.

Marx recognized, nevertheless, that political actions can sometimes have a system-changing effect, although his theory of superstructural consciousness cannot be readily applied in this connection. Innovative political events are part of the total natural-historical process. Politically induced changes in the form and in the distribution of productive property can result in the establishment of new organic systems. In his Introduction (1857) to *A Critique of Political Economy,* Marx wrote:

> A conquering nation may divide the land among the conquerers and in this way impose a distinct mode of distribution and form of landed property, thus determining production. Or it may turn the population into slaves, thus making slave-labour the basis of production. Or in the course of a revolution, a nation may divide large estates into plots, thus altering the character of production in consequence of this new distribution. . . Production has indeed its conditions and prerequisites which are constituent elements of it. At the very outset these may be naturally evolved. In the course of production, however, they are transformed from naturally evolved factors into historical ones, and although they may appear as natural pre-conditions for any one period, they are the historical result of another period (20).

Once a new organic system has been developed and consolidated, the distribution of the product that is created within the system cannot be altered in a way that would undermine the basic property relations. These relations are distributive in character. In discussing payments to wage-workers in capitalist and pre-capitalist societies, Marx says that the total available for

20. New York: International Publishers, 1970.

wage distribution is determined automatically, by the structure of the system:

> The relations and modes of distribution are thus merely the reverse aspect of the factors of production. An individual whose participation in production takes the form of wage-labour will receive a share in the product, the result of production, in the form of wages. The structure of distribution is entirely determined by the structure of production. . . the distribution of the product is automatically determined by that distribution which was initially a factor of production.

Distribution in *socialist* society will be determined in a similarly automatic way. Once the new social property form has been established through revolutionary political activity, political processes of a "superstructural" kind will not enter into the determination of how the product is distributed to the various individuals who constitute the working community (21).

Marx did not indicate, in his 1859 Preface, everything that was contained or implied in the term "forces of production" and "relations of production." In *The German Ideology* he had included international relations in the general class of "relations of production." External and internal relations were determined by an over-arching international system:

> The relations of different nations among themselves depend upon the extent to which each has developed its productive forces, the division of labour and internal intercourse. This statement is generally recognized. But not only the relation of one nation to others, but also the whole internal structure of the nation itself depends on the stage of development reached by its production and its internal and external intercourse (22).

Barbaric nations and tribal groups had been compelled by material need to invade, pillage and conquer the territory of other peoples. This need for new "means of production" was the primary material cause and "driving force" which accounted for this kind of aggression:

> This whole [materialist] interpretation of history appears to be contradicted by the fact of conquest. Up till now violence, war, pillage, murder and robbery, etc. have been accepted as the driving force of history. Here we must limit ourselves to the chief points and take, therefore, only the most striking example – the destruction of an old civilization by a barbarous people and the resulting formation of an entirely new organization of society. (Rome and the barbarians; feudalism and Gaul; the Byzantine Empire and the Turks.) With the barbarian people war itself is

---

21. Marx's theory of economic and social evolution in post-capitalist society, and the problems it entails, will be discussed in later chapters of this book.

22. Volume I, Part I, p. 32.

> still, as indicated above, a regular form of intercourse, which is the more eagerly exploited as the increase in population, together with the traditional, and for it, only possible, crude mode of production, gives rise to the need for new means of production (23).

When Marx referred to "needs" that were associated with the "driving force" of collective aggression in pre-capitalist societies, he was referring not to individual, private needs, but to the need of an entire society to maintain itself in existence, and to reproduce itself. Family production, the production of a new generation to take the place of the old, was an important aspect of material productive activity. Aggressive warfare develops when the group has no other way of meeting its material needs for self-maintenance and self-production.

THE OPPRESSION OF HUMANITY BY EXTERNAL SOCIAL POWER

Marx's kind of historical determinism included a dualism that was not derived from Hegel's philosophy of history. Hegel had said that there was an ineradicable tension between freedom and necessity. Freedom cannot exist except in relation to its antithesis, necessity. In his early writings, Marx believed that the "contradiction" between freedom and necessity would be resolved in the society of communism. But his primary emphasis was on the need for overcoming what he called "enslavement." The primary objective of the workers who will become the material force that will overthrow the system of capital is to emancipate themselves from enslavement.

What did Marx mean by enslavement? It is obvious that he was referring to wage slavery, as endured by the industrial workers who produced the material wealth that supported capital. But enslavement was a universal condition, and meant more than this. It was oppression experienced by all persons in modern society, and by humanity in general. Capital itself is enslaved by the system which sustains it, and the unfreedom of capital is also the unfreedom of humanity. When the working class succeeds in defeating the system of capital, the individuals who constitute society will be able to achieve an autonomy which is by definition freedom from the external compulsion that affects all persons in the age of capitalism. Marx's dialectics of history included a will-compulsion theory which denied that individuals in dominant political and economic groups, or in internally united dominant societies, have a power to act otherwise than as they do act, as demonstrated by the historical record. Hegel had said much the same thing, but he did not regard the determining power as oppressive. It was a power of "necessity" which was a means to spiritual freedom. In Marx's historical philosophy, all persons in internally divided class and caste societies are said to be constrained

23. *Ibid.*, pp. 33-34.

and compelled by a socially created, oppressive superforce. The power shared by persons in dominating social and political groups in the economic systems having this kind of division of labour is not "free" power. These persons are compelled to exercise domination over the under-classes. The enslavers are themselves coerced by the oppressive power of the system. The external power develops through the natural cooperation of the various different functional groups in the producing economy. Natural cooperation is distinguished from voluntary cooperation. In the slave economies, the slaves did not cooperate voluntarily with the master groups. Their cooperation was "natural." The power produced through natural cooperation is the result of the combined labours of all strata of the economic population. Marx was referring to the city-states of Greek and Roman antiquity when he wrote, in *The German Ideology,* that

> The citizens hold power over their labouring slaves only in their community, and on this account alone, therefore, they are bound to the form of communal ownership. It is the communal private property which compels the active citizens to remain in this spontaneously derived [natural] form of association over against their slaves (24).

Communal "private property" is property that is possessed exclusively by one section of the total economic population, i.e., by the politically dominant section. Private property belongs to individuals, but only in and through their membership in the political community.

Marx describes, in dramatic imagery, the condition of universal human powerlessness that has developed in the age of capitalism:

> The social power, i.e., the multiplied productive force, which arises through the cooperation of different individuals as it is determined by the division of labour, appears to these individuals, since their cooperation is not voluntary but has come about naturally, not as their own united power, but as an alien force existing outside them, of the origin and goal of which they are ignorant, which they thus cannot control, which, on the contrary passes through a peculiar series of phases and stages independent of the will, and action of man, nay even being the prime governor of these (25).

He then proceeds to identify this external, alien ruling force with Adam Smith's "Invisible Hand," transforming Adam Smith's Providence into Fate. He asks

24. Volume I, Part I, p. 33. In an earlier translation of Part I (International Publishers, 1947), the editor, R. Pascal, notes that in this and other passages Marx was using the German word "Naturwüchsig," which means "growing naturally." This is translated as "spontaneously derived" in the later version quoted above.

25. *Ibid.,* p. 46.

> . . . how does it happen that trade, which after all is nothing more than the exchange of products of various individuals and countries, rules the whole world through the relation of supply and demand, a relation which, as an English economist says, hovers over the earth like the Fate of the ancients, and with invisible hand allots fortune and misfortune to men, sets up empires and overthrows empires, causes nations to rise and to disappear – while with the abolition of the basis of private property, with communistic regulation of production (and, implicit in this, the destruction of the alien relation between men and what they themselves produce), the power of the relation of supply and demand is dissolved into nothing, and men get exchange, production, the mode of their mutual relation, under their own control again (26)?

The world wide extension of the capitalist economy, which renders each nation dependent on the supply and demand situation, is a necessary phase of the dialectical advance, laying the basis for universal emancipation:

> *All-round* dependence, this natural form of the work-historical cooperation of individuals, will be transformed by this communist revolution into the control and conscious mastery of those powers which, born of the action of men on one another, have till now overawed and governed men as powers completely alien to them (27).

In *Capital* Marx presented his will-compulsion theory in a somewhat different way. He denounced the evils of capitalist exploitation, and the far from admirable human traits which the system encouraged. But he also said that these evils develop naturally and inevitably. The capitalists cannot change the system, and their economic actions are governed by the compulsions of the economic system:

> . . . Capital is reckless of the health or length of life of the labourer, unless under compulsion from society. To the out-cry as to the physical and mental degradation, the premature death, the torture of over-work, it answers: Ought these to trouble us since they increase our profits? But looking at things as a whole, all this does not, indeed, depend on the good or ill will of the individual capitalist. Free competition brings out the inherent laws of capitalist production, in the shape of external coercive laws having power over every individual capitalist (28).

We note that here, although not in the earlier *German Ideology,* Marx

26. *Ibid.,* p. 47.
27. *Ibid.,* p. 49.
28. Volume I, Chapter X, p. 270.

refers to "society" as a protective and restraining power that has at least some limited effectiveness even in the capitalist system. This, however, is an aspect of Marx's later thought which never did affect his general interpretation of history, and the accompanying will-compulsion theory. He continued to affirm, in *Capital*, that

> As, in religion, man is governed by the products of his own brain, so in capitalistic production, he is governed by the products of his own hand (29).

THE BACKGROUND OF KANTIAN TELEOLOGY

There is good reason to believe that Kant was responsible for the initial teleological formulations that were later used in the construction of two major post-Kantian historical and cosmological philosophies, the Hegelian and the Marxist. Kant's teleological concepts were presented not only in his various political writings, but also in the last of his three great critiques, *The Critique of Judgement* (1790) (30).

Kant sought to adapt the teleological philosophy of nature developed by Aristotle in his capacity as a biologist, to the field of political and social history. He was searching for ways to carry forward into the age of Enlightenment and of modern science, a prophetic confidence in the eventual historical fulfillment of certain aims and aspirations which had originated in ancient Judaism. Human destiny on earth, he declared, could not be completed unless and until the rule of reason, identified with the rule of supra-national societal law, superseded the irrationality and the immorality of international anarchy, militarism and war.

Kant's rational optimism differed radically from the religious optimism of prophetic Judaism in important respects. Reliance on scriptural authority as a support for his own confidence about the human future was rigorously excluded. He was making use of a method that he regarded as analogous to though not reducible to procedures being used with conspicuous success in sciences of nature that were not concerned with the collective political and moral history of humanity.

Marx's morally critical view of his own society, of the present brought him closer to Kant than to Hegel, in ways that divided them both from Hegel. Like Kant, he believed that modern culture and civilization had made great strides in the modern, post-Catholic age of science, but that moral progress was by no means keeping pace with the civilizational advance. Moral changes affecting public collective life were called for, but present day humanity was suffering from defects of rational and moral will that seemed to be insurmountable. Kant and Marx both relied on what they called "natural"

---

29. Volume I, Chapter XXV, p. 621.
30. I shall not be concerned here with discussing the manifold difficulties and problems that are so evident in these works.

humanly unguided processes to create the circumstances that would produce the desired result.

The establishing, in historical time, of a condition of permanent world peace was Kant's primary, overriding political concern. The observable facts of political history were not encouraging. If such a peace were to be achieved, each nation would have to accept some restrictions on national autonomy and national freedom of action in relation to other nations and peoples. This they were presently not inclined to do. Kant implied that this resistance was "natural," being one of the indications that humanity as a species was morally and rationally limited by virtue to its tie to the rest of organic nature. It was possible, however, that the nature-given limitations of men who were organized into political societies might at the same time be manifestations of a higher purpose, and that they were serving some essential function in the total scheme of things. It was philisophically justifiable, and even necessary to posit that a teleological power, deriving from "a higher cause" beyond nature, space, and time, was acting within human natural history, through "hidden mechanisms" that could not be observed or even inferred by methods used in the empirical natural sciences.

Kant first presented this concept in his essay "An Idea for a Universal History with a Cosmopolitan Purpose" (1784). In the opening sentences of this essay, he makes it clear that he is viewing historical events as the outcome of human actions that are "freely willed' in the sense that they are not predetermined by unconscious instinct. They are, nevertheless, "naturally determined" by motives, desires and forms of rationality that are not the manifestations of "free will" in the *moral* sense of that term:

> Whatever conception of the freedom of the will one may form in terms of metaphysics, the will's manifestations in the world of phenomena, i.e., human actions, are determined in accordance with natural laws, as is every other natural event. History is concerned with giving an account of these phenomena, no matter how deeply concealed their causes may be. . .

To contemplate "the great world-drama" is by no means entirely edifying:

> . . . despite the apparent wisdom of individual actions here and there, everything as a whole is made up of folly and childish vanity, and often of childish malice and destructiveness. The result is that we do not know what sort of opinion to form of our species, which is so proud of its supposed superiority.

The philosopher cannot rest content with what is phenomenally given, however. He seeks to discover

> . . . a *purpose in nature* behind this senseless course of human events, and decide whether it is after all possible to formulate in terms of a definite plan of nature a history of creatures who act without a plan of their own.

Kant enumerates a number of propositions that must be accepted at the outset if this kind of natural-historical approach is to succeed in its aim. In the first proposition, he defines what he means by "the teleological theory of nature:"

> *All the natural capacities of a creature are destined sooner or later to be developed completely and in conformity with their end.* This can be verified in all animals by external and internal or anatomical examination. An organ which is not meant for use or an arrangement which does not fulfill its purpose is a contradiction in the teleological theory of nature. For if we abandon this basic principle, we are faced not with a law-governed nature, but with an aimless, random process, and the dismal reign of chance replaces the guiding principle of reason.

Kant notes, in the second proposition, that in searching for a "natural law" basis for optimism about the human future, he was not dealing with single "creatures" as biological organisms, but with humanity as a whole, and with uniquely human capacities that could have developed only on the species level:

> *In man* (as the only rational creature on earth), *those natural capacities which are directed toward the use of his reason are such that they could be developed only in the species, but not in the individual.*

In the third proposition, Kant notes that a natural law interpretation of species development must regard it as a process taking place over many generations. Teleological theory, limited as it is to terrestrial, organic existence, excludes the metaphysical idea that personal consciousness and personal development may continue on into a post-organic after life. The theory also, unavoidably, discriminates in favor of later as opposed to earlier generations:

> What remains disconcerting about all this is firstly, that the earlier generations seem to perform their laborious tasks only for the sake of the later ones. . . secondly, only the later generations will in fact have the good fortune to inhabit the building on which a whole series of forefathers (admittedly, without any conscious intention) had worked without themselves being able to share in the happiness they were preparing. But no matter how puzzling this may be, it will appear as necessary as it is puzzling if we simply assume that one animal species was intended to have reason, and that, as a class of rational beings who are mortal as individuals but immortal as a species, it was still meant to develop its capacities completely (31).

31. *Kant's Political Writings,* edited with Introduction and Notes by Hans Reiss. Cambridge University Press, 1971.

In spite of his emphasis on how much could be achieved through cumulative intergenerational gains, Kant as a teleological theorist was also saying that the optimal condition could not be reached solely through unaided human advances. In the essay entitled "On the Common Saying: 'This May be True in Theory, but it does not Apply in Practice' " (1792), he wrote that

> . . . it is not inappropriate to say of man's moral hopes and desires that, since he is powerless to fulfill them himself, he may look to *providence* to create the circumstances in which they can be fulfilled (32).

In the essay on "Perpetual Peace" (1795), teleological nature ". . . appears as the underlying wisdom of a higher cause, showing the way toward the objective goal of the human race and predetermining the world's evolution." Nature is portrayed as "a great Artist," and also as a designing, manipulative agency that achieves its effects externally and mechanically, through forms of compulsion. If not fully understood, these compulsions appear as *fate.* But when the purpose being achieved is fully known "we call it *providence.*"

The design and purpose , and also the mechanisms of operation are "visibly exhibited" to the philosophical understanding. Even though the hidden process cannot be observed or even inferred empirically ". . . we can and must *supply it mentally*. . ."

Kant seems to be saying three things: 1) The attainment of perpetual peace and all that this means to him is not impossible, even when the limitations of human nature are taken into account. 2) It is not legitimate to conclude that the theory as idea, as a basis for thought, is invalid because it cannot be proven true by methods used in the empirical sciences. 3) A pessimistic outlook which affirms, also without empirical evidence, that the goal cannot be reached, is morally unacceptable. The teleological theory of history which is in

> . . . conformity with the end which reason directly prescribes to us (i.e., the end of morality) can only be conceived as an idea. Yet while this idea is indeed far-fetched in *theory,* it does possess dogmatic validity and has a very real foundation in *practice,* as with the concept of perpetual peace, which makes it our duty to promote it by using the natural mechanism described above (33).

As a conceptual "designer," Marx, like Kant, was himself external to the process by which the future pattern of rational and moral order that he identified with ultimate communism was to be realized. Unlike Kant, he could not, of course, have represented cosmological nature as the instrument of a supersensible "higher cause."

---

32. *Op. cit.*
33. *Op. cit.*

Marx shared with Kant an *a priori* assumption that humanity's time on earth would be sufficient to accomplish the complete realization of human species-powers. In Hegel's philosophy, it seems as though no future time will be needed, since the Idea is already fully immanent and realized in the concrete life of the present. Nevertheless, Hegel presumed that humanity as species, although tied permanently to earth and to the organic substratum, is "immortal."

5

The Social Condition Of The Modern Working Class

Marx's theory of political and social revolution, the way that it would take place, and what it would achieve was inseparable from his belief that the industrial working class was the historically created instrument of universal redemption and emancipation. The workers would succeed in freeing themselves as a class, but only insofar as they acquired a form of consciousness, and a disposition to act, which would be in partial continuity with the preceding, equally necessary process of bourgeois emancipation. The appearance of the working class in history was part of a larger progressive movement that would culminate in the reconstruction of society. Working class victory would at the same time make it possible to eliminate from human culture a considerable number of traits and tendencies that were incompatible with a free condition of social and personal existence. The gains of civilization, many of which had been achieved in the capitalist era, would be preserved and extended through socialism. Marx's theory of revolution and of the conditions that would ensure its success cannot be abstracted from his more general views about the nature of bourgeois society, including its positive as well as its negative features.

Marx's idea of the proletarian mission was developed in response to the views given by Hegel in *The Phenomenology of Spirit* and in *The Philosophy of Right*. Hegel's exposition of the contradictions of capitalism and of the moral outlook and attitudes of the middle class beneficiaries of the system was extraordinarily penetrating. He had perceived and discussed a number of social, moral and economic difficulties arising on the systematic level which could not be resolved within the limits of the system. He had no solutions to offer, only pseudo-solutions. He took refuge in intellectual and moral evasions, ambiguities and abstractions in a way that was characteristic of his entire philosophy and theodicy of history. His analysis of capitalism almost invited the appearance of a social and economic philosophy that would repudiate his pessimistic conclusions. Hegel had accentuated the positive aspects of modern society and civilization in such a way that the negative aspects are discounted. Marx could not discount the negative, but his concept of the future and of the proletarian mission shows that he remained in fundamental agreement with Hegel in some respects, seeking to maximize a modern type of freedom.

Both Hegel and Marx stressed the importance of forms of autonomy which had not been available, they believed, to persons living in pre-modern societies. On one level, autonomy is personal, but personal autonomy must be supplemented by an autonomy that is collective, pertaining to the whole community, which possesses forms of public and societal power which is more than the sum total of separate personal powers. In Hegel's philosophy, autonomy on the personal level relates to the work that the individual who is a member of the middle class must perform in order to support himself and his immediate family. This middle class worker is responsible only to himself, and to his immediate family, if he is married. Unless he holds public office, he has no direct public responsibilities, although he must remain within the limits of the law in his economic conduct. Concentrating entirely on his own social and economic advancement and security, he "makes himself" through work activity. He is economically self-sufficient, in the sense that he is not dependent on external public or private sources of economic support. In a larger sense he is dependent like every one else on the economic system within which he functions. This individual is said to achieve self-respect through his work but also, at the same time, receives recognition and respect from other persons on his own level. Since he is also honest, not given to economic cheating, what he achieves for himself as a worker is a moral, material and social status, and a morally favorable estimation of himself. This middle class individual is potentially insecure, since he might conceivably forfeit his moral merit and his economic security, either through some fault of his own, or for some external reason beyond his control.

This personal economic and vocational autonomy, which developed in the laissez-faire economy of capitalism, was complemented by a condition of suprapersonal collective autonomy which was not economic but national, legal, political and moral. The nation is said to be a single, self-enclosed and self-sufficient entity. Unlike the autonomous individual, it does not have its own merit socially confirmed by social judgments arising from sources external to itself. It is above and beyond any kind of moral criticism. Its spiritual status is secure and inalienable, no matter what it does, and regardless of the consequences of actions undertaken on the collective level.

Marx indicted capitalism on more than one count. Among other things, the economy of capitalism made it impossible for the proletarians in modern industries to achieve a personal autonomy, as workers, that would be the moral and spiritual equivalent of the autonomy achieved by the self-reliant "self-making" middle class individual depicted by Hegel. But Marx was concerned not only with the extremely deprived situation of the proletarian workers. He was also concerned to a notable degree with the insecurity of the middle class situation. The proletarians, already at rock bottom, who had "nothing to lose but their chains," would be able to eliminate their own special handicaps through revolutionary victory, but the forms of insecurity that were experienced by individuals in the middle class would be eliminated through this same process. Personal autonomy, together with material and moral security of an inalienable kind, would become available to all. Collective autonomy, in Marx's system, was the socially shared autonomy of the community, considered as an economic productive entity.

THE GERMANIC COMPLEX IN MARX'S SOCIAL PHILOSOPHY

Although he conceived of the future society of communism as supranational, and its unity as chiefly economic, Marx's conception of the future condition of collective autonomy was modelled, originally, on the Hegelian conception of national collective autonomy. He did not believe that Germany, in its present condition, was capable of developing a kind of national, collective autonomy and power that Hegel had described, and had valued so highly. Germany was said to be deficient in qualities making for national greatness. England and France were greatly superior to Germany in this and other respects. The post-capitalist society that would be established through working class action was to incorporate a kind of strength that should also have been acquired by Germany as a nation had it been able to carry through a national bourgeois revolution and had thus been able to draw abreast of England and France. Most Germans had subjective psychological tendencies that were incompatible with the qualities required to carry through a bourgeois revolution. The importance of a struggle against such tendencies was emphasized especially in Marx's earliest revolutionary writings. Philosophy was being drawn into the struggle against forms of subjectivity that would impair the ability of philosophers to criticize the existing state of affairs in a sufficiently forceful, radical way, and to follow up this criticism with remedial social and political action. In a letter to Arnold Ruge, written in September 1843, Marx said:

> Now philosophy has become mundane, and the most striking proof of this is that philosophical consciousness itself has been drawn into the torment of the struggle, not only externally but also internally. But, if constructing the future and settling everything for all times are not our affair, it is all the more clear what we have to accomplish at present: I am referring to *ruthless criticism of all that exists,* ruthless both in the sense of not being afraid of the results it arrives at and in the sense of being just as little afraid of conflict with the powers that be (1).

What I am calling Marx's "Germanic complex" was related primarily to problems of Germany, but his way of perceiving and reacting to conditions in Germany was also the expression of a general Western ethnocentrism. In the political writings of his middle period, extending from 1845-46 through 1856, he was outspoken in endorsing Western colonialism and imperialism

---

1. *Collected Works of Marx and Engels.* New York: International Publishers, 1975, Volume III. This letter was published in the Deutsche-Franzosische Jahrbucher, 1844.

as the means by which cultures incompatible with socialism were being destroyed. He began his career as a revolutionary theorist by focussing on Germany, which he described as a backward, inadequately unified, feudal and patriarchal land. The German population lacked both the ability and the desire to free itself from its subordination to outworn forms and restrictions:

> In Germany. . . where practical life is as mindless as mental life is impractical, no class in civil society has any need or capacity for general emancipation until it is forced to it by its immediate condition, by *material* necessity, by its very *chains* (2).

The only German class that qualifies for national leadership is the working class, because only this class is forced by material necessity to overcome its subjective weakness:

> . . . in Germany every class lacks not only the consistency, penetration, courage and ruthlessness which could stamp it as the negative representative of society. There is equally lacking in every class that breadth of soul which identifies itself, if only momentarily, with the soul of the people – that genius for inspiring material force toward political power, that revolutionary boldness which flings at its adversary the defiant words; *I am nothing and I should be everything.*

In this same Introduction, Marx was also abstracting the proletarians from their national German setting. They cannot lead a merely national revolution, nor can they stop short at partial emancipation. The special national handicaps of the German workers will be offset when they come under the influence of the one aspect of German culture that is boldly radical, namely, the critical attack on religion carried on by neo-Hegelian philosophers:

> The weapon of criticism obviously cannot replace the criticism of weapons. Material force must be overthrown by material force. But theory becomes a material force once it has gripped the masses. Theory is capable of gripping the masses when it demonstrates *ad hominem,* and it demonstrates *ad hominem* when it becomes radical. To be radical is to grasp things by the root. But for man the root is man himself. The clear proof of the radicalism of German theory and hence of its political energy is that it proceeds from the decisive *positive* transcendence of religion. The criticism of religion ends with the doctrine that *man* is the *highest being for man,* hence with the *categorical imperative to overthrow all conditions* in which man is a degraded, enslaved, neglected, contemptible being. . .

---

2. Introduction to *A Critique of Hegel's Philosophy of Right,* translated by Easton and Guddat, *op. cit.*

By the time Marx reaches the end of this essay, he has accomplished the unification of theory with the revolutionary movement and has transformed the proletarians in Germany and elsewhere into a material-political force which will carry out the aims of theory:

> Where, then, is the *positive* possibility of German emanicpation? *Answer.* In the formation of a class with *radical chains,* a class in civil society that is not of civil society, a class that is the dissolution of all classes, a sphere of society that has a universal character because of its universal suffering and claiming no *particular right* because no *particular wrong* but *unqualified wrong* is perpetrated on it; a sphere that can invoke no *traditional* title but only a *human* title. . . a sphere, in short that is the *complete loss* of humanity and can only redeem itself through the *total redemption of humanity.* This dissolution of society as a particular class is the *proletariat. . .*
>
> As philosophy finds its *material* weapons in the proletariat, the proletariat finds its intellectual weapons in philosophy. And once the lightning of thought has deeply struck this unsophisticated soil of the people, the *Germans* will emancipate themselves to become *men.*

The aims of the proletarian revolution were in partial continuity with the world-conquering activities of the national political bourgeoisie outside of Germany. The proletarians had a special "world-historical" mission which was the second and last stage of a general Western planetary mission which was being partly accomplished by the "world-historical" bourgeoisie. The kind of degradation endured by the proletarians, and also the degraded status of Germany in the community of nations, was connected by Marx with tendencies to communal and personal subordination that were conspicuous also in certain backward non-Western cultures. In a newspaper article on the role of the British in India, he wrote:

> England has to fulfill a double mission in India, one destructive, the other regeneration: the annihilation of old Asiatic society, and the laying of the material foundations of Western society in Asia (3).

The suffering associated with the destructive aspects of human progress will come to an end, once the entire planet has come under the control of the most advanced, civilized Western nations, since the ground will then also be prepared for the passage into socialism:

---

3. Article dated July 22, 1853 on "The Future Results of the British Rule in India," reprinted in *The American Journalism of Marx and Engels,* edited by Henry M. Christman, New American Library, 1966.

> When a great social revolution shall have mastered the result of the bourgeois epoch, the market of the world and the modern powers of production, and subjected them to the common control of the most advanced peoples, then only will human progress cease to resemble that hideous pagan idol who would not drink the nectar but from the skulls of the slain.

India would have been conquered by militarily stronger peoples in any case, but it was better that the English, who were in the forefront of civilization, had arrived first:

> The question, therefore, is not whether the English had a right to conquer India, but whether we are to prefer India conquered by the Turk, by the Persian, by the Russian, to India conquered by the Briton.

The moral evils of bourgeois rule are clearly demonstrated by the actions of the British in India, but the good effects should also be kept in mind:

> England, it is true, in causing a social revolution in Hindustan, was actuated only by the vilest interests, and was stupid in her manner of enforcing them. But that is not the question. The question is, can mankind fulfill its destiny without a fundamental revolution in the social state of Asia? If not, whatever may have been the crimes of England she was the unconscious tool of history in bringing about that revolution (4).

Marx and Engels endorsed and approved the process of Westernization, even though they denounced the methods by which it was carried out, and the motives that inspired it. In his discussion of their views on this question, Horace B. Davis has noted:

> As between capitalism and pre-capitalist feudalism or barbarism, there was simply no choice at all in their view; capitalism with all its faults was immeasurably superior, if only because of the way it revolutionized production. . . For many years they defended the ruthless expansion of imperialism, provided only that it brought economic development in its wake.

With respect to India in particular, Davis notes that

> Contrary to a commonly accepted view, Marx did not in 1857-59 advocate independence for India, any more than Cobden and Bright did. . . and he still thought that British capitalism would perform a useful function in India, even if at tremendous cost, in shaking that country out of its centuries-old conservatism and backwardness. In 1862 he quoted with approval the hyperbolic

4. "The British Rule in India," article dated June 10, 1853, in Christman, *op. cit.*

> language of Mazzini, who had said that the English soldier seemed a demigod during the Indian insurrection! (5)

Marx had regarded the condition of life in the agricultural villages of India as degrading and sub-human. The culture of the passive, stagnating mass base of Asiatic society – the peasant population – had to be destroyed. The Indian villagers, by the very fact that they existed, had been responsible for calling out the forces of aggression and destruction which has been directed against them, most recently by the British, but previously by other invading groups. These "idyllic village communities" had

> . . . been the solid foundation of oriental despotism. . . they restrained the human mind within the smallest possible compass, making it the unresisting tool of superstition, enslaving it beneath traditional rules, depriving it of all grandeur and historical energies. . . We must not forget that this undignified, stagnatory, and vegetative life, that this passive sort of existence, evoked on the other part, in contradistinction, wild aimless and unbounded forces of destruction. . . (6).

Marx was expressing in more extreme form attitudes which had also appeared in some of the writings of Kant. In his "Metaphysical Principles of Virtue," Part III of a larger work, *The Metaphysics of Morals* (1797), Kant underlies the need to avoid religious and social servility. In the section devoted to a discussion of the duties of man to himself, he said that there could be no morally justifiable duty to submit to other people in a way that detracted from the dignity and status of the individual as a rational and spiritual being *(homo noumenon).* The ideally autonomous ethical individual who seeks to govern his own actions in accordance with the universal moral law must cultivate in himself a strength of will and character, and a power of self-defensive resistance to self-depreciating influences. He must maintain a certain independence and self-assertiveness. To act in a servile manner was inconsistent with his worth and dignity as a noumenal being.

Kant's precepts seemed to be addressed to persons above the lowest level of economic destitution and social powerlessness.

> Do not become the vassals of men. Do not suffer your rights to be trampled underfoot by others with impunity. Incur no debts for which you cannot provide full security. Accept no favors which you might do without. Do not be parasites nor flatterers nor (what really differs from these only in degree) beggars. Therefore, be thrifty so that you may not become destitute (7).

---

5. *Nationalism and Socialism: Marxist and Labor Theories of Nationalism to 1917,* Monthly Review Press, 1967, pp. 13, 14 and 67.
6. "The British Rule in India," *op. cit.*
7. *The Metaphysical Principles of Virtue,* translated by James Ellington, Bobbs-Merrill, Inc., 1964, Chapter I, Section III "Concerning Servility."

Religious vassalage, as well as social vassalage, was to be avoided. Symbolic, ceremonial gestures of submission to an unseen transcendental power, such as those associated with Catholic ritualism, were incompatible with human dignity. Religious image-making was idolatry:

> Kneeling down or groveling on the ground, even to express your reverence for heavenly things, is contrary to human dignity; as is also invoking heavenly things in actual images, for you then humble yourself not to an idea which your own reason sets before you but to an idol which is your own handiwork (8).

Kant called attention to the persistence of feudalistic manners and attitudes in Germany, as a notable instance of human tendencies to servility. These tendencies are reflected in language and behavior ". . . which the Germans of all people on earth (with the possible exception of the Indian castes) have developed to the utmost pedantry. But whoever makes himself a worm cannot complain when he is then trampled underfoot."

Kant distinguishes between the courtesy and respect that is due to every one, as a human being, and the special forms of exaggerated deference that connote servility:

> Bowing or scraping before another seems . . . to be unworthy of a man.
>
> Are not special manifestations of respect in words or manners, e.g., curtsies, bows, compliments, and courtly phrases designating distinctions of status with scrupulous punctilio (all of which are completely different from courtesy, which is necessary for mutual respect), even toward someone who does not hold public office, evidence of a widespread tendency to servility among men? (9).

Kant's attack on tendencies to servility and to self-victimization was carried forward into Marx's philosophy of revolutionary resistance. Marx wished to eliminate the objective conditions of economic dependency which placed the workers in a situation of being victimized by the capitalist overlord. At the same time it was equally necessary to eliminate those subjective tendencies to servility which had been defined as deficiencies of character by Kant. Kant's emphasis on the need for resistance to status degradation entered into Marx's attack on religion in general: "The criticism of religion ends with the doctrine that *man* is the *highest being for man,* hence with the *categorical imperative to overthrow all conditions* in which man is a degraded, enslaved, neglected, contemptible being . . . " (10).

---

8. *Ibid.*
9. *Ibid.*
10. Introduction (1843) to *A Critique of Hegel's Philosophy of Right,* translated by Easton and Guddat, *op. cit.*

ATOMISTIC DISSOLUTION IN MODERN SOCIETY

Marx accepted the abstract atomic view of bourgeois economic society which had been adopted by the classical laissez-faire economists and by the social contract theorists of the seventeenth and eighteenth centuries. From the dialectical standpoint, the benefits of atomization outweighed the evils. The atomization of society was a necessary condition of its social reintegration. Individuals in capitalist society had become detached from one another socially, morally, and psychologically, but they had also been freed from earlier restrictive societal bonds. In the earlier feudal society, individuals had been in subjection to restrictive customs, narrow jurisdictions, and various forms of external authority. They had also been limited by certain group-developed corporate constraints that had appeared in the free towns outside of the jurisdiction of the feudal landowners. Individuals of the medieval society had also been morally and psychologically subordinate to clerical, ecclesiastical authority. Even the landowning classes had been so constrained. When the medieval economy had been undermined by the rise of the post-feudal, early capitalist economy, the impersonal authority of tradition and the religious authority of Catholicism had also been undermined. Previously effective moral, social and religious restraints on individual freedom of action had lost their power.

In his discussion of civil society in *The Philosophy of Right* Hegel had said (section 183) that the political economists (he mentioned Smith, Say and Ricardo) had described a system of

> . . . complete interdependence, wherein the livelihood, happiness, and legal status of one man is interwoven with the livelihood, happiness, and rights of all. On this system, individual happiness, etc. depend, and only in this connected system are they actualized and secured. This system may be prima facie regarded as the external state, the state based on need, the state as the Understanding envisages it.

Although the individual in that external state was devoted exclusively to the pursuit of private ends, his dependence on society was as great as it had been in the past. Furthermore, the system of self-interest was a means for meeting ego-needs and for securing ego-satisfactions that were social, not reducible to material needs and satisfactions, in spite of the importance of material motivations. Although Hegel had conceived of the condition of the individual in the "state external" as atomic, this word did not have the same meaning for Hegel as it did for Marx (11). It was Marx, not Hegel, who seemed to regard the atomic individual as dependent on society only in an external, non-psychological, material sense. Both Hegel and Marx rejected the

11. See especially Hegel's definition of civil society as given in Part III of the Encyclopedia of the Philosophical Sciences, *Hegel's Philosophy of Mind.* Oxford: Clarendon Press, 1971, Section 523.

mythic anthropology of the social contract theorists, who had posited the existence of an isolated individual who had once lived in a pre-political and also a pre-social condition. Marx, however, implied that the non-social condition so described was the actuality of the present economic society. In the Introduction (1857) to *A Contribution to a Critique of Political Economy* he wrote that

> The individual in this [bourgeois] society of free competition seems to be rid of the natural ties, etc. which made him an appurtenance of a particular, limited aggregation of human beings in the previous historical epochs. The prophets of the eighteenth century on whose shoulders Adam Smith and Ricardo were still wholly standing, envisaged this eighteenth century individual – a product of the dissolution of feudal society on the one hand and of the new productive forces evolved since the sixteenth century on the other – as an ideal whose existence belonged to the past. They saw this individual not as an historical result, but as the starting point of history (12).

Marx regarded the atomic society of universal economic competition as a necessary break with the past, and as the first *real beginning* of history: "The prehistory of human society accordingly closes with this [bourgeois] social formation" (13). Socialism was to eliminate the negative aspects of the bourgeois external state, aspects to which Hegel had referred in *The Philosophy of Right:*

> Particularity [individuality] by itself, given free rein in every direction to satisfy its needs, accidental caprices, and subjective desires, destroys itself and its substantive concept in the process of gratification. . . In these contrasts and their complexity, civil society affords a spectacle of extravagance and want as well as of the physical and ethical degeneration common to them both. . .
>
> Individuals in their capacity as burghers in this state are private persons whose end is their own interest (14).

Hegel had also declared, however, that the evils of the external state condition were counteracted by the existence of the national political State. Although the evils of civil society could not be eliminated altogether, they could be held in check. The external civil society was morally as well as practically dependent on the higher State functions and on the activities which sustained the state. Marx declared that the opposite was the case. Not only was the modern state unable to counteract the evils of civil society. It was, on the contrary, the means by which these evils were being perpetuated.

In spite of his rejection of Hegel's political transcendentalism Marx

---

12. International Publishers, New York, 1970, p. 188.
13. Preface (1859) to *A Critique of Political Economy, op. cit.* p. 21.
14. *Op. cit.* Sections 185 and 187.

carried over into his own historical theory some of the most striking and unusual aspects of Hegelian philosophy. Both Hegel and Marx were concerned with the condition of the individual in a modern society no longer tied to the thought-ways of the past. Hegel was a philosopher of the future, as well as a philosopher of the on-going present. The individual who possessed a "universal" consciousness was also capable of detaching himself, mentally and emotionally, from any one particular national-institutional system and the forms of "objective mind" that accompanied these institutions. He was both inside and outside of his own political society. In some situations, detachment of a desirable kind could also take the form of spatial, geographical removal, a transfer of residence to a new location where problems appearing in the older environment could be left behind.

Marx regarded "labor" in modern civil society as a "universal" abstract category, supra-national and supra-local. "Labor" in this universal sense signified also a condition of personal detachment. The ideally detached workers included in the category of universal labor refused to be confined, as persons, to any one role and position in life. The universal worker was also able to uproot himself, without regret, from his homeland, his place of origin. Marx regarded America – especially the United States – as the land of the future. The emigrants to North America represented the category of universal free labor. They looked forward to the future, not backward to the past. They had been able to leave behind the environmental limitations that had surrounded them in the Old World. Marx wrote, in *The German Ideology* (1845-46):

> . . . in countries which, like North America, begin in an already advanced historical epoch, their development proceeds very rapidly. Such countries have no other natural premises than the individuals who settled there and were led to do so because the form of intercourse of the old countries did not correspond to their wants. Thus they begin with the most advanced individuals of the old countries, and therefore with the correspondingly most advanced form of intercourse, before this form of intercourse had been able to establish itself in the old countries (15).

Marx seems to have been referring especially, in this passage, to the absence of feudalistic distinctions and manners, i.e., to the greater prevalence of socially equalitarian attitudes and manners in the New World environment. At that time, he was still conspicuously affected by his anti-German, anti-feudal complex. In a footnote to the above passage, he had expressed his contempt for the German non-migrant "natural population" that had remained behind.

Hegel and Marx were philosophers of the Western frontier. This was partly a knowledge frontier, but it was also a way of getting beyond all boundaries of life in the present. As philosophers of progress and of modernity

15. Volume I, Part I, p. 89.

they looked westward, away from the old world of Europe to a new land where there was room for expansion and where great possibilities lay ahead. It is likely that Marx had been influenced by Hegel's statement that

> America is . . . the land of the future, where in the ages that lie before us, the burden of the World's History shall reveal itself – perhaps in a contest between North and South America. It is a land of desire for all those who are weary of the historical lumber-room of old Europe. Napoleon is reported to have said: *'Cette vielle Europe m'ennuie.'* It is for America to abandon the ground on which hitherto the history of the World has developed itself (16).

Marx continued to place the United States in a special category in his later writings. In his 1857 Introduction to *A Contribution to a Critique of Political Economy* the United States was described as the most modern, and therefore the most progressive, type of bourgeois society. Capitalists and workers seem both to be included in the abstract, symbolic category of universal labor:

> Labour, not only as a category but in reality, has become a means to create wealth in general, and has ceased to be tied as an attribute to a particular individual. This state of affairs is most pronounced in the United States, the most modern form of bourgeois society. The abstract category of "labour," "labour as such," labour *sans phrase,* the point of departure of modern economics, thus becomes a practical fact only there. The simplest abstraction, which plays a decisive role in modern political economy. . . appears to be actually true in this abstract form only as a category of the most modern society (17).

THE EXCLUSION OF THE WORKERS FROM MIDDLE CLASS STATUS

Marx began his theoretical work as a communist by accepting Hegel's description of the proletarian condition. The workers were excluded from the moral, social and political status available to middle class persons whose incomes might be derived from some form of non-manual labor, but also, in whole or in part, from their ownership of some form of private property. Hegel said that the condition of the modern working class was different from – and worse than – any previous condition of social and economic poverty. As Hegel saw it, there were two primary opposing moral categories in modern civil [external] society: 1) the active, industrious middle class workers who make their own way in the world through their own personal efforts, and

16. *The Philosophy of History,* Introduction, *op. cit.,* pp. 86-87.
17. *Op. cit.,* p. 210.

2) the degraded poor who do not measure up to this level. He summarized some of the contradictions and limitations of developing and maturing capitalism from the standpoint of a middle class insider who was able to see some of the defects of a system which he continued to endorse. The masses "begin to decline into poverty" in the modern civil (bourgeois) society. Their deprivation is economic, but it is also moral, political and spiritual. It was this idea of Hegel's to which Marx referred when he wrote, in the Introduction to *A Critique of Hegel's Philosophy of Right:*

> The proletariat is only beginning to appear in Germany as a result of the rising *industrial* movement. For it is not poverty from *natural circumstances* but *artificially produced* poverty, not the human masses mechanically oppressed by the weight of society but the masses resulting from the *acute disintegration* of society, and particularly of the middle class, which gives rise to the proletariat – though also, needless to say, poverty from natural circumstances and Christian-Germanic serfdom gradually join the proletariat (18).

Hegel had made no reference to a supposed process of middle class disintegration and impoverishment which Marx believed was producing an "artificial" modern kind of poverty. Hegel had meant that the poor in feudal society were once regarded as moral and spiritual members of society, in spite of their low estate. The general economic atomization of post-feudal civil society, however, had shattered the earlier community bonds, and the poor, those in the most precarious economic position, had suffered disproportionately:

> The poor still have needs common to civil society, and yet since society has withdrawn from them the natural means of acquisition and broken the bond of the family – in the wider sense of the clan – their poverty leaves them more or less deprived of all the advantages of society. . . The public authority takes the place of the family where the poor are concerned in respect not only of their immediate want but also of laziness of disposition, malignity, and the other vices which arise out of their plight and their sense of wrong (19).

Hegel seems to have relegated the entire proletariat to the category of a "penurious rabble," continually on the verge of pauperdom, even when fully employed. Their status is always nationally marginal and partly "surplus" both in the economic and the political sense:

---

18. Translated by Easton and Guddat, *op. cit.*

19. *The Philosophy of Right, op. cit.,* Section 241. Nathan Rotenstreich has pointed out in *Basic Problems of Marx's Philosophy,* that the term "civil society" appears in the original German of Hegel as "burgerliche Gesellschaft." This could be translated as "bourgeois society," but "civil society" has become the accepted term in English translations of Hegel.

> When the standard of living of a large mass of people falls below a certain subsistence level – a level regulated automatically as the one necessary for a member of the society – and when there is a consequent loss of the sense of right and wrong, of honesty and the self-respect which makes a man insist on maintaining himself by his own work and effort, the result is the creation of a rabble of paupers. At the same time this brings with it, at the other end of the social scale, conditions which greatly facilitate the concentration of disproportionate wealth into a few hands (20).

Marx accepted Hegel's conclusion that neither the objective nor the subjective handicaps of the modern industrial working class could be overcome within the limits of the present day economic system. Hegel had said that

> . . . despite an excess of wealth civil society is not rich enough, i.e., its own resources are insufficient to check excessive poverty and the creation of a penurious rabble. . . (21).

Hegel had outlined a socio-economic dialectic of capitalist expansion. The mass of econonic misery is bound to increase as the general wealth of bourgeois (civil) society increases. Owing to the mounting pressure of internal poverty relative to the amount of new wealth being created, markets for home-produced goods must be sought abroad. The workers in the home territories could not buy back enough of the product. Production outstripped the ability of the workers to consume:

> This inner dialectic of civil society thus drives it – or at any rate drives a specific civil society – to push beyond its own limits and seek markets, and so its necessary means of subsistence, in other lands which are either deficient in the goods it has over-produced, or else generally backward in industry, etc.

Marx could not accept Hegel's pseudo-solution for the problems of capitalism. Hegel had said that opportunities for out-migration to undeveloped territories outside the heavily populated European centers would help at least a section of the working class. The system could apparently continue indefinitely without entering into a stage of crisis in which this kind of escape from the crowded centers would no longer be available. Apparently, there was an indefinite amount of economic and geographic Lebensraum. The sea – which links together the "great progressive peoples" who "press onward to the sea" – provides some of the surplus population with a chance to "return to life" from a condition that is tantamount to spiritual death:

> This far-flung connecting link [the sea] affords the means for the colonizing activity – sporadic or systematic – to which the

20. *Ibid.*, Section 244.
21. *Ibid.*, Section 245.

> mature civil society is driven and by which it supplies to a part of its population a return to life on the family basis in a new land and so also supplies itself with a new demand and a field for its industry (22).

Marx, in opposition, believed that the capitalist economy, with all its internal contradictions, would be spread through the process of out-migration. The problems encountered in the original home bases would reappear elsewhere. As noted earlier in this chapter, he followed Hegel in conceiving that the new lands of open opportunity offered an escape from some of the limitations of Europe to those who were able to free themselves through out-migration. But the economy and society of capitalism was a single system. That system would continue to impose on the industrial worker conditions of work, and of existence, that were humanly degrading and intolerable.

Marx brushed aside as irrelevant Hegel's preoccupation with the so-called "laziness" of the modern poor. Dislike of work, a desire to escape from it, was due to the onerous conditions of work imposed on the proletarians. The worker living in the external civil society is subordinated to the external directing power of capital. He is forced to carry out a work project that is neither self-initiated nor self-directed. While he is "free" in a negative sense, as an atomic individual outside the bonds of feudal society, he is being subjected to a new kind of enslavement, described as "loss of self." When labor is external to the worker it is not "part of his nature:"

> . . . the worker does not affirm himself in his work but denies himself, feels miserable and unhappy, develops no free physical and mental energy but mortifies his flesh and ruins his mind. The worker, therefore, feels at ease only outside work, and during work he is outside himself. He is at home when he is not working and when he is working he is not at home. His work, therefore, is not voluntary, but coerced, *forced labor.* It is not the satisfaction of a need but only a *means* to satisfy other needs. Its alien character is obvious from the fact that as soon as no physical or other pressure exists, labor is avoided like the plague. External labor, labor in which man is externalized is labor of self-sacrifice, of penance. Finally, the external nature of work for the worker appears in the fact that it is not his own but another person's, that in work he does not belong to himself but to someone else. In religion the spontaneity of human imagination, the spontaneity of the human brain and heart, acts independently of the individual as an alien, divine or devilish activity. Similarly, the activity of the worker is not his own spontaneous activity. It belongs to another. It is the loss of his own self (23).

---

22. *Ibid.,* Section 246.

In these early writings, Marx was regarding materially productive work under normally "free" conditions as a process which demonstrates the unique capabilities which elevate humanity above the merely "animal" level. Under conditions prevailing in modern industry, however, the worker's entire life becomes sub-human:

> The result, therefore, is that man (the worker) feels that he is acting freely only in his animal functions – eating, drinking, and procreating, or at most in his shelter and finery – while in his human functions he feels only like an animal. The animalistic becomes the human and the human the animalistic.
>
> To be sure, eating, drinking, and procreation are genuine human functions. In abstraction, however, and separated from the remaining sphere of human activities and turned into final and sole ends, they are animal functions (24).

The workers in capitalist industry suffered from multiple deprivations, all of which contributed to the general "loss of self" that they were said to be experiencing. They are deprived of social respect and social recognition, because of the way in which they are regarded and treated by the middle class bourgeois society from which they are excluded. They will eliminate this social status handicap in a way that by-passes the Hegelian prescription, which applies to persons in middle class vocations. In raising themselves, through revolutionary action, to a more adequate social status level, they will be able to be free of certain restrictions which Hegel had associated with the modern class system. In *The Philosophy of Right* Hegel had written:

> A man actualizes himself only in becoming something definite, i.e., something specifically particularized; this means restricting himself exclusively to one of the particular spheres of need. In this class-system, the ethical frame of mind is therefore rectitude and *esprit de corps,* i.e., the disposition to make oneself a member of one of the moments of civil society by one's own act, through one's energy, industry, and skill, to maintain oneself in this position, and to fend for oneself only through this process of mediating oneself with the universal, while in this way gaining recognition both in one's own eyes and in the eyes of others (25).

The proletarians do not need to become specialized, or to move into middle class occupations in order to regain their human and social status. Their labor is "universal" and by definition not restricted or specialized. In their victory over capital, they will eliminate the disrepute which is attached to manual proletarian work by the bourgeois middle class society.

---

23. *Economic and Philosophic Manuscripts of 1844,* "Alienated Labor," translated by Easton and Guddat, *op. cit.*
24. *Ibid.*
25. *Op. cit.*, Section 207.

ECONOMIC DEPENDENCY AND MORAL DISCREDIT

In his writings of 1843 and 44 on economic alienation in modern society, Marx described a process of unequal social exchange in which the weaker party, the poor man acting under pressure of material need, was bound to suffer moral discredit when he entered into a dependency relation with a more powerful person or tried to establish such a relation. The situation of the person seeking economic credit because he did not have sufficient resources of his own was described in a way that seemed to refer back to Kant's precepts on the evils of economic dependency. In Kant's equalitarian moral economy, individuals who were born into a social stratum below the independent middle class level, or who had suffered some economic disaster that could not be regarded as a lapse from moral virtue, had no way of avoiding the kind of self-depreciation and social depreciation that Kant had deplored. No matter how worthy such a person might be in other respects, his economic and social dependency made it impossible for him to observe certain of the norms of middle class virtue prescribed by Kant. Marx was considering the situation of the individual who was not in the hopelessly destitute proletarian category when he described the evils of the debtor-creditor relation. This relation was to be eliminated in the economy of socialism. In the present, however, the poor man had to undergo an appraisal of his character which was based entirely on whether or not he could be relied upon to repay a debt which he wished to contract. The potential creditor who makes this appraisal has no moral right to do so, since his motives in lending money are wholly venal and self-interested. Even if he has other less venal impulses he must suppress them if he is not to lose whatever material and social advantage he has, impoverishing himself. The situation involves both parties in moral evils that could be avoided only if the relation itself were abolished. In economic notes written in 1844 Marx said that

> Mutual dissimulation, hypocrisy, and sanctimoniousness are carried to the point that a moral judgment is added to the simple statement that a man without credit is poor, a judgment that he is untrustworthy and unworthy of recognition, a social pariah and a bad man. On top of suffering from his destitution the poor man suffers from having to make a debasing *plea* to the rich for credit (26).

In later years, Marx continued to emphasize the evils of the debtor-creditor relation. The conflict between debtors and creditors was one kind of class conflict. It was less crucial and less important than the conflict between the proletarian workers in modern industry and the capitalist owners, but in times of antiquity it had been the primary class conflict. In *Capital,* he wrote that

---

26. Notes on James Mill's *Elements of Political Economy,* section on "Money and Alienated Man," translated by Easton and Guddat, *op. cit.*

> The class-struggles of the ancient world took the form chiefly of a contest between debtors and creditors, which in Rome ended with the ruin of the plebeian debtors. They were displaced by slaves. In the middle ages the contest ended with the ruin of the feudal debtors, who lost their political power together with the basis on which it was established (27).

The wage earner in modern industry was not applying for credit when he entered into the employ of a capitalist, but he was degrading and depreciating himself, entering into a dependency relation in which he was compelled to sacrifice his human status for the sake of maintaining himself in biological, physical existence. Marx followed Hegel in making a distinction between those economic systems which had included the institutions of slavery and serfdom and the modern economy. Master and slave categories had been replaced by universal free labor. All persons were formally free. For that very reason, however, the condition of the wage slave was more degraded than that of the chattel slave or serf. He is not under direct physical compulsion. His own action, his own need, is what brings him under the domination of the employer. As a legally free agent, he has certain self-powers, and powers of will, which he cannot use as long as he remains in a passive, dependent, subordinate role. As long as he continues to work under conditions imposed by capital, he is not only enslaving himself, he is also supporting, maintaining and even augmenting the oppressive power that is being turned against him. In his work activity, he widens the distance between himself and the human status which he should be asserting and affirming, i.e., his supra-animal status in the world of nature.

In the *Grundrisse* manuscripts of 1857-58, Marx described pre-modern types of economic subordination in a way which showed that he was familiar with Hegel's idea of the symbiotic unity of Master and Slave, as given in *The Phenomenology of Mind* [Geist]. In the Hegelian metaphysics, the will of the slave is absorbed into the will of the master and is actualized in a sublimated way. Man is distinguished from animals by the possession of a personal "will" that is capable of being used in ways that are determined by another human being, or by a social class that possesses some kind of dominating power. Marx, in referring to relations of domination and subordination in pre-capitalist slave societies, said that the will of the slave was "appropriated" by the master class:

> What we have here as an essential relation of appropriation is the *relationship of domination.* Appropriation can create no such relation to animals, the soil, etc., even though the animal serves its master. The appropriation of another's *will* is presupposed in the relationship of domination. Beings without will, like animals, may indeed render services, but their owner is not thereby *lord and master* (28).

27. Volume I, chapter 3, pp. 135-136.
28. *Pre-Capitalist Economic Formations, op. cit.,* p. 102.

In the writings of "the young Marx," the economic subordination of the proletarian worker to the "lords of capital" is closely identified with religious subordination. Both are equally intolerable forms of self-loss. The capitalist employer does not appropriate the will of the worker directly, as in the earlier slave relation. He appropriates it indirectly, by depriving the worker of the product that he has produced by means of his working will. The ego-will of the worker has passed into the object produced, which appears to be the entire world of non-human material objects. The capitalist, in appropriating the objectified products of labor activity, seems to the worker to be the supreme power to which he owes his own existence and which also creates the objective world. He does not know that he himself is the power and the creator. In a similar way, the religious man creates the religious object, which then becomes "alien" and opposed to him, and is mistakenly thought to derive from a power beyond himself. Marx made a distinction between the object that is alienated, and the creative source of the object, the labor activity of the worker. As the creating subject, the worker

> . . . is related to the *product of his labor* as to an *alien* object. For it is clear according to this premise: The more the worker exerts himself, the more powerful becomes the alien objective world which he fashions against himself, the poorer he and his inner world become, the less there is that belongs to him. It is the same in religion. The more a man attributes to God, the less he retains in himself. The worker puts his life into the object; then it no longer belongs to him but to the object. The greater this activity, the poorer is the worker. The greater this product is, the smaller he is himself. The *externalization* of the worker in his product means not only that his work becomes an object, an *external* existence, but also that it exists *outside him,* independently, alien, an autonomous power, opposed to him. The life *he* has given to the object confronts him as hostile and alien (29).

The "objective world" that is fashioned by the worker and is then externalized as "alien" developed as a result of a symbiotic union of two producing roles and functions, one dominating, and one subordinate. Alienation will not disappear until the subordinate role is excluded and the power of domination possessed by the capitalist class becomes universal social power, equally shared by the entire working community. Although the individuals in both of these major categories, the class that dominates and the class that is dominated, are in a condition of alienation, and are estranged from their true selves, it is only the proletarian who actually experiences self-loss. In *The Holy Family* (1844), he wrote:

> Private property as private property, as wealth, is compelled to maintain *itself,* and thereby its opposite, the proletariat, in *exis-*

29. "Alienated Labor," translated by Easton and Guddat, *op. cit.*

> *tence.* This is the *positive* side of the antithesis, self-satisfied private property.
>
> The proletariat, on the contrary, is compelled as proletariat to abolish itself and thereby its opposite, private property, which determines its existence, and which makes it proletariat. It is the *negative* side of the antithesis, its restlessness within its very self, dissolved and self-dissolving private property.
>
> The propertied class and the class of the proletariat present the same human self-estrangement. But the former class feels at ease and strengthened in this self-estrangement, it recognizes estrangement *as its own power* and has in it the *semblance* of a human existence. The latter feels annihilated in estrangement; it sees in it its own powerlessness and the reality of an inhuman existence (30).

In this same work, Marx referred to the proletarians as a mass group made up of separated isolated individuals each of whom was suffering from self-rejection. They are spiritually as well as materially oppressed. The former condition can be remedied only when they act aggressively and self-affirmatively to destroy the "material," i.e., the institutional, social and political power of bourgeois society, which their own self-debasing activity has produced:

> The enemies of progress *outside* the mass are precisely those *products* of *self-debasement, self-rejection* and *self-alienation* of the *mass* which have been endowed with an independent being and life of their *own.* The mass, therefore, turns against its *own* deficiency when it turns against the independently existing *products* of its *self-debasement,* just as man, turning against the existence of God, turns against his *own religiosity.* But as these *practical* self-alienations of the mass exist in the real world in an outward way, the mass must fight them in an *outward* way. It must by no means hold these products of self-alienation for mere *ideal* fantasies, mere *alienations* of *self-consciousness,* and must not wish to abolish *material* estrangement by purely *inward spiritual* action. As early as 1789 Loustalot's journal bore the motto:
>
> > The great appear great in our eyes
> > Only because we are kneeling.
> > Let us rise!
>
> But to rise it is not enough to do so in *thought* and to leave hanging over one's *real sensuously perceptible* head the *real sensuously perceptible* yoke that cannot be subtilized away with ideas (31).

---

30. *Collected Works of Marx and Engels, op. cit.,* Volume IV, The Holy Family, chapter 4, pp. 35-36.
31. *Ibid.,* chapter 6, p. 82.

MARX'S LATER VIEWS ON THE WORKING CLASS CONDITION

There is a definable difference between the views that Marx expressed in 1844 on the condition of the working class, and his later writings on the same subject. In 1844 Marx had focussed on the situation of the single individual – identified with the proletariat – who was outside of bourgeois society and who was not yet qualified to be in any kind of fully *human* society that would be beyond the bourgeois level. This individual is degraded below the still recognizably human though alienated level which persons inside of bourgeois society, identified as owners of private property, can maintain. This self-enslaving individual cannot overcome his deficiencies unless he joins with others like himself in a revolutionary resistance which will also be a self-redemptive process of status upgrading.

Beginning with *The German Ideology* (1845-46) Marx abandoned his earlier emphasis on the subjective ego-deficiencies on the proletarians. They are still objectively weak, and they also may still be isolated from one another, and in competition with one another. But in this respect they are not notably different from their bourgeois antagonists. They are more severely handicapped politically than the bourgeoisie, partly because their unity, as a political revolutionary class, must not be merely national or local but also international. Marx wrote that

> Competition separates individuals from one another, not only the bourgeois but still more the workers, in spite of the fact that it brings them together. Hence it is a long time before these individuals can unite, apart from the fact that for the purposes of this union – if it is not to be merely local – the necessary means, the great industrial cities and cheap and quick communications, have first to be produced by big industry. Hence every organized power standing over against these isolated individuals, who live in relationships daily reproducing this isolation, can only be overcome after long struggles. To demand the opposite would be tantamount to demanding that competition should not exist in this definite epoch of history, or that the individuals should banish from their minds relationships over which in their isolation they have no control (32).

It appears that the primary political problem, for the working class, is the overcoming of obstacles impeding the creation of a sense of common class interest strong enough to override the competitive, individualistic, irrational kind of social and economic behavior which is universal, common to all class groups, in the atomic era.

In *The Communist Manifesto,* Marx said that capitalist power had been

32. Volume I, Part I, p. 77n.

able to develop only because the workers were at first unable to overcome their own competitive disunity:

> The essential condition for the existence, and for the sway of the bourgeois class, is the formation and augmentation of capital; the condition for capital is wage-labour. Wage labour rests exclusively on competition between the labourers.

In *Capital,* Marx endorsed what he had written in *The Communist Manifesto,* but he also gave an expanded, politically pessimistic description of the various conditions which impaired the ability of the workers to acquire a revolutionary class consciousness:

> It is not enough that the conditions of labour are concentrated in a mass, in the shape of capital, at the one pole of society, while at the other are grouped masses of men, who have nothing to sell but their labour-power. Neither it is enough that they are compelled to sell it voluntarily. The advance of capitalist production develops a working-class, which by education, tradition, habit, looks upon the conditions of that mode of production as self-evident laws of Nature. The organization of the capitalist process of production, once fully developed, breaks down all resistance. The constant generation of a relative surplus-population keeps the law of supply and demand of labour, and therefore keeps wages, in a rut that corresponds with the wants of capital. The dull compulsion of economic relations completes the subjection of the labourer to the capitalist. Direct force, outside economic conditions, is of course still used, but only exceptionally. In the ordinary run of things, the labourer can be left to the "natural law of production," i.e., to his dependence on capital, a dependence springing from, and guaranteed in perpetuity by the conditions of production themselves (33).

Marx seems to have been referring here to conditions that had developed in the early stage of capitalist development, which he called the stage of "primary accumulation," in the process by which the former agricultural workers, forcibly driven from the land, had finally been absorbed, as wage earners, into the new manufacturing industries. His dialectical optimism overcomes his pessimism. He seems to have thought that the conditions he described were no longer operative in the later stage. His primary framework was dialectical, and therefore by definition optimistic. Political problems were consistently minimized. While he had called attention, in *The German Ideology,* to the difficulties that stood in the way of working class political unity, this observation appeared as a footnote to an optimistic passage in the test. He was confident that the growth of "big industry" would offset working class competition.

33. Volume I, chapter 28, p. 737.

> It is evident that big industry does not reach the same level of development in all districts of a country. This does not, however, retard the class movement of the proletariat, because the proletarians created by big industry assume leadership of this movement and carry the whole mass along with them, and because the workers excluded from big industry are placed by it in a still worse situation than the workers in big industry itself (34).

In *The Communist Manifesto* (1848) Marx was able to advance the optimistic thesis which he continued to develop in his later writings. The growth of large-scale manufacturing industries in which many workers were organized into a collective producing unit, was the means by which the capitalists were involuntarily helping to create the revolutionary political class power which would succeed them:

> The advance of industry, whose involuntary promoter is the bourgeoisie, replaced the isolation of the labourers, due to competition, by their revolutionary combination, due to association. The development of modern industry, therefore, cuts from under its feet, the very foundation on which the bourgeoisie produces and appropriates products. What the bourgeoisie, therefore, produces, above all, are its own grave-diggers. Its fall and the victory of the proletariat are equally inevitable.

There are two extant English versions of this passage. The one quoted here is the standard Moscow translation. In an alternate translation by Samuel Moore, approved by Engels for publication when it first appeared in 1888, the first sentence reads "The advance of industry, whose involuntary promoter is the bourgeoisie, replaces the isolation of the labourers, due to competition, by their involuntary combination, due to association" (35). Both versions make sense, in terms of Marx's dialectic. It is only *after* they come together "involuntarily," for reasons that are not social but personal, that a revolutionary combination emerges. The resulting power of association is stronger than the process of atomistic competitive disunification. In the *Manifesto* Marx noted that "The organization of the proletarians into a class, and consequently into a political party, is continually being upset again by the competition between the workers themselves. But it ever rises up again, stronger, firmer, mightier" (36). This optimistic thesis was expanded and elaborated in *Capital.*

In 1843 and 1844 Marx connected the economic subordination of the workers in modern industry with cosmological and religious subordination. He was also connecting the self-alienation of the worker with political subordination to governmental and legal authority. In *Capital,* on the other hand,

---

34. Volume I, Part I, p. 77.
35. The Samuel Moore version is available in the Penguin Books edition, also in the American edition issued by the Monthly Reveiw Press, 1964.
36. Samuel Moore translation.

the workers were no longer so closely identified with these problems. Only one section of the working class was reduced to the level of absolute poverty and degradation described as universal in the 1844 manuscripts. A good many workers, apparently the majority, are being welded into a militant effective mass force. These workers will not only be able to lead a successful political revolution, they will also be equipped to assume control of the producing economy after coming to power. The better organized workers have been able to improve their lot through class struggles within the capitalist system, but they have not thereby lost their incentives to revolution. Being more vigorous and self-confident, they will, on the contrary, become more militant and more dissatisfied with their still by no means satisfactory condition. They will be able also, when conditions are favorable, to arouse the more despondent, passive, less well organized individuals in the lower proletarian strata to take action against the system. Marx described two processes which took place at the same time. Their conjuncture ensured the inevitability of a mass working class revolution, and its ultimate success. The training and experience that the employed workers receive in capitalist industry strengthens their morale and develops qualities of character and of will, equipping them with the ability to carry on production in a fully competent way, in freedom from capitalist direction and management. At the same time, the incentives to revolution increase as the contradictions of the system intensify and the gap between the wealth-creating potentialities of that system and its existing limitations become ever more apparent:

> Along with the constantly dininishing number of the magnates of capital, who usurp and monopolize all the advantages of this process of transformation, grow the mass of misery, oppression, slavery, degradation, exploitation; but with this too grows the revolt of the working-class, a class always increasing in numbers, and disciplined, united, organized by the very mechanism of the process of capitalist production itself (37).

Marx, in *Capital* seems to have regarded the industrial workers, those in mass production industries, as standard setting leaders of the entire working class, directly linked with the political power of the socialist vanguard, the political working class movement, and with its program. Even though not all of those who work in the manufacturing industries are fully politicalized, they have a higher political potential than other sections of the class. As employed workers they were becoming an industrial army, capable of heroic and prolonged struggle against great odds. The industrial army is divided into active and reserve sections. The former are better paid, at less difficult work, more continually employed than those in other sections, but even the active workers can fall into the reserve (unemployed and disadvantaged) section in times of economic crisis. Marx referred also to a depressed, hopeless minority of workers capable of self-help. He refers to "the Lazarus layers" living at the

37. *Capital,* Volume I, chapter 32, p. 763.

bottom level of misery. These are the chronically unemployed, economically surplus or marginal even in times of prosperity, who are "officially accounted paupers" all of the time:

> . . . the relative mass of the industrial reserve army increases with the potential energy of wealth. But the greater this reserve army in proportion to the active labour-army, the greater is the mass of a consolidated surplus-population, whose misery is in inverse ratio to its torment of labour. The more extensive, finally, the Lazarus-layers of the working class and the industrial reserve army, the greater is the official pauperdom. *This is the absolute general law of capitalist accumulation.* Like all other laws it is modified in its working by many circumstances, the analysis of which does not concern us here (38).

Large sections of the middle class will support a working class regime once it has been established, since the workers will cancel the immense burden of debt which bears heavily on the middle class. A good many in this class are in any case being pressed down close to a proletarian level. The process of economic competition inevitably dooms the small, less profitable capitalist enterprises, who are swallowed up and absorbed by the larger firms. In the dialectical perspective, this consolidation is progressive. Large scale units of production, investment and management are more efficient, economically more rational, than smaller units. The concentration of capitalist economic power into a few hands prepares the way for the future control and direction of the socialized economy by the united working class, a single collective power. Concentrated, monopolistic capital is a social power, alienated from the community because it has been "usurped" by a small number of individuals, used for their own ends:

> We have seen that the growing acculumation of capital implies its growing concentration. Thus grows the power of capital, the alienation of the conditions of social production personified in the capitalist from the real producers. Capital comes more and more to the fore as a social power, whose agent is the capitalist. This social power no longer stands in any possible relation to that which the labour of a single individual can create. It becomes an alienated, independent, social power, which stands opposed to society as an object, and as an object that is the capitalist's source of power. The contradiction between the general social power into which capital develops, on the one hand, and the private power of the individual capitalists become ever more irreconcilable, and yet contains the solution of the problem, because it implies at the same time the transformation of the conditions of production into general, common, social conditions (39).

38. *Ibid.,* Chapter 25, p. 644.
39. *Capital,* Volume III, Chapter 15, p. 264.

In Marx's early writings on the alienation of labor in capitalistic society, the worker, as an individual, was alienating his own personal labor product when he entered into a wage contract with an employer. He was thereby also alienating himself. But in *Capital* Marx is no longer viewing the situation in this way. He says that powers and resources created by society are being usurped, i.e., illegitimately appropriated, by a small number of powerful capitalists. The wealth-creating technology, which now operates mostly for their benefit, is social, developed through a long historical process. It is the common heritage of mankind. The individuals who are magnates of capital also appropriate, as surplus value, a more directly social and psychological energy and producing power which arises in group cooperation. The workers of the industrial army have a power of social production derived in part from the instruments of production, i.e., from the technology that is socially created and that is rightfully the possession of society. But they also have an irreducibly social power of production that both includes and transcends the energy and power that they could develop in isolation, as independent workers. What the worker produces in his work activity, in association with others, is indivisible, not to be sub-divided into separate personal work contributions. This enhanced, supra-individual power which arises from the fusion of many forces into a single force, is value added in cooperative activity. It does not belong to any individual worker:

> Not only have we here an increase in the productive power of the individual, by means of cooperation, but the creation of a new power, namely, the collective power of masses (40).

In the capitalist exchange economy the worker appears on the labor market as a private owner of his personal labor power, which he has a legal right to sell (or to refuse to sell), in return for wages. But he does not have a legal right to sell (or alienate) this *social* power, which emerges only in the actual labor process, after he has become incorporated into capital as a "living component." The value added in social cooperation cannot be a part of the original wage transaction between a single worker and the employer. It can never be a *personal* possession. Yet the capitalist is able to appropriate, as surplus value, this added supra-individual component.

From the very first, beginning with Marx's earliest writings as a socialist, society was always the supra-personal power which, like the Hegelian transcendental Idea, is finally restored to wholeness after being divided against itself. In Marx's later writings, however, the single individual is no longer, so conspicuously, the center of moral concern. He is no longer personally divided and self-alienated, struggling against inner tendencies which keep him in subjection to outer powers. The older Marx did, indeed, continue to emphasize not only the objective but also the subjective degradation of the modern proletarians, and their spiritual as well as material misery. But these evils were natural results of the unfavorable social situation. They were offset,

40. *Capital,* Volume I, Chapter 13, p. 326.

among a significant portion of the working class, by the development of economic and political class consciousness through organized activities of resistance against capitalist power. Marx, especially in his later years, was aware of the various difficulties, psychological as well as social and circumstantial, that were handicapping the workers in their struggle against the existing system, yet it was also in these years that his transcendental idea of the proletarian mission became more rather than less important. His confidence in the ability of the workers to carry through that mission was strong enough to survive the negative indications and setbacks. Above all, time was working on the side of the proletarians, on the side of socialism. The present, already receding into the past, was less real than the future that was in the process of coming to be.

6

Socialism As A Program For Moral Change

In this chapter I will focus on Marx's approach to problems of the moral life. The two chapters that follow after this one will continue the discussion begun here. The subject, a vast one, cannot be neatly contained within formal limits. Neither will it be possible for me to discuss, philosophically, the various problems involved. My aim is merely to clarify the nature of Marx's views. The materials presented in each of the preceding chapters of this study have indicated certain aspects of his moral outlook. I will refer in this chapter chiefly to his earlier writings, up to and including *The Communist Manifesto* of 1848.

T.B. Bottomore has raised questions about possible contradictions in Marx's socialism with respect to moral questions. The difficulty, in his opinion, arises in connection with Marx's "theory of ideology." Bottomore believes that this theory is a form of sociological, scientific determinism which "excludes science from the realm of socially determined ideas" and which "makes moral ideas relative." He notes that Marx "also expresses what appear to be absolute moral judgments. If this is indeed the case, there is a contradiction in his thought." He suggests that this apparent contradiction might be cleared up by a study of Marx's early writings, i.e., those written prior to the formation of his theory of ideology:

> The controversy over this question has recently come to be expressed in somewhat different terms as a result of the interest in Marx's early writings. Is there, for Marx, a permanent, unchanging essence of man, which is alienated in certain forms of society, but which in others can find full expression, and which can thus be treated as a moral ideal in some version of a morality of self-realization? Or is the essence of man a purely historical phenomenon, so that no universal ideal or criterion of morality can be formulated at all? I shall not attempt to resolve this problem here. Marx did not attempt to do so, and to say the least his thought is obscure on this subject (1).

1. "Karl Marx: Sociologist or Marxist," paper read August 30, 1965 at the 60th annual meeting of the American Sociological Association, published in *Science and Society, 30:*11-31 (Winter 1966) and in *Sociology and Social Criticism,* Morrow, NY 1974.

There are a number of contradictions and ambiguities in Marx's moral outlook. He operates in more than one frame of reference, in a way that is often hard for the reader to follow. But even the most casual reader cannot help but be aware that Marx does indeed conceive of the future society of socialism as being morally preferable, in an absolute sense, to the society of capitalism. The desirable moral changes that will come about through socialism will include the elimination of all forms of abstract ideological thinking that have any relation to the moral life. Indeed, the kind of self-realization which Marx, in his essays of 1843 and 1844, identified with the actualization of the human "essence" required the elimination of such ideological functions. In other words, it is not possible to turn to these early writings, as if they might provide some way of reconciling the "apparent contradiction" between Marx's materialistic theory of the origin and function of moral ideas, and the absolute criteria of judgment which he uses when he criticizes and condemns the evils of the capitalist economy and society.

Under the cover of an attack on the evils of ideological abstraction, Marx was also, at the same time, engaged in an even more significant operation. He was declaring that the origin, the aims, and the program of modern socialism could be entirely disconnected from the ethical concepts and precepts contained in the Old and New Testaments. Socialism, both as a movement and as a future system of society, was being dissociated, in an absolute sense, from the moral and religious background out of which it had developed (2). The proletarian worker was an ideally post-religious, wholly secular individual. He was also ideally "practical," not given to any kind of thinking about moral, religious, or philosophical questions that had no direct relation to practical social and economic life.

MORALITY AND IDEOLOGY

Marx's theory of ideology appeared in its first, most radical form in *The German Ideology* (1845-46). It was linked with the epistemological materialism which Marx had first endorsed in his doctoral dissertation of 1841 and which he had connected with the philosophy of Epicurus. Essential or true knowledge derived from and was verifiable by means of universal sense perception (3). In his materialist conception of history, first presented in *The German Ideology,* Marx gives primary weight to productive activity which he classes as "material," and which resulted in the production or the transformation of objects that were "material," existing outside of consciousness in external physical space. The superstructural phenomena that were not in this

2. In an article on "Religion and the Socialist Movement in the United States," published in the symposium on "Marxism and Christianity," Humanities Press, 1968, I have discussed some aspects of the conflict between Marx's secular socialism and non-Marxist varieties of American socialism that drew upon the Judeo-Christian ethic and the authority of the Bible as a support for the socialist program.

3. See the discussion in chapter 1, this book, "From Christianity to Communism."

category were ideas and constructs that could not be objectified materially. They existed, but only on a mental level. They were either illusory products of ideological activity or else mental copies or images of what was primarily material and objective. No material, objective, non-illusory basis could be found for "morality, religion and metaphysics." Marx wrote, in *The German Ideology,* that

> We set out from real, active men, and on the basis of their real life process we demonstrate the development of the ideological reflexes and echoes of this life-process. The phantoms formed in the human brain are also, necessarily, sublimates of their material life-process, which is empirically verifiable and bound to material premises. Morality, religion, metaphysics, and all the rest of ideology and their corresponding forms of consciousness thus no longer retain the semblance of independence. They have no history, no development; but men, developing their material production and their material intercourse, alter, along with this their real existence, their thinking and the products of their thinking (4).

Marx could not overlook the fact that consciousness appearing on the superstructural level can sometimes be critical of existing relations, but it is still merely a "sublimate" or an "echo" of the real, material life-process:

> But even if this theory, theology, philosophy, ethics, etc. comes into contradiction with the existing relations, this can only occur as a result of the fact that existing social relations have come into contradiction with existing forces of production. . . (5).

This kind of critical relation to the existing order will disappear once the *primary* contradiction, which exists on the material sub-ideological level of social and economic life has been eliminated.

Marx divided humanity into two major types which cut across class divisions. The downgraded category, to be excluded from the fully human and social life of the future, was associated with past and present ruling class functions which would no longer be required in the classless society. Modern ideologists produced ideas which helped to maintain and consolidate ruling class power. The hegemony of the ruling classes in the alienated societies of Western civilization depended to a considerable degree on productions of an abstract, ideological kind:

> The ideas of the ruling class are in every epoch the ruling ideas, i.e., the class, which is the ruling *material* force of society, is at the same time its ruling *intellectual* force. The class which has the means of material production at its disposal, has control at the

4. *Op. cit.,* Volume I, Part I, pp. 37-38.
5. *Ibid.,* p. 43.

> same time over the means of mental production, so that thereby, generally speaking, the ideas of those who lack the means of mental production are subject to it. The ruling ideas are nothing more than the ideal expression of dominant material relationships grasped as ideas; hence of the relationships which make the one class the ruling one, therefore, the ideas of its dominance (6).

As Marx goes on to develop this theory, it appears that "ruling ideas" are not *just* "material relations grasped as ideas." A distinctive, negative function of the ideologists is the development of self-deceptive illusions of the ruling class about itself and about its value to the community.

The majority of individuals within the ruling political society are not directly implicated in activities of self-deception. They passively receive the ideas produced by the intellectual wing of their class:

> The division of labour, which we already saw above. . . as one of the chief forces of history up till now, manifests itself also in the ruling class as the division of mental and material labour, so that inside this class one part appears as the thinkers of the class (its active, conceptive ideologists, who make the perfecting of the illusion of the class about itself their chief source of livelihood), while the other's attitude to these ideas and illusion is more passive and receptive, because they are in reality the active members of this class, and have less time to make up ideas and illusions about themselves. Within this class this cleavage can even develop into a certain opposition and hostility between the two parts, which, however, in the case of a practical collision, in which the class itself is endangered, automatically comes to nothing, in which case there also vanishes the semblance that the ruling ideas were not the ideas of the ruling class and had a power distinct from the power of this class (7).

Although Marx was referring to activities of the intellectual wing in any modern class society, his attack was aimed chiefly at those German philosophers whose moral and metaphysical views were symptomatic of the special national weakness and backwardness of Germany. The German philosophers were treated as if they were latter-day priests, promoting a belief in the existence of a detached, supra-historical consciousness beyond material life. The division of labor in society had become objectionable – and a major problem which had to be overcome – when priests had first appeared. "Division of labour only becomes truly such when a division of material and mental labour appears" (8). In a marginal note, Marx wrote that priests were "the first form of ideologists," going on to say that

---

6. *Ibid.*, p. 60.
7. *Ibid.*, p. 61.
8. *Ibid.*, p. 43.

> From this moment onwards consciousness *can* really flatter itself that it is something other than consciousness of existing practice, that it *really* represents something without representing something real; from now on consciousness is in a position to emancipate itself from the world and to proceed to the formation of "pure" theory, theology, philosophy, ethics, etc.

"Practical" individuals are obviously in the preferred category. The most effective, history-making representatives of the bourgeois ruling class were individuals whose consciousness was wholly secular, and who were therefore able to act collectively, as a national political class, to promote their own class interests in domestic and foreign affairs and thereby also the economic and political power of their nation. Marx objected to Kant's moral philosophy, calling it a petty-bourgeois Germanic outlook:

> We find again in Kant the characteristic form which French liberalism, based on real class interests, assumed in Germany. Neither he, nor the German burghers, whose whitewashing spokesman he was, noticed that these theoretical ideas of the bourgeoisie had as their basis material interests and a *will* that was conditioned and determined by the material relations of production. Kant, therefore, separated this theoretical expression from the interests which it expressed; he made the materially motivated determinations of the will of the French bourgeois into *pure* self-determinations of *"free will"* . . . Hence the German petty bourgeois recoiled in horror from the practice of energetic bourgeois liberalism as soon as this practice showed itself, both in the Reign of Terror and in shameless bourgeois profit-making (9).

The proletarian revolutionary movement has eminently practical aims, and the workers who will lead the revolution are practical individuals. When they become a political ruling class there will be no division, within the class, between material and mental labor. The working class will not wish or need to support a specialized ideological wing of their own class whose full time occupation is intellectual and theoretical in the downgraded ideological sense. Scientific specialists and theorists seem not to have been included in Marx's attack on ideologists. Science, unifying theory and practice, extended man's practical control over nature, and at the same time refuted the claims of theology and of ideological philosophy. It appeared as though material labor was a category of "universal labor" that could include various activities carried on by middle class workers and that in *The German Ideology* Marx was not referring to proletarian manual labor only, when he contrasted material with mental labor.

In later works, Marx's approach to the problem of the unification of material and mental labor was broadened, so as to include issues not being

9. *Ibid.*, Volume I, Part III, p. 209.

considered in *The German Ideology* (10). His chief aim, in the earlier work, was to eliminate all functions that had anything to do with the formation of a "superstructural" consciousness that included reference to moral and religious ideas.

Marx's way of treating the superstructural aspects of human life and expression in the version of the materialist conception of history which he presented in his 1859 Preface to *A Critique of Political Economy* was less polemical and negative in tone than in the first version of *The German Ideology*, but underlying assumptions were unchanged. He was still saying that all moral ideas and actions were predictable, rationally intelligible responses to conditions that were sub-moral and sub-ideological: ". . . the mode of production in material life determines the social, political and spiritual processes of life in general."

In his comments on Marx's theory of history, Rotenstreich concluded that Marx had represented man as being "totally historical." In the process of historical evolution man has become separated (alienated) from himself:

> Marx assumed that practice in history up to the present creates alienation, and that the self-same practice will ultimately abolish it. Hence in his view man is totally historical. As for the historical situation as it is in the present, man is a split historical being, but he is about to become a rounded, self-identical historical being. The only way, according to Marx, to make man totally unified is to submerge him totally in the realm or stream of history. In other words, man is bound to go along with the course of history without an external yardstock of norms and principles to apply to it. History bears its own value criteria (11).

Marx did project such a complete psychological and moral submergence in the historical flux in *The Poverty of Philosophy* (1846-47) when he declared that "M. Proudhon does not know that all history is nothing but a continuous transformation of human nature" (12), and when he said that

> The same men who establish their social relations in conformity with their material productivity, produce also principles, ideas and categories, in conformity with their social relations.
>
> Thus these ideas, these categories, are as little eternal as the relations they express. They are *historical* and *transitory* products.
>
> There is a continual movement of growth in productive forces, of destruction in social relations, of formation in ideas; the only

10. Other aspects of the material and mental labor question will be discussed in Chapter 10, below, on "The Necessity of Labor in Communist Society."

11. *Basic Problems of Marx's Philosopny, op. cit.,* chapter 7, p. 161.

12. International Publishers, NY, 1963, chapter 2, p. 147.

immutable thing is the abstraction of movement – *mors immortalis* (13).

Marx did not undertake to demonstrate that the morally critical ideas and the positive aims that he supported and that he identified with socialism were in an historically exceptional category. He provides no philosophical or scientific basis for such a claim. He seemed not to think that there was any conflict between his historical relativism and the kind of universalism he identified with the objectives and the values of the working class movement. There were no contradictions to be overcome in this respect. According to his theory, the moral ideas of socialism could be just as time bound, just as relative to a particular, historically developed social form and system, as the ideas and values that were being condemned and displaced. He by-passed the problem by emphasizing the *practicality* of the revolutionary movement and the "material" means by which it was to succeed. Materiality in this context included his representation of the workers as a human "material force" which could dispense with the ideological weaponry used by their opponents, and by preceding ruling classes of history. As a philosopher he relegated all conceptual-level "abstract" moral norms, ideas, and principles to an epiphenomenal plane of reality, i.e., to a cultural superstructure that was supported by a primary structural social and economic base. But he also expected that the communist form of society that would finally emerge out of the earlier phases of socialism would be an enduring one. Further evolutionary changes could occur on this structural and social foundation, but they would not *undermine* the foundation, culturally, morally, or politically.

THE PROJECT OF UNIVERSAL SELF-CHANGING

Marx expected that socialist political revolution would establish new conditions and relations and production and that it would *reverse* the process of political alienation described by Rousseau in *The Social Contract.* Rousseau had implied that *political* power, in the social contract society that he was depicting, was a desirable, morally redemptive form of *social* power, and that human nature transcended the limitations of private individuality through the constitution of the nation as a political entity. Marx, on the other hand, believed that favorable changes of this kind could not take place until the power that had been alienated from individuals by the institution of national political rule had been restored to the individuals who comprised the nation. They had been deprived and weakened, rather than strengthened, in the alienating process. At the conclusion of his first essay on "The Jewish

13. *Ibid.,* pp. 109–110. *Mors immortalis* means "immortal death." As noted by the editors, the Latin phrase refers to Lucretius's poem *On The Nature of Things* (Book II, line 869) "immortal death hath taken away mortal life."

Question" (1843), he quoted directly from the original French of Rousseau, but added his own italics:

> Whoever dares to undertake the founding of a nation must feel himself capable of *changing,* so to speak, *human nature* and *transforming* each individual who is in himself a complete but isolated whole, into a *part* of something greater than himself from which he derives his life and existence, substituting a *partial* and *moral* existence for physical and independent existence. *Man* must be deprived of *his own powers* and given alien powers which he cannot use without the aid of others (14).

According to Marx, this was a correct depiction of ". . . the abstraction of political man." The process of political alienation so described had been a loss, not a gain. The atomized, self-sufficient, pre-political individuals postulated by Rousseau were products of historical disintegration and social dissolution that coincided with the rise of capitalism and of economic individualism. The political power that was established on the atomic foundation could not eliminate the evils of isolation. It had compounded these evils, forcing individuals to surrender a self-power which they had, apparently, once possessed. The loss of power through political alienation will be remedied through the social reunification that will be brought about through communism:

> Only when the actual, individual man has taken back into himself the abstract citizen and in his everyday life, his individual work, and his individual relationships has become a *species-being,* only when he has recognized and organized his own powers as *social* powers, so that social force is no longer separated from him as *political* power, only then is human emancipation complete (15).

Marx is proposing to found, not a political nation, but a classless society that will be beyond all national antagonisms and national forms of competition and aggression. The individual will have access to non-alienating forms of social power that he can acquire only by acting in unity with others. He will surrender nothing of his essential self-hood in becoming united with others in a universal society, but he will have freed himself from the evils of the isolated or "abstract" condition.

The writings of two neo-Hegelian philosophers, Ludwig Feuerbach and Max Stirner, influenced the way in which Marx proceeded, after 1844, to develop his ideas about the process of universal self-changing that would take place through the working class revolution. Marx had found, in Feuerbach's *Essence of Christianity,* published in 1841, some support for his own different kind of materialism and humanism. But in his critical comments on Feuerbach, appearing both in the *Theses on Feuerbach* (1845) and in *The German Ideology* (1845-46) he was defining his own revolutionary and philosophical position. He discarded the Hegelian term "essence," which he

14. *Collected Works of Marx and Engels, op cit.,* Volume III, 1975, p. 167.
15. Translated by Easton and Guddat, *op. cit.*

himself had used freely in his philosophical essays of 1844, because he objected to the way in which Feuerbach was using the word. In the 1844 writings, Marx had defined essence to mean the *true nature* of Man, the species, as it would one day become, after the false, deceptive illusions of "appearance" had been stripped away in the post-alienated condition of ultimate communism. "Essence" referred to a general condition of *social* existence, shared by all, not located in individual "human nature" except in so far as the individual was *also* a member of a moral and social whole. In his attack on Feuerbach, however, Marx said that the word "essence" could also be used in a non-idealist sense, to mean a general defective, alienated condition of the present, affecting all persons within the alienated society. It was this defective general "essence" that had to be overcome through a revolutionary process of "self-changing."

In his third Thesis on Feurbach, he wrote that "The concurrence of the changing of the circumstances and of the human activity, or self-changing, can be conceived as *revolutionary practice*" (16). This cryptic statement was expanded in *The German Ideology*, in the course of an attack on the anti-communism of Max Stirner:

> . . . the communist proletarians who revolutionize society and put the relations of production and the form of intercourse on a new bases – i.e., on themselves as new people, on their new mode of life. . . would only remain "as of old" if. . . they "sought the blame in themselves;" but they know too well that only under changed circumstances will they cease to be "as of old," and therefore they are determined to change these circumstances at the first opportunity. In revolutionary practice the changing of oneself coincides with the changing of the circumstances (17).

The transformation of the self was to be inward, affecting the subjective life and consciousness of each person. But it must be supported by supra-personal economic, social and circumstantial changes. The isolated individual cannot change himself by his own efforts, as a social and economic person relating to other persons in his own society, because he cannot change, by himself, the institutional conditions of that society. But the individual need not remain in a morally static, passive condition. The workers and their allies can, as individuals, participate in a self-changing collective effort when they join with others in a common revolutionary task which will bring about the necessary institutional changes. The essential change cannot be completed, however, until all individuals are included in a new kind of society, and live under new conditions.

Marx thought that Feuerbach placed too much emphasis on the psychological individual, and too much also on subjective differences between one individual and another. Feuerbach had said that some persons are prone to

16. Translated by Rotenstreich, *op. cit.*
17. *The German Ideology, op. cit.*, Volume I, Part III, pp. 229–230.

experience a religious kind of self-rejection. Marx was refuting but also partly misinterpreting Feuerbach when he wrote, in his Sixth Thesis on Feuerbach that

> Feuerbach resolves the religious essence into the *human* essence. But the human essence is not an abstract, inherent in the single individual. In its reality it is the ensemble of the social conditions.
>
> Feuerbach does not go into the criticism of this real essence and is, therefore, compelled (1) to abstract from the historical course of events, to fix a religious mental disposition, and to presume an abstract – *isolated* – human individual. . . . (18).

He went on to say, in Thesis Seven, that

> Feuerbach does not see, therefore, that "the religious mental disposition" itself is a social product and that the abstract individuum, whom he analyzes, belongs to a particular form of society.

Feuerbach had said that humanity could be divided into two psychological types. The "religious man" was contrasted with the "natural man." The great majority of persons were both "natural" and "rational." The irrational religious individual is one who has a tendency to regard himself as being morally *below* the general level of his fellow human beings. He is, therefore, "separated from himself," dissatisfied with himself and with the world in general. Feuerbach offered therapeutic counsel to the religious person. He was advised to overcome his sense of alienation from the majority of his fellows, and his own sense of personal insufficiency, by contemplating the greatness of the species to which he belonged. The species incorporates the good and admirable qualities not merely of one person, but of all persons. The defects of one are offset by the assets of another. The assets vastly outweigh the deficits, and the whole, the totality, is the "absolute nature" of each person: "It is ludicrous and even culpable error to define as finite and limited what constitutes the essence of man, the nature of the species, which is the absolute nature of the individual" (19). God was the "absolute Self" (20). The implication was that the distressed person could participate in the "perfection" of the essential condition merely by realizing that the "human

---

18. Translated by Rotenstreich, *op. cit.* In most translations of this thesis, the last sentence of the first paragraph reads: "In its reality it is the ensemble of the social relations." Rotenstreich, in his introductory chapter, notes that he had made a literal translation from the original German text as written by Marx, which was later revised and republished in German by Engels. Apparently Marx had written "conditions." This word is more consistent with his general historical-causal logic than "relations." In the materialist conception of history the relations of individuals to one another are always dependent on the conditions of production. These include the degree and kind of practical knowledge affecting the control over nature that a given community has acquired.

19. *The Essence of Christianity,* translated by George Eliot, Harper and Row, chapter 1, p. 17.

20. *Ibid.,* chapter 8, p. 82.

essence" was indeed his own "absolute," quasi-divine nature. No change in outer conduct or in social relations seemed to be required.

Marx objected to the implication that the individual who felt himself to be degraded below an ideal-essential "absolute" condition of self-being could remedy this psychological distress by achieving a sense of identity with humanity as a whole, as it presently existed. He was also objecting to Feuerbach's way of differentiating between a religious minority and a "natural" majority. He said that all individuals were, presently, in an equally "abstract," i.e., alienated condition. They were abstracted from the true community of the future. All were equidistant from a whole which could not exist, or be identified with the true essence of Man, until the moral evils and also the irrationality of the present social and cultural order had been left behind.

The moral and cognitive unity of communism – the unity of the individual self with others – to which Marx looked forward, excluded the possibility of innate personal diversities of mind or temperament that might produce differences in the moral and also in the religious responses of individuals belonging to the same community and in the same cultural environment. Religious tendencies manifested by individuals in modern society were related in one way or another to the alienating, disunifying conditions of community life, and to the inability of modern society to satisfy the human, non-religious, essential needs of all. Personal diversities in religious outlook flourished in the de-communalized era, but there was no enduring psychic foundation either for religion as such, or for abstract "morality" as such, and also no natural foundation for *personal* differences in these fields.

Marx was not, of course, advocating the political suppression, under socialism, of religious diversity and religious organization; he was definitely opposed to such a policy. But he did assume that the "changing of the circumstances" and the changing of self would come to be all-inclusive, affecting all persons in a similar way. All persons were presumed to be alike in one specific negative sense. All were devoid of "natural" religious tendencies that might reappear in various types of society, even under communism. The arrival of communism would liberate all persons from "religion." But Marx did not believe that all were naturally equal with respect to talents and capacities that had no connection with the religious life. He had ended by discarding the proposition that all persons are intellectually equal which he associated with the outlook of the French "Cartesian materialists." In *The Holy Family* (1844), he had stressed the relation of his communism to this form of materialism, when he wrote that

> There is no need for any great penetration to see from the teaching of materialism on the original goodness and equal intellectual endowment of men, the omnipotence of experience, habit and education, and the influence of environment on man, the great significance of industry, the justification of enjoyment, etc. how

> necessarily materialism is connected with communism and socialism (21).

In the *Theses on Feuerbach,* he was indicating not only his disagreement with Feuerbach, but also that his own idea of communism required a rejection of some of the doctrines of eighteenth century materialism and rationalism. Marx never specifically rejected the idea of the "original goodness" of men, which would imply also an equality in "goodness." His own kind of historical anthropology, however, cannot be accommodated to this sort of doctrine. Personal "individuality" was said to have developed historically out of a tribalistic, instinctual form of group consciousness. This simply exists, not *beyond* good and evil, but *below* the level at which these words have any meaning. He did explicitly reject the equal intellectual endowment thesis in various writings. In *Capital* III he divided the society of the European, Catholic feudal era into two sections, clergy and laity, which cut across economic class divisions:

> . . . the circumstance that the Catholic Church in the Middle Ages formed its hierarchy out of the best brains in the land, regardless of their estate, birth or fortune, was one of the principal means of consolidating ecclesiastical rule and suppressing the laity. The more a ruling class is able to assimilate the foremost minds of a ruled class, the more stable and dangerous becomes its rule (22).

The future rule of the working class in the first, political stage of post-capitalist development will be neither stable nor dangerous, in this sense. Individuals with the "foremost minds" will no longer be able to separate out from the remainder, so as to constitute a special source of moral and ideological influence not only within their own class but within society as a whole. When Marx placed political government in the superstructure, separated from material life, he was referring to government by a class minority, as opposed to a collective majority. The working class movement, in the class struggle phase of history, represents the union of the majority. Individuals joined together in the movement lose their "abstraction," i.e., their moral isolation, and also the ideological-intellectual functions which Marx associates with institutional political religion.

THE SOCIAL DESTRUCTION OF THE MORAL CATEGORY

In his philosophy of socialism, Marx wished to exclude from the society of the future a good deal more than the oppressive ideological, political functions of minority governing power. He wished also to eliminate, from the universal consciousness of the future social (and practical) individuals any need to refer to "abstract" ideational norms of social or moral conduct.

21. *The Collected Works of Marx and Engels,* Volume IV, chapter 6, p. 130.
22. *Op. cit.,* chapter 26, pp. 600–601.

These aspects of culture would disappear, once the oppressive ideological-political functions carried on by ruling class minorities in previous periods of history, and especially in modern capitalist society, had been eliminated through working class revolution. The fully "human" and social individuals depicted in Marx's writings of 1844 would neither have, nor need to have, any awareness of ideal or obligatory standards of moral performance, which they might possibly fail to meet. These individuals will be incapable of acting in ways that would violate certain moral norms which Marx himself regarded as necessary to community life. These norms, when realized in practice, need no longer exist on the level of "idea," i.e., in the "abstract" cultural consciousness of the individuals who will make up the future transformed society.

Marx expected that the future society would be a rationally ordered system of relations and arrangements which would enable persons to act toward one another in a way which conformed to Kant's conception of a universal "kingdom of ends." This, according to Kant, was "admittedly an ideal." In his *Groundwork of the Metaphysics of Morals,* Kant had said:

> The practical imperative will therefore always be as follows: Act in such a way that you always treat humanity, whether in your own person, or in the person of any other, never simply as a means, but always at the same time as an end (23).

Kant had gone on to say "We will now consider whether this can be carried out in practice." He was unable to demonstrate how this kingdom of ends morality could be practiced in economic and political life. It was a personal imperative which the ethical individual should endeavor to carry out in his relations with others. Marx undertook to elimiate the various obstacles which impeded the actualization of this ideal kingdom of ends in public, economic and social community relations. The individuals of the future classless society were expected to exemplify this norm because their feelings toward one another would naturally incline them to act in a way that is *social.* There would be no opposition between what the individual wanted to do and what he ought to do.

In the social, post-Kantian kingdom of ends society, the personal self was to be included within a transformed larger whole, the community, in such a way that previously existing barriers which had walled off the single "abstract" atomic self as a separate unit of consciousness from the mind and the consciousness of other people would no longer exist. In his philosophical essays of 1844, Marx was projecting a future condition of self-being that would come about as the result of the transformations of self and of society that would be brought about through communism. The transformed individuals would have an enhanced capacity for life enjoyment, including a marked

---

23. Translated by H.J. Paton, *op. cit.,* chapter 2, p. 96. See also the reference to Kant's kingdom of ends conception and its relation to Marx's humanism in chapter 2, this book, on "The Cosmological Philosophies of Hegel and Marx."

increase in satisfactions of a *social* nature. In their previously self-enclosed atomic condition, they had been unable to experience these satisfactions. The quality of their experiences in relations with other people would be transformed in the post-alienated society. Harmony would replace conflict, friendliness and trust would replace hostility and mistrust, competition would give way to cooperation. The satisfactions and security available to one person would not be gained or retained at the expense of others. The reverse would be the case. The individual's personal happiness would be increased by his knowledge that he was depriving no one else, and that others were equally well off. He would share empathetically in the satisfactions of others.

The condition of alienation which was universal in bourgeois society was the antithesis of this condition of community. It was an estrangement, a radical separation of the single self from all other selves. Marx was not referring to the separation of an entire group of persons in one country or in one culture from other persons who lived far away, in different locations and cultures outside the home base. The estrangement was internal, affecting interpersonal life within the same linguistic, territorial and cultural group. People in the alienated society were literally "alien" to one another, strangers to one another, even though they may be living side by side, in close physical contiguity, and may even have certain egoistic interests in common (24). In the alienated society, people need others, but only as a means to their own ends. These ends, if and when attained, yield no true satisfaction. The individual becomes obsessively concerned with acquiring more for himself. He is driven by various forms of ego-centric compulsion, striving always to get more for himself, some material or social assets which give him some kind of real or imagined advantage over others, or seem to be an addition to himself. This pattern of individualistic, acquisitive and competitive striving was to be broken when community is restored following the process of universal alienation and atomization.

In these early essays, Marx was conveying a vision of the future that bordered on mysticism, of the kind that is called "monistic." He was not able to recapture, or at least to express, this singular vision in his later works, i.e., those written after 1844. Mysticism of the monistic variety contrasts with other forms of more distinctly religious mysticism in which the individual has a sense of being in touch with a higher power which originates outside of himself, and which *remains* outside. In the latter case, the person does not lose the sense of being morally distinct from or in some way subordinate to the higher order power. In Marx's early metaphysical socialism, the experiencing subject is unified with a totality which is a social cosmos, one that will

24. In his political novel "Sybil: or The Two Nations" (1845), Benjamin Disraeli gave a description of the disintegration of community in urban industrial England which had something in common with Marx's description of the general condition of bourgeois society: "In great cities men are brought together by the desire of gain. The are not in a state of cooperation, but of isolation, as to the making of fortunes; and for all the rest they are careless of neighbours. Chirstianity teaches us to love our neighbour as ourself; modern society acknowledges no neighbor" (from Chapter 5).

not be morally distinguishable from the "self" that is joined to this cosmos. The boundaries of self-ness are partly obliterated, in such a way as to produce what William James described as "the mystical feeling of enlargement, union, and emancipation. . . " (25). In Marx's social transcendentalism, the individual and society are wholly one. No opposition is possible or conceivable. In "Private Property and Communism" (1844) Marx described communism as ". . . the restoration of man as a *social,* that is human being." He was not referring to "society" as an entity possessing powers that could be directed, repressively or punitively, against any individual member of the whole: "To be avoided above all is establishing 'society' once again as an abstraction over against the individual. The individual *is* the *social being"* (26). It seems as though the being of community is morally and metaphysically identical with the being of the single self.

Marx could not have described his own unity concept as mystical. According to James, a "well-developed mystical state" is one that is recognized by the subject as an extraordinary, super-normal experience. Such states therefore serve to "break down the authority of the non-mystical or rationalistic consciousness, based on the understanding and the senses alone. They show it to be only one kind of consciousness." Marx explicitly and forcefully reject any attempt to "break down the authority" of the non-mystical. He wrote in the eighth of his *Theses on Feuerbach:*

> All social life is essentially *practical.* All mysteries that induce the theory to mysticism find their rational solution in human practice and in the conception of this practice.

"Ideology," which developed on a non-practical "abstract" level, in separation from "material" life, was associated with mysticism, as well as with morality and religion, and with any form of philosophical consciousness which seemed to preclude the total moral absorption of the single self into the higher level unity.

THE ELEVATION OF THE HEROIC ABSOLUTE

When Marx looked forward to the society of classless communism, he was also looking forward to a time of universal world peace, beyond all forms of international war and beyond all forms of class struggle. But he was a philosopher of war, of class struggle, as well as a philosopher of peace. The social person was one who would naturally be inclined to act heroically, in certain types of combat situations. Marx did not say this explicitly, because he did not include situations of this kind in his concept of the future life. It

---

25. *The Varieties of Religious Experience,* Random House, NY. The Gifford Lectures on Natural Religion delivered at Edinburgh in 1901-02. Lectures 16 and 17 on Mysticism, pp. 416-417.

26. Translated by Easton and Guddat, *op. cit.*

was implied, however, in his attitude toward the morally defective, alienated existence of the bourgeois age.

Marx elevated the workers who were carrying out the class struggle to an heroic dimension, as a collective solidarity group. The individuals who participated in such groups were capable of acting heroically, for the sake of defending and advancing a common, wholly justified cause. They were united by a group morale and a group spirit, and were able to identify themselves, immediately and completely, with the group cause. The working class struggle was likely to include directly military confrontations with the political class enemies. The less military types of economic and political struggle carried on by the workers in their conflict with the employers also called out a spirit of heroic solidarity and a sacrificial effort. The workers supported one another in a willingness to share in the hardships which had to be suffered in their struggle against oppression.

Marx also conceived of other situations, not related to the working class struggle, in which heroic qualities were demonstrated in situations deserving of absolute, unqualified moral support. He linked the sacrificial solidarity of working class struggle with certain forms of national heroism. Whole peoples – national and tribal communities – had defended themselves against threats to their communal existence. The individuals in the self-defending group had a personal stake in the outcome, identifying with a society that extended beyond their own particular life span.

In this long political essay on "The Jewish Question," Marx had stigmatized the bourgeoisie of the French revolutionary period as insufficiently patriotic. Individuals in the bourgeois class were all too readily inclined to put private self-interest and private security ahead of national security and national survival to an extent amounting to betrayal:

> It is somewhat curious that a nation just beginning to free itself, tearing down all the barriers between different sections of the people and founding a political community, should solemnly proclaim (Declaration of 1791) the justification of the egoistic man, man separated from his fellow men and from the community, and should even repeat this proclamation at a moment when only the most heroic sacrifice can save the nation and hence is urgently required, when the sacrifice of all the interests of civil society is highly imperative and egoism must be punished as crime (Declaration of the Rights of Man of 1793) (27).

The particular proclamation to which Marx referred was the right of private property. He quoted from the French Constitution of 1783: "The right of property is that belonging to every citizen to enjoy and dispose of his goods, his revenue, the fruits of his labor and of his industry *as he wills.*" Marx said that "The right of property is thus the right to enjoy and dispose of one's possessions as one wills, without regard for other men and indepen-

27. Translated by Easton and Guddat, *op. cit.*

dently of society. It is the right of self-interest." He also said that security regulations enforced by political power in the bourgeois society of private property and egoistic right upheld the security of private property even when this ran counter to national security needs:

> *Security* is the supreme social concept of civil society, the concept of the *police,* the concept that the whole society exists only to guarantee to each of its members the preservation of his person, his rights, and his property. In this sense Hegel calls civil society "the state as necessity and rationality."
>
> Civil society does not raise itself above its egoism through the concept of security. Rather, security is the *guarantee* of this egoism (28).

The heroism of the workers in their struggle against capital was not identical with national heroism, but this was because the class struggle was invested by Marx with an exceptional moral significance going beyond all previously recorded manifestations of national heroism. The difference, however, is obscured in certain of Marx's writings on the political situation in France. In his 1871 address on *The Civil War in France* the defense of Paris by the Communards was likened to the defense of Rome by its citizens who had resisted barbarian invasion:

> . . . the real women of Paris showed again at the surface – heroic, noble, and devoted, like the women of antiquity. Working, thinking, fighting, bleeding Paris – almost forgetful, in its incubation of a new society, of the cannibals at its gates – radiant in the enthusiasm of its historic initiative!. . . Paris people die enthusiastically for the Commune in numbers unequalled in any battle known to history. . . The women of Paris joyfully give up their lives at the barricades and on the place of execution. . . Working men's Paris, with its Commune, will be for ever celebrated as the glorious harbinger of a new society. Its martyrs are enshrined in the great heart of the working class (29).

It does seem that a continuing potentiality for acting in an heroic way if and when the occasion should arise is inherent in Marx's conception of the future social, essentially human condition, i.e., that it is an indispensable quality of acceptably human selfhood. But Marx does not regard this kind of sociality as a "moral ideal." It is a capacity that the individual either does or does not manifest. It is altogether unforced, free and voluntary. The acting group is not forcing its members into this sort of action. The moral virtue and value of the action lies in its voluntary character. This kind of volition, as described by Marx, develops in group situations. Each of the individuals participates in a group spirit which could not arise if the individuals were atomistically separated from one another.

28. *Ibid.*
29. Selected Works of Marx and Engels, Volume II, *op. cit.*

THE NEGATION OF SACRIFICIAL TENSION

In Marx's early writings, the future liberation of the individual from modern forms of oppression and restriction is the overriding aim. The destruction and the reconstruction of society is a means to that end. Personal death – i.e., the death of the physical self – is not represented as a form of sacrifice which detracts from the necessity of the struggle, and the benefits it confers on the individual. The emotional importance of death fear and death resistance is being discounted.

Marx described the struggle in symbolic language that had theological overtones and implications. The individual who was seeking to overthrow the existing conditions of society was also struggling against a cosmic kind of justice. This modern Everyman was peculiarly the product of the capitalist age. He was victimized by Fate, i.e., by historically created circumstances not of his own making for which he and other human beings could not be held morally accountable. Possessing a modern type of self-consciousness, he was more acutely oppressed in a subjective sense than the oppressed individuals of past generations. Marx conveys this feeling in several key passages in *The German Ideology,* and also in his 1843 Introduction to *A Critique of Hegel's Philosophy of Right,* where the proletarians are described as

> . . . a class with *radical chains*. . . a sphere of society having a universal character because of its universal suffering and claiming no *particular* right because no *particular wrong* but *unqualified wrong* is perpetrated on it; a sphere that can invoke no *traditional* title but only a *human* title. . . (30).

In *The German Ideology* he said that modern individuals had achieved a kind of freedom unknown to pre-modern individuals: "Never in any earlier period, have the productive forces taken on a form so different to the intercourse of individuals as individuals, because their intercourse itself was formerly a restricted one (31). The modern individual, as a self-center has been abstracted from ego-restrictive forms of class of caste identity, and from an ego-restrictive range of associations and fundtions that persons in pre-modern periods had accepted as natural:

> The division between the personal and the class individual, the accidental nature of the conditions of life for the individual, appears only with the emergence of the class, which is itself the product of the bourgeoisie. . . Certainly the refugee serfs [of the feudal era] treated their previous servitude as something accidental to their personality. But here they were only doing what every class that is freeing itself from a fetter does; and they did not free themselves as a class but separately. Moreover, they did

30. Translated by Easton and Guddat, *op. cit.*
31. Volume I, Part I, p. 82.

> not rise above the system of estates, but only formed a new estate. . . (32).

The historical atomizing process, i.e., the dissolution of feudal society, has resulted in the emergence of an "absolute" individual who is conscious of being essentially *more* than can be defined or expressed in any particular accidentally given role of functions. The society of communism was to provide conditions which would be wholly nonoppressive and nonrestrictive. Individuality was to be freed from all limiting roles and attachments not expressive of the absolute personal self. Oppressive restrictions were presently being imposed by the economic organization and institutional structure of modern class society. The implication was that people would relate to one another as individual persons, and that these relations would be wholly positive and free of tension, once the specialized roles and functions which created a sense of social distance and of difference, had been eliminated.

In *The German Ideology* Marx discussed the question of "self-sacrifice" in relation to socialism and communism. He was repudiating the unfavorable view of communism given by Stirner, in *The Ego and its Own.* He had been in partial agreement with Stirner before he undertook to refute him. He endorsed certain of the views of Stirner, and even made use of Stirner's language. He used certain of the sharpest ideas of Stirner as weapons with which to attack his opponent, as if the latter had said something quite different.

Stirner had called communism a form of "social liberalism." Under communism people will be expected to live "for one another." "Each of us exists only through the other, who, caring for my wants, at the same time sees his own satisfied by me." Furthermore

> The beautiful dream of a 'social duty' still continues to be dreamed. People think again that society *gives* what we need, and we are *under obligations* to it on this account, owe it everything. They are still at the point of wanting to serve a 'supreme giver of all goods.' That society is no ego at all, which could give, bestow, or grant, but an instrument or means, from which we may derive benefit; that we have no social duties, but solely interests for the pursuance of which society must serve us, but, if we sacrifice anything, sacrifice it to ourselves – of this the socialists do not think, because they – as liberals – are imprisoned in the religious principle, and zealously aspire after – a sacred society, such as the State was heretofore (33).

---

32. *Ibid.,* pp. 93 and 94.

33. *Max Stirner: The Ego and His Own,* English translation by S.T. Byington, 1907, Selected and Introduced by John Carroll, Harper and Row, 1971, pp. 101-102. A few advance copies of this work were circulated late in 1844, but the official publication date was 1845. It is likely that Marx did not come to grips with Stirner until after he had finished writing *The Holy Family* (1844), where other neo-Hegelian philosophers, but not Stirner, had been severely attacked.

Marx did indeed make the individual who was social radically independent on the society of other people. The presence of these others was a good deal more than merely a means to non-social personal ends. But the future society to which Marx referred would not in any way suppress or restrict the freedom or the rights of the Ego. The emancipated society could exert no external pressure on the individual, and could exact no duties or obligations that could be construed as "self-sacrifice." Sacrifice, to Marx, meant self-subordination to an enslaving external power. The working class struggle did not involve the participants in enslaving subordination either to a cause or to an entity apart from themselves. In one respect only was society elevated above the individual, but this difference of levels was decreed by nature. Although "society" is never an "abstract over against the individual," it is nevertheless a continuing process and reality whose life is of indefinite duration, having no biologically given terminal point. The case is otherwise with the biological individual. In "Private Property and Communism" (1844) Marx wrote that

> *Death* seems to be a harsh victory of the species over the particular individual and to contradict the species unity, but the particular individual is only a *particular generic being* and as such mortal (34).

It seems as though the form of non-natural death that the individual may undergo as a result of his participation in the self-changing, redemptive struggle against the existing social and economic order is not this kind of "harsh victory." One of the most remarkable aspects of Marx's transcendental process philosophy, as it appears in his early works, is the way in which he reduces to insignificance the personal and biological reality of death and of temporal finitude when he is referring to the working class movement. The reality of death as the final end of personal existence seems to be suspended. The individual is sacrificing only his present alienated self-existence in order to achieve a future more fully human life. The struggle in which he is engaged leads away from spiritual and social death into a more fully realized condition of personal life fulfillment. In his reply to Stirner, whom he called "Saint Max," Marx declared that

> Saint Max believes that the communists wanted to "make sacrifices" to "society," when they want at most to sacrifice existing society; in this case he should have described their consciousness that their struggle is the common cause of all people who have outgrown the bourgeois system as a sacrifice that they make to themselves (35).

Marx denied the charge that the communists are expecting or desiring the elimination of "egoism," i.e., of the individual's right to enjoy life and to fulfill himself as a person, for the sake of himself:

34. Easton and Guddat, *op. cit.*
35. *The German Ideology,* Volume I, Part III, p. 229.

> *Communism* is simply incomprehensible to our saint [Stirner] because the communists do not put egoism against self-sacrifice or self-sacrifice against egoism, nor do they express this contradiction theoretically either in its sentimental or in its highflown ideological form; on the contrary, they demonstrate the material basis engendering it; with which it disappears of itself. The communists do not preach *morality* at all, such as Stirner preaches so extensively. They do not put to people the moral demand: love one another, do not be egoists, etc.; on the contrary, they are well aware that egoism, just as much as self-sacrifice, *is* in definite circumstances a necessary form of the self-assertion of individuals. Hence the communists by no means want, as Saint Max believes . . . to do away with the 'private individual' for the sake of the 'general' self-sacrificing man (36).

The "self-sacrifice" that occurs in the struggle for communism is a form of self-affirmation, an affirmation of the value and status of the self as a human being. The human person who participates in the working class struggle has justifiably egoistic and hedonic motives. He is claiming his human right to life-enjoyment, self-expression, and self-affirmation, which will become possible after victory. The anticipated outcome seems to outweigh the reality of the present. It is almost as though the oppressed person has the prospect of attaining the final goal within the span of his own lifetime. The interval between time present and time future is being obliterated.

Marx, independently of Stirner, had used the word "egoism" in a positive as well as in a negative way in some of his 1844 manuscripts. In notes which were comments on certain sections of James Mill's *Elements of Political Economy,* he had said:

> The *exchange* of human activity within production itself as well as the exchange of *human products* with one another is equivalent to the *generic activity* and generic spirit whose actual, conscious, and authentic existence is *social* activity and *social* satisfaction. As *human* nature is the *true common life* [Gemeinwesen] of man, men through the activation of their *nature create* and produce a human *common life,* a social essence which is no abstractly universal power opposed to the single individual, but is the essence or nature of every single individual, his own activity, his own life, his own spirit, his own wealth. *Authentic common life* arises not through reflection; rather it comes about from the *need* and *egoism* of individuals, that is, immediately from the activation of their very existence (37).

---

36. *Ibid.,* pp. 266-267. The reader of Stirner will find it hard to believe that he was, in any way, a preacher of morality. But in *The Holy Family* Marx had also insisted on calling all other neo-Hegelian ideologists (with the exception of Feuerbach) by the negative title of "saint."

37. Translated by Easton and Guddat, *op. cit.,* pp. 271-272.

The economic and philosophic manuscripts of 1844 followed immediately after the drafting of these notes. In these manuscripts, Marx was describing an hedonic, entirely post-sacrificial condition. In the new society the individual was to obtain from other people a self-sustaining reaction of recognition and respect. The individual who became a member of that society was to suffer no kind of self-diminution or loss in his social exchanges with other people. He was to be active and self-assertive, able to put himself across to the other people in his immediately present social and human environment. The society was an equalitarian peer group formation. Persons not sufficiently active in presenting themselves to others were somewhere on the outside of a closed system of ideal mutuality and reciprocity. Within the closed system, each person who dispenses love to others like himself receives love in like measure in return. Marx warns the individual not to waste himself in any kind of love expenditure which is not effective in eliciting a reciprocal response:

> Assume *man* to be *man,* and his relationship to the world to be a human one; then you can exchange love only for love, trust for trust, etc. . . . Every one of your relations to man and to nature must be a *specific expression* corresponding to the object of your will, of your *real* individual life. If you love without evoking love in return – that is, if your loving as loving does not produce reciprocal love; if through a loving expression of yourself you do not make yourself a *beloved one,* then your love is impotent – a misfortune (38).

This balanced system of interpersonal mutuality and reciprocity excludes a variety of unequal power and unequal responsibility situations in which the exchange formula, giving "love for love" and "trust for trust," could not readily apply. In the manuscripts of 1844 Marx was excluding the inequalities and the various tensions and imbalances of nuclear family life, especially obligations, economic and supra-economic, relating to the carrying out of parental roles and functions. The dependent relation of children to parents, a relation in which the parent adult can hardly be perceived by a child except also in connection with some sort of family function, is also being excluded. In "Private Property and Communism," Marx referred to the process of production and to general laws of production as tending, inevitably, to the final obliteration of family roles and nuclear family life:

> Religion, family, state, law, morality, science, art, etc. are only *particular* forms of production and fall under its general laws. The positive overcoming of *private property* as the appropriation of *human* life is thus the positive overcoming of all alienation and the return of man from religion, family, state, etc. to his *human,* that is, *social* existence (39).

---

38. *Collected Works of Marx and Engels, op. cit.,* Volume III, Economic and Philosophic Manuscripts of 1844, essay on "The Power of Money in Bourgeois Society."
39. Translated by Easton and Guddat, *op. cit.*

In *The German Ideology* he said that slavery had always been latent in the family group, but whether this potentiality became overt, and an important source of oppression, depended on economic conditions in the community outside of the family. There was no doubt that familial as well as other forms of oppression were especially intolerable in the bourgeois era. The family would disappear along with all other forms of enslavement, as bourgeois society was transcended: "That the abolition of individual economy is inseparable from the abolition of the family is self-evident" (40). Private property, which permits the development of inequalities of economic distribution within the larger community and fosters major supra-familial power inequalities, originates in a communal division of labor that exists also within the family. The division of labor creates ". . . property: the nucleus, the first form of which lies in the family, where wife and children are slaves of the husband. . ." (41).

When Marx defined bourgeois society as the dissolution of community, which had resulted in the emergence of the isolated, abstract atomic individual, he was abstracting the individual from family roles. Alienation was omnipresent within as well as outside of the family relation. Hegel had made a comparable kind of abstraction when he was describing the nature of the bourgeois individualistic laissez-faire economy whose workings and laws had been disclosed by outstanding political economists. Hegel mentioned Adam Smith, Say, and Ricardo. He pointed out that the primary economic unit in this political economic theory is the individual, and that it makes no difference whether that individual is a single person responsible only for himself, or a supporter of a family group. In discussing "the transition of the family into civil society," Hegel said that

> The family disintegrates (both essentially, through the working of the principle of personality, and also in the course of nature) into a plurality of families, each of which conducts itself as a self-subsistent concrete person and therefore as externally related to its neighbours (42).

In the "civil state" described by political economic science ". . . individuals in their capacity as burghers. . . are private persons whose end is their own interest" (43). This abstract unit of particularity is the ground of Marx's political economic theory also. The adult individual, as a separate person distinct from the family group, was the exclusive center of Marx's moral concern, in his early writings. (44).

---

40. *Op. cit.*, Volume I, Part I, p. 40n.
41. *Ibid.*, p. 44.
42. *The Philosophy of Right, op. cit.*, section 181.
43. *Ibid.*, section 183.
44. The modification of this exclusiveness in Marx's later writings is discussed later in chapter 10 on "The Necessity of Labor in Communist Society."

THE EXTERNALIZATION OF EVIL IN THE HISTORICAL PROCESS

Marx conceived of revolutionary self-changing as a process that would culminate in a condition that was beyond the evils of past and present history. Good was to prevail universally. This expectation had been combined with an evolutionary nihilism. Progress toward a morally desirable outcome was occurring in ways that were natural but not moral, and that should not be interfered with. Socialist revolutionaries had to develop a theory and an attitude which was accommodated to moral and political reality, as manifested in past and present natural societies, if they were to succeed in changing that reality. Like Hegel, Marx had a dialectical faith in the humanly ungoverned processes of political and economic history. In Marx's system, historical evil was the *thesis* which had to be posited before the movement to overcome social and moral evils could be called into existence. The socialist movement was working to realize the future good, but until the ultimate condition had been achieved, it was necessary that certain existing evils be condoned rather than opposed, on grounds of dialectical necessity. Marx's nihilism was formulated as a logical doctrine in *The Poverty of Philosophy,* where he wrote that "It is the bad side that produces the movement which makes history, by providing a struggle." He argues that if hypothetical economists living "during the epoch of the domination of feudalism" had given way to an ill-considered zeal for reform, and had "set themselves the problem" of eliminating the evils of feudalism in order to preserve the good aspects of that social order, the progress made under capitalism would not have occurred: "All the elements which called forth the struggle would have been destroyed and the development of the bourgeoisie nipped in the bud. One would have set oneself the absurd problem of eliminating history" (45).

A titianic battle between good and evil forces is to take place within the confines of modern Western civilization. The entirety of humanity must first be included within that civilization. Western colonialism and imperialism, as carried on by the bourgeoisie, must be allowed to run their course, on account of their utility in creating the conditions required for world socialism and world unification. Such activities, no matter how objectionable morally, were a means to a greater good. It was not merely one segment of the world that was to be transformed. Humanity as a whole was to be raised to a higher level. Less advanced civilizations immersed in backward forms of culture and religion must give way to the higher civilization which had learned to dominate and conquer all aspects of nature except "human nature." The bourgeoisie had been the chief historical agency for bringing about this Westernization of the planet. The bourgeoisie of the Western capitalist nations were accomplishing a necessary task of destruction. This was, indeed, their "world-historical mission." In *The Communist Manifesto* Marx declared that

45. Chapter 2, pp. 121–122.

> The bourgeoisie has through its exploitation of the world-market given a cosmopolitan character to production and consumption in every country. . . In place of the old local and national seclusion and self-sufficiency, we have intercourse in every direction, universal interdependence of nations. As in material, so also in intellectual production. The intellectual creations of individual nations become common property. National one-sidedness and narrow-mindedness become more and more impossible, and from the numerous national and local literatures there arises a world literature.
>
> The bourgeoisie. . . compels all nations to adopt the bourgeois mode of production; it compels them to introduce what it calls civilization into their midst, i.e., to become bourgeois themselves. In a word, it creates a world after its own image.

Socialism is to eliminate the bourgeois image and the bourgeois reality, in such a way that it will preserve, in a higher civilization, all the gains of the bourgeois liberal era. But this can be done only when the image has been clearly objectified on the screen of history, made visible to the working class and its allies. The evils of the system will then be presented in an objectified external form. These are also the evils of the present-day human essence, of alienated non-social individuality.

The anti-bourgeois proletarian mission was to be carried out by workers who represented the good forces of the future. The revolutionary masses were to destroy evils that appeared to them as *external,* thus confirming their own moral status as representatives of the future. In his Introduction to *A Critique of Hegel's Philosophy of Right,* Marx had said that in order to overcome the condition of universal alienation, capitalist society must be split up into two parts, one of which represents the emerging post-corrupt, post-alienated society. The *other* side is the one in which the generalized evils of the unredeemed, universal self-condition are concentrated and objectified. The working class was to carry through to completion the interrupted process of popular revolution which had begun in France. For a short time, during the anti-feudal revolution, the people of that nation had joined forces with the rising bourgeoisie in a common, nationally liberating attack on the feudal regime. The bourgeoisie had acquired, temporarily, a "positive, general significance." Marx made a psycho-political generalization which applied also to the final class war, to the proletarian struggle against the bourgeoisie:

> If a *popular revolution* is to coincide with the *emanicpation of a particular class* of civil society, if *one* class is to stand for the whole of society, all the defects of society must conversely be concentrated in another class. A particular class must be the class of general offense and the incorporation of general limitation. A particular social sphere must stand for the *notorious crime* of society as a whole so that emancipation from this sphere appears

> as general self-emancipation. For *one* class to be the class of emancipation *par excellence,* conversely another must be the obvious class of oppression. The negative, general significance of the French nobility and clergy determined the positive, general significance of the bourgeoisie standing next to and opposing them (46).

In the revolutionary struggle of the workers against capital, the bourgeois ruling class becomes the class of "general offense." It appears that the workers are being encouraged to project on to an external class enemy, evils that are also "within themselves," but are to be treated *as if* entirely external:

> Theory is capable of gripping the masses when it demonstrates *ad hominem,* and it demonstrates *ad hominem* when it becomes radical. To be radical is to grasp things by the root. But for man the root is man himself (47).

During the revolutionary continental upheavals of 1848-49, Marx and Engels had actively encouraged the expression of militant proletarian moral antagonism, to be directed against the external class enemy. The spirit of ruthlessness that had characterized the successful and powerful bourgeoisie in nations outside of Germany would have to become, for a brief time, part of the fighting strength of the proletariat.

In an article published in *Die Neue Rehinische Zeitung,* Marx held the weak, contemptible German bourgeoisie responsible for the victory of their own opponents, the Prussian reactionaries:

> The bourgeoisie in *Germany* meekly joins the *retinue* of the absolute monarchy and of feudalism before securing even the first conditions necessary for its own civic freedom and its rule. In France it played the part of a tyrant and made its own counter-revolution. In Germany it acts like a slave and carries out the counter-revolution for its own tyrants. . . History presents no example of *greater wretchedness* than that of the *German bourgeoisie* (48).

In Germany, the republican, social revolution must also be a socialist, working class revolution. In order to achieve success, the movement will have to become, in its initial stage, as uncompromising as the bourgeois revolution in France had been. Addressing the bourgeoisie of Germany in the name of the revolutionists, Marx wrote that

---

46. Translated by Easton and Guddat.
47. *Ibid.*
48. Article on "The Victory of the Counter-Revolution in Vienna," published on November 7, 1848. Reprinted in *The Revolution of 1848-49:* Articles from the Neue Rehinische Zeitung, by Marx and Engels, International Publishers, NY, 1972.

> We are ruthless and want no consideration from you. When our time comes, revolutionary terrorism will not be sugar-coated. There is but one way of simplifying, shortening, concentrating the death agony of the old society as well as the bloody labour of the new world's birth – revolutionary terror (49).

A circular signed and written jointly by Marx and Engels in 1850 was in the same vein:

> . . . the proletarian is not to abdicate the dictatorship too soon. Let vengeance triumph; like a blue flame, let it blaze in the cities and the towns. The leaders of the proletariat must see to it that the revolutionary excitement shall not subside immediately after victory is won. On the contrary, this excitement must be kept up as long as possible. Far from stopping the so-called excesses, examples of popular vengeance upon hated individuals and public buildings, with which bitter memories are associated, one must not only tolerate these examples but lead and conduct them (50).

Marx's writings on the German political situation must be interpreted in the light of his anti-patriarchal complex which applied specifically to German national culture. He associated what he called the deficiencies of German national character with tendencies to submit to external moral authority of a paternalistic kind, lodged in the political State. The bourgeoisie of other nations had overcome patriarchalism when they had ascended to political dominance. They were no longer handicapped by moral standards emanating from a source outside of themselves. In *The German Ideology* he had denounced Kant as a "petty bourgeois" moralist who objected to bourgeois ruthlessness, but he was at the same time reserving the right to condemn these same bourgeois activities in a way that by-passed Kant's moral philosophy:

> The state of Germany at the end of the last century is fully reflected in Kant's *Critik der Practischen Vernunft* [Critique of Practical Reason]. While the French bourgeoisie, by means of the most colossal revolution that history has ever known, was achieving domination and conquering the continent of Europe, while the already emancipated English bourgeoisie was revolutionizing industry and subjugating India politically, and all the rest of the world commercially, the impotent German burghers did not get further than "good will." . . . Kant's good will fully corresponds to the impotence, depression and wretchedness of the German burghers, whose petty interests were never capable of developing into the common, national interests of a class and who were

49. *Op. cit.*, article published May 19, 1849.

50. Circular issued by the Central Committee of the Communist League, 1850, in *Selected Works of Marx and Engels, op. cit.*, Volume I.

> therefore constantly exploited by the bourgeois of all other nations (51).

At the time that he wrote *The Poverty of Philosophy* Marx was accepting the temporary appearance of chattel slavery in the United States as a necessary evil. As a form of subordination, it was less repulsive than the submission of legally free workers to patriarchal power. The United States was classed as the most progressive of all the Western capitalist countries, the one farthest removed from patriarchalism. In a letter to P.V. Annenkov (December 28, 1846) he said that chattel slavery in the American South ought not to be abolished prematurely:

> Direct slavery is as much the pivot of our industrialism today as machinery, credit, etc. Without slavery no cotton; without cotton no modern industry. . . Slavery is therefore an economic category of the highest importance. Without slavery North America, the most progressive country, would be transformed into a patriarchal land. You have only to wipe North America off the map of the nations and you get anarchy, the total decay of trade and of modern civilization (52).

Marx did, of course, change his position on this question during the American Civil War. He then perceived the historical situation from the standpoint of the internal working class struggle against capital that was going on in the United States:

> In the United States of North America, every independent movement of the workers was paralysed so long as slavery disfigured a part of the Republic. Labour cannot emancipate itself in the white skin where in the black it is branded (53).

In his early writings, and also in *Capital,* Marx's attitude toward feudal civilization in general, considered apart from the German situation, had not been entirely negative. In certain respects, feudalism had been preferable to capitalism. Its dissolution, however, had been dialectically necessary, as part of the process whereby moral illusions were being dispelled.

In his long essay on "The Jewish Question," Marx had said that "Feudal society was dissolved into its foundation, into *man.* But into man as he actually was the foundation of that society, into egotistical man." This dissolution had been a good thing. The negative potentialities of man as an "abstract" individual that were formerly hidden from view now emerged in open and public form. In one of his economic and philosophic essays of 1844, "Rent of Land," Marx said that the economic feudal relations between

---

51. *The German Ideology,* Volume I, Part III, p. 207. See also the discussion of Marx's Germanic complex in chapter 5 of this book on "The Social Condition of Modern Working Class."

52. Published as an Appendix to *The Poverty of Philosophy,* International Publishers.

53. *Capital,* Volume I, chapter 10, p. 301.

the landlord and his tenants and serfs had at first been pre-commercial and therefore less venal, less tainted with the corruption of money and the egoism of the bourgeois commercial age which followed: ". . . the feudal lord does not try to extract the utmost advantage from his land. Rather he consumes what there is and calmly leaves the worry of producing to the serfs and the tenants. Such is *nobility's* relation to landed property, which casts a romantic glory on its lords." The rise of commercialism had demonstrated that this non-venality was a "false appearance," masking the reality underneath:

> It is necessary that this [romantic] appearance be abolished, that landed property, the root of private property, be dragged completely into the movement of private property and that it become a commodity: that the rule of the proprietor appear as the undisguised rule of private property, of capital, freed of all political tincture. . . and that the land should likewise sink to the status of a commercial value, like man. It is essential that that which is the root of landed property – filthy self-interest – make its appearance, too, in its cynical form (54).

By "cynical form" Marx apparently meant open, undisguised, unabashed forms of amoral activity and bourgeois "shamelessness." Those who engage in such activity do not feel the need for moral self-justification.

Marx, when referring to Germany, had said that the bourgeoisie of the major non-Germanic capitalist nations were free of "petty bourgeois" moral scrupulosity. But he nevertheless accused these same non-Germanic ruling groups of duplicity and hyporcrisy. They operated with a double standard, one of which applied to internal national affairs, the other to foreign policies. As upholders of internal law and order, the bourgeoisie enact and advocate the enforcement of restraints on violence and on personal freedom of action within the borders of their own nation. This same class abandons all pretense of restraint in relations with external peoples, especially when these peoples are unable to resist and to retaliate. They claim a certain moral respectability and virtue as upholders of internal law and order. This false appearance is unmasked in their external actions. This kind of hypocrisy is compounded by the fact that these bourgeois nations profess to adhere to Christianity. In his newspaper article on "The Future Results of British Rule in India" (July 22, 1853), Marx wrote that

> The profound hypocrisy and inherent barbarism of bourgeois civilization lies unveiled before our eyes, turning from its home, where it assumes respectable forms, to the colonies, where it goes naked. They are the defenders of property but. . . While they prated in Europe about the inviolable sanctity of the national debt, did they not confiscate in India the dividends of the rajahs, who had invested their private savings in the Company's own funds? While they combated the French Revolution under the

54. *The Collected Works of Marx and Engels,* Volume III.

> pretext of defending "our holy religion," did they not forbid, at the same time, Christianity to be propagated in India. . . (55).

The majority of the people in the Western nations, the working classes in particular, are not implicated in the barbaric undertakings of bourgeois national leaders. When the people come to power, there will be no moral dualities, no hypocritical concealments, and no discrepancy between the standards of conduct that are applied to external as opposed to internal relations.

Marx's political and moral condemnation not only of the system and the society of capitalism but also of its upholders and defenders, was always somewhat in contradiction of his scientific frame of reference. The natural process of social and economic evolution had included, inevitably, the formation of various caste and class systems. The relations maintained by persons in upper stratum groups to persons in subordinate groups were determined by the requirements of these particular, naturally devleoped economic systems. Marx did not attribute to the majority of upper stratum individuals in any age of history a concern for ideas and ideals of economic and social justice which, if carried out in practice, would require them to renounce their economic, moral and social advantages. He was staying within the limits of the recorded historical facts. In times of class struggle, the underclasses rose up against the dominant groups because they found their position to be intolerable. This did not mean, however, that they possessed any special moral virtues or qualifications that gave them an inherent right to judge and condemn their opponents as human beings. All absolute condemnations and judgments of this kind were suspended and nullified in the logical, scientific frame of reference. Nevertheless, this deterministic logic broke down at certain pressure points. This occurred, in a particularly notable way, at the conclusion of one of his most impressive speeches. He tried to censor this speech, written in English, by saying that he did not intend to have it printed. In a letter to Engels (dated April 16, 1856) he wrote that

> . . . the day before yesterday there was a little banquet to celebrate the anniversary of the People's Paper [an English Chartist publication]. On this occasion I accepted the invitation, as the times seemed to demand it, and all the more so since I *alone* (as announced in the paper) of all the refugees had been invited and the first toast also fell to me, in which I was to hail the sovereignty of the proletariat in all the countries. So I made a little English speech which I, however, shall not have printed (56).

In the concluding paragraph of this address, Marx expressed ideas about a supra-legal, secret, collective tribunal, invested with a power and right of punitive justice, a justice to be meted out by revolutionists to persons in posi-

55. *The American Journalism of Marx and Engels, op. cit.*
56. *Selected Correspondence of Marx and Engels,* Progress Publishers, Moscow, 1965.

tion of ruling class power. These power holders deserved to be dislodged and overthrown. They are also an integral part of the economic, moral and cultural order that, more impersonally, deserves to be doomed by history. Marx decreed death to the system together with the symbolic obliteration of its defenders:

> To revenge the misdeeds of the ruling class, there existed in the middle ages in Germany a secret tribunal, called the "Vehmgericht." If a red cross was seen marked on a house people knew that its owner was doomed by the "Vehm." All the houses of Europe are now marked with the mysterious red cross. History is the judge – its executioner, the proletarian (57).

This passage is strange for more than one reason. The punishing tribunal does not render a judgment in the usual sense. It does not possess, in any rational, conceptual way, a norm of judgment. In any case the accused and marked individuals are guilty as charged. The tribunal merely executes a judgment. It is the vehicle of a transcendental judgment pronounced by an almost personified History.

Marx displaces moral culpability on to symbolic entities. Individuals, apart from their symbolic function, are not being judged. In *Capital* he said that the nature of the capitalist economy made it inevitable that material wealth and the power of domination that he associated with wealth, was being concentrated increasingly in the hands of a numerically insignificant ruling class. These were the "lords of capital." In using this term, Marx was carrying over the emphasis on the discrepancy between social appearance and moral reality that he had identified earlier with the possession of feudalistic upper class status. The lords of capital, possessing money, have acquired a false superficial glitter and a social prestige that is not an indication of their personal qualities. These power holders are to be condemned not as persons, but absolutely, in a symbolic manner. They incarnate the evils of an isolated, non-social condition which had not existed earlier, in the traditional feudal society. The capitalist who represents the system of capital is a larger than life archtype. He is a product of a late stage of capitalist economic evolution. The actions he carries out are ". . . the effect of the social mechanism of which he is but one of the wheels." As an economic individual he is ". . . a mere function of capital – endowed as capital is, in his person, with a consciousness and a will. . . " (58). He is also, for Marx, a figure on which to project the detested characteristics of non-social egoism. He represents the disposition of the egoist to aggrandize self at the expense of others. Such persons are indifferent to the plight of all but themselves:

> Capital that has such good reasons for denying the sufferings of the legions of workers that surround it, is in practice moved as much and as little by the sight of the coming degradation and

57. Selected Works of Marx and Engels, *op. cit.,* Volume I.
58. *Capital,* Volume I, chapter 24, p. 592.

> final depopulation of the human race, as by the probable fall of the earth into the sun. In every stock-jobbing swindle every one knows that some time or other the crash must come, but every one hopes that it may fall on the head of his neighbor, after he himself has caught the shower of gold and placed it in safety (59).

The capitalist is also described as a power-hungry Ego who alienates, as surplus value, what has been produced by society. He wants to negate the very existence of society and of all other persons, absorbing all into himself: "To accumulate, is to conquer the world of social wealth, to increase the mass of human beings exploited by him, and thus to extend both the direct and the indirect sway of the capitalist" (60). In a footnote following this sentence, Marx quoted a lengthy passage from Martin Luther, which he prefaced by saying that "Taking the usurer, that old-fashioned but ever renewed specimen of the capitalist for his text, Luther shows very aptly that the love of power is an element in the desire to get rich." Luther had referred to

> . . . a usurer and a money-glutton, such a one would have the whole world perish of hunger and thirst, misery and want, so far as in him lies, so that he may have all to himself, and everyone may receive from him as from a God, and be his serf forever. . . the usurer would deceive the world, as though he were of use and gave the world oxen, which he, however, rends and eats all alone. . .

The capitalist, he whose sole function is to "appropriate more and more wealth in the abstract" is wholly given over to ". . . the restless never-ending process of profit-making." He symbolizes the capitalist system, i.e., he is ". . . capital personified and endowed with a consciousness and a will" (61). As such he is like the usurer, extracting *more* than is his due, not by direct robbery, but by legal means. However, his function can also be historically justified. Capitalism was lialectically necessary as the precursor of socialism.

In his preface to the first edition of *Capital* (July 25, 1867) Marx said that the ultimate aim of his book was ". . . to lay bare the economic law of motion of modern society." The knowledge so achieved shows that the progress of that society toward its ultimate form can take place only at the pace set by natural laws of economic development: ". . . it [the society] can neither clear by bold leaps, nor remove by legal enactments, the obstacles offered by the successive phases of its normal devleopment. But it can shorten and lessen the birth-pangs." All persons, whether capitalists or workers, were within that society and were subject to certain nature-imposed historical limitations:

---

59. *Ibid.*, chapter 10, pp. 269–270.
60. *Ibid.*, chapter 24, p. 592.
61. *Ibid.*, chapter 4, pp. 152–153.

> . . . to prevent possible misunderstandings, a word. I paint the capitalist and the landlord in no sense *coleur de rose*. But here individuals are dealt with only in so far as they are the personifications of economic categories, embodiments of particular class-relations and class-interests. My standpoint, from which the evolution of the economic formation of society is viewed as a process of natural history, can less than any other make the individual responsible for relations whose creature he socially remains, however much he may subjectively raise himself above them (62).

Marx says that no single person can be held responsible for the economic system which he obviously did not create, nor can entire classes of persons be held responsible. Is it also the case that they are being given a blanket immunity from judgment, no matter what policies they promote and what actions they carry out? In *Capital* Marx condemns certain human qualities and traits of character that are encouraged by the system, detaching the qualities of the act from the personalities, the specific individuals, who are the authors of these actions. It is hard to know what he means when he suggests that the individual may be able "to subjectively raise himself" above the system. Are some persons more likely than others to be able to do this? if so, how? Perhaps by recognizing the evils of the system, or even by working to change it. Whatever the case, Marx does not say or imply that persons in the capitalist class should abdicate their own positions, nor does he blame them for failure to do so. The class as a whole could not do so, and exceptional, personal acts of renunciation would leave the system intact. Other people would be on hand to fill the vacated roles.

Marx had his sights set on a future condition of existence which would eliminate certain problems and evils of subjectivity, as well as those that were social and institutional. Eventually all persons would share in a condition of social consciousness that would be "beyond morality," and also beyond philosophy, i.e., beyond the various tensions, conflicts and disturbances which Marx associated with the moral and the intellectual, as distinct from the *social* life.

---

62. The word "relations" is replaced by the word "conditions" in an alternate English translation of this preface by Eden and Cedar Paul, International Publishers, NY, 1929.

7

Problems Of Law, Crime, Authority And Justice

Marx conceived of communism as a program and process that would eventually eliminate crime, and with it the necessity of legal coercion. Both individual and society would be emancipated from the rule of law, and also from subordination to any form of moral authority. I will indicate certain of the difficulties involved in his freedom philosophy, and some of its broader implications. The relation of Kant's moral philosophy to Marx's anti-legalism and to his concept of freedom will be examined at some length.

Marx was second to none in his desire to secure and to uphold the freedom of the individual. This freedom could be obtained only in and through society, and only when the individual was delivered not only from economic class oppression, but also from other forms of oppression, moral and political. In his early writings especially, he placed such an emphasis on the importance of abolishing the political State and the legal authority of the state that his communism seemed very close to anarchism. Throughout his entire life, however, he objected strongly to anarchistic forms of socialism and communism. He stressed the necessity of public power and public control. He declared in *The Communist Manifesto* that

> When, in the course of development, class distinctions have disappeared, and all production has been concentrated in the hands of a vast association of the whole nation, the public power will lose its political character. Political power, properly so called, is merely the organized power of one class for oppressing another...

The elimination of political power was identified with the elimination of the need for a division of society into two parts, one of which had become morally external to the other part, endowed with an oppressive kind of public and social power. In the classless society, this kind of moral division, and this relation of domination and subordination, would no longer exist. The life of freedom that Marx projected when he referred to the classless condition was one in which there need be no consciously developed rules, regulations, or standards of moral and social performance accepted as valid and as necessary – either for practical or for moral reasons – by the society to which the individual belonged and with which he was wholly united.

Henri Lefebvre, the French Marxist, has concluded from his study of Marx that a fully realized communist society ". . . will be able to dispense with a formal body of laws, norms, formal maxims, and gradually, in unforseen ways, go back to the rule of custom" (1). There is some justification for this impression, but Marx did not anticipate any kind of rule by custom which would subject the individual to social condemnation if he failed to live up to norms and expectations maintained through the power of public opinion or of custom. Marx had associated rule by custom with the limitations of the feudal economy and society. These had been cast aside by the bourgeoisie in course of their rise to a ruling class position. The future society of communism would not restore earlier, pre-capitalist forms of moral and psychological constraint.

In the last volume of *Capital,* Marx implied that the future society would not develop, in connection with socially necessary productive work, any system of rules, norms or obligations relating to work performance. He was aware that a considerable amount of productive work had been carried on in the free towns of the middle ages, in urban societies which had won substantial political and economic independence from the feudal estate system. These societies, he said, represented an incipient form of capital and labor division. Both capital and labor were said to be "trammeled" by the corporate rules and regulations of the guild economy, and by duties and obligations relating to work performance:

> Even in the medieval guild system neither capital nor labor appear untrammeled, but their relations are rather defined by the corporate rules, and by the same associated relations, and the corresponding concepts of professional duty, craftsmanship, etc. Only when the capitalist mode of production . . . (2).

Here the manuscript breaks off. If Marx had completed the passage in accordance with the libertarian views he had developed earlier, he would have had to say that capitalism, in going beyond the restrictions of the medieval era, had liberated both capital and labour from the earlier "trammeling" conditions and that labor in socialist society would be altogether untrammeled.

Marx's conception of freedom had originated much earlier, in connection with issues that had no direct bearing on work performance. His chief concern as a communist was to eliminate the evils of existing economic and political society. These evils included the authority of the State, and the moral duality of the political condition. The necessary radical changes would have to be made in a way that avoided the kind of moral teaching effort which had been advocated by certain French philosophers of the eighteenth century enlightenment, those whom Marx classed as materialists. In the first paragraph of his third Thesis on Feuerbach, he had said that

---

1. *The Sociology of Marx,* Pantheon Books, NY, 1968, Chapter 4, p. 115 (French edition published in 1966).
2. *Op. cit.,* Chapter 48, p. 810.

> The materialistic teaching on the changing of the circumstances and education forgets that the circumstances are changed by men, and it is necessary that the educator himself be educated. This teaching, therefore, is bound to split society into two parts, one of which is superior to the other (3).

These materialists were said to have affirmed "the omnipotence of experience, habit and education, and the influence of the environment of man." In *The Holy Family* (1844) he had expressed considerable sympathy with this environmental emphasis. He concluded, however, that these philosophers had been unable to develop an approach to social change which would achieve the objectives of communism. Although individuals in the working class movement were engaged in a process of self-changing, they were not taking on functions of moral instruction, setting themselves up as superior, morally, to the rest of society.

MARX'S PRE-SOCIALIST PHILOSOPHY OF STATE AND LAW

Marx had started out, in the period of his political career that preceded his acceptance of communism, with a neo-Hegelian conception of an "ethical State" in which there was no differentiation between the educator and the educated. At that time, he was vigorously protesting the reactionary policies of the German government, which regarded the people of Germany as if they were morally immature and incompetent, requiring external moral instruction and moral supervision. The Prussian State was establishing a theocratic kind of government control. Restrictions on freedom of speech and press were being imposed in the name of Christianity and of Christian morality. Marx charged that this reactionary idea of the State was incompatible with the true concept and reality of the State as an ethical entity. The citizens of the ethical State did not have to accept the religion of Christiantiy, or submit to any particular kind of religious guidance and instruction. The ethical state was indeed an educational agency, but of a wholly different kind:

> . . . the true "public" education of the state is rather the rational and public actuality of the state. Even the state educates its members by making them part of the state, by transforming the aims of the individual into universal aims, by transforming raw impulse into ethical inclination, by transforming natural independence into spiritual freedom, and by the individual finding his satisfaction in the life of the whole and the whole in the attitude of the individual.

The state was ". . . an association of free men mutually educating one another," but the defenders of the government were portraying the people of

3. Translated by Rotenstreich, *op. cit.*

the nation as "... a crowd of grown-ups destined to be educated from above and to pass from the 'narrow' schoolroom to the 'broader' one" (4). Marx was referring here to an article written by a government defender, the editor of the *Kölnische Zeitung.* Marx's rebuttal was published in July 1842. This was one of a series of articles written and published in 1842 and the early part of 1843, which dealt with Marx's pre-socialist philosophy of state and law. Government spokesmen were saying that the people of the nation could not be trusted with the management either of their own political affairs or their own private lives. The "individual" might be led astray by "bad opinion" publicized in a free press that was critical of the sacrosant authority of Church and of State. Marx observed that "To combat freedom of the press, one must defend the permanent immaturity of the human species" (5). He also said, however, that freedom of the press could not be established by the mere elimination of a theocratic kind of moralistic repression. This kind of freedom from governmental control could very well co-exist with a materially motivated, secular perversion by special interests, especially the interests of big business:

> The French press is not too free; it is not free enough. It is not subject to intellectual censorship, to be sure, but subject to a material censorship, the high security deposit. This affects the press materially, because it pulls the press out of its true sphere into the sphere of big business speculations. In addition, big business speculations need big cities. Hence, the French press is concentrated in a few points, and when material force is thus concentrated, does it not work demonically, as intellectual force does not? (6).

The press that is truly free reflects the spirit of the whole people, urban and rural sections alike. The entire people are the rightful legislators of the nation. They are above all limited material interests. In relation to the internal German situation, Marx objected especially to the elevation of "a few privileged individuals," the government authorities, over the rest. One defender of the government had said that the views circulated in the liberal press indicated "... the impurity of the heart and the imagination that is titillated by obscene pictures." Marx replied that the censors were revealing their own state of mind, not the condition of the people:

---

4. This article was entitled "The Leading Article in No. 179 of the *Kolnische Zeitung:* Religion, Free Press, and Philosophy." It was an editorial written by Marx as editor of the *Rheinishe Zeitung.* English translation by Easton and Guddat, in *Writings of the Young Marx on Philosophy and Society, op. cit.*

5. *Karl Marx on Freedom of the Press and Censorship,* edited and translated by Saul K. Padover, The Marx Library, McGraw Hill Book Co., from "Debates on Freedom of the Press and Publication," a series of six articles appearing in the *Reinische Zeitung* during May 1842, p. 21.

6. *Ibid.,* pp. 33-34.

> It is despair over one's own salvation that makes personal weakness into mankind's weakness to shift it from one's own conscience; it is despair over the salvation of mankind that forbids it to follow its inherent natural laws, and which preaches immaturity as a necessity; it is hypocrisy that makes God into a hollow pretext without a belief in his own reality, the omnipotence of the good; it is selfishness that puts private salvation higher than the salvation of the whole.

The people of Germany were achieving their own salvation. The government censors

> . . . despair over mankind in general and canonize individuals. They project a frightening picture of human nature and demand that we genuflect before the icon of a few privileged individuals. We know that the individual person is weak, but we know at the same time that the totality is strong (7).

Marx did not deny that the law must define some actions as socially impermissible, nor that the state had certain rights over the individual whose conduct threatened the civil order: "The right of an individual citizen is folly if the right of the state is not recognized" (8). But he declared that no verbal, intellectual attack on those in positions of State authority could undermine public security and public morality. The justifiable, legitimate laws of the State were said to incorporate ". . . positive, clear, universal norms, in which freedom has won an impersonal, theoretical existence independent of the caprice of any individual." The democratic ethical State – the people's sovereignty – is composed of persons who observe these norms naturally, without effort and without taking thought, acting in "accordance with the unconscious natural law of freedom." These natural laws become dead letters when they are incorporated into legal statues. The living spirit can never be contained in law. The laws do become active, but only when certain persons, a small minority, fail to act naturally in accordance with "the law of freedom."

> The law prevents only as command. It becomes active law only when it is violated, for it is true law only when within it the unconscious natural law of freedom has become the conscious law of the state. Where law is real law – that is, where it is the essence of freedom – it is the real essence of the freedom of man. Hence laws cannot prevent man's activities, for they are, after all, the inner life laws of his behavior, the conscious mirror images of his life. Thus law steps back before the life of man as a life of freedom; and until his real action shows that he has stopped obeying the natural law of freedom, the law of the state compels him to be free, just as physical laws emerge as alien only after

7. *Ibid.*, p. 35.
8. *Ibid.*, p. 39.

> my life has ceased to be the life of these laws, when it is sick. Hence a preventive law is a senseless contradiciton (9).

The public function of the free press is to serve as a vehicle of the spirit. The opinions published and circulated can do no harm unless some of them are prescribed by the censoring authority. Suppression suggests the presence of something that ought to be concealed:

> Every mystery corrupts. Where public opinion is a mystery to itself, it is from the outset corrupted by all writings that formally break through the mysterious bounds. The censorship makes all forbidden writing, good or bad, extraordinary writing, while freedom of the press robs all writing of special importance.

The free press helps the people to achieve a national self-consciousness that is true self-knowledge, dispelling all mysteries and concealments, bringing all imperfections out into the open, and inspiring the people with vigor and self-confidence:

> The free press is the omnipresent open eye of the spirit of the people, the embodied confidence of a people in itself, the articulate bond that ties the individual to the state and the world, the incorporated culture which transfigures material struggles into intellectual struggles and idealizes its raw material shape. It is the ruthless confession of a people to itself, and it is well known that the power of confession is redeeming. The free press is the intellectual mirror in which a people sees itself, and self-viewing is the first condition of wisdom (10).

Marx also had something to say about the function of the legislator in the ideal-ethical state, i.e., of the individual who drafts the laws and may also be called upon to modify them. He did so in an article that was not concerned with the free press issue, but was discussing a proposed revision of the divorce law. He was here treating law as a public power that could and did serve a protective function in recognizing and maintaining the bond of marriage. Marriage was a legal and secular but also an ethical relation. He objected to a proposed liberalization of the divorce law, a change which would allow marriages to be broken up at the wish of either of the two parties. The advocates of this position

> . . . take an eudaemonistic view. They think only of two individuals and forget the *family.* They forget that nearly every dissolution of a marriage is the dissolution of a family and that the children and what belongs to them should not be dependent on arbitrary whims, even from a purely legal point of view. If mar-

9. *Ibid.,* pp. 29-30.
10. *Ibid.,* p. 31.

> riage were not the basis of the family, it would not be subject to legislation, just as friendship is not.

What he called the "will of marriage" was not reducible to the individual will of two persons, but was related to the essential function of marriage. The legislator has to take into account the "ethical substance" of marriage:

> The legislator . . . must consider himself a naturalist. He does not *make* laws; he does not invent them; he only formulates them. He expresses the inner principles of spiritual relationships in conscious, positive laws. The legislator would have to be accused of gross arbitrariness if he permitted his whims to replace the nature of things. But it is his right to regard it as gross arbitrariness if private persons want their whims to prevail against the nature of things (11).

The legislator in the ethical state, who acts as the agent of the people, can grant a legal divorce only in the presence of clear factual evidence which demonstrates that the relation is already dead in an ethical sense:

> . . . as precise unmistakable proof is required for *physical* death, the legislator can declare an *ethical* death only in the presence of the most indubitable symptoms.

The guarantee that the law, which allows divorce in some cases but not in others, will be properly administered ". . . will be present only when the law is the conscious expression of the will of the people, created with and through it."

Marx abandoned his concept of the ethical state in an abrupt way when he became a communist. The family ethical relation disappeared, along with the legal protection of that relation which he had advocated a short time before. In his writings of 1844 and also in *The German Ideology* (1845-46) he declared that the program of communism had to include "the abolition of private property, family, and State."

The marriage relation was external only, just as all other relations in the bourgeois atomic society were external. The ethical relation did not need legal protection because it did not exist. But the external relation as it still survived and was recognized in law had to be eliminated since it was a hollow sham, a dead form devoid of living substance. All mention of the family as a child-nurturing relation disappeared (12). The elimination of the family occurred after Marx had written his *Critique of Hegel's Philosophy of Right* (1843). This negation was a logical correlary of his rejection of Hegel's legal and political idealism. Society was now the atomized civil society of the external economy. The individual who was viewed as a member of civil society had been treated by Hegel as a single person. The ethical bond of the

---

11. Article entitled "On a Proposed Divorce Law," published in the *Reinische Zeitung,* December 19, 1942. Translated by Easton and Guddat, *op. cit.*

12. Marx's views on the family are discussed at greater length in Chapter 11 of this book on "The Necessity of Labor in Communist Society."

family did not affect the external economic relations that the family man maintained with other persons in the laissez-faire economy.

In eliminating. the family, Marx was also eliminating some of the internal complexities of his earlier ethical state conception. In the ethical state, there had been two primary ethical relations, one of which was familial, the other being public, communal and supra-familial. In the familial relation, the will of the community – the sovereign people – took precedence. The community had an inherent moral right to exert some kind of external legal and moral control over private persons in those cases where the marriage bond needed this kind of reinforcement. The same individual who joined with others on a public level, as part of the sovereign power, might as a private person elect to follow his or her personal wishes, regardless of the effect on the children of the marriage. These inclinations would be subject to community disapproval. In private life, the individual would be "willing" against the will of the people, in at least one respect, and therefore could not be wholly united in spirit with that will.

There was also the other, major problem of the criminal offender, a person who has committed some act which violates those essential positive norms that are supported by the sovereign legislative power of the people's state. Marx said that the law which might be invoked, in the ethical state, against an individual when the laws of freedom had not been observed, had no preventive power. Nevertheless, in some unspecified way, the existence of these laws had some function in supporting the life of freedom. It "compels all individuals to be free." They are "alien" only when the individual is no longer able to follow them in an entirely "natural" and voluntary way. The laws of the ethical state support the life of freedom only when they do not impose restrictions that would impair the health and vitality of the community as an ethico-spiritual entity, and therefore also of the individuals who comprise that community. Marx became involved in an insuperable difficulty. He was unable to demonstrate that laws which were by definition "alien" from the point of view of the criminal law-breaker, could "compel him to be free," if freedom were defined as an ability to act, voluntarily, "in accordance with the natural laws of freedom." In coming before the law, the individual would have demonstrated that he was not then capable of this kind of volition. The one clear point that Marx was making was that no legal power either can or ought to oppose, on moral grounds, what the people as a united sovereign power naturally wish to do. Their collectively shared aims and aspirations were, by definition, incapable of violating "the unconscious natural laws of freedom." Only the desires and aims of the single individual might, under some conditions, have to be opposed and frustrated by public authority for morally legitimate reasons.

The unification to be achieved through communism was to eliminate crime, i.e., to eliminate the psychological separation of the deviant norm-violator from the public majority. In the time of the present, the power of the public society, as it had existed on the level of spirit in the ethical state, had gone into eclipse. It was no longer available in the atomized external civil society. The power was to be restored through communism. The community, however, would no longer be the national community. It would be a world community. The unity of the individual with the whole would include his unity with his own nation, but the condition of wholeness comparable to that which Marx had described in his writings on the national ethical State was contingent on the unification of all nations into a world community. This union would be voluntary. It could not be maintained through law.

Marx's opposition to "ideological" morality, coincided with his shift to a universalism that excluded the ethical State conception. In his neo-Hegelian period, when he was attacking the repressive measures of the Prussian government, he had made a sharp distinction between religion, as a condition of dependency, and morality as a condition of autonomy. The government was setting itself in opposition to universal ethical religion:

> Morality recognizes only its own universal and rational religion, and religion only its own particular and positive morality. Following the Instruction, censorship will have to repudiate such intellectual heroes of morality as Kant, Fichte, Spinoza for being irreligious and threatening discipline, morals and outward loyalty. All of these moralists proceed from a principled opposition between morality and religion, because *morality,* they claim, is based on the *autonomy,* and *religion* on the *heteronomy* of the human spirit (13).

The autonomy of the ethical State, however, had not been complete, since it included a partial dependency on the power of internal law. This dependency was to be eliminated in the society of communism. The unity would then be sustained by conditions which would eliminate the need for law, and thereby also any opposition between the will of the individual and the will of the whole.

COMMUNISM AS THE ABOLITION OF CRIME

Marx expected that communism would eliminate crime. It would therefore also resolve the problem of how society ought to relate to the offender whose acts were defined as criminal. In *The Critique of the Gotha Programme* (1875), he referred to offenses committed by private individuals in civil society. Anti-social acts of this private kind would not disappear instantly, when the working class came to power. There would still be the need for public protective action. But he did expect that in socialist society, the problem of crime would be reduced to simple and manageable proportions. He mentioned, briefly, his own ideas about the program for the treatment of

13. "Comments on the Latest Censorship Instruction," completed in February 1842 and published in February 1843, translated by Easton and Guddat, *op. cit.*

criminal offenders which working class parties should support. The movement should adopt a morally non-punitive, socially redemptive attitude toward the "ordinary criminal," i.e., toward persons who endanger the lives of others and the security of public order or who commit offenses that cannot be allowed to go unchecked. The treatment of criminals was to be humane, in keeping with their human status. The function of incarceration was to restrain, but also to re-educate, to provide opportunities for the offender to change, so that he could be restored to society. Capital punishment was ruled out. Marx had made his view on this form of punishment clear, more than twenty years earlier, in an article published in the New York Daily Tribune, February 18, 1853. In *The Critique of the Gotha Programme* he objected to the German party demand for "regulation of prison labour." He questioned the meaning of this phrase, which might really be a defense of the economic interests of free, non-condemned wage workers, at the expense of those in prison:

> A petty demand in a general workers' programme. In any case, it should have been clearly stated that there is no intention from fear of competition to allow ordinary criminals to be treated like beasts, and especially that there is no desire to deprive them of their sole means of betterment, productive labour. This was surely the least one might have expected from socialists.

In this paragraph, Marx treats the question of the socialist attitude toward the criminal as one that is already settled and agreed upon by most people in the movement, scarcely needing to be mentioned in a political party programme. His philosophically primary writings on the subject of crime, society, and law had not been so uncomplicated. They contain the characteristic opposition between his naturalistic, scientific non-judgmental perspective and the morally judgmental perspective that came to the fore when he referred to the actions of people in the ruling class sections of modern society (14). Naturalism predominates whenever crime and law are treated as social disorders, symptoms of a pathogenic condition affecting alike both the individual who must be subordinated to the law, and those in positions of law-making, rule-making and law enforcing authority. The program of communism was to eliminate the causes of the divided condition. In the classless era, human relations and social actions would conform to the "unconscious natural law of freedom" to which Marx had referred earlier, in his ethical state writings, but there would no longer be a need for "a conscious law of the State." There would be no conflict between the natural inclinations of the individual and the needs of the public society. Crime, as the action of an individual law-breaker, and the law, as the defensive action of society, are both natural and inevitable phenomena that testify to universal unfreedom. The necessity of law, under these unfree conditions, does not mean that those who administer the laws and uphold their authority are

14. See Chapter 6 of this book, section on "The Eternalization of Evil in the Historical Process."

superior, in a moral sense, to those who are, as individual offenders, the "objects" of the law.

In 1844, Marx declared that law would no longer be required, just as the State would no longer be required, after the presently existing contradiction between private life and private good and public life and good had been eliminated through communism. This discrepancy was the primary cause of individualistic crime, and therefore also the cause of law. The inherent contradictions of present day society reduced the State to a condition of moral impotence. None of the evils of life in the modern age could be abolished by political means. In a journal article entitled "Critical Notes on 'The King of Prusia' and Social Reform" (1844) he was not referring to the problem of crime. He was pointing out the futility of social reform efforts that might be initiated by a politically idealist administration hoping to bring about morally beneficial changes in the civil society. Such efforts were doomed to fail. The very existence of the State proved the impossibility of this kind of reform. The State was

> . . . based on the contradiction between *public* and *private* life, on the contradiction between *general interests* and *particular interests*. . . Its power ceases where civil life and its working begins. Indeed, as against the consequences which spring from the unsocial nature of this civil life. . . *impotence* is the *natural* law of the administration (15).

In *The Holy Family* (1844) written shortly thereafter, Marx anticipated that the abolition of the conflict between public and private life would also eliminate crime, i.e., the action of an offender against the laws of the State.

> If man draws all his knowledge, sensation, etc. from the world of the senses and the experience gained in it, then what has to be done is to arrange the empirical world in such a way that man experiences and becomes accustomed to what is truly human in it, and becomes aware of himself as man. If correctly understood interest is the principle of all morality, man's private interest must be made to coincide with the interests of humanity. If man is unfree in the materialistic sense, i.e., free not through the negative power to avoid this or that, but through the positive power to assert his true individuality, crime must not be punished in the individual but the anti-social sources of crime must be destroyed, and each man must give social scope for the vital manifestation of his being. If man is shaped by environment, his environment must be made human. If man is social by nature, he will develop his true nature only in society, and the power of his

15. Translated by Easton and Guddat, *op. cit.*

> nature must be measured not only by the power of separate individuals but by the power of society (16).

"Correctly understood interest" is an essential qualifying phrase in this passage. "Interest" when "correctly understood" is not the same as what the individuals who are in the ruling class sections of modern, atomistic society *believe* to be in their own interest.

In *The German Ideology* (1845-46) Marx defined the nature of crime and the functions of law in a way that was consistent with the naturalistic and materialistic interpretation of history which he was then developing. There was a rational explanation and cause for the existence of law and of crime. Both had developed because the underlying conditions and relations of production were such as to make conflicts between individual existence and the existence of society inevitable. Crime, in this context, was the self-defensive and self-assertive activity of an individual who was struggling alone against oppressive conditions. Society, however, also had to maintain and defend its own existence through the enforcement of laws that might oppress the individual:

> Like right [law], so crime, i.e. the struggle of the isolated individual against the prevailing conditions, is not the result of pure arbitrariness. On the contrary, it depends on the same conditions as that rule. The same visionaries who see in right and law the domination of some independently existing general will can see in crime the mere violation of right and law. Hence, the State does not exist owing to the ruling will, but the State which arises from the material mode of life of individuals has also the form of a ruling will. If the latter loses its domination, it means that not only has the will changed but also the material existence and life of individuals, and only for that reason has their will changed (17).

Marx was able to uphold the necessity of law, as the right of a political society to defend itself against anarchical forms of disruption, without also conceding to that society the right to condemn such disruptive actions on moral grounds. Punishments inflicted by society, through law, might be defended, but only on practical, non-moral grounds. In a newspaper article published in the New York Daily Tribune, February 18, 1853, he declared his opposition to capital punishment. He also said

> Is it not a delusion to substitute for the individual with his real motives, with multifarious social circumstances pressing upon him, the abstraction of "free will" – one among the many qualities of man for man himself? This theory, considering punishment

---

16. *Collected Works of Marx and Engels,* Volume 4, *op. cit. The Holy Family,* Chapter 6, pp. 130–131. It should be noted that Engels was the author of only the first twenty pages of this supposedly joint work, which totals 211 pages in the English language translation cited here.

17. *Op. cit.,* Volume I, Part III, p. 358.

> as a result of the criminal's own will, is only a metaphysical expression of the old "jus talionis," eye against eye, tooth against tooth, blood against blood. Plainly speaking, and dispensing with all paraphrases, punishment is nothing but a means of society to defend itself against the infraction of its own vital conditions, whatever may be their character (18).

Sometimes Marx attacked and ridiculed the law-abiding individuals in the "respectable" bourgeois strata who supported the established economy and State in a way that recalled his previous attacks on the German government authorities who were setting themselves in opposition to the free expression of the people's life and spirit. The isolated individual who offended against the restrictive rules of bourgeois society could be represented as a rebel and as a creative disruptor. In *Theories of Surplus Value* (1862-63) he launched into a heavily sarcastic, tongue-in-cheek description of the criminal as "producer." This individual seemed to be a universal type, appearing in life and in literature long before the advent of capitalism and of industrial civilization.

Under modern conditions he has a greater disruptive power than in earlier times. He forces bourgeois society to divert a considerable portion of its resources, the surplus value acquired through the exploitation of proletarian labor, in vain efforts to contain those types of crime that are individualistic protests:

> The criminal produces not only crimes but also criminal law, and with this also the professor who gives lectures on criminal law. . .
>
> The criminal produces an impression, partly moral and partly tragic, as the case may be, and in this way renders a "service" by arousing the moral and aesthetic feelings of the public. He produces not only compendia on Criminal Law, not only penal codes and along with them legislators in this field, but also art, belles-lettres, novels, and even tragedies, as not only Mullner's *Schuld* and Schiller's *Rauber* show, but also [Sophocles'] *Oedipus* and [Shakespeare's] *Richard the Third.* The criminal breaks the monotony and everyday security of bourgeois life. In this way he keeps it from stagnation. . . (19).

The proletarians of capitalist society were outside of that society, and outside of the bourgeois moral system. From the point of view of the working class, the entire system of bourgeois law, morality, and justice was external and alien. Individuals in the criminal category, in bourgeois society, might or might not be proletarians, but they did at least have the negative virtue of not covering up or concealing those tendencies and impulses which

18. Translated by T.B. Bottomore, in *Karl Marx: Selected Writings in Sociology and Social Philosophy,* McGraw Hill, 1956, pp. 228-229.
19. Progress Publishers, Moscow, 1963, Volume I, pp. 387-388.

persons in positions of outward respectability were able to mask and to hide from public view. The idea of punitive justice, administered through the State, was disconnected from the program of communism. Marx declared, in his address on *The Civil War in France* (1871) that "The civilization of justice and of bourgeois order comes out in its lurid light whenever the slaves and drudges of that order rise against their master. Then this civilization and justice stand forth as undisguised savagery and lawless revenge. . . ."

The proletarians were the primary victims of bourgeois justice, regardless of whether they were or were not, as individuals, in a criminal category. Certain types of non-political crime were more likely to be committed by poor persons than by persons in middle and upper strata. Such persons were then tried and condemned, legally and morally, by the representatives of the same class that enslaved them economically, as wage-earners, even when they were law-abiding. It is evident, in *Capital* and in Marx's later political writings, that the proletarians who form the industrial army and will one day defeat the barbarians and the justice of bourgeois civilization are not in the criminal category. The proletarian army excluded the demoralized, and also the bohemian sections of the economic under-population. Some of these were parasitic hangers-on, whose way of life was symptomatic of the corruption of the entire system. In addition, certain degraded and criminal sections of the working class, the "lumpenproletariat," were actual or potential hirelings of the ruling classes, ready and willing to carry out the messier, more brutal functions of upper class power.

The upholders of internal law and justice were engaged, routinely, in acts of external military and economic aggression, directed against external peoples. Those who decried private violence at home, and denounced the offenders, were quite willing to aid and abet the criminal activities of national citizens abroad, and to engage in national wars for the sake of expanding the resources of wealth available to the national ruling classes. These activities were criminal in a supra-legal, moral sense, regardless of the fact that they were regarded as non-criminal by the ruling classes who supported internal "law and justice" at home.

Marx defined the *modern State as an association.* In capitalist society it was a class-based association carrying out certain group-sanctioned functions. These functions could in no way serve any higher objective that could override and check the evils of bourgeois egoism and atomism. The working class were not included in this political association. As individuals they were negatively free from the complicity in bourgeois political projects. Marx also represented the workers, in 1844, as initially atomistic individuals who were coming together, for the first time, in an association of their own, the essence of which was not political, but social, and which was the antithesis of bourgeois forms of political association. This is described as their first entry into society, i.e., their first social experience that is other than merely external and utilitarian. They acquire a need for each other, a need for society, for association as such. In an essay on "Human Requirements and the

Division of Labour under the Rule of Private Property," Marx described his impression of the working men's meetings which he had visited in Paris:

> When communist *artisans* associate with one another, theory, propaganda, etc. is their first end. But at the same time, as a result of this association, they acquire a new need – the need for society – and what appears as a means becomes an end. In this practical process the most splendid results are to be observed whenever French socialist workers are seen together. Such things as smoking, drinking, eating, etc. are no longer means of contact or means that bring them together. Association, society and conversation, which again has association as its end, are enough for them; the brotherhood of man is no mere phrase with them, but a fact of life, and the nobility of man shines upon us from their work-hardened bodies (20).

The ends of association in the classless society must be consistent with the positive good of social life. Sociality of this ideal-transcendental kind cannot be implicated in the evils of bourgeois justice or transformed into a force of which will carry out ends that are by definition "inhuman."

THE REJECTION OF KANT'S DUALISM

An examination of Marx's early liberation philosophy leads back in the direction of Hegel, but also back toward Kant. The systems of Kant and of Marx can be aligned with one another in ways that by-pass Hegel. Marx rejected the distinction which Kant had made between two types of "will," one of which was "natural," and belonged to humanity as a species tied to nature. The other was "free," possessed by humanity as a "noumenal" species, partly separate from nature, and tied to the noumenal supersensible power beyond nature. According to the logic of Kantian dualism, this meant that evil in the moral sense, as a condition of self-being, could not exist in the absence of the "noumenal" will. Marx eliminated the noumenal will. It, therefore, followed that social punishment could not be a morally just, i.e., morally deserved, reaction of the public authority to criminal offenses. The criminal could not be condemned on moral grounds, as one who had committed an intrinsically evil act in going against the laws of society.

In his writings on law, Marx was setting himself in opposition to Hegel as well as to Kant, minimizing the differences between the two. In *The Holy Family* he had reacted against Hegel's "speculative idea" that the condemned criminal, in being judged and sentenced by others in his own society, is really also passing judgment on himself, and thereby "willing his own punishment." This idea had been current in German intellectual circles some time before

20. *Collected Works of Marx and Engels, op. cit.,* Volume III, p. 313.

Hegel had incorporated it into his own philosophy. Kant, before the time of Marx, had disagreed with this view, saying that

> . . . a person does not suffer punishment because he wished to have the *punishment itself,* but because he wished to commit *a punishable deed.* After all, it is not a punishment if a person is subjected to something he wishes, and it is impossible to *wish* to be punished (21).

According to Marx, Hegel's theory was ". . . a mere speculative interpretation of the current empirical punishments for criminals." It was ". . . the *speculative disguise* of the old *jus talionis,* which *Kant* expounded as the *only juridical* penal theory." Hegel, in other words, was trying, in an evasive way, to mitigate the harshness of judicial punishment, which was necessarily always external and alien, from the point of view of the condemned person. Marx also said that all external punishments were necessarily inhuman, because the law could not make allowances for the particular personal and social situation of the offender. Marx did not object to this rigidity. Any other approach, even had it been feasible, would still have been objectionable. There was also the specific content of the law to be considered. Insofar as the laws sought to enforce the rules of a given historic society, their moral and rational content was open to question. The rational and moral evaluation of this content, from an external position beyond the law of any specific society, would, however, become unnecessary, if the law itself were to be eliminated:

> According to Hegel, the criminal in his punishment passes sentence on himself. . . For Hegel, self-judgment of the criminal remains a mere *"Idea,"* a mere speculative interpretation of the *current empirical punishments for criminals.* He thus leaves the mode of application to the respective stage of development of the state, i.e., he leaves punishment as it is. . . A *penal* theory which at the same time sees in the criminal the *man* can do so only in *abstraction,* in imagination, precisely because *punishment, coercion,* is contrary to *human* conduct. Moreover, it would be impossible to carry out. Purely subjective arbitrariness would take the place of the abstract law because it would always depend on the official "honourable and decent" men to adapt the penalty to the individuality of the criminal. Plato long ago realized that the *law* must be one-sided and *take no account* of the individual(22).

Law by its very nature must support standards which apply equally to all persons. It must call persons to equal account. It must necessarily reduce all persons to an enslaved condition. They became "objects" of the law, not persons in their own right. In his newspaper article dealing with capital punishment and legal philosophy (1853), Marx said that although the inten-

21. *The Metaphysics of Morals* (1797), Part I, translated by H.B. Nisbet, in *Kant's Political Writings, op. cit.,* p. 158.
22. *Op. cit.,* Chapter 8, p. 179.

tion of Kant and of Hegel had been to uphold and affirm the inalienable human dignity of the criminal, in *reality,* the condemned person was reduced to a mere object, a "slave of justice," robbed of his human status:

> From the point of view of abstract right, there is only one theory of punishment which recognizes human dignity in the abstract, and that is the theory of Kant, especially in the more rigid form given to it by Hegel. Hegel says: "Punishment is the *right* of the criminal. It is an act of his own will. The violation of right has been proclaimed by the criminal as his own right. His crime is the negation of right. Punishment is the negation of this negation, and consequently an affirmation of right, solicited and forced upon the criminal by himself."
>
> There is no doubt something specious in this formula, inasmuch as Hegel, instead of looking upon the criminal as a mere object, the slave of justice, elevates him to the position of a free and self-determined being. Looking, however, more closely into the matter, we discover that German idealism here, as in most other instances, has but given a transcendental sanction to the existing rules of society (23).

This comment was brilliantly acute, as far as it went. But it does not shed much light on the specific nature of Kant's moral outlook, or on the meaning of Kant's "free will" conception. Kant had adopted a harshly punitive attitude toward the criminal offender who had violated the laws of the State. He insisted that the practice of capital punishment be retained, opposing persons who were advocating its abolition. He was reluctant to concede that extenuating circumstances should be taken into account in moderating the sentence imposed for a capital offense. He conceded only that the law might be unjust in specific cases, because an individual might be falsely accused and condemned. He invested the authority of public law with a noumenal, i.e., a theological, sanction. The continual presence of this power was essential to the life of modern, civilized society, and also to the life of the individual as a noumenal being.

Kant's moral philosophy was inherently political and social, concerned with the maintenance of public order and public morality, as well as with the moral condition of the individual. On both levels, the public and the personal, he distinguished between processes and conditions that were within the realm of nature, and those that were related to the noumenal, supra-sensuous aspects of human life. Considered as "natural beings" no individuals could incur moral blame, since their actions were determined by natural necessity, by laws of nature acting through them, or by forms of self-will that could not be classed as moral will. But Kant also said that it was impossible to divest the

---

23. Translated by T. B. Bottomore, *op. cit.*

condemning authority of law of a noumenal element, just as it was also impossible to divest human beings of the noumenal component of their existence.

All traits that human beings possessed through "nature" could be regarded as good, since nature would not have endowed the species with impulses and dispositions that had no utility or justification in the general plan of nature (24). In *Religion within the Limits of Reason Alone,* Kant had said that the radical evil in human nature cannot be blamed on sensuous physical nature and "the natural inclinations arising therefrom" (25). But human beings had an inner moral sense, a noumenal capacity to distinguish between good and evil. This existed even in primitive societies before the development of modern political society and modern civilization. There was also a universal propensity to evil, derived not from nature, but from the human connection with the supersensible power of creation. Kant associated "radical evil" with "negative will," a will that cannot exist unless the moral sense is also present. Negative will was, therefore, a noumenal self-will. It appeared in consciousness as a desire to defy and reject the moral restrictions imposed by external social and legal authority, i.e., by those moral norms of society that were upheld and enforced by law. It was also resistance to the dictates of moral reason arising from within the self, apart from societal law. Nothing was more dangerous to the moral life of the self, or to society, than this kind of noumenal negativity. Kant regarded all morally culpable offenses against the law as manifestations of noumenal negativity or "noumenal will." Since all persons shared in the same noumenal status, all offenders should be treated by the law as abstract spiritual (noumenal) beings, irrespective of any differences in social class position. No human power could rob them of their equal human status. The law recognized their human status – and their human freedom from nature – when it penalized them as possessors of negative will.

As a philosopher of law, Kant reduced the differences in the outer social and economic circumstances of individuals to insignificance. He also disregarded differences in their inner state of consciousness and their moral personality traits. This was so in spite of the fact that he also recognized that persons might differ from one another in psychological respects, especially in their capacity for what he called "ethical legislation," i.e., in their capacity for self-restriction in response to inner moral directives and commands that might exist even when external restrictions were absent.

Marx equalized all persons in a similarly abstract way. Negative will was no longer an essential attribute of man. In the equalitarian society of communism, it would no longer be an attribute of any person. All individuals would be "natural," but not "noumenal" in the Kantian sense. They would have a "natural" will, but not a "noumenal" will. Society, as a public power, and as

24. See the discussion of Kant's "idea for a universal history," in Chapter 4, on "Marx's Dialectical Interpretation of History."

25. Translated by Greene and Husdon, Harper and Row, NY, 1960, Book I, Part III.

the upholder of societal norms, would also be divested of its noumenal authority. The distinction which Kant had made between "ethical legislation" and "juridicial legislation" would be eliminated, because both kinds of legislation would no longer exist.

Kant had said that some individuals had to be controlled externally, by "juridicial legislation," i.e., by the threat of external coercion and legal punishment. In others, the capacity for internal legislation, i.e., for ethical legislation, was better developed. The individual who is a moral self-legislator, capable of giving the law to himself, lives within a legal jurisdiction. Under no circumstances does he have a private moral right, an inner moral authorization, to violate the laws of his own legal and political society. But insofar as he is an ethical legislator, he will obey the authorities not because of fear of external punishment, but from motives of moral duty. The individual who is capable of ethical legislation must abide, voluntarily, by the prevailing laws, regardless of whether or not he approves of their content. He does have a right to voice public criticism of certain laws and policies of the State, and even a moral duty to participate in legislative review and reform, but he is still morally culpable if he undermines the sacrosant authority of the "head of State" by any act of overt civil disobedience, regardless of the nature of the sovereign's laws and commands.

The ethical individual comes within the jurisdiction of two courts of justice, an internal court of conscience, and an external public court of law. An individual who lacked internal conscience need encounter only an external judge, whose moral authority he might resist and reject. Kant declared, however, that all persons have internal powers of self-judgment, which can serve as an incentive for engaging in a process of self-perfecting which would render them morally "self-sufficient," capable of governing their own actions according to laws prescribed by moral reason. Self-perfecting begins with self-knowledge, a moral self-appraisal which indicates to the person that he or she has a good many internal hindrances to overcome before "negative will," or "bad will," can be eliminated. "Good will," which is a noumenal will, exists to begin with as potentiality, but it can be actualized in such a way that it can entirely displace the negative will, only through a prolonged process of self-perfecting:

> Moral self-knowledge, which tries to fathom the scarcely penetrable depths of the heart, is the beginning of all human wisdom. For this wisdom, which consists in the accord of one's own will with his ultimate end, requires a man first and foremost to remove the internal hindrances (of bad will seated within him), and then try and develop his inalienable original predisposition of a good will. Only descent into the hell of self-knowledge prepares the way for godliness (26).

---

26. *Metaphysical Principles of Virtue, op. cit.,* Introduction, pp. 18–19.

The ethical individual experiences a kind of external constraint which comes from *within* the psyche, not from the external legal power. This higher rational and moral power within the self is conscience. Conscience has a punitive force that is in some way less severe than the penalties that can be inflicted by public authority. No man is morally obligated or entitled to condemn himself to death, i.e., to commit suicide, nor to incarcerate himself. But conscience is also more inescapable than public judgment:

> The consciousness of an internal court of justice within man. . . is *conscience.*
>
> Every man has a conscience and finds himself observed by an internal judge, who threatens him and keeps him in awe (respect combined with fear). This authority watching over the laws within him is not something which he himself (arbitrarily) creates, but is incorporated in his being. If he tries to run away, his conscience follows him like his shadow. To be sure, he can stupefy himself with pleasures and diversions or can put himself to sleep; but he cannot avoid coming to himself now and then or waking up, at which time he immediately hears its awful voice. . . conscience must be conceived as the subjective principle of being accountable to God for one's deeds (27).

In the event that the self-accused is able to acquit himself, the favorable decision may

> . . . contain the joy of having escaped the danger of being found culpable. Therefore, satisfaction in the comforting encouragement of one's conscience is not positive (as enjoyment) but only negative (as relief following previous anxiety)(28).

In *The Critique of Practical Reason* Kant had said that an ethical individual who makes a morally just decision to respect the rights of another person, may sometimes have to surrender, voluntarily, certain advantages which he could have retained had he not been committed to uphold the moral law. But this kind of moral self-limitation is freedom, not bondage:

> The heart is freed from a burden which has secretly pressed upon it; it is lightened when in instances of pure moral resolutions there is revealed to man, who previously has not correctly known it, a faculty of inner freedom to release himself from the impetuous importunity of the inclinations, to such an extent that not even the dearest of them has an influence on a resolution for which he now makes use of his reason. In a case where I alone know that injustice lies in what I do, and where an open confession of it and an offer to make restitution is in direct conflict

27. *Ibid.,* section 13, pp. 100–102.
28. *Ibid.,* p. 103.

> with vanity, selfishness, and an otherwise not illegitimate antipathy to the man whose rights I have impaired, if I can set aside all these considerations, there is a consciousness of an independence from inclinations and circumstances and of the possibility of being sufficient to myself which is salutary for me in yet other respects (29).

The desire for self-respect, which must be earned through the observance of moral duty, i.e., through obtaining command over morally disapproved, resistant aspects of the self, is perhaps the most important of all motives to morally good action:

> The law of duty, through the positive worth which obedience to it makes us feel, finds easier access through the respect for ourselves in the consciousness of our freedom. If it is well established, so that a man fears nothing more than to find himself on self-examination to be worthless and contemptible in his own eyes, every good moral disposition can be grafted on to this self-respect, for the consciousness of freedom is the best, indeed the only guard that can keep ignoble and corrupting influences from bursting in upon the mind (30).

In Marx's post-Kantian philosophy, the unification of public and private interest eliminated the need for external legal coercion and for external moral control and punishment, coming from a source of authority outside of the self. This meant also that the individual would have nothing to fear from the law, or from condemnation by the public opinion of his own society. But there remained the possibility that he might still experience personal moral distress, feelings of self-blame and moral unworthiness. In a section of *The Holy Family* cited earlier in this chapter, Marx had said that ". . . *punishment, coercion,* is contrary to *human* conduct." He was referring here to external moral condemnation by the society of other people. There was to be no external, social court of justice, and no punitive external judging process, legal or supra-legal, to which the individual might be subjected. But the *internal* court of justice as described by Kant, in which the individual is divided against himself, and acts as his own judging authority, must also be abolished. In the human society, other people would not reinforce, through their concurrence, the individual's self-rejecting tendencies. They would do the reverse. They would assure him that in reality there was no justifiable basis for his private self-rejecting reactions. It was this kind of reassurance to which Marx referred in "Private Property and Communism" (1844) when he said that socialism represented man's "positive self-consciousness, no longer attained through the overcoming of religion. . ." It was being attained through the negation of the internal power of the isolated conscience and the

29. *Op. cit.,* p. 165.
30. *Ibid.*

"internal court of justice" as conceived by Kant. In *The Holy Family,* Marx had said that

> . . . under *human* conditions punishment will *really* be nothing but the sentence passed by the culprit on himself. No one will want to convince him that *violence* from *without* done to him by others, is violence which he had done to himself. On the contrary, he will see in *other* men his natural saviours from the punishment he has imposed on himself; in other words, the relation will be reversed (31).

This implies also that the person who is helped by others – saved from himself – will also then be able to perceive himself in the same positive way as he is perceived by others. His true self will be affirmed by others, and he will substitute the positive appraisals and judgments of others for his superseded negative self-judgment.

In *The German Ideology* Marx presented a radically anti-Kantian definition of communism as the realization of "good will." His way of opposing Kant, however, also demonstrated the strength of the Kantian influence. He affirmed the connection which Kant had established between the outer legal order and the internal court of justice, by eliminating them both simultaneously. All persons were to be regarded as "natural" beings. As natural beings, living in a transformed natural society, they could not, as persons, have self-inhibiting, morally self-constraining powers operating against natural inclination and need. The external source of commanding and judging moral authority, originating on the social level, would also be non-existent. Freedom of personal self-expression and self-assertion would be total, but would have no socially harmful consequences. The pressure of duty, of moral obligation, would disappear, along with "negative will" which had been, for Kant, an aspect of noumenal self-hood and of radical evil which the ethical person must strive to overcome.

Marx declared that communism was to make possible a *summum bonum* condition of personal and social existence which would be the actual, practically feasible realization of a *summum bonum* condition which Kant had projected as conceivable and as possible, but which could not be attained in the mortal life that was bounded and limited by nature. In the course of his attack on Kant, Marx had said that

> The state of Germany at the end of the last century is fully reflected in Kant's *Critik der Practischen Vernunft* [Critique of Practical Reason]. . . the impotent German Burghers did not get any further than "good will." Kant was satisfied with "good will" alone, even if it remained entirely without result, and he transferred the *realization* of this good will, the harmony between it and the needs and impulses of individuals, to the *world beyond* (32).

---

31. *Op. cit.,* Chapter 8, p. 179.
32. *The German Ideology, op. cit.,* Volume I, Part III, p. 207.

Kant had defined a perfected state of good will as a condition of self in which the individual would no longer have to struggle against various inclinations and tendencies, whether natural or noumenal, that might induce him to set aside the various imperatives of rational morality. The individual would be transformed in the sense that he would be incapable of wishes and desires that were not entirely in accordance with the imperatives of moral duty and moral law. No individual, with the possible exception of a few saints, could expect to achieve this condition in his mortal, terrestrial life. He could, however, at least begin to progress toward that condition with the expectation that he would continue to advance in a condition of existence beyond earthly life:

> This infinite progress is possible, however, only under the presupposition of an infinitely enduring existence and personality of the same rational being; this is called the immortality of the soul. Thus the highest good is practically possible only on the supposition of the immortality of the soul. . . (33).

Kant was referring to the limited life in nature when he wrote:

> If a rational creature could even reach the state of thoroughly liking to do all moral laws, it would mean that there was no possibility of there being in him a desire which could tempt him to deviate from them, for overcoming such a desire always costs the subject some sacrifice and requires self-compulsion, i.e., an inner constraint to do that which one does not quite like to do. To such a level of moral disposition no creature can ever attain. For since he is a creature, and consequently is always dependent with respect to what he needs for complete satisfaction with his condition, he can never be wholly free from desires and inclinations which, because they rest on physical causes, do not themselves agree with the moral law, which has an entirely different source. . .(34).

No amount of moral effort in society could rectify the inevitable injustices suffered by many individuals. Moral striving alone could not ensure personal and general happiness and a condition of absolute justice. Optimum happiness, which is also optimum freedom, can be attained only when the individual's own wish and will have been brought into complete harmony with the requirements of moral reason and moral law. The achievement of such a state is open to all, but only because each person will have ample time for self-perfecting, in a future condition of existence.

> Happiness is the condition of a rational being in the world, in whose whole existence everything goes according to wish and will. It thus rests on the harmony of nature with his entire end

33. *Critique of Practical Reason, op. cit.*, p. 127.

34. *Ibid.*, p. 86. It is hardly necessary to point out that Kant's moral philosophy, no less than that of Marx, was involved in certain internal ambiguities and contradictions in connection with the status of "natural inclinations" as well as in other respects.

> and with the essential determining ground of his will. . . there is not the slightest ground in the moral law for a necessary connection between the morality and proportionate happiness of a being which belongs to the world as one of its parts and as thus dependent on it. . . Therefore also the existence is postulated of a cause of the whole of nature, itself distinct from nature, which contains the ground of the exact coincidence of happiness with morality (35).

In Marx's conception of the future life condition, universal self-realization would be a state of happiness, a "heaven on earth," that would supplant not only the Christian idea of heaven, but also Kant's conception of the *summa bonum* condition. Unlike Kant, Marx did not expect that past injustices could be rectified, for individuals. But absolute justice would be established in a different way. All persons would be treated as equal in human value, and each would have an equal opportunity for personal life development. Although belonging to the world "as one of its parts," dependent on nature and society, the individual would exist in a state of freedom from inner and outer constraint resembling the kind of freedom which Kant had identified with the termination of moral striving and moral self-division, in a life beyond nature.

POLITICAL CONSCIENCE IN THE SOCIALIST MOVEMENT

There is a discrepancy between two frames of reference and two kinds of language in Marx's thought. He separated his determinism and naturalism, and his transcendental materialism, from those aspects of his socialism which required the recognition of the historical – though transitory – reality of political consciousness and political conscience, as these developed within the working class movement. He did not try to reconcile the contradictions involved. They would disappear, as problems, after the political movement had fulfilled its function and had gone out of existence. His primary logical and metaphysical system, which was self-consistent within certain formal limits, was comparable to the cosmological unification which Kant had projected when he wrote that ". . . existence is postulated of a cause of the whole of nature, itself distinct from nature, which contains the ground of the exact coincidence of happiness with morality" (36). The ground, in Marx's philosophy of the future, is nature itself. Although he did, of course, declare that human productive activity, human work, was the initiating cause of historical development and civilizational progress, this was a naturally neces-

35. *Ibid.*, p. 129.

36. Hegel, in his post-Kantian cosmology, did not claim that such an "exact coincidence" could ever be established through the noumenal power that he identified with God. The Hegelian God of Philosophy could do nothing whatsoever for the individual whose lot in life excluded him from any kind of human existence.

sary activity, and also an expression of human powers, carried on by individuals who were a part of the general system of nature. Their powers of will, reason and consciousness remained within natural limits. The most distinctive, nature-transcending powers of man had no connection with political life and with political authority.

Marx and Kant were in partial agreement. Nature itself could not be the source of moral norms, laws and judgments, nor could it be the source of an inner subjective moral sense, identified by Kant as conscience. In Marx's theory of history, society, which was also a natural phenomenon, was the source of the mores and the laws that were invested with some kind of oppressive force and authority, when embodied in political law and when connected with punishment. The origin of such authority, and the origin of whatever content might be included therein, was outside of the individual psyche. The various historical, societal systems of the past and present could not supply the unifying moral or ideological ground of the future world society, the society in which the Kantian "kingdom of ends" morality would be realized in fact and not only in philosophical imagination. The process of revolutionary self-changing which was taking place through political working class struggles would eventually make it possible to break through to a social condition that would be beyond radical evil and also beyond sacrificial effort. In his early writings, Marx represented the workers as individuals who were already beyond inner moral conflict and moral stress. Their world-historical task was to strike down the externalized, objectified, oppressive powers and evils of the anti-human system of which they were the principal victims. The workers need not be subordinated to moral laws, and had apparently no connection with moral rules.

Occasionally Marx went beyond the limits of his own metaphysical naturalism. At the close of the Inaugural Address which he delivered, in English, at the Working Men's International meeting in London, September 1864, he had said that it was the task of the enlightened sections of the working class, the politically conscious vanguard, to ". . . vindicate the simple laws of morals and justice, which ought to govern the relations of private individuals, as the rules paramount of the intercourse of nations." By taking a stand based on adherence to these simple moral laws, the working class could resist the attempt of the bourgeoisie to secure proletarian cooperation in ". . . foreign policy in pursuit of criminal designs, playing upon national prejudices, and squandering in piratical wars the people's blood and treasure." According to Marx, the struggle for a foreign policy based upon ". . . the simple laws of morals and justice . . . forms part of the general struggle for the emancipation of the working classes"(37). Later, in a short pamphlet written in October 1871, he formulated "General rules of the International Working Men's Association." This association required among other things "That all societies and individuals adhering to it will acknowledge truth, justice and

37. *Selected Works of Marx and Engels, op. cit.,* Volume II.

morality as the basis of their conduct toward each other and toward all men, without regard to color, creed, or nationality" (38).

In his speech of May 1871, in commemoration of the defeated workers of Paris, Marx adhered to his usual dialectical language. In praising the heroic actions of the Communards, he declared that the workers ". . . have no ideals to realize, but to set free the elements of the new society with which the old collapsing bourgeois society itself is pregnant"(39). These elements are, of course, the forces of production now bottled up within the womb of capitalism. They also designate the good, positive, social aspects of human nature, which had been associated by Kant with an "inalienable original predisposition of good will."

In *The Critique of the Gotha Programme* (1875) Marx used the word "conscience" in a special political context. In his attack on the party program of the German social democrats, he exclaimed:

> Does not the mere fact that the representatives of our party were capable of penetrating such a monstrous attack on the understanding that has spread among the mass of our party, prove by itself with what criminal levity and with what lack of conscience they set to work in drawing up this compromise programme!

In this same commentary, he also attacked the German party leadership for including a demand for "freedom of conscience:"

> *"Freedom of Conscience!"* If one desires at this time of the Kulturkampf to remind liberalism of its old catchwords, then it surely could have been done in the following form: Everyone should be able to attend to his religious as well as his bodily needs without the police sticking their noses in. But the Workers' Party ought at any rate in this connection to have expressed its consciousness of the fact that bourgeois "freedom of conscience" is nothing but the toleration of all possible kinds of *religious freedom of conscience* and that for its part in endeavors rather to liberate the conscience from the spectre of religion. But there is a desire not to transgress the "bourgeois" level.

When Marx referred to a conscience that ought to prevail within the working class movement, he was conceiving it as loyalty to the aims and tasks of the revolution. The task is voluntarily assumed, but once undertaken, it becomes a binding social and personal commitment. It includes an obligation to abide by certain standards of intellectual integrity. Individuals within the movement are condemned, morally, for failure to live up to expectations and obligations that should be binding on all. He is criticizing persons in positions of intellectual influence. The importance of theory is being underlined. It is not that Marx is advocating blind acceptance of previously developed views

38. *Ibid.*
39. *Ibid.*

of whose soundness he is himself convinced. But he does demand that carefully reasoned conclusions which he has worked out, should not be lightly and capriciously, i.e., "arbitrarily," set aside. A failure of conscience on this level subverts the generally recognized moral aims of the working class movement.

As a dialectical philosopher, Marx denied the historical importance of certain "abstract" manifestations of moral consciousness. He also assumed that their appearance in culture could not be attributed to permanent qualities and tendencies in human nature. When formulating his practical materialism, he said, in *The Holy Family* (1844), that morally critical ideas had no power to change society, apart from the "practical force" required to carry them out: "Ideas can never lead beyond the old world order but only beyond the ideas of the old world order. *Ideas cannot carry out anything at all.* In order to carry out ideas men are needed who can exert practical force" (40). He had already, in the preceding year, predicted that the working class would carry out forms of practical revolutionary action which would ensure the eventual achievement of ultimate communism. The extent to which individuals in that class had any "abstract" moral ideas of their own is left in doubt. As a philosophical materialist, Marx preferred to represent the working class as non-ideological and on that account as lacking in moral ideas. But he did not maintain this view consistently. It breaks down in certain contexts.

In *Wages, Prices, and Profit* Marx assumed that the workers whom he was addressing responded to moral language and to the call of duty, and that they possessed moral ideas about distributive economic justice which were in the category of ideals not being applied in practice. At the same time he was trying to discourage a radical egalitarian idealism which might cause the workers to disregard the need for practical compromise and accommodation to the realities of a particular situation. The workers have a duty to struggle against the encroachments of capital, but they should do so in a way that is consistent with what is rationally possible and economically advisable. He was discussing strategies they should adopt in their present day struggles against the capitalist system. They could reasonably expect to achieve a substantial reduction in the working day. This had been extended beyond previously customary and tolerable limits, to an extent that was economically irrational, even from the capitalist standpoint. Through their attempts to reduce ". . . the working day to its former rational dimensions . . . working men fulfill only a duty to themselves and their race. They only set limits to the tyrannical usurpations of capital. Time is the room of human development. A man who has no free time to dispose of is . . . a mere machine for the production of foreign wealth, broken in body and brutalized in mind" (41).

Marx warned the workers that they could not expect to receive more

---

40. *Op. cit.,* Chapter 6, p. 119.

41. *Selected Works of Marx and Engels,* Volume II, written in May and June 1865, pp. 68–69.

wage income than the capitalist economy could tolerate. But they did have a moral obligation to avoid being unnecessarily defrauded. Although they will have to accept cuts in wages in times of stagnation and of falling prices, they should try to block attempts by employers to reduce wages more than is economically necessary. They must not ". . . renounce their resistance against the encroachments of capital. . . By cowardly giving way in their every day conflict with capital, they would certainly disqualify themselves for the initiating of any larger movement" (42).

The capacity of the workers for practical action would be reduced if they were to promote unrealistic radical demands for an "equalization of wages." They must not try to go beyond the prevailing practices: ". . . as the costs of producing labouring powers of different quality vary, so must differ the values of the labouring powers employed in different trades. . . To clamour for *equal* or *even equitable distribution* on the basis of the wages system is the same as to clamour for *freedom* on the basis of the slavery system. What you think just or equitable is not the question. The question is: What is necessary and unavoidable within a given system of production?" (43).

Political conscience that is rational includes the willingness to exclude certain moral ideas relating to distributive justice from the practical revolutionary program. In *Wages, Prices and Profit* Marx is not denying the *existence* of ideas which have to be compromised in action. But he seems to be doing just this in his *Critique of the Gotha Programme* (1875). Here he reaffirms his opposition to any direct political attempts to equalize the wages received by different grades of workers. The system established in the capitalist economy is to be carried over into the first stage of socialism. But it appears that in the *socialist* economy, no ideas about a future more equitable state of affairs *can exist,* since "Right [justice] can never be higher than the economic structure of society and the cultural development thereby determined." The actual distributive system is represented as the sole source of ideas about existing practice. These ideas are apparently not critical of what presently exists, i.e., they are not formed in reaction against existing practice. Rather, social consciousness, insofar as it is ideational, is shaped by that practice and is in conformity with it. But these accepting or conforming ideas have no practical force, i.e., no power to obstruct future changes in distributive practice that will occur as the new economy develops beyond its beginning phase.

During the pre-socialist phase of revolutionary struggle, ideas that are distinctly moral and that are critical of existing conditions do exist among the workers, but such ideas are by no means also useful or practical. They may cause complications. They will no longer be in evidence when the workers have succeeded in their practical aim, which is to take possession of the means of material production.

---

42. *Ibid.*, p. 75.
43. *Ibid.*, pp. 55-57.

Various material income inequalities will persist for some time in the socialist era, but these will have no *moral* significance. In the period of struggle against capital, before success is achieved, the unity and solidarity of the workers does not depend on this kind of material levelling. So also, when power is attained, the collective unity of working class rule is based on a common sense of equal individual worth that undercuts all differences in occupation, skill, and personal abiltiy. The inequalitarian social economy of capitalism supported false, superficial discriminations and appraisals. The degree of respect given to individuals, and to some extent their feelings of self-worth, depended a good deal on their materially based social class position. Competitive ranking of this kind would disappear in the working class economy, along with the disposition to develop abstract moral ideas that were out of line with practice. All kinds of socially judging and ranking processes relating to the personal moral qualities of individuals seem to go into permanent eclipse. This includes public responses to anti-social or criminal actions. The approach to the social offender is to be rational and practical, but not moralistic. He may have to be restrained, but as an individual he is not being morally judged or deprived of an inalienable human status.

Marx expected that the demise of political capitalism would be accompanied by a cultural revolution in moral attitudes and values. But he does not conceive of socialism as a *culturally* revolutionary program which will also require a significant change in working class cultural mentality or in the general mentality of the people in the advanced capitalist nations. From the very beginning, he had elevated the working class as a world-historical formation whose internal unity, when finally achieved, would conform naturally to the liberationist model of the ultimate classless society, as depicted in his early philosophical writings. In this society there would be no need for functions of moral judgment and moral decision-making. All persons would relate to one another positively and supportively, united by a recognition of their material and spiritual interdependence as individuals, and by an awareness of their common collective dependence on the efficient, rationalized operation of the producing economy.

8

The Relation Of Marx To Hobbes

Marx's socialism was a program for overcoming all forms of social conflict, all forms of social, political and economic anarchy, and all forms of warfare in modern Western civilization. It was to provide a remedy for the "war of all against all," *the bellum omnium contra omnes,* which was introduced as a major concept into modern political philosophy by Thomas Hobbes, in his *Leviathan.*

In this chapter, and in the one that follows, I will focus on the relation of Marx to Hobbes. Hobbes has been used, adapted, partly rejected, partly assimilated, by a good many social and political philosophers. Leo Struass has noted that

> . . . the moral philosophy, not merely of eighteenth century rationalism, but also of Rousseau, Kant, and Hegel, would not have been possible without Hobbes's work (1).

He could have added the name of Marx. Marx's philosophy of communism was the outgrowth of a movement of thought that culminated in the political philosophy of Hegel. Marx turned back in the direction of the original Hobbesian theory in 1843, as soon as he had discarded his own neo-Hegelian idea of the "ethical state." At that time he declared that all forms of the State had to be eliminated. Hobbes had said that the Leviathan State was necessary, but socialism would establish conditions that would make it unnecessary. Communism was to transfer the public power that was presently invested in the political state. It was to restore that power to the rightful sovereigns, the united community of the poeple. This power, when returned to the base out of which it had originated, would be divested of its political, i.e., of its alien character. It would be social, not political. The legal status of political citizenship would be eliminated, in a universal society that had no morally significant political boundaries (2).

---

1. *The Political Philosophy of Hobbes,* 1936, Introduction, p. 1, University of Chicago, 1952.
2. First of two articles on "The Jewish Question" (1843), translated by Easton and Guddat, *op. cit.*

Marx found Hobbes congenial for several reasons. 1) Hobbes was holding a mirror up to nature, i.e., describing the society of capitalism as it really was, while demonstrating at the same time why nothing could be done to remedy its primary evils. 2) Hobbes was a philosophical materialist, who denied the existence of "free will" as this term had been used by Kant and by Hegel in connection with their justification of punitive law. Hobbes had disposed of the question, briefly and finally, when he wrote (*Leviathan,* chapter 21):

> . . . from the use of the word *free will,* no liberty can be inferred of the will, desire, or inclination, but the liberty of the man; which consisteth in this, that he finds no stop, in doing what he has the will, desire, or inclination to do.

Thirdly, Hobbes had denied that persons who were invested with political authority were in any way superior, morally, to those in the governed society. 4) Hobbes had exposed, in his discussion of the bourgeois monetary economy, the fact that labor power was reduced to the status of a commodity, and that the market price which a worker received for his work was not a true measure of the value of the individual, or of his labor. 5) Hobbes had represented the law as being above the level of custom. Law was necessary because local customs and general mores were ineffective politically, and could not secure a condition of internal civil order. Marx expected that the power that was to be restored to the base community of Hobbesian subjects and citizens, the vast majority, would likewise be above the level of custom, and free from the limitations of custom.

In his first essay on "The Jewish Question," he identified "the spirit of civil society" with "the sphere of egoism, of the bellum omnium contra omnes." In later years he came to associate Hobbes's universal war with the Malthusian and Darwinian concept of the "struggle for existence."

In *The German Ideology* (1845-46) he placed Locke and Hobbes in the same category. Both were philosophers of the bourgeois era whose views on society, economy and State were descriptive of the historical conditions of their time:

> The apparent absurdity which transforms all the various interrelations of men into the single relation of utility, an apparently metaphysical abstraction, follows from the fact that in modern civil society all relationships are in practice subordinated to the single abstract relation of money and speculation. This theory made its appearance with Hobbes and Locke, at the time of the first and second English revolutions, the first blows with which the bourgeoisie conquered power for itself. . . (3).

---

3. Volume I, Part III, as translated by Bottomore in *Karl Marx: Selected Writings In Sociology and Social Philosophy, op. cit.,* p. 161.

Years later, in *Capital,* Marx stated again that the atomic condition was an historical actuality, i.e., that it was not a merely metaphysical abstraction. Referring to bourgeois society he wrote

> In the form of society now under consideration, the behavior of men in the social process of production is purely atomic. Hence their relations to each other in production assume a material character independent of their control and conscious individual action (4).

Hobbes had been preoccupied with problems of "civil war," i.e. with internal conflicts that might develop within the political boundaries of each of the separate "Christian Commonwealth" nations. Marx's primary frame of reference was the international world community and economy that was emerging in the present. But in spite of his supra-political universalism, Marx might be called a civil war theorist. The unity of the future world society would be comparable, in important respects, to national forms of unity.

Unlike Hobbes, Marx was concerned chiefly with economic competition and economic anarchy, not with political anarchy. The most important socialist task was to establish rational socialist control over the producing system. The standards of rational management that individual capitalists applied within their own businesses, would be applied universally, when the ownership and management of the industrial process had been transferred to the working class. In *Capital* he wrote that

> The capitalist mode of production, while on the one hand, enforcing economy in each individual business, on the other hand begets, by its anarchical system of competition, the most outrageous squandering of labour-power and of the social means of production, not to mention the creation of a vast number of employments, at present indispensible, but in themselves superfluous (5).

THE NATURAL LIMITATIONS OF POLITICAL POWER

Hobbes's expectations as to what the Leviathan political power could accomplish in natural historical time were definitely on the sober side. State political power could maintain civil peace but could not eliminate international war. Marx expected that the kind of supra-political power that would be obtained through socialism would establish universal peace, even though the moral limitations of *political* power were much as had been described by Hobbes.

---

4. Volume I, chapter 1, pp. 92-93. Since Marx in his university years had concentrated not only on philosophy but also on law and legal philosophy, he had probably read Hobbes at that time. The influence of Hobbes is just as evident in *Capital* as in the early works, but the emphasis is somewhat different in the later writings.

5. Volume I, chapter 17, p. 530.

In an article published in *Vorwartz* (August 1944) Marx objected to the views of French political theorists who had hoped to bring about moral changes in society by using the power of the State:

> The classical period of political thought is the *French Revolution* . . . The principle of politics is *will.* The more one-sided and thus the more perfected *political* thought is, the more it believes in the *omnipotence* of the will, the blinder it is to the *natural* and spiritual *restrictions* on the will, and the more incapable it is of discovering the source of social ills (6).

The state was ". . . based on [i.e., made necessary by] the contradictions between *public* and *private* life, on the contradiction between *general interests* and *particular interests*." It could not "transcend the contradiction" without "transcending itself." It could not change the organization of society: ". . . its power ceases where civil life begins." Because its functions to maintain the existing "organization of society" it also reinforces the social evils which it is powerless to remedy. In order to break through this impasse, it is necessary to abolish both State and the organization of society which makes the state necessary. In countries like Germany and France where the State was especially powerful, thinking about social problems and how to resolve them was especially weak

> The more powerful the state and hence the more *political* a country is, the less it is inclined to seek the basis and grasp the *general* principle of *social* ills in the *principle of the state* itself, in the *existing organization of society* of which the state is the active self-conscious and official expression. *Political* thought is political precisely because it takes place *within* the bounds of politics.

The abolition of the state power would not nullify the natural and spiritual restrictions on the will that had formerly existed both in the civil society and on the political level. To change the organization of society, a new kind of power would be needed:

> In actual history, those theoreticians who regard *power* as the basis of right [law], were in direct contradiction to those who looked on *will* as the basis of right. . . If power is taken as the basis of right, as Hobbes, etc. do, then right, law, etc. are merely the symptoms, the expression of *other* relations upon which the State power rests. The material life of individuals, which by no means depends on their "will," their mode of production and their form of intercourse, which mutually determine each other –

---

6. Article entitled "Critical Notes on 'The King of Prussia' and Social Reform," translated by Easton and Guddat, *op. cit.*

> this is the real basis of the State and remains so at all stages at which division of labour and private property are still necessary, quite independently of the *will* of individuals (7).

Marx expected that the future transformation of the material life would overcome the conflict between public and private ends which Hobbes said the state could not abolish. Under socialism, private anti-social ends would be transformed into social ends. They would be personal, but socially shared and universal. The pursuit of these ends would not threaten the public good or the maintenance of public order, but would rather contribute to their maintenance. Economic life would be so arranged that individuals would not have to choose between public and private aims and interests, since these would coincide.

Hobbes had said that public and private interests could be identical only for individuals who occupied the supreme political office. He preferred a monarchical government to a parliamentary government. The latter was merely an extension of the battleground of the civil society. Particular interests and factions compete against one another in Parliament. Each group tries to promote its particular aims, regardless of national security and well-being. Hobbes said that a monarch ". . . cannot disagree with himself, out of envy or interest, but an assembly may; and that to such a height as to produce a civil war" (8). All persons are naturally inclined to protect and promote their own private interests first when a conflict arises between that interest and the public, national interest. In the case of the monarch, this conflict is eliminated because he can promote his private interests at the same time that he also promotes the public (9).

THE MYTH OF THE SOCIAL COVENANT

Marx disregarded Hobbes's myth of the social covenant. Yet it could be said that he replaced it with a functional equivalent, in his own system, when he elevated the proletarians to a transcendental level and endowed the class with a world-historical mission. A comparison of the two systems brings out the essential differences as well as the similarities.

Hobbes's political philosophy was also, in part, a political theology. The myth of the social covenant does not come across as a wholly secular idea. The theological aspects of Hobbes's political philosophy are often shoved aside, as if they had played no part in determining the content of a more important residue. Leslie Stephen, in his study of Hobbes, noted that Hobbes had managed to find a way of reconciling his cosmological materialism with his theology, arriving at a definition of God which would somehow get

---

7. *The German Ideology,* Volume I, Part III, P. 357.
8. *Leviathan,* chapter 10.
9. *Leviathan,* chapter 19.

around the seemingly insurmountable objections that he himself could have raised:

> It would be superfluous to examine this singular hypothesis in which Hobbes is driven by the desire to reconcile his materialism with his theology. It is enough to remark that his system would clearly be more consistent and intelligible if he simply omitted the theology altogether (10).

This comment applies with equal force to Hobbes's political and moral philosophy. It would be more intelligible and self-consistent if the theological elements could be excised.

The authority of the Leviathan State was said to have been derived from an initial social covenant. This covenant had been formed because the majority of persons who had been living in a pre-political "state of nature" had somehow become convinced that it was to their own private advantage to institute a governing, law-enforcing, fear-inspiring power which could do what they, as separate individuals, could not do. In his myth of the covenant, Hobbes provided a theological sanction for the morality of nationalism. The State need have no concern about the effects of its political and economic policies on peoples outside the home territory.

Originally, according to Hobbes, there had been only one covenantally unified nation, the community of ancient Israel. The Judaic covenant had bound the people in a relation of common, national subordination to the power and authority of God, or to a political and religious authority directly connected with God. In the modern era, however, there was a plurality of nations, each acknowledging Christianity as their religion. The God of Israel was now supra-national and remote, detached from the political world. Instead of one covenantally unified nation there were now a good many. The latter-day national covenants could not establish a privileged, exclusive relation of one particular nation to the universal God.

One of the chief reasons for setting up a Leviathan State was the fear of aggression and violence and of death at the hands of other individuals in the ungoverned condition. It was also necessary to establish a power of military defense to repel external attacks. There was to begin with a common language and a common territory. Within that territory, however, anarchy was so acute that the people could not defend themselves from outside enemies.

In the initiating act of covenant, all the people joined together as "one will." They established "a real unity:"

> The only way to erect such a common power, as may be able to defend them from the invasion of foreigners, and the injuries of one another, and thereby to secure them in such sort, as that by their own industry, and the fruits of the earth, they may nourish themselves and live contentedly; is to confer upon one man, or

10. *Hobbes,* chapter 3, p. 152, by Sir Leslie Stephen, republished by the University of Michigan Press, 1961.

> an assembly of men, that may reduce all their wills, by a plurality of voices to one will. . . and therein to submit their judgment, to his judgment. This is more than consent, or concord, it is a real unity of them all in one and the same person, made by covenant of every man with every man. . .

Warfare against outsiders helped to maintain the internal unity. Aggressive wars could be undertaken by the sovereign in order to add to the economic resources of the commonwealth. All wars, whether aggressive or defensive, were to be regarded by the subjects and citizens as "just wars," when sanctioned by the authority of the sovereign. The unity that developed naturally, among the people of the Leviathan society, in times of war, had to be secured in times of peace by the punitive, coercive, fear-inspiring power of the State:

> . . . Nor is it enough for the security which men desire should last all the time for their life, that they be governed, and directed by one judgment, for a limited time; as in one battle, or one war. For though they obtain a victory by their unanimous endeavor against an enemy; yet afterwards, when either they have no enemy, or he that by one part is held for an enemy, is by another part held for friend, they must needs by the difference of their interest dissolve, and fall again into a war against themselves (11).

Herbert A. Deane has noted that Hobbes's description of humanity in the ungoverned condition of "mere nature" resembles Augustine's concept of libidinal compulsion, by which the natural man is bound and enslaved:

> . . . Hobbes's graphic description of the *bellum omnium contra omnes* comes to mind when Augustine depicts the consequences of the fierce competition for inevitably scarce goods carried on by self-centered men, each of whom is driven by infinite and insatiable desires (12).

Deane notes also the differences between Hobbes and Augustine. Hobbes emphasizes the drive for self-preservation and security, seeing the acquisitive impulse as one of the major means by which this need for security is satisfied. In neither case, however, is there any way of getting beyond the "natural" condition in historical society.

Hobbes developed his own post-Augustinian version of the Christian expectation that natural time would some day come to an end, through supernatural means. The Leviathan state was a "mortal God." At some unpredictable date in the future, the need for political power might be abolished through supernatural intervention. This would mean the end of war in all of its forms. It would be the time of advent, the Second Coming of Christ.

11. *Leviathan,* chapter 17.
12. *The Political and Social Ideas of St. Augustine,* chapter 2, p. 46, Columbia University Press, 1963.

Advent would coincide with the bodily resurrection of the dead and the Day of the Last Judgment. All persons would be judged by a divine authority. Some would live on; others would undergo a swift and final death, without hell and without punishment after death. Those who continued to live would eventually die in a natural way, since no human being could be immortal. Christ would become supreme commander and ruler over all the nations. The various national sovereigns would surrender their authority. People would no longer have children at this final stage of planetary life.

Hobbes had nothing to say about the nature of absolute judgment. But he accepted the Christian belief that all persons, in the final day, will be considered by the supreme Judge only when they had first been divested of their external class and status differences. The final judgment would also disregard the political judgments that had been rendered against persons by the State.

In his condemnation of capitalist society, Marx was closer in some respects to Augustine and to the outlook of the medieval Church than to Hobbes. R. H. Tawney commented, in *Religion and the Rise of Capitalism*

> The medieval theorist condemned as a sin precisely that effort to achieve a continuous and unlimited increase in material wealth which modern societies applaud. . . The true descendant of the doctrines of Aquinas is the labor theory of value. The last of the Schoolmen was Karl Marx (13).

EQUALITY AND PRICE IN THE LABOR MARKET ECONOMY

Marx and Hobbes were equally inclined to discount the moral significance of the external ranking system of economic society. Marx was especially concerned with differences deriving from the unequal possession of money and credit. The pecuniary system in the bourgeois age was exposing to public view the falseness of all economic evaluations of personal worth. There was no "just price" for any kind of human labor. The labor market economy had destroyed the feudal system of caste inequality, together with attitudes regarding the "natural" superiority of the feudal landlord class and the natural inferiority of the under-castes which had prevailed throughout the society, according to Marx's account. In *Capital* he said that the modern concept of human equality could not have been known to Aristotle because "Greek society was founded upon slavery and had, therefore, for its natural basis the inequality of men and their labour-powers." Today, however, the idea of human equality "has already acquired the fixity of a popular prejudice." Such a belief is possible

> . . . only in a society in which the great mass of the produce of labour takes the form of commodities, in which, consequently, the dominant relation between man and man is that of the owners of commodities (14).

13. Chapter 1, p. 39, Harcourt Brace and World, Mentor Book reprint, 1963.
14. Volume I, chapter 1, p. 60.

In bourgeois society, money is the great leveller:

> Just as every qualitative difference between commodities is extinguished in money, so money, on its side, like the radical leveller that it is, does away with all distinctions (15).

In his chapter on "The buying and selling of labour power," Marx said that capital comes into existence in its modern form

> . . . only when the owner of the means of production and subsistence meets in the market with the free labourer selling his labour-power. And this one historical condition comprises a world's history. Capital, therefore, announces from its first appearance a new epoch in the process of social production (16).

In support of this statement, he appended a footnote quoting from Hobbes's *Leviathan,* chapter 10. He cites a truncated version of a longer sentence, putting a period in place of a semicolon:

> The value or worth of a man, is as of all other things his price – that is to say, so much as would be given for the use of his power.

Hobbes had gone on to say

> . . . and therefore is not absolute, but a thing dependent on the need and judgment of another.

Hobbes's language, throughout this entire chapter, entitled "Of Power, Worth, Dignity, Honour and Worthiness" was ambiguous. "Honour" and "dishonour" are labels attached to persons of high or low social standing and power, but apparently they do not refer to traits of inner moral character. On the other hand, these same terms can sometimes be used to refer to moral qualities that individuals possess or acquire, regardless of their external social position. The individual who is not recognized by society as having worth is at a great disadvantage, whatever his personal "worthiness" may be:

> To be conspicuous, that is to say, to be known, for wealth, office, great actions, or any eminent good, is honourable; as a sign of the power for which he is conspicuous. On the contrary, obscurity, is dishonourable.
>
> To be descended from conspicuous parents, is honourable, because they the more easily attain the aids, and friends of their ancestors. On the contrary, to be descended from obscure parentage is dishonourable.

The individual who covets much, who has great ambitions, is more honourable than he who covets little:

15. Volume I, chapter 3, p. 132.
16. Volume I, chapter 6, p. 170.

> Covetousness of great riches, and ambition of great honours, are honourable; as signs of power to obtain them. Covetousness, and ambition, of little gains, or preferments, is dishonourable.

In the paragraph cited by Marx, Hobbes was dealing with the buying and selling of labor power, the capacities and skills of individuals. The "true value" of an individual in this context is said to be determined by the utility of his labor from the point of view of the buyer of labor power. The individual's own favorable estimation of the value or worth of his work, apart from this utility, is of no account:

> An able conductor of soldiers, is of great price in time of war present, or imminent; but in peace not so. A learned and uncorrupt judge, is much worth in time of peace; but not so much in war. And as in other things, so in men, not the seller but the buyer determines the price. For let a man, as most men do, rate themselves at the highest value they can; yet their true value is no more than it is esteemed by others.

An individual has no moral basis for claiming priority over others who are equally well qualified. There is also no moral basis for the external social appraisals that individuals receive from others. These appraisals are the effects produced by the possession of some kind of dominating power:

> Dominion, and victory is honourable; because acquired by power; and servitude, for need, or fear, is dishonourable.

> Good fortune, if lasting, honourable; as a sign of the favour of God. Ill fortune, and losses, dishonourable. Riches are honourable; for they are power. Poverty, dishonourable.

A number of virtues are represented as qualities attached to persons who are in socially dominant, prestigeful positions: "Magnaminity, liberality, hope, courage, confidence, are honourable; for they proceed from the conscience of power. Pusillanimity, parsimony, fear, diffidence, are dishonourable." The emphasis in this chapter is on the importance of external insignia and of social display, as these contribute to social reputation.

Marx expected that power inequalities and external status differentials would disappear in communist society. The monetary economy had already exposed the falseness of these differences. After the commodity pricing system had been abolished, all persons would possess and manifest desirable forms of social power, and the virtues that were associated with such power. The value of all will be appreciated, levelled upward, after the false system of differential social appraisal had been eliminated. There would be no discrepancy between the external public and social esteem that individuals receive, and their true worth or value, which would be *absolute*. It is not to be measured in terms of price, or in terms of any kind of economic or social reward for work performed, or any special quality of personal outstandingness.

THE GENERAL WILL IN THE CAPITALIST STATE

Like Hobbes, Marx was morally centered on problems developing in the "Christian Commonwealth" block of nations. He paid no attention to those aspects of Hobbes's convenantal and legal philosophy that were intended to justify caste distinctions and feudalistic forms of economic, social and political subordination. He did not bother to refute Hobbes's claim that "government by institution" was set up to represent the interests of the nation as a whole. He regarded Hobbes as being primarily a secular political and economic philosopher of the early bourgeois age. Discounting his elaborate myth of the social covenant, it was obvious that he was describing the atomistic condition of bourgeois society, not a "state of nature" existing before the development of the modern legal State. Marx did, however, make use of Hobbes's positivistic, relativistic approach to law and government. The law and justice of the capitalist State was positive law, which served the interests of the capitalist class. The content of that law was determined by its utility to the class. Political policies and political laws expressed the "general will" of the bourgeois class.

The theory of law that he formulated in *The German Ideology* (1845-46) applied to the bourgeois class State. The individuals who constituted that state ruled as a class. They had no need to set up an autocratic sovereign whose judgment was to be placed above the class judgment and class will. They were not as incompetent, nor as irrational, as the subjects and citizens who had to be governed by the Leviathan State. The political bourgeois were morally autonomous, free of the need to submit to any kind of external rule, and free also from the need to regard any interests but their own, except when it was necessary for them to make concessions for the sake of retaining power.

Marx's conception of the future freedom that was to be possessed by individuals in the emancipated society of communism was predicated on his views about the nature of political society, government and law in the modern, post-feudal societies of the advanced capitalist nations. The freedom of communism was to be built on the foundation of the already achieved bourgeois freedoms. To a considerable extent these freedoms were moral and psychological and were descriptive of the self-condition of individuals in the top ruling class circles of the bourgeoisie. Marx had a positive attitude toward some of the character traits exhibited by the "haute bourgeoisie." The individuals in the category exemplify a desirable power of self-confidence, and an ability to reject all forms of external moral, social or traditional authority. They are free from despised traits of humbleness, submissiveness, and readiness to defer to higher social authority. They are subjectively immune from external moral judgments of their political conduct that might be rendered by some transcendental supra-class authority (17).

17. See also chapter 5 in this book, section on "The Germanic Complex in Marx's Social Philosophy"; and chapter 6, section on "The Externalization of Evil in the Historical Process."

The sweeping political generalizations that Marx advanced in *The German Ideology* were ostensibly applicable to all historical, political societies. Marx, however, was basing his remarks on the record of political events which had taken place in the course of the bourgeois revolution. His description of the process by which the bourgeois conquered power has something in common with Hobbes's model of "government by acquisition." Bourgeois government was also nationalistic, helping the people in a formerly feudal cultural territory to progress beyond the limitations of feudal and ecclesiastical rule. The bourgeoisie could not have acquired power in the first place, except by appealing to a broader public which was later excluded from the actual exercise of national power. During the period of active political revolution, individuals leading the revolution regard and represent their own interests and aims as being in harmony with universal common interests and aims:

> The class making a revolution appears, from the very start. . . as the representative of the whole society; it appears as the whole mass of society confronting the one ruling class. It can do this because, to start with, its interest really is more connected with the common interest of all other non-ruling classes, because under pressure of hitherto existing conditions, its interest has not yet been able to develop as the particular interest of a particular class. Its victory, therefore, benefits also many individuals of the other classes which are now winning a dominant position, but only insofar as it now puts these individuals in a position to raise themselves into the ruling class. . . Every new class, therefore, achieves its hegemony only on a broader basis than that of the class ruling previously, whereas the opposition of the non-ruling class against the new ruling class later develops all the more sharply and profoundly (18).

In this discussion, Marx was killing several birds with one stone. He was denying that morally significant ideas and values that were culturally dominant in particular political periods had an "independent existence," i.e., that they had any enduring significance. The "ruling classes" may believe that they are representing certain ideal values, but this is only an illusion of ideology. Because the dominating political and social power of any ruling class could not be maintained in the absence of the economic property base which was the material support of that power, it therefore followed that when the property base was destroyed, the ideas of the class also disappear. Charging that "the German ideologists" had ignored the material basis of political and cultural life, he said that

> If now in considering the course of history we detach the ideas of the ruling class from the ruling class itself and attribute to them an independent existence. . . we can say, for instance, that during

18. Volume I, Part I, pp. 61-62.

> the time the aristocracy was dominant, the concepts of honour, loyalty, etc, were dominant, during the dominance of the bourgeoisie the concepts of freedom, equality, etc. The ruling class itself on the whole imagines this to be so. For each new class which puts itself in the place of the one ruling before it, is compelled, merely in order to carry through its aims, to represent its interest as the common interest of all the members of society, that is, expressed in ideal form; it has to give its ideas the form of universality, and represent them as the only rational, universally valid ones (19).

This kind of falsely abstracted ideality and rationality, which does not correspond to the actualities of social and economic life, is an illusion of appearance:

> This whole semblance, that the rule of a certain class is only the rule of certain ideas, comes to a natural end, of course, as soon as class rule in general ceases to be the form in which society is organized, that is to say, as soon as it is no longer necessary to represent a particular interest as general or the "general interest" as ruling.

Marx emphasized the sharp break between the earlier forms of the State and the bourgeois form:

> By the mere fact that it is a *class* and no longer an *estate,* the bourgeoisie is forced to organise itself no longer locally, but nationally, and to give a general form to its mean average interest. Through the emancipation of private property from the community, the State has become a separate entity, beside and outside of civil society; but it is nothing more than the form of organization which the bourgeois necessarily adopt both for internal and external purposes, for the mutual guarantee of their property and interests. The independence of the State is only found nowaways in those countries where the estates, done away with in the more advanced countries, will have a part to play, and where there exists a mixture; countries, that is to say, in which no one section of the population can achieve dominance over the others. This is the case particularly in Germany. The most perfect example of the modern State in North America. The modern French, English and American writers all express the opinion that the State exists only for the sake of private property, so that this fact has penetrated into the consciousness of the normal man (20).

When the State becomes a separate entity, freed from community control, the power of the State becomes an instrument of the general will of the

19. *Ibid.*
20. *Ibid.*, p. 78.

bourgeois class. This is by no means a "free will." The bourgeois civil law, which ". . . develops simultaneously with private property out of the disintegration of the natural community," is not the result of "general will," because the property relations which the law sanctions were not created by an act of general will, but were historically and naturally developed, part of the system of production relations and conditions that changed and developed in time.

The limited general will concept which Marx applied to the capitalist state did have something in common with earlier general will theories. The class will transcended the anarchy prevailing in the bourgeois civil society beyond the State. Each of the individuals composing the class base of the state was in a psychologically atomic condition. The class as a whole, however, has access to a form of self-interested rationality that is objectified in the general will of the bourgeois State, which is said to be identical with the law of the State. The bourgeois State is a political association. Through this association ". . . individuals who are independent of one another assert themselves and their own will, which on this basis is inevitably egoistical in their mutual relations. . ." (21). Only class-limited aims can be pursued by means of the political will, and the rationality of the class is confined within these limits:

> These actual relations are in no way created by the State power; on the contrary they are the power creating it. The individuals who rule in these conditions, besides having to constitute their power in the form of the *State,* have to give their will, which is determined by these definite conditions, a universal expression as the will of the State, as law – an expression whose content is always determined by the relations of this class, as the civil and criminal law demonstrate in the clearest possible way (22).

Individual diversities of opinion within the class on matters affecting class interest must be overridden by a political consensus embodied in state and law, if the class hegemony is to be maintained:

> Just as the weight of their bodies does not depend on their idealistic will or on their arbitrary decision, so also the fact that they enforce their will in the form of law, and at the same time make it independent of the personal arbitrariness of each individual among them, does not depend on their idealistic will. Their personal rule must at the same time be constituted as average rule. Their personal power is based on conditions of life which they, as ruling individuals, have to maintain against others and, at the same time, maintain that they hold good for all. The expression of this will, which is determined by their common interests, is law (23).

---

21. *The German Ideology,* Volume I, Part III, p. 358.
22. *Ibid.,* p. 357.
23. *Ibid.,* pp. 357–358.

Marx also represented the individuals of the bourgeois class as being restricted in the free expression of their personal inclinations by the need to abide within the limits of the rational class will. They could be disciplined by this ruling will if they failed to observe the most essential regulations. Like the consenting individuals depicted in Hobbes's myth of the social covenant, however, the great majority of the class perceive the need for some kind of rational unifying power. They voluntarily consent to restrict their personal freedom. They recognize the necessity of some kind of "self-denial" which must be enforced by a group power that is not available to a single individual:

> . . . it is precisely because individuals who are independent of one another assert themselves and their own will, which on this [bourgeois, atomistic] basis is inevitably egoistical in their mutual relations, that self-denial is made necessary in law and right, self-denial in the average case which therefore, not *they*, but only the 'egoist in agreement with himself' regard as self-denial (24).

The reference to "the egoist in agreement with himself" is a negative comment on Stirner's anti-political individualism. Stirner had said that all laws, even if they are laws upholding the right of the individual to complete freedom for "self-development, self-activity, self-creation" (25), entail a sacrifice of private independence, which is always threatened by dependence on social, supra-personal power. The individual must undertake a solitary struggle to achieve aims derived from the self alone, rejecting all forms of common action with others, for the sake of common ends. Any dependence on political law is servitude, an abject submission to an external "ruling will":

> States last only so long as there is a *ruling will* and this ruling will is looked upon as tantamount to the own will. . . The State is not thinkable without lordship and servitude (subjection); for the State must will to be the lord of all it embraces, and this will is called 'the will of the State' (26).

Marx denies that the utilization of State and law by the individuals of the bourgeois class entails this kind of feudalistic lordship and bondage relation. The substantial degree of personal power and freedom presently possessed by individuals who constitute the bourgeois ruling clsss can be maintained only through the power of political law, i.e., through the agency of the State. But in the argument he advances against Stirner, Marx had divided the individuals of the ruling class into a rational majority who support the rule of law because they perceive its necessity as a matter of enlightened self-interest, and an irrational, anarchistic minority. The irrational minority is subjected to external restraints, not deriving from their own will and consent, which are imposed by the rational majority of their own class.

24. *Ibid.*, p. 358.
25. *Max Stirner, The Ego and His Own, op. cit.*, p. 134.
26. *Ibid.*, p. 131.

In *The German Ideology* Marx presented his own communist philosophy of freedom in its most radical form. He expected that in communist society, the distinction between the rational majority and the irrational minority would have been eliminated. The external imposition of law upon a recalcitrant minority would therefore no longer be needed. Marx, in his "general will" conception of the bourgeois State, had implied that there was also a certain tension between personal inclination and enlightened class rationality that affected persons in the majority (ruling class) group. These persons had consented for prudential reasons to have certain restraints imposed on their own actions, but they are, nevertheless, restraints. In communist society, on the other hand, there will be no such inner duality, i.e., "self-denial" will not have to be rationally self-imposed by voluntary assent to the decisions and laws of public, social, legal power in the future classless era. The social individuals will have acquired access to another kind of social power which will make the rational restrictions of law unnecessary. There will be no kind of political rationality and political will in the universal society. Marx dropped all references to political will and to "general will" when he projected the conditions of the future. Even in the first political class phase of socialism, the period of the proletarian dictatorship, the unity of the working class need not be reinforced by the will that is embodied in law.

THE RELATION OF LAW TO CUSTOM

The theory of law that Marx developed in *The German Ideology* in reference to the capitalist State, was historically related to Hobbes's concept of positive law. In both systems, the sovereign power is set above the level of custom, precedent and tradition. In the *Leviathan,* the rationality of the sovereign is contrasted with the irrationality and also the variability and diversity of custom. Hobbes wrote, in *Leviathan,* chapter 11:

> Ignorance of the causes, and original constitution of right, equity, law, and justice, disposeth a man to make custom and example the rule of his actions; in such a manner, as to think that unjust which it hath been the custom to punish; and that just, of the impunity and approbation of which they can produce an example, or, as the lawyers which only use this false measure of justice barbarously call it, a precedent. . .

Hobbes argued that in any case individuals are not effectively restrained by the power of custom. They are ready to overturn custom when it profits them to do so, and equally ready to justify an action by reference to custom or precedent, if this is to their advantage. They

> . . . appeal from custom to reason, and from reason to custom as it serves their turn; receding from custom when their interest requires it, and setting themselves against reason, as oft as reason

> is against them: which is the cause that the doctrine of right and wrong, is perpetually disputed, both by the pen and the sword.

There is nothing to indicate whether or to what extent the Sovereign authority is absorbing and then externally enforcing the prevailing mores, including concepts of right and wrong, good and evil, justice and injustice, that are current in the general society or in decisive sections thereof. The Sovereign is placed at such a distance from the society which he governs, in such a position of autonomous power, as to suggest that Hobbes is giving no weight at all to public opinion or to the prevailing mores. The question of how much the Sovereign power is itself psychologically influenced by established customs or by the prevailing and changing content of the mores seems not to arise. The presumption is that the sovereign will be able to counteract at least some of the most dangerous irrationalities in the base society.

In Marx's general will theory of capitalist sovereignty and law, the individuals who make use of the power of law to implement their common class interests have already been emancipated from the rule of custom. The power of custom may be useful to them, helping them to consolidate and maintain their rule over the economic underclass, the proletariat. But it appears that they themselves are not limited morally by general societal mores, in any way that would impede the pursuit of their class aims.

In the first volume of *Capital,* when Marx was describing the way in which the rural population of England had been forcibly driven off the land and compelled to become wage earners, deprived of the security they had had under the feudal system, he had said that

> The advance of capitalist production develops a working-class which by education, tradition, habit, looks upon the conditions of that mode of production as self-evident laws of Nature. The organization of the capitalist process of production, once fully developed, breaks down all resistance. . . (27).

Marx seems here to be referring to the sporadic, disorganized, largely personal resistance of individuals who had not yet been fully broken to bridle. This initial resistance is destroyed. But it is superseded by another resistance movement which develops after the workers have been subjected to the socializing discipline of capitalist industry and after they have acquired collective self-confidence, recognizing their own ability to master and to manage the social process of production, and recognizing also that the capitalist class is performing no essential functions that could not be carried out as well or better by the united working class.

At first, before this self-confidence developed, the workers had become habituated to the capitalist system, which had enslaved them culturally as well as economically. He had written, in *The German Ideology:* "The ideas

27. Chapter 28, p. 737.

of the ruling class are in every epoch the ruling ideas: i.e., the class which is the ruling *material* force of society, is at the same time its ruling *intellectual* force" (20).

The power of class ideology and of general forms of habituation to the routines of capitalism is offset when the industrial workers develop not only an awareness of their own power, but also an insight into the nature of the class ideology which has been used to uphold the system. They are then able to break away. They thereby achieve the degree of subjective freedom from custom and tradition that their antagonists, the political bourgeoisie, had had to begin with. When the workers come to power, ideology, which had supported the class power of the bourgeoisie, will no longer be needed. It will disappear, along with the class restricted political general will.

What will be re-established, in a new way, in the post-capitalist economy, is a desirable kind of stability, security and order which Marx had associated, in the last volume of *Capital,* with the power of custom and tradition. He had done so in the context of discussion of pre-capitalist agricultural economies, in a section on "the genesis of capitalist ground-rent." Ground-rent, in its primitive, pre-capitalist form was labor expended by the non-owner, the serf, in producing for the landlord. The amount of labor to be given up in this way to the property owner was regulated by tradition. The serfs were sometimes able to accumulate independent property and wealth under these custom-protected conditions. They were not, in any case, subjected to the same degree of unregulated exploitation that was the lot of the proletarians in the post-feudal, commercial society:

> . . . it is evident that tradition must play a dominant role in the primitive and undeveloped circumstances on which these social production relations and the corresponding mode of production are based. It is furthermore clear that here as always it is in the interest of the ruling section of society to sanction the existing order as law and to legally establish its limits given through usage and tradition. Apart from all else, this, by the way, comes about of itself as soon as the constant reproduction of the basis of the existing order and its fundamental relations assumes a regulated and orderly form in the course of time. Any such regulation and order are themselves indispensable elements in any mode of production, if it is to assume social stability and independence from mere change and arbitrariness. Under backward conditions of the production process as well as the corresponding social relations, it achieves this form by mere repetition of their very reproduction. If this has continued on for some time, it entrenches itself as custom and tradition and is finally sanctioned as an explicit law (29).

---

28. Volume I, Part I, p. 60. See the discussion of this passage in chapter 6 of this book, pp. 125–126.

The generalization given here about the nature of ruling class legalism is less simplistic than the one Marx had given earlier in *The German Ideology,* but it is not a radical departure from the earlier formulation. He is still attributing to individuals in the dominant classes a politically rationalistic class-egoistic psychology. They are able to make use of tradition, which seems always to work in their favor, and they are presumably not handicapped by it. It seems, however, that law might also include a traditional content that has developed in a natural process of economic and social evolution, even in capitalist society. What is most evident in the passage just cited, is that Marx associates the power of law with an indispensable kind of regulation and order. The fact that law is codified and administered by a dominant class in its own interest does not detract from its stabilizing value, which derives partly from its continuity with tradition and custom. The freedom that is to be attained in the future society of communism will be freedom from legalized traditions, and also from the supra-legal power of customs carried over from the past into the present.

29. Chapter 47, p. 793.

9

Scarcity And Necessity: The Technological Leviathan

Marx's thesis that the world society of classless communism could not be realized until material scarcity had been abolished is a major aspect of his philosophy of the future. He never abandoned his emphasis on the importance on material abundance. In *The Critique of the Gotha Programme* (1975) he said that the evolution of socialism from its early stages to the fully developed period of classless communism would require an expansion of material production and of labor productivity beyond the level that existed at the beginning of the socialist era:

> In a higher phase of communist society, after the enslaving subordination of individuals under division of labour, and therewith also the antithesis between mental and physical labour, has vanished; after labour, from a mere means of life, has itself become the prime necessity of life; after the productive forces have also increased with the all-round development of the individual, and all the springs of cooperative wealth flow more abundantly – only then can the narrow horizon of bourgeois right be fully left behind and society inscribe on its banners: from each according to his ability, to each according to his needs!

This chapter will focus chiefly on Marx's early writings, those in which the personal, subjective elements in his freedom philosophy were most in evidence. He was then utilizing the work of Hobbes to demonstrate the non-necessity of any form of ego-restrictive, inhibiting social authority in the future post-capitalist age. The emphasis on the need for abundance appears in its most radical form in the earlier works.

THE LOGICAL POSSIBILITY OF CIVILIZATIONAL COLLAPSE

In *The German Ideology* Marx declared that neither State, law, nor the bourgeois private property economy, could be abolished safely until an adequate replacement had become available. The communist revolutionaries must not call prematurely for the abolition of the capitalist state and the system of private property. An alternative control system must first have developed:

> . . . so long as the productive forces are still insufficiently developed to make competition superfluous, and therefore would give rise to competition over and over again, for so long the classes which are ruled would be wanting the impossible if they had the "will" to abolish competition and with it the State and the law (1).

Marx gives his readers the impression that a future society of communism might collapse like a house of cards unless a condition of economic want were not continuously forestalled by the production of sufficient material supplies. The spectre of scarcity, as a logical possibility, seems to be haunting the society of the future, threatening it with instant dissolution:

> . . . this development of productive forces (which itself implies the actual empirical existence of men in their *world-historical* instead of local, being) is absolutely necessary as a practical premise; firstly for the reason that without it only *want* is made general, and with want the struggle for necessities and all the old filthy business would necessarily be reproduced. . . (2).

A few pages earlier, he had listed a number of conditions that would have to co-exist along with the high development of the productive forces if communism were to achieve its aims. Prior to the development of capitalism

> . . . the abolition of private property was impossible for the simple reason that the material conditions governing it were not present. The setting-up of a communal domestic economy presupposes the development of machinery, of the use of natural forces and of many other productive forces – e.g., of water-supplies, of gas-lighting, steam-heating, etc., the removal of the antagonism of town and country. Without these conditions a communal economy would not in itself form a new productive force; lacking any material basis and resting on a purely theoretical foundation, it would be a mere freak and would end in nothing more than a monastic economy. . . (3).

The reader is left to wonder what would happen to this future non-monastic way of life if the new economy were to encounter a serious material shortage, or have to operate in a contracting economic situation. The economy is to be a means for sharing wealth, not a means for sharing common poverty and hardship. The inhabitants of the future society are not expected

1. Volume I, Part III, p. 358.
2. Volume I, Part I, p. 46.
3. Volume I, Part I, p. 40n.

to cope with problems of decreasing rather than increasing abundance. The possibility of economic contraction on a socialist economic foundation is excluded both in the earlier and later writings. Marx never again referred, in a direct way, to the theoretical possibility of civilizational collapse. But he established a moral dependency of the society on the material power of social production which was analogous to the dependency of Hobbes's political citizens and subjects on the Leviathan State, the State instituted through the social covenant. The Hobbesian myth was being supplanted by another kind of rationalistic construction. The "abstract" individuals who are to become collectively united and sovereign in the classless age combine together for the purpose of appropriating and gaining control over the productive forces. The appropriating association becomes thereafter radically dependent on the operation of these forces, just as the citizens of the Leviathan convenantal state, once having installed the Sovereign, are reduced to a condition of radical political dependence.

In Hobbes's conception of the Leviathan State, the dependency of the subjects on that state, once it has been instituted, is so great that there can be no temporary lapse of a personal kind of authoritarian continuity, such as might arise when the office of state has been left vacant by the death of an incumbent sovereign. The citizens cannot be relied upon to elect a human replacement and to keep the functions of government going. In *Leviathan,* chapter 10, Hobbes wrote that

> . . . the death of him that have the sovereign power in propriety leaves the multitude without any sovereign at all; that is, without any representative in whom they should be united, and capable of doing any one action at all; and therefore they are incapable of election of any new monarch.

It appears that there has been some kind of regression, a loss of rational capacity that had been present at the beginning, at the time when the multitude of future subjects had recognized the need for a political authority and had combined voluntarily to install that authority.

According to Hobbes, individuals in modern political societies are elevated above a frightful condition of primitive savagery, a way of life in which "every man is an enemy to every man." The outbreak of civil war in post-barbaric political societies could bring on a relapse into the primitive condition:

> . . . it may be perceived what manner of life there would be where there were no common power to fear, by the manner of life, to which men that have formerly lived under a peaceful government, use to degenerate into, in a civil war (4).

In Marx's system, there is a possible relapse into a vaguely conceived competitive and anarchical condition below the level of civilization attained

4. *Leviathan,* chapter 13.

in capitalist society. But once the necessary power has been appropriated, previous "natural limitations" can be set aside. In the appropriating act the individuals regain powers of which they had been deprived in the private property economy:

> . . . standing over against these productive forces, we have the majority of the individuals from whom these forces have been wrested away, and who, robbed thus of all real life-content, have become abstract indiviudals, but who are, however, only by this fact put into a position to enter into a relation with one another *as individuals*. . . in the appropriation by the proletarians, a mass of instruments of production must be made subject to each individual, and property to all. . .
>
> Only at this stage does self-activity coincide with material life, which corresponds to the development of individuals into complete individuals and the casting-off of all natural limitations. . . With the appropriation of the total productive forces through the united individuals, private property comes to an end (5).

The emancipation of the productive forces from the limitations of the capitalist economy is also the emancipation of the individual from the restrictions imposed by various specialized roles which Marx associated with the division of labor. The division of labor had been imposed by historical necessity. All formerly unavoidable unfree forms of labor will be eliminated in community society (6). In *The German Ideology* Marx was referring to society as it would operate after the division of labor had been left behind. In this context he used the term "society" in two ways. It was a voluntary association of "abstract" individuals. It was also an impersonal regulating power which operates in an automatic way to free these individuals from their former limiting situations and from the need to engaged forms of work that are imposed by necessity:

> . . . as soon as the distribution of labour comes into being, each man has a particular, exclusive sphere of activity, which is forced upon him and from which he cannot escape. . . while in communist society, where nobody has one exclusive sphere of activity but each can become accomplished in any branch he wishes, society regulates the general production and thus makes it possible for me to do one thing today and another tomorrow, to hunt in the morning, fish in the afternoon, rear cattle in the evening, criticize after dinner, just as I have a mind, without ever becoming hunter, fisherman, shepherd or critic (7).

5. Volume I, Part I, pp. 82-84.
6. The modification of his early freedom philosophy introduced by Marx in his later writings will be discussed in chapter 11 on "The Necessity of Labor in Communist Society."
7. *The German Ideology, op. cit.* p. 44.

Marx had said that competition would become superfluous only when the productive forces had been sufficiently developed. Once their development has reached an optimal point, State and law can be eliminated. This optimum coincides with the abolition of the division of labor and the disappearance of those forms of necessary labor needed in earlier, pre-communist societies:

> . . . the proletarians, if they are to assert themselves as individuals, will have to abolish the very condition of their existence hitherto (which has, moreover, been that of all society up to the present), namely, labour. Thus they find themselves directly opposed to the form in which, hitherto, the individuals, of which society consists, have given themselves collective expression, that is, the State. In order, therefore, to assert themselves as individuals, they must overthrow the State (8).

THE ADAPTATION OF HOBBES'S THEORY OF COMPETITION

In his early writings, Marx had been making use of Hobbes to demonstrate the non-necessity of political law and government in a future society of absolute material abundance. Marx did not refer to "absolute abundance." I am using the phrase to mean that condition of freedom from material want which is sufficient to maintain the future classless society in a condition of conflict-free unity, and to avoid the possibility of civilizational and rational regression.

Marx appears to have accepted certain of the arguments that Hobbes had used to demonstrate the necessity of laws relating to the establishment of private property rights. These rights were decreed by the State. They did not exist in the "state of nature." Their enactment and enforcement was one of the most important functions of the Leviathan State. The rights of private property were basic to the maintenance of civilized order in the internal life of each of the Christian Commonwealth nations.

It is possible to infer from Hobbes's arguments in support of these rights, that an absolute sufficiency of material supply would eliminate the need for such laws. That Marx did indeed make this inference is demonstrated by the nature of his social and economic logic, as given in the economic and political essays of 1844 as well as in *The German Ideology.*

In chapter 24 of *Leviathan,* entitled "Of the Nutrition and Procreation of a Commonwealth," Hobbes gives the impression that the sovereign State in some way gathers up the total wealth of the nation, derived from resources of land and sea, and then distributes it to the people of the nation. But the sovereign does not really distribute in this way. Hobbes recognized that the State legalizes the presently existing *status quo,* whatever that may be.

8. *Ibid.,* p. 95.

In Hobbes's political economics, private economic activities were the chief means for increasing national wealth. One of the important functions of the state was to establish a uniform currency and standard of exchange. Money was "the blood of the commonwealth." By circulating within the nation, and also in transactions between nations, money ". . . nourisheth by the way every member of the body of man."

Propriety, i.e., the principle and power of governmental restraint, was identified with laws protecting individual property owners from the violent encroachments of other individuals, now deprived, who feel equally entitled – in a human sense – to the benefits derived from possession. Hobbes stressed the benefits to all, not the economic deprivation of some or of many, which result from the legal protection of private property rights:

> The distribution of the materials of this nourishment, is the constitution of *mine,* and *thine* and *his:* that is to say in one word *propriety:* and belongeth in all kinds of commonwealth to the sovereign power. For where there is no commonwealth there is, as has already been shown, a perpetual war of every man against his neighbour, and therefore everything is his that getteth it, and keepeth it by force; which is neither *propriety,* nor *community,* but *uncertainty* . . .

Pre-political "natural rights" of individuals living in a state of nature include the right to appropriate the property of others by force. This right must be surrendered on entering into the social covenant. Henceforward, property transfers are to take place in the internal life of the nation by legal and peaceful means, by buying and selling, not by force. In particular, industrial and commercial wealth produced by individual work effort is to be protected. People are to have a legal right to retain what they have worked for, and to be safeguarded from economic aggressions by others.

Material "scarcity" seems to be the primary cause of those economic aggressions that must be proscribed and penalized by the power of the State, which protects the security of those who have some property to defend. But it was not material scarcity as such, but scarcity relative to the natural sense of human equality and equal natural right that had been responsible for a good deal of the violence and insecurity of the ungoverned condition. In chapter 13 of *Leviathan* Hobbes wrote that

> Nature hath made men so equal in faculties of body and mind; as that. . . when all is reckoned together the difference between man and man is not so considerable as that one man can thereupon claim to himself any benefit to which another may not pretend, as well as he. . .

Natural equality creates an "equality of hope" in regard to the secular goods of this world:

> From this equality of ability, ariseth equality of hope in the attainment of our ends. And therefore if any two persons desire the same thing, which nevertheless they cannot both enjoy, they become enemies, and in the way to their end, which is principally their own conservation, and sometimes their delectation only, endeavor to destroy, or subdue one another.

According to this account, relations of caste inequality that existed in the feudal system in England had developed out of an earlier, more natural equalitarian condition. Hobbes had defended the existing feudal system and the formalized inequalities of power and of status that divided individuals from one another in that society. Nevertheless he had been, as Marx perceived, primarily a philosopher of the early bourgeois age of commercial and industrial expansion. Post-feudal forms of wealth and property were becoming increasingly important. Sentiments of "natural equality" among the expanding middle classes contradicted and partly undermined attitudes fostered by the feudal system. Once the feudal relations had been completely undermined, there was nothing to prevent all persons from becoming psychologically and morally a part of the competitive open class system. The new economy, however, could not provide equal satisfactions and equal opportunities for all.

In his theory of natural equalitarian competition Hobbes stressed the inherently social nature of some of the "passions and appetites" that were generally more powerful than reason. The desire for honor and glory was emphasized and tied closely to the economic system. Glory means special personal distinction. Wealth brought power and honor and was desired for these reasons as well as for the material amenities it made possible. People were by no means all alike in what they wanted, and some were more competitive and acquisitive than others. But all desired security, and all would like to "live well" in a material sense as far as they can. The composite situation was summed up by Hobbes in such a way as to suggest that modern civilization is consumed with restlessness and driven by the need to expand:

> So that in the first place, I put for a general inclination of all mankind, a perpetual and restless desire of power after power, that ceaseth only in death. And the cause of this, is not always that a man hopes for a more intensive delight, than he has already attained to; or that he cannot be content with a moderate power; but because he cannot assure the power and means to live well, which he hath present, without the acquisition of more. And from hence it is, that kings, whose power is greatest, turn their endeavors to the assuring of it at home by laws, or abroad by wars; and when that is done, there succeedeth a new desire: in some, of fame from new conquest; in others, of ease and sensual pleasure; in others, of admiration, or being flattered for excellence in some art, or other ability of the mind (9).

9. *Leviathan,* chapter 11.

Marx's society of communism was to be in a condition of status and power equality. The "equality of hope" to which Hobbes had referred would have been transformed into an equality of fulfillment. Marx associated the bourgeois revolution with the rise of equalitarian sentiments and demands for the destruction of caste privilege. The individuals who united politically in a struggle against feudal privilege were on their way up. They had refused to be impressed by the claims of the aristocracy. In the months during which he was making the transition to communism. Marx had begun by identifying the working class movement as an extension of the bourgeois revolution. In October 1843 he wrote and published an article in the *Rheinische Zeitung* of which he was editor. He cited a passage from a speech delivered by a radical French scientist at a scientific congress which had just been held in Strasburg. The speaker had said that

> The position of the middle estate today resembles that of the nobility in 1789; at that time, the middle estate claimed for itself the privileges of the nobility and obtained them; today the estate that owns nothing demands to share in the wealth of the middle classes, which are now at the helm.

A conservative critic had accused the *Rheinische Zeitung* of communistic leanings because it had publicized this address. Marx replied, in a subsequent article, that the statement in question was simply a reporting of the facts:

> That the estate that today possesses nothing [the proletariat] *demands* to share in the wealth of the middle classes is a fact which, without the talk at Strasburg, and in spite of Augsburg's silence, is obvious to everyone in Manchester, Paris and Lyons (10).

He soon broke with this interpretation of proletarian aspirations. He labelled it "crude communism" in his essay on "Private Property and Communisn" (1844), where he was referring to stages in the development of *the idea* of communism. The demand to share in already existing material wealth would result in regression below the bourgeois level, not in advance, since it was not aimed at appropriating the means of production and the resources of culture and civilization:

> How little this overcoming of private property is an actual appropriation is shown precisely by the abstract negation of the entire world of culture and civilization, the reversion to the *unnatural* simplicity of the *poor* and wantless man who has not gone beyond private property, has not yet even achieved it (11).

10. *Marx and Engels Collected Works,* Volume I. Oscar Berland, in an article on "Radical Chains: The Marxian Concept of the Proletarian Mission," has called attention to this interchange. (*Studies on the Left,* Volume VI, Sept.-Oct., 1966.)

11. Translated by Easton and Guddat, *op. cit.*

Marx is here accepting Hobbes's premise that during the time of scarcity, "private property" is essential to the maintenance and advancement of civilization.

An intermediate stage in the development of the idea was free of the defects of the crude first stage. It included an awareness that an ultimate stage which would eventually be reached, but also the necessity of a preceding transitional stage, which may be

> . . . (a) still of a political nature, democratic or despotic; (b) with the overcoming of the state, but still incomplete and influenced by private property, that is, by the alienation of man. In both forms communism already knows itself as the redintegration or return of man to himself, as the overcoming of human self-alienation. . .

When the "return to self" has been accomplished, possessiveness, greed, and envy are to disappear. There will also be no need for government or for any kind of restricting, prohibiting and censoring authority. Hobbes had said that numerous individuals were competing for a limited supply of material and social assets. The State had therefore to establish and enforce private ego-claims to various forms of acquired personal property. Economic inequality was unavoidable, but at least the state could curb economically motivated acts of aggression by preventing individuals from taking what they wanted by force from other persons. In Marx's post-alienated society of absolute plentitude, the condition which he called "ultimate communism," there will be no incentives to this kind of aggression and violence. There will be no need for a social authority with the function of establishing "propriety" in the Hobbesian sense, i.e., of establishing distinctions between what is "mine," "thine," and "his." In the ultimate society, these distinctions will no longer exist. There can be no encroachments on private property rights because there will be no need for such rights. Marx describes a situation in which each person will have a direct, socially unmediated access to an unlimited source of material supply. All persons draw on this common source. No matter how much any one takes, there is still plenty left over. Material goods are consumed by individuals but are not retained for any length of time as personal property over which the individual might establish an ego-claim, a right to hoard, or to reserve the use of the product or consumable object for a later time. In such a case, another person might want to appropriate and to use immediately what is being retained and saved by the first party. There will be no public agency with functions of saving, withholding, and setting aside for future use. There will be no process or power that might mediate between the single individual and his free appropriation of whatever he might need or want. Such need satisfying activities will not have to be curbed by a public agency on the grounds that the supply might be exhausted at a given current level of consumption. Nature constitutes the open, inexhaustible reserve. There need be no other socially maintained reserve. The only mediating power between the individual as a dynamic, self-affirmative object-appropriating center of needs and wants and the unlimited resources of Nature is the social technology. This appears to operate automatically, with no need for a personal labor input to keep it going (12).

The elimination of labor eliminates the need for any kind of economic exchange. That is, individuals do not have to receive from a public consumption fund a certain allocation of material goods in exchange for a contribution of working time. There will likewise be no material trade exchanges among individuals. People will associate with others for enjoyment, companionship, and the like. The emphasis is on consuming, utilizing, enjoying, experiencing. There will be no need for a science of political economy, which is a science of asceticism, i.e., of scarcity:

> This political economy – despite its wordly and voluptuous appearance – is a true moral science, the most moral of all the sciences. Self-renunciation, the renunciation of life and of all human needs, is its principal thesis (13).

Exchanges in which an individual has to give up something in order to get something else he wants and does not have are in essence monetary exchanges. In the alienated society of private property, lack of money stands between the individual and the realization of his needs and powers:

> The difference between effective demand based on money and ineffective demand based on my need, my passion, my wish, etc., is the difference between *being* and *thinking*, between the idea which merely *exists* within me and the idea which exists as a *real object* outside of me (14).

When private property is abolished, there will be no obstacle – temporal, social, or moral – to impede the immediate translation of a merely subjective, and ineffective, wish, passion, or need into an objectively experienced and possessed actuality. In bourgeois society, socially produced objects desired by an individual can be obtained by him legally, without force, only if something else is given in exchange. In this legal exchange transaction the individual alienates a part of himself. He ought not to have to alienate, i.e., to give up anything at all. Each of the produced material objects is part of the individual's own universal nature. He can therefore claim them as his own, while at the same time not denying the equal claim of others:

> Apart from the situation of force, what causes me to externalize [alienate] *my* property to another person? Economics answers correctly: *need* and *want*. The other person is also a property

12. I am giving here an interpretation of the content of the 1844 manuscripts, cosmological essays of a highly abstract nature, as indicated in Chapter 2 in this book.

13. *Collected Works of Marx and Engels,* Volume III, Economic and Philosophic manuscripts of 1844, essay on "Human Requirements and Division of Labour under the Rule of Private Property."

14. *Op. cit.,* "The Power of Money in Bourgeois Society."

> owner, but of *another* object which I lack and which I neither can nor want to be without, an object which to me seems to be something *needed* for the redintegration of my existence and the realization of my nature. . . For the need of an object is the most evident and irrefutable proof that the object belongs to *my* nature and that the existence of the object for me and its property are the property appropriate to my essence (15).

The needs and wants of "my nature" are expressions of my "generic nature," my humanness as a needing and wanting being, which is social, while the objects desired are also social, produced by "generic activity." This does not mean that I and other persons have precisely identical wants, but it means that all such wants are equally valid and will be equally fulfilled in communist society. Desired objects cannot become "my property" in such a way that they do not also belong to all other persons who desire them in the society of absolute abundance.

The evil of egoistic greed, the desire to acquire possession, for oneself, of something which another must do without, will disappear. There can be no conflict between the desire to keep for oneself and the impulse to respond to the need (or demand) of another by sharing or giving away what is possessed by the self, i.e., by alienating property which is presently mine but not also that of another. Nor can a moral tension arise in connection with a desire to cut oneself a larger than average portion of a total communal pie, leaving less for the rest. The amount available on the communal level will expand in proportion as individual needs expand.

In the 1844 essays, the society of communism was conceived as being beyond forms of competition that could not be classed as merely economic. Both Hobbes and Marx had stressed the importance of economic competition, but Hobbes had referred also to competition for social assets that were often the by-products of superiority of economic position and power. Economic goods, according to Hobbes, are sought after quite justifiably, for their own sake. Poverty as such is undesirable. But there is also an inequality in the distribution of supra-economic, social assets. Superior status and esteem in the eyes of the world, the possession of forms of personal honor and distinction not available to others, is an important aspect of the general scarcity situation. These social assets are by definition always in short supply, in the competitive society. They are available to some only because others are excluded. No purely economic remedy, no sufficiency of material goods, could eliminate those forms of social competition that were not just a competition for economic property.

Marx seemed to be reducing Hobbes's theory of competition to purely economic dimensions when he placed such a major emphasis on the appropriation of the forces of production by the great mass of individuals presently

---

15. Excerpts from notes on the economics of James Mill (1844), from section on "Money and Alienated Man," translated by Easton and Guddat, *op. cit.*

excluded from power. But communism was to provide an absolute sufficiency of supra-material goods. In the post-competitive society, individuals who have equal access to an unlimited material abundance will also have equal access to a fully adequate human status. Their own sense of personal worth will be derived from their membership in a transcendental equalitarian society. The economy of abundance will underwrite the personal psychological and moral security of every one who participates fully in the life of that society.

THE NECESSITY OF ECONOMIC EXPANSION

Marx conceived of a single universal society and economy, inclusive of all nations. The elimination of the need for the defense of personal private property in land and in movable goods against encroachments by other persons who are either propertyless, or desire to acquire more than they have at present, will be, at the same time, the elimination of the need for national political boundary defenses against external aggression. In the nationally based Leviathan economy of Hobbes, however, there is no possibility that national territorial aggression can be averted. Each national economy is under pressure to expand. While wars are needed to consolidate internal unity under the military command of the sovereign, they are also needed for economic reasons. Some of the competitive pressures that fragment the nation internally can be alleviated on the collective economic level. While the aggressiveness of individuals with respect to their fellow citizens was to be kept in check, the economic acquisitiveness of the citizens, and their desire for material improvement and increased security, becomes a contributing cause of aggressive war. The economic gains secured at the collective level accrue to the entire Commonwealth. An increase in the national wealth, however unequally divided that wealth may be, still benefits all of the subjects. By no means all of the economic efforts to be undertaken by the Sovereign lead to war. Peaceful trade with other nations was to be encouraged. But the possibility of war always remains. The economic policies of the Sovereign must be flexible, so as not to frustrate the economic ambitions of the citizens. In spite of the great emphasis Hobbes gave to the fear-inspiring punitive power of the state, that political power depended to a large extent on voluntary support. While the Leviathan state was called "a great machine," it was also a corporate entity. Economic commodities are called "the nutrition of the commonwealth," Hobbes declared, in *Leviathan,* chapter 24:

> *The nourishment of a commonwealth consisteth in the commodities of sea and land.* The NUTRITION of a commonwealth consisteth in the *plenty,* and *distribution of materials* conducing to life; in *concoction* or *preparation;* and, when concocted, in the *conveyance* of it, by convenient conduits, to the public use.

The nutritive materials are partly native and partly foreign:

> And because there is no territory under the dominion of one commonwealth, except it be of very vast extent, that produceth all things needful for the maintenance, and the motion of the whole body; and few that produce not some thing more than necessary; the superfluous commodities to be had within become no more superfluous, but supply those wants at home, by the importation of that which may be had abroad, either by exchange, or just war, or labour. For a man's labour also, is a commodity exchangeable for benefits, as well as any other thing. . .

In this same chapter Hobbes also declared that "the public is not to be dieted." In his "natural capacity" as a private person, the sovereign may wish to set aside certain national resources for his own use, but because of his public function he is unable to do this if he is to retain power. The internal reserves must be opened up, if necessary, to those citizens who want to use them. Otherwise they might act to overturn the authority of the state which denies them this access. As far as possible, the state must serve, not frustrate, the economic aims of the private citizens.

If, for some reason – usually on account of poor management by the sovereign – the material nutriment available to the public should decline, the pressure on publicly owned resources of land will be intensified:

> *The public is not to be dieted*. . . The nature of man being what it is, the setting forth of the public land, or of any certain revenue for the commonwealth, is vain, and tendeth to the dissolution of government, and to the condition of mere nature, and war, as ever the sovereign power falleth into the hands of a monarch, or an assembly, that are either too negligent of money, or too hazardous in the engaging the public stock, into a long and costly war. Commonwealths can endure no diet; for seeing their expense is not limited by their own appetite, but by external accidents, and the appetites of their neighbours, the public riches cannot be limited by other limits than those which the emergent occasions shall require.

In Marx's philosophy, the elimination of material scarcity and of inter-individual competition for limited supplies is at the same time the elimination of all pressure again internal territorial resources. The sovereign – in this case the producing system instituted by the proletarians at the beginning – functions flawlessly, subject to none of the human failings which the sovereign described by Hobbes is all too likely to possess. All the resources of the earth will of course be internal. There will be no "appetites" of neighboring countries to place limits on internal expansion. Nor will nature itself become such a limit. It appears, however, that the future public, like the public of Hobbes, is one that cannot be dieted. There is a pressure for economic expansion that nothing can counteract. The bourgeois class state has been the guardian of a class monopoly. Needed productive resources in capital and in land were being withheld from public use. The elimination of the class monopoly will open up these reserves. The economy from that time on will expand as much as needed. The pressure of increased demand will never outrun the supply. Scarcity will never recur, as long as the productive process functions as it should.

Although Marx's views with regard to the post-capitalist economy were modified in his later works, he always stressed the importance of economic expansion on the socialist foundation, pointing out that the defeat of capitalism would eliminate those causes of modern poverty that were due to the nature of the economic system. In Volume III of *Capital* he wrote that

> . . . the consuming power of the workers is limited partly by the law of wages, partly by the fact that they are used only as long as they can be profitably employed by the capitalist class. The ultimate reason for all real crises always remains the poverty and restricted consumption of the masses as opposed to the drive of capitalist production to develop the productive forces as though only the absolute consuming power of society constituted their limit (16).

The elimination of the poverty, the restricted consumption, of the masses establishes an expanding economy which resembles the middle class economy described by Hegel in *The Philosophy of Right.* Hegel had written

> An animal's needs and its ways and means of satisfying them are both alike restricted in scope. Though man is subject to this restriction too, yet at the same time he evinces his transcendence of it and his universality, first by the multiplication of needs and the means of satisfying them. . . at the standpoint of needs what we have before us is the composite idea which we call *man.* Thus this is the first time, and indeed properly the only time, to speak of *man* in this sense. . . The multiplication [of needs] goes on *ad infinitum.* . . to be confined to mere physical needs as such and their direct satisfaction would simply be the condition in which the mental is plunged in the natural and so would be one of savagery and unfreedom (17).

In *The German Ideology* Marx tied need expansion to a power-acquiring process which had been going on since the beginning of history. Tool-making activities designed to satisfy primary biological requirements existing at the beginning of historical evolution are said to create additional needs which develop out of the tool-making achievement:

---

16. Chapter 30, p. 484.
17. *Op. cit.,* sections 190, 191 and 193.

> . . . men must be in a position to live in order to be able to "make history." But life involves before everything else eating and drinking, a habitation, clothing and many other things. The first historical act is thus the production of the means to satisfy these needs, the production of material life itself. And indeed this is an historical act, a fundamental condition of all history, which today, as thousands of years ago, must daily and hourly be fulfilled in order to sustain human life. . .
>
> The second point is that the satisfaction of the first need (the action of satisfying, and the instrument of satisfaction which has been acquired) leads to new needs; and thus production of new needs in the first historical act (18).

Two inseparable processes, the meeting of biological needs required for survival, and the creation of new needs, blend into a single "first historical act." The desire to satisfy acquired needs which have developed naturally out of a previous need-fulfilling activity, becomes an incentive to further inventive activity. There seems always to be a gap between a level of need existing at the outset of a productive project and an expanded level of need that emerges during the course of the project. Man, the productive worker in nature, seems to be impelled forward by a pressure of needs and wants that can never be overcome.

A good many of the acquired needs are social. They become needs and wants for an individual because the objects that are desired are also desired by others. They have value for the self because they are also valued by others. In lectures on economics given in 1847 before a British working class audience, Marx adopted an abstract, highly positive view of a process of social and material emulation which would seem to be characteristic of a middle level bourgeois economy and society. The attitudes he described revealed the presence of social motives and social needs, demonstrating the social nature of man. To be influenced by the values of others, and even to experience emotions of envy because other persons have managed to acquire conscipuous material accoutrements of an impressive kind is better than a condition of isolated "self-sufficiency" and total indifference to the opinion of others that is apparently the only alternative:

> A house may be large or small; as long as the surrounding houses are equally small it satisfies all social demands for a dwelling. But let a palace arise beside the little house, and it shrinks from a house to a hut. The little house shows now that its owner has only very slight or no demands to make; and however high it may shoot up in the course of civilization, if the neighboring palace grows to an equal or even greater extent, the occupant of the relatively small house will feel more and more uncomfortable, dissatisfied and cramped within its four walls.

---

18. Volume I, Part I, p. 39.

A noticeable increase in wages presupposes a rapid growth of productive capital. The rapid growth of productive capital brings about an equally rapid growth of wealth, luxury, social wants, social enjoyments. Thus, although the enjoyments of the worker have risen, the social satisfaction that they give has fallen in comparison with the state of development of society in general. Our desires and pleasures spring from society; we measure them, therefore, by society and not by the objects which serve for their satisfaction. Because they are of a social nature, they are of a relative nature (19).

The refusal of individuals to acknowledge their material dependence on society had been associated by Marx with the evils of an isolated self-condition, and also with philosophical solipsism. In *The Holy Family* (1844) he had charged that the neo-Hegelian philosophers, ignoring the economic realities, were concerned only with the condition of a mythical, unreal individual who they portrayed as wholly detached and self-sufficient, independent of the material economy and therefore also independent of society:

Speaking exactly, and in the prosaic sense, the members of civil society are not *atoms.* The specific property of the atom is that it has *no* properties and is therefore not connected with beings outside it by any relationship determined by its own *natural necessity.* The atom *has no needs,* it is *self-sufficient;* the world outside it is an absolute *vacuum,* i.e., it is contentless, senseless, meaningless, just because the atom has *all fullness* in itself. The egoistic individual in civil society may in his non-sensuous imagination and lifeless abstraction inflate himself into an *atom,* i.e., into an unrelated, self-sufficient, wantless, *absolutely full,* blessed being. Unblessed *sensuous reality* does not bother about his imagination, each of his senses compels him to believe in the existence of the world and of individuals outside him, and even his *profane* stomach reminds him every day that the world *outside* him is not *empty,* but is what really *fills.*

Marx went on to say that

. . . it is *natural necessity,* the *essential human properties,* however estranged thay may be, and *interest* that hold the members of civil society together; *civil,* not *political* life is their *real* tie. It is therefore not the *state* that holds the *atoms* of civil society together, but the fact that they are *atoms* only in imagination, in the heaven of their fancy. . . (20).

---

19. *Wage Labour and Capital,* published in 1849, reprinted in *Selected Works of Marx and Engels, op. cit.* Volume I.

20. *The Collected Works of Marx and Engels, op. cit.,* chapter 6 of "The Holy Family," p. 120.

In the post-capitalist society, the real ties between human beings will be social and material. The fallacies of solipsism and of abstract philosophy will have been left behind. Individuals will then be united by ties of "natural necessity" in such a way that the withdrawn and detached ego-condition will no longer be projected as desirable. The relativity and the mutability of the needs, desires and satisfactions which "spring from society" is part of their moral value. Marx did not anticipate the development in socialist society of individualistic forms of competitive emulation in relation to material consumption, nor did he expect that there would be radical contrasts between the "palace" and the "hut" in that society. In the cited passage from *Wage Labour and Capital* he shows his preference for an extraverted kind of self-condition, and for attitudes that are passively open and receptive to external social impressions. The sense of "greatness" or of aspiring to greatness that is associated with this sociality will be largely collective, a participation in the greatness of man as species. The desires and pleasures that spring from society counteract the evils of the egoistic, non-social condition.

Marx projects unceasing changes of style and form in social production rather than an unlimited quantitative increase in material production and consumption. Nevertheless the two are bound together, in his deterministic logic, in such a way that one seems always to include the other. The emphasis is on the transcendence of instinct and of nature-given tendencies that might resist absorption into the process of socially determined change. In this respect, socialist society will be continuous with the society of capitalism. Socialism will accomplish what capitalism is only striving to accomplish. In the *Grundrisse,* Marx had written that

> . . . capital drives beyond national barriers and prejudices as much as beyond nature worship, as well as [beyond] all traditional, confined, complacent, encrusted satisfactions of present needs, and reproductions of old ways of life. It is destructive of all this, and constantly revolutionizes it, tearing down all the barriers which hem in the development of the forces of production, and the exploitation and exchange of natural and mental forces.
>
> But from the fact that capital posits every such limit as a barrier and hence gets *ideally* beyond it, it does not by any means follow that it has *really* overcome it. . . (21).

Material expansion in socialist society is associated with labor-saving technology, and also with continuous activities of invention and innovation which bring a whole series of desirable consequences in their wake. There will be no advertising pressures, no profit-motivated stimulation of consumer demand, no deliberate attempts to create "new needs." Marx expected that wasteful expenditures required to maintain the economy and society of

21. *Pre-Capitalist Economic Formations, op. cit.*, p. 93.

capitalism, would be eliminated. But new modes of production inevitably displace earlier, outmoded forms. New kinds of consumer goods become desired as "objects" by the consuming society. The logic of the need expansion process seems to preclude the possibility that the process could ever be brought to a halt, or that the new could ever be rejected in favor of the old.

10

The Proletarian Dictatorship

Marx's conception of the proletarian dictatorship is an important part of his theory of socialist revolution. It has had a good deal of historical impact, but has also given rise to much confusion and controversy. In a letter to J. Wedemeyer (March 1, 1852) he wrote that

> . . . no credit is due to me for discovering the existence of classes in modern society or the struggle between them. Long before me bourgeois historians had described the historical development of this class struggle and bourgeois economists the economic anatomy of the classes. What I did that was new was to prove: 1) that the *existence of classes* is only bound up with *particular historical phases in the development of production;* 2) that the class struggle necessarily leads to the *dictatorship of the proletariat;* 3) that this dictatorship itself only constitutes the transition to the *abolition of all classes and to a classless society.*

S. Avineri is one of the interpreters of Marx who have tried to downplay this aspect of Marx's socialist theory. He argues that Marx only used the term two or three times and ". . . always in what is basically a private communication" (1). David Fernbach takes a different view, and he also provides useful background information on the origin of this concept. It was first formulated by Auguste Blanqui, a French communist prominent in the revolutionary uprisings of 1848. Fernbach notes that Marx had publicly endorsed Blanqui's call for a proletarian dictatorship in 1850, and that he referred to the necessity of this dictatorship in public as well as in private communications in later years (2).

It appears, from Marx's various statements, that all forms of working class government are classed as "dictatorships," and also that these governments cannot disappear until the class struggle phase of history has come to an end. This implies that the dictatorship in any one country cannot be termi-

1. *The Social and Political Thought of Karl Marx,* chapter 8, Cambridge University Press.
2. *Karl Marx: Political Writings,* Volume III, Introduction, edited and introduced by David Fernbach, The Marx Library, Random House, NY, 1974.

nated until all countries have achieved political socialism, though Marx did not state this explicitly. He did, however, repeatedly emphasize the international aspects of the class struggle.

The period of class struggle was the period in which the workers had to be prepared, when necessary, to take up arms, either to achieve power, or to defend it once it had been achieved. In an article written in January 1873, he seemed to identify the abolition of the working class state with a condition of security that would permit the workers to "lay down their arms":

> . . . if the workers replace the dictatorship of the bourgeois class with their own revolutionary dictatorship. . . in order to satisfy their miserable profane daily needs and to crush the resistance of the bourgeois class, they, instead of laying down their arms and abolishing the state, give to the state a revolutionary and transitory form (3).

In spite of this emphasis on the need for armed defense, Marx seems not to have envisaged a situation in which a proletarian State would find it necessary to divert a substantial part of its energies and resources to military defense. In his address on *The Civil War in France* (1871), he had said that a working class regime, such as that outlined but never established in the Paris Commune program, would reduce the expenses of government to a considerable extent, by destroying "the two greatest sources of expenditure – the standing army and State functionalism" (4). The people were to be armed, as a National Guard, or as a popular militia capable of defending the new social order in emergencies. In the first draft of this address he had written that

> The Communal organization once firmly established on a national scale, the catastrophes it might still have to undergo would be sporadic slaveholders' insurrections, which, while for a moment interrupting the work of peaceful progress, would only accelerate the movement, by putting the sword into the hands of the social revolution (5).

THE PROLETARIAN DICTATORSHIP AS A TRANSCENDENTAL CONCEPT

In his writings on the Paris Commune, Marx had been projecting his own concept of socialism into the consciousness of the future governing working class. It is a hopeless task to try to interpret his writings on political theory and on political socialism except in the light of his primary philosophical and moral concerns. His political thought is highly abstract, often obscure or ambiguous. Controversies have developed, especially in regard to the question of whether or not he anticipated the total disappearance of political

3. Article on "Political Indifferentism," reprinted in Fernbach, *op. cit.*
4. *Selected Works of Marx and Engels,* Volume II, Progress Publishers, Moscow, 1969.
5. Reprinted in Fernbach, *op. cit.*

government in the classless society. It was Engels, not Marx, who had said that the State would "wither away" at that later time (6).

Insofar as Marx used the terms "political government" and "State" to signify a divided condition of society, a separation between the rulers and the ruled, he did expect that the need for this duality would be eliminated in the condition of "perfected communism."

The proletarian dictatorship is a transcendental formation. It displaces Hegel's transcendental concept of the modern Nation-State. It is morally continuous with Marx's concept of the world-historical working class mission. The Hegelian State possessed a corporate moral identity, an autonomy based on the existence of the nation as a legal and cultural unit. When an individual is morally and psychologically included in the corporate "particularity" of the State, this negates those evils of personal particularity (subjective individuality) which might otherwise remain were it not for the transcendental connection. A comparable type of transcendental connection was established by Marx, which applies to the period of the dictatorship. The working class government has functions of power and authority not possessed by other members of society excluded from the dictatorship. Only after the latter has become unnecessary, can society be transformed into an indivisible whole, with no special public authority that does not belong to all. The condition of unity need not coincide, according to Marx, with the eclipse of all governmental functions, but it does coincide with the eclipse of the political movement and class sttuggle phase of history. In *The Communist Manifesto* Marx predicted that ". . . public power will lose its political character. Political power, properly so called, is merely the organized power of one class for oppressing another."

The working class state is the hegemony of the advanced, vanguard section of the total working class. This vanguard is to assume command of the nation, directing its social and economic policies. Although Marx wrote in *The Critique of the Gotha Programme* that the material conditions of production will have become "the cooperative property of the workers themselves," the town and city sections of the proletarian class will be the initial custodians of this property.

The primary task of the vanguard is to inaugurate a national plan of economic development, one which will extend the large-scale rationalized and collectivized mode of social production established in manufacturing industries into the countryside. In a brief article on "The Nationalization of the Land," written in the spring of 1872, Marx said that national property in agricultural land should not be leased by the working class government to individual cultivators. Neither should it be given over to a collective association of rural producers. Referring to proposals made by another socialist, with whom he partially disagreed, he wrote that

---

6. Ralph Miliband, *Marxism and Politics,* Introduction, Oxford University Press, 1977. Miliband calls attention to the influence of Engels on the political philosophy of Marxism.

> . . . the social [socialist] movement would lead to this decision that the land can but be owned by the nation itself. To give up the soil to the hands of associated rural labourers, would be to surrender society to one exclusive class of producers (7).

The urban workers were to be the planners and coordinators for the entire nation. They represented the enlightened rationality of modern scientific culture and civilization. They were therefore a universal, non-exclusive class. Under their management

> Agriculture, mining, manufacture, in one word, all branches of production, will gradually be organized in the most adequate manner. *National centralisation of the means of production* will become the national basis of a society composed of free and equal producers, carrying on the social business on a common and rational plan. Such is the humanitarian goal to which the great economic movement of the nineteenth century is tending.

In this same article Marx said that when class distinctions have disappeared and no one is able to live on the labor of other people ". . . there will no longer be any government or state power, distinct from society itself!"

The proletarian dictatorship was to be a collective rule. Monarchy, the reign of a single person as head of state, had been preferred by Hobbes. A monarch ". . . cannot disagree with himself, out of envy or interest, but an assembly may. . ." The working class state includes but also transcends, rationally and morally, the unitary power of the Hobbesian monarch. There will be no problem of factionalism, nor of division between minority and majority opinion, within the new sovereignty system. The persons who assume command have already been united in their aims and program before coming to power. The unity had been forged in their struggle against the forces of capital.

The proletarian dictatorship was linked to the popular sovereignty concept that Marx had supported in his pre-socialist writings on state and law, at the time when he was opposing the censorship laws enacted by the Prussian government (8). At that time, he said that the people of the nation, united in spirit, were the only legitimate moral and political authority. They constitute the unity of "the ethical state." The repressive policy of the Prussian government, aimed at suppressing internal dissent

> . . . cancels the equality of the citizens before the law. It divides rather than unites; and all dividing laws are reactionary. . . In *an ethical state the view of the state* is subordinate to its members, even though they *oppose an organ of the state* or the *government.*

7. *Marx and Engels Selected Works,* Volume II, *op. cit.*
8. See chapter 7 of this book, section on "Marx's Pre-socialist Philosophy of State and Law."

Writing many years later as a socialist, Marx said that the national economy was to be centralized and administered according to a national plan, but that the proletarian dictatorship was also to decentralize certain essential public functions outside of the category of material production. In the more advanced, republican countries it was to restore to the people in the locally based communities within the nation certain powers and forms of authority of which they had been deprived during the time of bourgeois ascendancy. The supra-local political center, the national state, would no longer operate as before.

Marx ranked different forms of modern political government according to certain criteria. The republican capitalist countries were in a preferred category. Germany and countries whose situation resembled that of Germany were in the lowest category. Between the two extremes, there were various gradations. In his remarks on the political system of the United States, he indicated that the cultural and moral groundwork for a socialist popular sovereignty had already been formed in the various localities. The nationally federated governmental system allowed for a substantial degree of local autonomy in the states whose federation constituted the national union. The federated structure of the Swiss republic was in the same class. In the local jurisdictions, the people were already exercising a direct type of sovereign authority and supervisory control over the agencies and policies of the local governments.

In *The Critique of the Gotha Programme* Marx represented the majority of the people in the advanced republican countries as being morally qualified to take over national sovereignty, even though the bourgeoisie was still in control. This view was stated when he was condemning the German Party for advocating, in the name of socialism, "universal and equal elementary education through the state. Universal compulsory school attendance. Free instruction." According to Marx, the Party was saying that the State was to determine the content of what was taught in the schools. It was implying that the state was especially qualified to act in an instructional capacity. This revealed a characteristic German tendency to elevate the central, national state as a special moral authority. In actuality, this elevation was an inversion of the true situation. The people of the nation, those who did not hold national political office, were morally superior to the central power:

> Defining by a general law the financial means of the elementary schools, the qualifications of the teachers, the branches of instruction, etc., and, as happens in the United States, supervising the fulfillment of these legal prescriptions by means of state inspectors, is a very thing from appointing the state as the educator of the people! Government and church should rather be equally excluded from any influence on the school. Particularly, indeed, in the Prusso-German empire (and one cannot take refuge in the rotten subterfuge that one is speaking of a 'state of

> the future,' we have seen what that is), the state has need, on the contrary, of a very stern education by the people.

The people in the advanced republican countries cannot obtain power on the national level until the working class movement in these countries has succeeded in overcoming the nationally centralized political class power of the bourgeoisie, and has taken over the management of the national economy. But once this has been done, it would seem that the proletarian dictatorship in these countries can scarcely be distinguished from a populist government, i.e., a people's sovereignty. The overwhelming majority of the people in the various localities would willingly accept the dictatorship as the only national power capable of upholding and advancing their own interests, which are also the interests of the nation.

In the working class State, social and economic policies and administrative procedures were to be decided by a process which Marx called "universal suffrage," which was superseding "individual suffrage." His address on *The Civil War in France* (1871) included a description of the system of government which *would* have been established by the Paris Communards if they had been able to retain power. Marx wrote that

> . . . universal suffrage was to serve the people, constituted in Communes, as individual suffrage serves every other employer in the search for the workmen and managers in his business. And it is well known that companies, like individuals, in matters of real business generally know how to put the right man in the right place, and, if they for once make a mistake, to redress it promptly. On the other hand, nothing could be more foreign to the spirit of the Commune than to supersede universal suffrage by hierarchic investiture (9).

Marx here uses the term "suffrage" to mean decision making and managerial power. "Universal suffrage" is collective decision making and management. The group functions as if it were a single psyche. In the Commune system, the appointment of an individual to a particular position separates him from the collective authority of which he had previously been a part. It also subordinates him to that authority. All appointees will presumably be chosen from the ranks of the people. But the people who are members of the sovereign body must exercise close surveillance over their appointed functionaries and representatives. According to Marx, the Paris Commune

> . . . was formed of the municipal councillors, chosen by universal suffrage in the various wards of the town, responsible and revocable at short terms. The majority of its members were naturally working men, or acknowledged representatives of the working class. The Commune was to be a working, not a parliamentary, body, executive and legislative at the same time. Instead of con-

9. *Marx and Engels Selected Works,* Volume II, *op. cit.*

> tinuing to be the agent of the Central Government, the police was at once stripped of its political attributes and turned into the responsible and at all times revocable agent of the Commune. . .

The emphasis on the need for group control and surveillance was especially marked in relation to those policing and judiciary functions which will still be necessary in the first stages of socialism. In the Commune system

> The judicial functionaries were to be divested of that sham independence which has but served to mask their abject subservience to all succeeding governments to which, in turn, they had taken, and broken, the oaths of allegiance. Like the rest of public servants, magistrates and judges were to be elective, responsible, and revocable.

The united people, in other words, were to become the supreme judging and punitive authority.

Civil liberties of the kind that had developed in the more liberal bourgeois nations were given short shrift in the government of the dictatorship. Marx's lack of concern with civil liberties in socialist society was in contrast to the position he took when protesting against the repressive policies of the anti-liberal Prussian government. There was, however, no real contradiction involved. In protesting against repression, he had been defending the right of anti-government critics to advocate the overthrow of the existing political state authorities. He did so in the name of the people who were being oppressed by the political regime in office. He made it clear that he was not advocating anarchy, but merely the elimination of a reactionary, paternalistic type of political control. Some of these anti-censorship statements appeared in 1842, before he became a communist. Others were written in 1849, during the time when he was acting as an attorney for the defense in the Cologne sedition trials. He was himself one of the accused, and was able to win an acquittal. At that time he declared that "It is the function of the press to be the public watchdog, the tireless denouncer of the rulers, the omnipresent eye, the omnipresent mouth of the spirit of the people that jealously guards its freedom" (10).

When the workers become sovereign, they do not require the "watchdog" function that had been necessary when they – and the people – were out of power. They constitute their own defense and are guardians of the freedom of the nation in which they are, temporarily, the ruling class. There need be no explicit, socially sanctioned and legally enforceable right of the individual to dissent, to give public voice to criticism of particular policies and decisions that have been adopted by the government of the dictatorship through "universal suffrage."

---

10. Speech delivered on February 7, 1849, published the following week in the *Neue Rheinische Zeitung.* Translated by Padover, in *Karl Marx on Freedom of the Press and Censorship,* McGraw Hill Book Co., 1974.

In *The Critique of the Gotha Programme* Marx had mentioned only one civil freedom of the bourgeois liberal era that was to be carried forward into the period of the dictatorship. This was called "freedom of conscience," which was nothing more nor less than private freedom of religion (11).

On the question of religion in relation to the state, Marx's theory of socialist government was in marked contrast to the theory of Hobbes. In the society of seventeenth century England, religious dissention was very much a public and political issue. The Hobbesian Sovereign was to eliminate by decree the religious differences dividing the population into warring factions. A single State religion, a politicalized Christianity, was to be established by the Sovereign for practical, political reasons. Marx, in a later age, believed that religion had become so entirely privatized, so publicly irrelevant, that it could pose no threat to the working class state. As long as it existed, however, it was a threat to the believing individual, who is less free, subjectively, than he or she would otherwise be. The worker's party and movement is attempting to ". . . liberate the conscience from the spectre of religion," not by political suppression, but by eliminating fears which Marx associates with religion.

In Marx's theory of the popular-proletarian State, the individuals who exercise the sovereign power are morally elevated above the level of egoistic self--interest. The Sovereign of Hobbes's Leviathan State, in contrast, had not been so elevated. As an individual he is morally indistinguishable from his subjects. It is his office, and the nature of his function, that confers on the State power its moral authority and legitimacy. In all socialist nations, the working class vanguard is at the helm, guiding the foreign policies and also the economic policies of the nation. As a class it is still carrying out a world historical mission. It is also merged with, and reinforced by a direct, localized authority of the people in the more enlightened modern societies. Whatever the local situation, "dictatorship" is the omnibus term Marx applies to all socialist governments that come to power in the period of transition:

> Between capitalist and communist society lies the period of revolutionary transformation of the one into the other. There corresponds to this also a political transition in which the state can be nothing but the *revolutionary dictatorship of the proletariat* (12).

11. See the paragraph on "freedom of conscience," in *The Critique of the Gotha Programme,* quoted in chapter 7 of this book, section on "Political Conscience in the Socialist Movement."

12. *The Critique of the Gotha Programme.*

11

The Necessity Of Labor In Communist Society

The philosophy of work that Marx developed in his later years included a number of remarkable features. He expected that "the division of labor" would be eliminated in the society of communism, and also that the age of scarcity would have given way to the age of abundance. In his earlier works, however, he had also assumed that labor itself, as a public necessity, would likewise have been abolished. This view was in marked contrast to the philosophy of work which appears in *Capital* and in other works written after 1856.

Marx's philosophy of work, and his conception of the meaning of proletarian labor, had always been linked to a great many other issues. Problems that become evident in his later views are tied in with his belief that the economy of socialism will develop naturally and inevitably beyond the first, imperfect and inequalitarian stage of the beginning until society finally reaches the fully equalitarian condition of universal abundance. In the early part of his theoretical career, Marx had implied that future progress would result simply from the material expansion that would become possible in the socialized economy. In the later works, the emphasis on material expansion is retained, but other changes relating to the allocation of work and of time, also become important.

The abolition of the "division of labor," which was also the separation of mental and physical labor, would have to be preceded by a stage in which the proletarians of socialist society would continue to perform the same kind of work that they had been forced to carry on for capitalist employers. Their conditions of work would be greatly improved, and their hours of work shortened, but they would retain their class and occupational identity. Gradually, as society evolved toward a classless condition, they would be absorbed into a community of universal labor. In his address on *The Civil War in France* (1871), Marx said that the Paris Commune had been

> . . . essentially a working class government, the product of the struggle of the producing against the appropriating class, the political form at last discovered under which to work out the economic emancipation of labour. . . The political rule of the producer cannot coexist with the perpetuation of his social slavery. The Commune was therefore to serve as a lever for uprooting the

> economic foundation upon which rests the existence of classes, and therefore of class rule. With labour emancipated, every man becomes a working man, and productive labour ceases to be a class attribute (1).

The industrial technology that had developed in the age of capitalism and that would be carried forward into socialism had created the need for a kind of work which Marx regarded as burdensome and unpleasant. The tasks performed by the majority of unskilled and semi-skilled workers were devoid of intrinsic interest, being repetitive and uncreative. In *The German Ideology* (1845–46) he seemed to expect the modern worker to welcome the deterioration of work experience with open arms. This loss was merely a prelude to a condition in which no labor of this kind would be needed, and in which the individual would also be freed from other past and present restrictions:

> . . . there is found with medieval craftsmen an interest in their special work and in proficiency in it, which was capable of rising to a narrow artistic sense. For this very reason, however, every medieval craftsman was completely absorbed in this work, to which he had a contented, slavish relationship, and to which he was subjected to a far greater extent than the modern worker, whose work is a matter of indifference to him (2).

In *Capital,* Marx left his readers in no doubt as to the continued need for collectivized, routinized, mechanized labor in communist society. Subordination to the impersonal disciplines and exacting requirements of this kind of work would be required of the manual workers – the proletarians of capitalism – in the first stage of socialism. In the society of communism, this kind of subordination will be universal, required of all who are physically and mentally capable.

THE DUALITY OF FREEDOM AND NECESSITY

Marx regarded work as a moral and spiritual necessity for the individual. The personal fulfillment of the individual dependent to a considerable degree on his ability to engage in meaningful work. He objected strongly, in the *Grundrisse* (1857–58) to Adam Smith's assumption that work is a curse, an externally imposed affliction from which individuals try to escape whenever they can. For Smith, a state of "tranquillity," or rest

> . . . appears as the adequate state, as identical with 'freedom' and 'happiness.' It seems quite far from Smith's mind that the individual 'in his normal state of health, strength, activity, skills, facility,' also needs a normal portion of work, and of the suspen-

1. *Selected Works of Marx and Engels, op. cit.,* Volume II.
2. *Op. cit.,* Volume I, Part I, p. 67.

> sion of tranquillity. Certainly labour obtains its measure from the outside, through the aim to be attained and the obstacles to be overcome in attaining it. But Smith has no inkling whatever that this overcoming of obstacles is in itself a liberating activity – and that, further, the external aims become stripped of the semblance of merely external natural urgencies, and become posited as aims which the individual himself posits – hence as self-realization, objectification of the subject, hence real freedom, whose action is, precisely, labour.

Work has indeed often been an affliction, but only when carried out under oppressive conditions:

> He [Adam Smith] is right, of course, that, in historic forms as slave-labour, serf-labour, and wage-labour, labour always appears as repulsive, always as *external forced labour,* and non-labour, by contrast, as 'freedom, and happiness' (3).

When these conditions no longer exist, work can be seen in its true light. In this argument against Smith, Marx was contrasting onerous forced labor with "attractive work," which was primarily work undertaken by the single individual on his own initiative. It is chiefly this kind of work which is a means to self-realization. Work as self-realization is a serious undertaking. It never

> . . . becomes mere fun, mere amusement, as Fourier, with *grisette-like* naivete, conceives it. Really free working, e.g. composing, is at the same time precisely the most damned seriousness, the most intense exertion (4).

When Marx in his early writings anticipated the elimination of work in communist society, he was not declaring that self-realizing work of the "free" kind would become unnecessary. He was, however, eliminating the tension and duality, the opposition between "free" and "necessary" labor that appeared as soon as he came to expect that individuals in the classless era would have to make a public contribution of labor time, reducing thereby the amount of time left over for free work and other activities. In the *Grundrisse* manuscript, a transitional work, Marx reverted to an Hegelian metaphysical style of language and thought. Some passages are therefore difficult to decipher. He adopted a device previously used by Hegel. He declared that the contradiction between freedom and necessity could be nullified or "suspended" by an act of mental comprehension, even though the contradiction persists on the non-mental level of social and working life. In the *Grundrisse* Marx distinguished between "free work" undertaken on the individual creative level and necessary work, which he called "material production." Material labor is largely physical, but it is also possible for the

3. Translated by Nicolaus, *op. cit.,* p. 611.
4. *Ibid.,*

worker so engaged to use his mental as well as his physical powers, provided he grasps the historical significance of material production. After referring to the really free working time that is not in the "material production" category, Marx had gone on to say that

> The working of material production can achieve this [free] character only 1) when its social character is posited, 2) when it is of scientific and at the same time general character, not merely human exertion as a specifically harnessed natural force, but exertion as subject, which appears in the production process not in a merely natural, spontaneous form, but as activity regulating all the forces of nature (5).

In a later passage of the manuscript, he said that under these conditions there would be a "suspension of the contradiction between free time and labor time" (6).

In *Capital,* Marx established a clearcut dualism. Work that is classed as "socially necessary" material production is not as free as that which can be carried on by each person on the level above this social necessity. He conceived of persons in the society of communism as living on two levels. One was the level of freedom beyond necessity. On the other, material level, they would have to devote a portion of their time to less free kinds of productive labor which had to be carried on in order to meet the subsistence requirements of the producers as consumers. In *Capital* III he wrote that

> . . . the realm of freedom actually begins only where labour which is determined by necessity and mundane considerations ceases; thus in the very nature of things it lies beyond the sphere of actual material production. Just as the savage must wrestle with Nature to satisfy his wants, to maintain and reproduce life, so must civilized man, and he must do so in all social formations and under all possible modes of production. With his development this realm of physical necessity expands as a result of [the expansion of] his wants; but, at the same time, the forces of production which satisfy these wants also increase. Freedom in this field can only consist in socialized man, the associated producers, rationally regulating their interchange with Nature, bringing it under their common control, instead of being ruled by it as by the blind forces of Nature; and achieving this with the least expenditure of energy and under conditions most favourable to, and worthy of, their human nature. But it nonetheless still remains a realm of necessity. Beyond it begins the development of human energy which is an end in itself, the true realm of freedom, which, however, can blossom forth only with this realm of necessity as its basis. The shortening of the working day is its basic prerequisite (7).

5. *Ibid.,* pp. 611-612.
6. *Ibid.,* p. 711.
7. Chapter 48, p. 820.

Marx referred here to "the realm of physical necessity." What does he mean by this? The word "physical" is being used to indicate the operation of "laws of nature" that cannot be set aside by any powers available to Man. Marx is not referring to mechanical laws, or to biological laws. He is classing *social* necessity as *physical* necessity. In the preceding volumes of *Capital* he had emphasized the concept of "socially necessary" labor. The examination of this concept sheds light on the term "physical necessity" as this is applied to human affairs. Wants that are in the "physically necessary" category are those which must be met by labor that is socially necessary.

Socially necessary labor, in socialist society, will be undertaken as a means to an external end. Materials goods will no longer be produced, as in the capitalist economy, on account of their exchange value, i.e., their market value, but on account of their use value. It is the use value placed upon the goods produced in the socialized economy that makes them necessary in a social as well as in a biological sense. The requirements of the standard of living in communist society that must be met by social production will be determined in much the same way that the wages of labor were said by Marx to have been determined in various societies where "free wage labor" had put in an appearance. In the socialist economy, wage labor will be abolished. Like the wage workers in times gone by, the material producers of socialism will have "natural wants," but they will also have other "so-called necessary wants." "Natural wants" are apparently those required to maintain the worker in a physical condition fit for work, throughout the duration of his working life:

> Given the individual, the production of labour-power consists in his reproduction of himself or his maintenance. For his maintenance he requires a given quantity of the means of subsistence. Therefore the labour-time requisite for the production of labour-power reduces itself to that necessary for the production of those means of subsistence. . . If the owner of labour-power works today, tomorrow he must again be able to repeat the same process in the same conditions as to health and strength. His means of subsistence must therefore be sufficient to maintain him in his normal state as a labouring individual (8).

Marx went on to say that

> His [the wage worker's] natural wants, such as food, clothing, fuel, and housing, vary according to the climatic and other physical conditions of his country. On the other hand, the number and extent of his so-called necessary wants, as also the modes of satisfying them, are themselves the product of historical development, and depend therefore to a great extent on the habits and degree of comfort in which the class of free labourers has been formed.

8. *Capital,* Volume I, chapter 6, p. 171.

> In contradistinction therefore to the case of other commodities, there enters into the determination of the value of labour-power an historical and moral element.

This theory that wages are automatically determined by a combination of natural and historically modified wants shows that Marx is regarding the "moral element" of custom as binding not only on the wage earners but also on the employers of labor power. Marx's concept is similar to the "natural price" theory of wages developed by Ricardo. The natural price was said to vary considerably, when different countries were compared. Within the same country, it also varied, when different times were compared. Customs were alterable in time and place. Ricardo, however, had included in the "natural price" the cost of family reproduction:

> The natural price of labour is that price which is necessary to enable the labourers, one with another, to subsist and to perpetuate their race, without either increase or diminution [in numbers] (9).

Marx made no specific mention of family reproduction in his wage theory. He followed the procedure adopted by Hegel in *The Philosophy of Right.* The "abstract" individual is the activity unit who is then included within a system of economic relations and who becomes morally, socially and materially dependent on that system. His wage theory was highly abstract, and could not easily be applied to the situation of the workers in the capitalist economy. In many passages in *Capital* he referred to the absolute impoverishment of workers in capitalist industry. The lives of factory workers, including those of women and children employed in industry, were being shortened, their strength depleted, through the combined effect of intolerably long hours, low wages, and bad working conditions. In this situation, the level of wages seems not to be determined by "subsistence requirements," even when such requirements are confined to what Marx called the "natural wants" of a single worker, quite apart from the question of family reproduction. A major difference between the economy of capitalism and socialism will be the return, under socialism, to a determination of living standards by a process that includes not only the natural wants but also a socially determined increment of so-called necessary wants. All workers, including those who were formerly unemployed or underemployed, the "industrial reserve army" of capitalism, and those who had been reduced to pauperdom and to dependence on public relief, will be brought up to the more adequate, socially modified standard.

In his discussion of the functions that would have to be carried out on the public level in the society of socialism, Marx assumed the existence of rational, decision-making and resource allocating public powers. A certain portion of the total material product would have to be withheld from imme-

9. Cited by Wesley C. Mitchell, in *Types of Economic Theory,* Lecture 19.

diate consumption. No such functions had been projected in his early writings (10). But in spite of the changes introduced in the later works, serious deficiencies in Marx's theory of economic socialism could not be eliminated. As an historical determinist, he maintained that economic distribution of the material product to different sectors of any social economy was determined automatically by powers beyond rational control. Society was to be invested with regulatory functions, but the natural and socially modified material wants of the individuals who make up society seem at the same time to be determined by psychological and social processes, as well as by physical (i.e., biological) processes outside of rational control. The producers are psychologically compelled to meet certain material production goals which they cannot rationally appraise in the light of other goals that might, under some conditions, be given a higher priority. Yet Marx was looking forward to a future social economy in which some forms of rationality would be increased. Rational social planning to meet the needs and wants of all would supersede the irrationality of capitalism which could not provide for all. Powers of instrumental and technical reason will be adequately developed and applied. The rationality of the producers will be sufficient to provide means to the realization of ends that cannot be rationally appraised or altered except indirectly, through general processes of historical change.

A major aim of socialist economic management will be to increase the amount of private free time available to each worker. Marx refers to only one method of accomplishing this. It is a method which is bound to maximize the dependence of the society on large-scale mechanized, collectivized forms of labor in industry and in agriculture. The greater the degree of mechanization and rationalization, and the more all labor becomes collective group labor, the greater the amount of free time produced. The worker, in his free time, may produce something that is of value to himself or to others beside himself, but this personal product in no way enters into the material standard of living, which consists only of those items that have been produced by time-saving rational, mechanical and collective methods. A significant reversion to handicraft production, or to non-collective small scale agriculture, would be impossible in Marx's divided time system. His philosophy of work is notably different from the philosophy of the British socialist William Morris, who had hoped that socialist society would eventually get beyond the stage at which mechanical production was promoted at the expense of all other methods (11).

10. See chapter 9, in this book, on "Scarcity and Necessity: The Technological Leviathan."

11. In his utopian novel *News from Nowhere* (1890) Morris, reporting from the future, wrote that ". . . we have now found out what we want, so we make no more than we want; and as we are not driven to make a vast quantity of useless things, we have time and resources enough to consider our pleasure in making them. All work which it would be irksome to do by hand is done by immensely improved machinery: and in all work which it is a pleasure to do by hand machinery is done without. . . there is such a vast number of things which can be treated as works of art, that this alone gives employment to a host of deft people."

The methods of work rationalization that were developed in capitalist industries for the sake of maximizing surplus value were to be carried forward into the socialist economy. The definition of socially necessary (unfree) labor time that applies to capitalist production applies also to socialist production. Marx was describing capitalist production for profit when he wrote

> . . . only so much of the time spent in the production of any article is counted, as, under the given social conditions, is necessary. The consequences of this are various. In the first place, it becomes necessary that the labour should be carried on under normal conditions. If a self-acting mule is in general use for spinning, it would be absurd to supply the spinner with distaff and spinning wheel. The cotton too must not be such rubbish as to cause extra waste in being worked, but must be of a suitable quality. Otherwise the spinner would be found to spend more time in producing a pound of yarn than is socially necessary, in which case the excess of time would create neither value nor money. . . labour power itself must be of average efficacy. . . This power must be applied with the average amount of exertion and with the usual degree of intensity (12).

Referring to what might be possible in a socialist economy, Marx wrote that

> Only by suppressing the capitalist form of production could the length of the working-day be reduced to the necessary labour-time. But even in that case, the latter would extend its limits. On the one hand, because the notion of "means of subsistence" would considerably expand, and the labourer would lay claim to an altogether different standard of life. On the other hand, because a part of what is now surplus-labour, would then count as necessary labour; I mean the labour of forming a fund for reserve and accumulation (13).

The socialist economy will, of course, operate from the very first within the limits of certain humane protections both as to the number of hours worked and the conditions of work, protections not voluntarily adopted by capitalist employers. Marx did not expect that productivity and total production would decline from the level attained in the capitalist economy. While the capitalist was careful to avoid waste in his own industry, the economy as a whole was extravagantly wasteful. Under socialism, waste will be avoided not only in specific industries but also on the general level of planning. There will also be rational economic conservation aimed at preserving and renewing the natural resources that must remain available to future generations. Capitalism, on the other hand, is incapable of such foresight.

12. *Capital,* Volume I, chapter 7, pp. 195-196.
13. *Ibid.,* chapter 17, p. 530.

THE FUTURE REALIZATION OF ABSOLUTE EQUALITY

Marx included in his idea of the future, an ideal norm of equity which applied to material distribution and also to the distribution of free time. The ideal equalization could not be attained directly through conscious moral efforts of a public kind. On this question, Marx stayed strictly within the limits of the deterministic logic he applied to all of history. He had denied that economic and political societies, considered as functionally integrated, natural-organic entities, have the power to alter the internal system of production relations, which are also relations of distribution, in accordance with an ideal norm that goes beyond the status quo. In *The Critique of the Gotha Programme* (1875) he described the conditions that would exist in the higher phase of communist society "after the enslaving subordination of individuals under the division of labour, and therewith also the antithesis between mental and physical labour, has vanished" (14). The concept of enslavement, as noted earlier (chapter 3) implied the existence of an oppressive system-integrating power which could be eliminated only through a process of natural historical evolution. He referred also to the "narrow horizon of bourgeois right" (justice) which also could not be left behind until the higher phase had been reached.

The arguments he used to demonstrate that the ideal of the French communists: "From each according to his ability, to each according to his needs" could not be achieved in the early phases of socialism also reveal the meaning that this ideal had for Marx. The distributive equity that will be realized in the higher phase of communism will be a rectification of injustices that have their origin in nature as well as in society. Socialism will be able to apply, at first, only the principle of "equal pay for equal work," which had developed in bourgeois society in connection with a formal legalistic concept of "equal right." In *The Critique of the Gotha Programme* Marx said that ". . . *equal right* is still in principle – *bourgeois right,* although [in the future socialist economy] principle and practice are no longer in conflict." In the "equal pay for equal work" economy of transitional socialism, each worker will receive a certificate of consumption entitling him to draw from the public stock an amount proportional to the measurable, objective value of his material work contribution. The material inequality that results from this application of the equal pay principle is due in large part to the fact that

> . . . one man is superior to another physically or mentally and so supplies more labour in the same time, or can labour for a longer time; and labour, to serve as a measure, must be defined by its duration or intensity, otherwise it ceases to be a standard of measurement. This *equal* right is an unequal right for unequal labour. It recognizes no class differences, because every one is only a worker like every one else; but it tacitly recognizes

14. See paragraph cited in chapter 9 of this book on p. 204.

> unequal individual endowment and thus productive capacity as natural privileges. *It is therefore a right of inequality in its content, like every right.* Right by its very nature can only consist in the application of an equal standard. . .

Material inequality will arise also for reasons having no relation to differences of natural privilege. The personal expenses of workers may differ: ". . . one worker is married, another not; one has more children than another, and so on and so forth. Thus with an equal output, and with an equal share in the social consumption fund, one will in fact receive more than another, one will be richer than another, and so on." He said that theorists of socialism do not have to be concerned with future problems of material distribution, which will correct themselves. It must be recognized that

> . . . these defects are inevitable in the first phase of communist society as it is when it has just emerged after prolonged birth-pangs from capitalist society. Right can never be higher than the economic structure of society and the cultural development thereby determined.

Initial material inequities will be eradicated gradually after the working class has taken over the ownership of the means of production:

> The capitalist mode of production, for example, rests on the fact that the material conditions of production are in the hands of non-workers in the form of property in capital and land, while the masses are only owners of the personal condition of production, *viz.* labour power. Once the elements of production are so distributed, then the present day distribution of the means of consumption results automatically. If the material conditions of production are the cooperative property of the workers themselves, then this likewise results in a different distribution of the means of consumption from the present one.

In the higher equalitarian condition, individuals will continue to differ in degree and kind of natural ability and in family circumstances. They will then receive a personal return commensurate with their personal need. Every worker will have an equal moral claim against the socially produced material resources. Although workers will be receiving different material amounts, according to need, they will be receiving *equal* amounts of another, important supra-material asset. An implicit norm of abstract, formal (bourgeois) "equal right" will apply in the distribution of the supremely valuable asset of free, private time. This equalization is not classed by Marx as a "right." He excludes the term "equal right," perhaps because he also excludes the concept of equal obligation or duty. Duties of a moral kind will be non-existent, being metaphysically excluded from the future post-sacrificial free condition of personal and social life (15). At first, the distribution of free time will not be equitable, since all persons will not yet be engaged in material production. In the higher condition of communism, all persons will be making an equal social contribution of time and effort on the necessary work level, even though the material value of one person's work time may be greater than that of another, and even though the material needs and the material income of individuals will differ.

Marx's socialist economic theory, as given in *Capital* and in *The Critique of the Gotha Programme* included a transcendental moral logic. Material productivity, and therefore the amount of free time available to all persons in socialist society will be maximized when all share equally in the tasks of material production, i.e., when each spends an equal amount of time in such work. The securing of material abundance requires rational planning and management, but also other elements not reducible to rationality. The inequalities associated with the division of labor and especially with the antithesis of mental and physical labor must be eliminated if optimum material productivity is to be attained. The optimal condition which Marx called the higher stage of communism will be reached only through the interaction of rationally planned material expansion with other processes of spiritual and general development taking place in the working class economy.

THE ANTITHESIS OF PHYSICAL AND MENTAL LABOR

The primary inequity in the first stages of socialist development is not material but temporal. All individuals will at first be enslaved and subordinated by the inequalitarian system of relations which they have no power to overturn. Certain groups of workers would not, at first, be engaged in necessary material labor. Persons who had been living at a middle class cultural and vocational level would retain their advantages The manual workers would have initial disadvantages relative to this other group. Nothing can be done, or ought to be done, about this inequality. In *The Critique of the Gotha Programme* Marx made this clear when he raised questions about the wording of the German party's recommendations regarding education. He insists that there be no cultural regression in the process of changing from capitalism to socialism. Educational opportunities available to middle class children will at first be greater than those available to children of the working class, i.e., to the great majority:

> *Equal elementary education?* What idea lies behind these words? Is it believed that in present-day society (and it is only with this one has to deal) education can be *equal* for all classes? Or it is demanded that the upper classes also shall be compulsorily reduced to the modicum of education – the elementary school – that alone is compatible with the economic conditions not only of the wage workers but of the peasants as well.

15. See the discussion of Marx's moral outlook in chapters 6 and 7 of this book.

Although Marx seems here to be thinking only of present conditions in capitalist society, he expected that these conditions would persist for some time in the socialist economy. He was not referring only to inherited class inequalities, however, when he anticipated the continuance of the "enslaving subordination of individuals under division of labour" in the early stages of socialism. He was referring also to the persistence of certain individualistic attitudes which had been widespread in the open-class society of capitalism. In *Capital* III he wrote that in present day society ". . . a man without fortune but possessing energy, solidity, ability and business acumen" may be able to obtain commercial credit on the basis of his abilities and thus become a capitalist. The availability of this kind of opportunity is

> . . . greatly admired by apologists of the capitalist system. Although this circumstance continually brings an unwelcome number of new soldiers of fortune into the field and into competition with already existing individual capitalists, it also reinforces the supremacy of capital itself, expands its base and enables it to recruit ever new forces for itself out of the substratum of society (16).

Did Marx expect that some of those who has been in the substratum of capitalist society, would continue to rise out of their class of origin, i.e., out of the ranks of physical laborers, to join those who were engaged in mental rather than in physical work? Certain passages in *Capital* and elsewhere suggest that he expects this might happen, but he makes no clear statements. What does come across clearly is his opposition to "hierarchy," i.e., to the perpetuation under socialism of any special occupational stratum of cultural, social and intellectual leaders endowed with special forms of power and influence. In the middle ages, according to Marx, the Catholic Church had "formed its hierarchy out of the best brains of the land, regardless of their estate, birth or fortune." The ruling power of the Church had been consolidated chiefly by this means (17). He added that "The more a ruling class is able to assimilate the foremost minds of a ruled class, the more stable and dangerous becomes its rule."

Although the proletarian workers will become the ruling class in the first stages of socialism, they will rule collectively. They will have no special privileges to defend. Their accession to power does not endow them with such privileges. They remain as they had been, the essential working foundation of modern society, committed to their collective social tasks. Their rule will be neither stable nor dangerous, blocking the further advance to the fully realized condition. In the evolution taking place under socialism, the "foremost minds" of the time will ultimately be incorporated into a system of "generalized labor." Mental and physical work will lose their antithetical

16. Chapter 36, pp. 600–601.
17. See also the discussion of Marx's exclusion of ideological power from socialist society in chapter 6 of this book, pp. 125–128.

character. At first, there will be a considerable minority of non-physical workers who will not identify themselves with the majority of their fellow human beings. They will not voluntarily wish to give up the occupational advantages they possess. The problem of giving up does not exist among the masses of workers, who therefore have less of a moral handicap to overcome than persons at the middle stratum level. As time goes on, persons in the latter category will be increasingly deprived of the power to avoid the burden of necessary material labor that is the lot of the majority. Marx was referring to the first stage of socialism when he wrote, in *Capital:*

> The intensity and productiveness of labour being given, the time which society is bound to devote to material production is shorter, and as a consequence, the time at its disposal for the free development, intellectual and social, of the individual is greater, in proportion as the work is more and more evenly divided among all the able-bodied members of society, and as a particular class is more and more deprived of the power to shift the natural burden of labour from its shoulders to those of another layer of society. In this direction, the shortening of the working-day finds at last a limit in the generalisation of labour. In capitalist society spare time is acquired for one class by converting the whole life-time of the masses into labour-time (18).

The rate of advance toward the optimum condition of personal and social development will accelerate as the earlier inequalitarian condition is outgrown. In the passage just quoted, Marx did not indicate in what way the non-proletarian strata would be "more and more deprived" of their burden-shifting tendencies, nor did he ever discuss this question.

In the *Grundrisse,* Marx referred to a process of personal self-development that would take place in the free time segment of total life time. Here he was assuming that the unity of mental and physical work was an accomplished fact. Under these conditions, an increase in free time improves total productivity. But he also emphasized the importance of economic rationalization as a means to increasing free time:

> The less time the society requires to produce wheat, cattle, etc., the more time it wins for other production, material or mental. Just as in the case of an individual, the multiplicity of its development, its enjoyment and its activity depends on economization of time. Economy of time, to this all economy ultimately reduces itself. Society likewise has to distribute its time in a purposeful way, in order to achieve a production adequate to its overall needs; just as the individual has to distribute his time correctly in order to achieve knowledge in proper proportions or in order to satisfy the various demands on his activity. Thus,

18. Volume I, chapter 17, p. 530.

> economy of time, along with the planned distribution of labour time among the various branches of production, remains the first economic law on the basis of communal production (19).

In another *Grundrisse* passage Marx said that

> The saving of labour time [is] equal to an increase of free time, i.e., time for the full development of the individual, which in turn reacts back upon the productive power of labour as itself the greatest productive power.

It appears that Marx is referring in part to an increase in personal productivity which will take place in connection with private work projects that are not in the public material category. The saving of labor time

> . . . can be regarded as the production of *fixed capital,* this fixed capital being man himself. It goes without saying, by the way, that direct labour time itself cannot remain in the abstract antithesis to free time in which it appears from the perspective of bourgeois economy. Labour cannot become play, as Fourier would like. . . (20).

Marx retained, throughout the years, his organic, Hegelianized vision of a future developing system in which necessity and freedom interact in a supra-rational way, just as "individual" and "society" will also interact. Necessary work includes work on the private free time level as well as work on the collective "socially necessary" level. Productivity on both levels is enhanced; wealth – material and supra-material – is increased, as more and more free time becomes available, under ideally equalitarian conditions. In *The Critique of the Gotha Programme* he declared that the higher stage of communism will emerge ". . . after labour, from a mere means of life, has itself become the prime necessity of life; after the productive forces have also increased with the all-round development of the individual, and all the springs of co-operative wealth flow more abundantly. . ."

Marx's equalitarian and communal emphasis created more than one kind of difficulty. He did, of course, not propose to eliminate mental labor. Nevertheless, mental work is morally subordinated to physical work, in spite of the fact that it, too, will continue to be necessary in the carrying on of material production, in general public and economic planning and administration, and in the maintenance of a variety of publicly essential functions and services.

When he discussed material production as it would be carried on in specific industries in the socialist economy, Marx expected that the production workers would administer and manage their own particular enterprises, and that they would in this way be engaging in mental as well as in physical work. But he sidestepped the problem of technical, scientific and professional

---

19. Translated by Nicolaus, *op. cit.,* pp. 172-173.
20. *Ibid.,* pp. 711-712.

specialization in these same industries. Certain functions might require specialized education and the development of aptitudes not needed by the majority. Either there will be no vocational specialization, which seems ridiculous, or else the relatively small category of mental, professional workers will be dividing their time, spending just as much of their total day in unskilled or semi-skilled forms of group work as the average non-specialist. This could mean that their total working day would be longer than average. The time spent on the "mental work" level would count as "free time," and not as time spent in sharing the tasks and burdens of physical work. This is indeed what Marx seems to be implying. His vision of unity and of burden-sharing cannot be contained within the bounds of "common sense."

In *Theories of Surplus Value* (1862-63) Marx defined "immaterial labor." He said that economic science could disregard this kind of work, which did not belong to the sphere of capitalist production proper, which is chiefly large-scale mass production. Immaterial production

> . . . cannot be separated from the act of producing, as is the case with all performing artists, orators, actors, teachers, physicians, priests, etc. Here too the capitalist mode of production is met with only to a small extent, and from the nature of the case can only be applied in a few spheres. . . All these manifestations of capitalist production in this sphere are so insignificant compared with the totality of production that they can be left entirely out of account (21).

From the standpoint of the time calculus to be used by economic science in the time of socialism, any kind of specialized mental labor and any kind of immaterial labor can be left out of account, treated as if belonging in the "free time" category. In *The Critique of the Gotha Programme* Marx did say that some of the "proceeds of labour" will have to be retained at the public, social level, not only in order to accumulate a reserve fund for the replacement of equipment and for production expansion, but also for certain communal purposes that fall into a secondary, non-material category. It will be necessary to deduct from the total material product "First, the general costs of administration not belonging to production. . . Secondly, that which is destined for the communal satisfaction of needs, such as schools, health services, etc. . . . Thirdly, funds for those unable to work, etc., in short, what is included under so-called official poor relief today." In spite of this cursory reference to "communal needs' for a considerable variety of services that are in the "immaterial labor" category, Marx seems to adhere to his expectation that all able-bodied persons should participate in material (physical) labor at the unskilled or semi-skilled collective group level. He leaves his readers to infer that persons engaged in other occupations will be earning their keep in a *moral* sense only insofar as they also engage in necessary material work.

21. Part I, pp. 410-411, Progress Publishers, Moscow, 1963.

TRANSFORMATION OF HEGEL'S PHILOSOPHY OF WAR

The freedom and necessity dualism which Marx developed in connection with his philosophy of labor can be interpreted as a transformation of Hegel's philosophy of war, including Hegel's conception of the way in which war relates to the economy and society of capitalism. Marx's economic collectivism supplanted Hegel's political collectivism. Marx had invested the proletarians in mass industry with heroic attirbutes. They were said to have acquired desirably social qualities and powers, and essential capacities for discipline, as a result of having been conscripted by history to work in capitalist industry, becoming a para-military industrial army (22).

Hegel was an upholder of what has been called "the work ethic" in its most individualistic form. The worker who exemplifies this ethic is a member of the middle class. He is self-motivated. His work is a testimony to his human freedom, to his autonomous power of personal "self-making." He receives in return for his efforts, benefits that are material, social and also moral. He develops desirable moral character traits through work, and thereby acquires an acceptable social standing and meritoriousness in the eyes of other people in the same middle class society, and also in his own eyes. For the "ethical individual," who is by definition a member of the middle class, there is ". . . the precept of action to acquire goods through one's own intelligence and industry, – of honesty in commercial dealing, and in the use of property – in short moral life in the socio-economic sphere" (23). This same individual is also a member of a national spiritual collective. On this level he participates in a unity of action and of spirit which includes persons who are not in the middle class occupational range. The ethical individual must stand ready, at all times, to forfeit his earthly possessions, including life itself, for the sake of the nation. It is his duty to act so as to maintain ". . . this substantive individuality, i.e., the independence and sovereignty of the state, at the risk and the sacrifice of property and life, as well as of opinion and everything else naturally comprised in the compass of life" (24). Hegel denied the moral validity of any program for establishing "perpetual peace," referring especially to Kant's anti-war position:

> War is that state of affairs which deals in earnest with the vanity of temporal goods and concerns – a vanity at other times a common theme of edifying sermonizing. This is what makes it the moment in which the ideality of the particular attains its rights and is actualized. War has the higher significance that by its agency, as I have remarked elsewhere, "the ethical health of peoples is preserved in their indifference to the stabilizing of finite institutions; just as the blowing of the winds preserves the

22. See chapter 6 of this book, section on "The Elevation of the Heroic Absolute."
23. *Hegel's Philosophy of Mind, op. cit.,* section 551. See also the discussion of Hegel's socio-economic morality in chapter 5 of this book.
24. *The Philosophy of Right, op. cit.,* section 324.

> sea from the foulness which would be the result of a prolonged calm, so also corruption in nations would be the product of prolonged, let alone 'perpetual' peace" (25).

The ethical individual need not undergo, in reality, the total loss of his secular assets or of his life in times of national mobilization. But he must stand ready to do so. His personal fate will be determined by accidental factors that operate independently of his personal sacrificial will. It is the *will* that must be in accord with the divine necessity.

Hegel had excluded the industrial proletariat of capitalistic society, from the "ethical life" of independent, personal self-making. The middle class was at the moral center of the nation. The proletarians were on the periphery. Marx placed these same workers at the economic and moral center of modern universal society. They represent the great majority within the various industrial nations. The middle class strata, on the other hand, are reduced to moral and economic marginality.

Hegel's collectivism did not nullify nationally internal, morally discriminatory class status differences except in a transcendental manner. The socially and morally marginal proletarians will be called upon to make the same military sacrifices as the higher status groups. For purposes of military action, they are included as equal members of the spiritual whole. There is, in other words, a double standard of moral ranking in Hegel's system. The spiritually equalitarian standard applies also in the relation of the particular individual to the law. Persons in the category of the "penurious rabble" have the same "right" to legal punishment as persons in middle and upper groups. The class differences are to be disregarded, since the law represents "equal justice," i.e., equal right, for all who come under the national jurisdiction. The marginal underclasses who are not, according to Hegel, upholders of the existing legal system, and who are not qualified to serve as representatives of legal authority, must endure the disadvantages of living in modern bourgeois national society, while being denied access to the compensating benefits.

In his concept of universal participation in necessary social labor, Marx was eliminating the inequities and moral ambiguities of the bourgeois system described by Hegel. There would be equal justice for all, i.e., an equality of rank and of merit, and an equality of free personal life-time, based on an equality of effort and of time contribution in relation to necessary material labor tasks. Marx eliminated the contrast between the secular institutional routines of socio-economic life and the extraordinary interruptions of the normal routine in times of war. There need be no readiness to undergo sacrificial death for the sake of preserving society as a whole from corruption. Neither will there have to be a willingness to risk material security. In place of the constant, voluntary readiness for *total* sacrifice which is required of the ethical, middle-class individual in the Hegelian system, there will be a normal universal rendering of a voluntary work contribution. In Hegel's system, the

---

25. *Ibid.,*

ethical individual who has achieved, through personal spiritual development, a complete "self-mastery," has attained a condition in which his own will is identical with the will of the State. Conflict between self-will and the universal imperatives has been eliminated. In Marx's system, the necessity of material labor will not be experienced by the individuals as a social or moral exaction, a limitation on freedom imposed from without, against the wishes or the will of the acting subject. Individuals who have become fully social will not have a tendency to resist such participation. In collective work, they will have acquired, in a natural and social way, a power of self-discipline which is also self-subordination to a collective group project. He (the universal worker)

> . . . not only effects a change of form in the material on which he works, but he also realizes a purpose of his own that gives the law to his modus operandi, and to which he must subordinate his will. . . And this subordination is no mere momentary act. . . The less he is attracted by the nature of the work, and the mode in which it is carried on, and the less, therefore, he enjoys it as something which gives play to his bodily and mental powers, the more close his attention is forced to be (26).

In both systems, Hegelian and Marxist, the autonomy of the working individual is highly prized, but it is always linked to collective autonomy, the autonomy of the whole to which the individual belongs. In Hegel, autonomy on a national level already exists. The "ethical individual" participates in the freedom and autonomy of the nation, which is subject to no external moral or social authority, and to no law except that of its own internal life-development and destiny. In Marx, collective autonomy was yet to be attained by the workers. They could not be autonomous as a working association and society as long as capitalism endured:

> That a capitalist should command on the field of production, is now as indispensable as that a general should command on the field of battle. . . An industrial army of workmen, under the command of a capitalist, requires, like a real army, officers (managers) and sergeants (foremen, overlookers), who, while the work is being done, command in the name of the capitalist (27).

After the rule of capital has ended, the formerly external command functions will be internalized and exercised collectively. The workers will become their own managers, supervisors, and directors. In his Inaugural Address before the meeting of the First International Workingman's Association, October 1864, Marx hailed the success of experimental producer cooperatives as a demonstration of what the future could become. These cooperatives were a

---

26. *Capital,* Volume I, chapter 7, pp. 177-178. This passage has been cited earlier, in chapter 3 in connection with Marx's philosophy of evolution.

27. *Ibid.,* chapter 13, pp. 330 and 332.

> . . . victory of the political economy of labour over the political economy of property. We speak of the cooperative movement, especially the cooperative factories raised by the unassisted efforts of a few bold "hands." The value of these great social experiments cannot be overrated. By deed, instead of by argument, they have shown that production on a large scale, and in accord with the behests of modern science, may be carried on without the existence of a class of masters employing a class of hands. . . and that, like slave labour, like serf labour, hired labour is but a transitory and inferior form, destined to disappear before associated labour plying its toil with a willing hand, a ready mind, and a joyous heart (28).

Hegel had represented the practice of war as a necessity of national spiritual autonomy. This autonomy included the freedom to embark on grand national designs which might lead to disaster, military defeat, and even to the death of the particular nation of which the ethical individual was a member. The autonomy of associated labor, as conceived by Marx, cannot lead to destruction or to the infliction of death. The work of the association is directed to the maintenance and realization of life.

THE DEVALUATION OF THE FAMILY IN THE LABOR PROCESS

Marx's high evaluation of collective group labor went hand in hand with his devaluation of family functions and family roles. Certain parental functions were being absorbed and partly nullified in a collective process above the family level. So considered, the necessity of sharing in the burden of physical labor was also a form of emancipation, insofar as it was also a means for relieving the individual of certain other, formerly burdensome responsibilities and problems. Marx's position on the family, in *Capital,* was not as negative as it had been in his early communist writings (29). The family would persist, albeit in a "higher form," in communist society. Nevertheless, it was still being devalued. Individuals will no longer have to exercise a significant degree of personal moral and disciplinary authority over their children. Nothing in Marx's later writings on family and society was contradictory to what he had written in *The Communist Manifesto:*

> The bourgeois family will vanish as a matter of course when its complement vanishes, and both will vanish with the vanishing of capital.

---

28. *Selected Works of Marx and Engels, op. cit.,* Volume II.

29. See also the discussion of Marx's pre-communist approach to marriage and the family, in chapter 7 of this book, section on his presocialist philosophy of state and law.

> Do you charge us with wanting to stop the exploitation of children by their parents? To this crime we plead guilty.
>
> But, you will say, we destroy the most hallowed of relations, when we replace home education by social.
>
> And your education! Is not that also social, and determined by the social conditions under which you educate, by the intervention, direct or indirect, of society by means of schools, etc.? The Communists have not invented the intervention of society in education; they do but seek to alter the character of that intervention, and to rescue education from the influence of the ruling class.

In *Capital,* Marx said that socialism was to eliminate those forms of parental right that led to the victimization of children. Parental economic exploitation of children was one result of the general atomization process by which all previously established familial ties and moral restraints of a protective kind had been dissolved: ". . . modern industry, in overturning the economic foundation on which was based the traditional family, and the family labor corresponding to it, had also unloosened all traditional family ties." The British Parliament had been reluctant to pass protective laws regulating labor carried on by children in home industries, i.e., outside the factories, viewing such regulation as ". . . a direct attack on the patria potestas, on parental authority." In finally passing such legislation, the members of Parliament blamed the parents for the evils of child exploitation in the home. Marx blamed the system of capital, but he also believed that the parents, as well as the employers, had been engaging in a "mischievous misuse of power" which is the hallmark of capitalism:

> . . . it was not. . . the misuse of parental authority that created the capitalistic exploitation, whether direct or indirect, of children's labour; but, on the contrary, it was the capitalistic mode of exploitation which, by sweeping away the economic basis of parental authority, made its exercize degenerate into a mischievous misuse of power (30).

The economy that leads to this degeneration is laying the basis for a dialectical leap which will not restore the earlier, tradition-bound form of family life. Instead, it will eliminate the possibility that parental power will continue to exist to any important degree:

> However terrible and disgusting the dissolution, under the capitalist system, of the old family ties may appear, nevertheless, modern industry, by assigning as it does an important part in the process of production outside the domestic sphere, to women, to young persons, and to children of both sexes, creates a new economic foundation for a higher form of the family and of the

30. Volume I, chapter 15, p. 489.

> relations between the sexes. . . Moreover, it is obvious that the fact of the collective working group being composed of individuals of both sexes and all ages, must necessarily, under suitable conditions, become a source of humane development. . . (31).

Personally exercised functions of authority and parental control appearing in earlier forms of family life are being replaced by an impersonal discipline which regulates the activities of all in the working group. Previously existing differences between masculine and feminine functions are being minimized as much as possible. Women will not retain any special family functions and responsibilities. When masculine family authority is excluded, feminine authority disappears also.

It is hardly surprising that Marx, in his outlook on the future, made no room for a category of labor – partly material and partly mental – that was unpaid labor in capitalist society, and which was not the source of surplus value derived by capital from industrial production and paid proletarian work. Marx seems to sssume either that the need for domestic household functions will not exist in socialist society, or that no provision at all need be made for such work, which will apparently be counted as a "free time" occupation, along with those middle class occupations classed as "immaterial labor." Marx treats the proletarian way of life as if it included no domestic sphere at all. It is the middle class family, in which the men, women and children are not working side by side, collectively, for the capitalist employer, that is to be extinguished. He makes it clear that women will be expected to work in non-domestic, material production the same number of hours as men, both in the political economy of the working class, and in the final classless society.

Non-domestic collective work is a character-training and character-transforming process which adults and children undergo involuntarily, in capitalist society, if they are proletarians. This form of training will one day be universalized. The process is needed especially by children, since they no longer have a family environment. Marx objected strongly to the Gotha Programme demand of the German party, calling for "the restriction of women's labour and the prohibition of child labour." Women, he said, should come under the same protective regulations in regard to the length of the working day that are suitable for men, and should be restricted only by being excluded from "branches of industry that are specifically unhealthy for the females body or are objectionable morally for the female sex." He went on to say that

> A general prohibition of child labour is incompatible with the existence of large-scale industry and hence an empty, pious aspiration.

---

31. *Ibid.*, p. 490.

> Its realization – if it were possible – would be reactionary, since, with a strict regulation of the working time according to the different age groups and other safety measures for the protection of children, an early combination of productive labour with education is one of the most potent means for the transformation of present-day society.

In the *Grundrisse* manuscripts, at the time when Marx was abandoning his earlier idea that labor on the necessary level of material production might be completely eliminated in the classless society, he implied that children will be able to become adults capable of further independent self-development only if they first undergo the discipline of the group work experience:

> The process [of material labor] is then both discipline, as regards the human being in the process of becoming; and, at the same time practice [Ausubung], experimental science, materially creative and objectifying science, as regards the human being who has become, in whose head exists the accumulated knowledge of society. For both, insofar as labour requires practical use of the hands and free bodily movement, as in agriculture, [it is] at the same time exercize (32).

Both Hegel and Marx had devalued the family, along with specifically feminine functions, in their philosophies of history. Hegel, however, had attached a good deal of importance to the family as a child-caring institution. The modern proletarians, according to him, were morally deprived, not qualified for full participation in the authority of society, because their extreme impoverishment had made family life impossible for them. Non-scholastic educational and disciplinary functions taking place within middle class families were an essential preparation for later adult life:

> . . . the right of the parents over the wishes of their children is determined by the object in view – discipline and education. . . this education has the negative aim of raising children out of the instinctive, physical level on which they are originally, to self-subsistence and freedom of personality and so to the level on which they have the power to leave the natural unity of the family (33).

It is only the young adult male who must take his place in the wider, supra-familial world of economic and political life. The woman's activities, on a mature level, are still confined to the domestic sphere as she leaves her original natural family to function in a new family relation as a wife and a parent. While Hegel did not exclude women from the ethical life, they never achieve that degree of "abstract" independence and especially that degree of rationality and of intellect, which the man can achieve. Women, as adults, share in an "ethical mind" union with their husbands in regard to family mat-

32. Translated by Nicolaus, *op. cit.*, p. 712.
33. *The Philosophy of Right*, sections 174 and 175.

ters. The bond of marriage produces a common "ethical mind" within the family domain: "The identification of personalities, whereby the family becomes one person and its members become accidents. . . is the ethical mind" (34). As an economic unit, the family also has a single identity. It ". . . has its real external existence in property," which is family capital and which becomes "the embodiment of the substantial personality of the family" (35).

In Hegel's dialectics, the development of Reason in history culminates in the emergence of a personal self-consciousness and a power of personal self-making which is associated with masculine identity, and which becomes, in the political sphere, a participation of the individual in the "ethical substance" of the State. The woman is excluded from this political relation, which is not required for the attainment of the highest level of feminine spiritual life. The family, an ethical sphere which is sub-political, has therefore no "world-historical" significance, i.e., feminine functions as such have no world-historical significance:

> In this social relation [of the family], morality consists in the members behaving toward each other *not as individuals* – possessing an independent will; not as persons. The family, therefore, is excluded from that process of development in which History takes its rise (36).

Marx, as we have seen, substituted character training in the collective working group for education in the middle class family. The Hegelian emphasis on the development of philosophical intellect and reason in history was subordinated to an emphasis on the development of technological power over nature. This progressive activity, like the activity of philosophy, was identified with masculine initiatives and powers. History had progressed beyond the primitive state of immersion in original nature. The mind and will of the universal worker developed beyond the first, instinctual level, through an interaction with the materials of nature which had brought out the dormant potentialities of passive matter by inducing changes in form. In this way, Man had evolved himself. Further changes in social, economic and political institutions and structures, and in culture, had come about as a result of this primary interactivity. In Aristotelian philosophy, the vitalizing, form-developing Nous components of teleological Nature signify masculine powers. The passive, form-receptive attributes of matter are identified as feminine.

Marx associated the achievement of rational scientific power over nature, and a practical, instrumentalist attitude toward nature, with the accession of humanity to a mature, adult level of self-consciousness. Primitive communal life, in which such power had not developed, and in which the prevalent attitude toward nature, Marx believed, had been religious, was iden-

34. *Ibid.*, section 163.
35. *Ibid.*, section 169.
36. *The Philosophy of History,* Introduction

tified with childhood dependency. In the evolutionary perspective, he sometimes treated the human species as if it were a single super-entity changing and maturing in time. Even when the dividing line between pre-history and history had been crossed, historical individuals at a low level of development were socially in a "pre-natal" condition. Societies somewhat more advanced represented various stages and forms of cultural childhood. Full cultural adulthood – in an alienated form – was reached in bourgeois society, at which time the individuals had been freed by history from feudalistic and patriarchal dependency ties. The bourgeois break with feudal culture and with Catholic clerical authority was therefore the historical equivalent of the passage of a single person from later childhood to adulthood in the course of his personal life history. The rupture with the pre-adult past, both in personal and in social history, seemed to be complete.

In describing the social experience of the individual in modern rational society, and the way in which he acquires self-consciousness, Marx minimized and indeed almost obliterated references to childhood experience. In one of the most interesting of the many interesting footnotes in *Capital* he had written:

> In a sort of way, it is with man as with commodities. Since he comes into the world neither with a looking glass in his hand, nor as a Fichteian philosopher, to whom "I am I" is sufficient, man first sees and recognizes himself in other men. Peter only establishes his own identity as a man by first comparing himself with Paul as being of like kind. And thereby Paul, just as he stands in his Pauline personality, becomes to Peter the type of the genus homo (37).

This passage is compatible with Marx's abstract atomic theory, with his formal supposition that adults in the atomized society have no social experience which gives them a sense of identity with others, until they encounter such others in non-familial relationships of a positive kind. Obviously, he cannot be referring to the early impressions received by a child who normally must relate to, and in some way become forcefully aware of, the different-from-self identity of his parents, of other adults, of older and younger children and of persons of the opposite sex, to mention only some of the most obvious "non-identical" categories likely to be encountered.

When Marx excluded the family as an educational agency, he was at the same time eliminating from his own philosophy of the future the personal dialectic of negation and of the "negation of the negation" which Hegel had included when he referred to the spiritual development of the "ethical individual" who achieves a transcendental unification with the objective Spirit and Mind of the State. The individual so described also participates in the universal Reason and Mind of philosophy at the highest modern level of absolute enlightenment. This ethical individual starts out as a youth imbued with an

37. Volume I, chapter 1, p. 52. See also chapter 7 of this book, pp. 169 and 170.

ideal about the world and his role in it which is not compatible with the actuality. ". . . he feels that both his ideal and his own personality are not recognized by the world, thus the youth, unlike the child, is no longer at peace with the world." As the youth matures, he must come to recognize that the ideal which he seeks is already present and actualized in the objective world outside of himself. He then recognizes his own activity as part of the ideal process. Only if he becomes afflicted by a "diseased state of mind" and is unable to "give up his subjectivity" will the adult man be "unable to overcome his repugnance to the actual world, and by this very fact finds himself in a state of relative incapacity which may become actual incapacity." But the stronger persons manage to overcome this subjectivity:

> If, therefore, the man does not want to perish, he must recognize the world as a self-dependent world which in its essential nature is already complete, must accept the conditions set for him by the world and wrest from it what he wants for himself. As a rule, the man believes that this submission is only forced upon him by necessity. But, in truth, this unity with the world must be recognized, not as a relation imposed by necessity, but as rational. The rational, the divine, possesses the absolute power to actualize itself, and has, right from the beginning, fulfilled itself. . . The world is this actualization of divine Reason: it is only on its surface that the play of contingency prevails. . . therefore the man behaves quite rationally in abandoning his plan for completely transforming the world, and in striving to realize his personal aims, passions, and interests only within the framework of the world of which he is a part (38).

Although Hegel seems to refer to a representative middle class individual, it is only the philosopher who recognizes the "divine" nature of necessity. It is apparent that Marx proposed to transform the actuality, in such a way as to eliminate the initial period of youthful negativity and opposition to the world as it exists. In so doing, he also eliminates the breaking away period of adolescence which Hegel had described in such an interesting way. He eliminates the Hegelian contrast between the early family environment and the wider, initially alien environment of the world in which the young man must learn to find himself, and to realize himself. The society of socialism, from the very beginning, will be beyond radical, critical negation, since it will have passed through that stage. The negative action of the working class revolutionary movement in defeating the powers of capital displaces or absorbs the dialectical critical negativity of the Hegelian single self. Once the crisis is passed, actuality, even in the first, still highly imperfect stage of socialist development, will be recognized and accepted as tending inevitably toward the higher condition. In the economy of socialism, all significant relations, even those experienced by young children, will be extra-familial. The

38. *Hegel's Philosophy of Mind, op. cit.,* section 396.

individual will be included as soon as possible in a collective work group which will be his moral and social environment. This group will be composed of persons of both sexes and of nearly all ages. The individual will not pass through a period in which he becomes critical of the existing world or insecure in his relation to it.

In his political unity philosophy, Hegel had made an implicit distinction between the ethical individual who finally, after undergoing some degree of stress, achieves a transcendental unity with the State and the great majority of non-philosophical individuals who comprise the nation. The single ethical individual had first negated this own personal critical reactions before becoming united with the Divine Reason of the State. This dialectical unification seems to be by-passed in the case of the great majority, the people who become united into a spiritual whole under the influence of political soul-leaders and military heroes. The Volkgeist is a collective spirit that undercuts the level of rational critical consciousness. Persons are united sub-rationally into a collective whole, in response to external leadership and direction. This spirit is first

> . . . in a state of unconsciousness which the great man in question aroused. Their fellows, therefore, follow these soul-leaders; for they feel the irresistible power of their own inner Spirit thus embodied (39).

This collective spirit, guided by the leadership, is part of the history making progressive, divinely guided force that will continue to operate indefinitely in the future.

There was a less conspicuous division, in Marx's system, between the individual who passes smoothly from childhood into maturity in the society of socialism and the collective unity of the working group of which he will also become a part. In the *Grundrisse,* the individual who has gone through the stage of "becoming," i.e., a process of personal maturation, becomes mentally detached from the group work in which he is engaged, perceiving it in its world-historical perspective. Here the mind of the Hegelian philosopher reappears, without being so labelled. However, there were passages in *Capital* where Marx was describing the collective spirit and form of social empowerment that developed naturally and spontaneously in group labor activities. Here the group was described as being under external direction. The mentality that initiates the work project, directs and manages it, is external to the group. Something resembling the Hegelian *Volkgeist* develops under these conditions. The mind of philosophy, the mind of the detached knower, is wholly in abeyance. The collective spirit is social, not political, but the unifying work activity is analogous to a military activity:

---

39. *The Philosophy of History,* Introduction. See also the discussion of Hegel's philosophy of national Spirit, in chapter 4 of this book, section on "The Oppression of Humanity by External and Social Power."

> Just as the offensive power of a squadron of cavalry, or the defensive power of a regiment of infantry, is essentially different from the sum of the offensive or defensive powers of the individual cavalry or infantry soldiers taken separately, so the sum total of the mechanical forces exerted by isolated workmen differs from the social force that is developed, when many hands take part simultaneously in one of the same undivided operation. . . Not only have we here an increase in the productive power of the individual, by means of cooperation, but the creation of a new power, namely, the collective power of masses.
>
> Apart from the new power that arises from the fusion of many forces into one single force, mere social contact begets in most industries an emulation and a stimulation of the animal spirits that heighten the efficiency of each individual workman. . . The reason of this is that man is, if not as Aristotle contends, a political, at all events a social animal (40).

In Hegel's philosophy, the political collective that is being mobilized by "soul leaders" is to be aroused to a condition of enthusiasm for collective aggression, destruction, and sacrifice. There must be a readiness on the part of the male individual to sacrifice a good deal more than his own personal life and his own personal assets and interests. In spite of the fact that Marx, in his vision of the future society of associated labor, eliminates the family as a moral unit, his socialism was more child-protective than Hegel's political nationalism. The "ethical health of peoples" which, according to Hegel, can be preserved from corruption only by war, requires the periodic sacrifice of family security and the security of children. Women and children, as well as men, are imperilled in the essential masculine activity of war. The duty of the adult male to the State, a duty which links him to the "divine life," overrides any duty he might have toward his own family. The lives and security of families in those other nations which might be subjected to attack by the individual's own nation, also count for nothing in the spiritually cleansing ritual of war.

When Marx replaced Hegel's political collectivism with an economic collectivism, and the nationally unifying project of war with the unifying, world-universal activities of associated labor, he was including the entire family – men, women, and children – within the same life-protective and security maintaining system. He was also concerned with ensuring the maintenance and replenishment of the natural resources required by future generations. Hegel, on the other hand, had been indifferent to such concerns.

---

40. Volume I, chapter 13, pp. 325–326. See also chapter 5 of this book, p. 121.

THE CONTINUING NECESSITY OF STRUGGLE

In his mature works, Marx had modified his perspective on the future. In his early period, he was ignoring the process of childhood development that all persons born into the future social economy would have to undergo. The focus was on the society of adults who were to achieve self-emancipation and autonomy, becoming free of the need for external legal and social constraint and external social authority, once they had gained control of the material means by which this freedom would be achieved. In the later works, the period of childhood is recognized. The individual who begins as a child will have to go through a socializing and disciplining process before he can become a fully mature member of society. Marx's resemblance to Hegel was in some ways more pronounced in his later period. This was partly the result of his emphasis on non-scholastic childhood education. In addition, the continued necessity of material labor on the adult level of life guarantees the persistence of a kind of social solidarity and morale that the "young Marx" had not included in his vision of ultimate communism.

In the mature works, individuals united in associated labor will be bound together by the continued necessity of struggle against a non-human external, potentially inimical power – the power of Nature. The social struggle against external Nature becomes the means by which the internal morality of the society will be maintained in future generations beyond the time of political and social class struggle.

In the early writings, the essential condition for the maintenance of peace, unity and freedom in the future society seemed to consist almost entirely in the avoidance of material scarcity. The conflict of interests and the universal competition prevailing in bourgeois society would be eliminated when scarcity was overcome. That same society, however, might conceivably disintegrate into a collection of atomistic individuals in situations of economic decline and recurring material scarcity. Individuals who had become psychologically accommodated to a particular material standard of living might again compete against one another economically, if there were not an almost unlimited supply of material goods made continually available by a transcendental, collectively appropriated technological and social power that seemed to operate automatically.

In the later writings, the situation is not so unstable, although there is still a major emphasis on the need for material expansion as a means for bringing about the higher stage of communism. Marx's basic moral outlook, throughout every phase of his career, was always connected with a metaphysical atomism. The isolated atomic individual was treated as the root source and cause of the competitive, aggressive, acquisitive and destructive potentialities of universal human nature. These are likely to reappear, and to express themselves again in action, provided there is no social environmental system which can effectively offset them. The older Marx, thinking of the future society, begins with the child. The child is born into society as an "abstract" non-social individual, containing within himself or herself diverse potentialities, negative and positive. The disapproved potentialities will be counteracted in the socializing and training experience of the group environment. In this process, the child will become attached directly to the collective whole, and will be brought under the influence of the collective group spirit.

In the early writings, the future social individual was perceived as the member of a consuming society, not also as a material worker and producer. with a publicly necessary contribution to make. His consumer needs and wants were said to be derived from "society." As such, they would inevitably expand, increasing and also changing as a result of unceasing technological innovations and improvements, in a situation of expanding material productivity. The socialized consumer's expectations as to what he should rightfully get and even demand in the way of a material standard of living were determined by his passive, uncritical dependency on the group value system, i.e., by his readiness to accept the value judgments of other people as his own. Insofar as he is fully immersed in the ongoing "life process of society" he will be incapable of developing a negative reaction to any aspect of the ever-changing material consumer need system. The process of continuous technological change testifies to the presence of higher faculties of scientific and practical reason. It is complemented by consumer passivity and by the morally desirable social irrationality of the need determining process.

Marx's technological emphasis was by no means diminished in his later writings. The future social individuals are still being considered as material consumers who are perpetually under the influence of socially determined needs and wants. These requirements are called "mundane." But the mundane consumer needs system is transcended in the unity of the collective work effort. A continuous struggle with Nature is required because of the need pressure, i.e., the need to combat nature. This same work necessity is also a socially essential moral training ground for the younger generation, a substitute for the Hegelian family system.

In *Capital* III Marx had said that humanity would never be free from the need to "wrestle with nature" in order to satisfy his wants. In socialist society, nature will always yield a sufficiency, but only when an input of common activity, of collective discipline, and of time-sacrificial effort is being contributed. Under such conditions, there will be a unifying morale, a constantly renewed sense of common purpose, which provides a substitute for the politically unifying class struggle that has been left behind. It is also a substitute for Hegel's activity of war. The class struggle had been a unity against a common social enemy. In the period of classless communism, there will be no external social opponent, but the necessity of material labor will maintain, in practice, a combat solidarity and an equality of moral ranking which was in continuity with Marx's heroic ideal. The collective work endeavor which is socially necessary is a struggle not directed primarily against *outer* nature. It is a means for keeping a potentially troublesome internal field of "human nature" under permanent, morally sufficient control.

12

Sociology And Social Theory

This concluding chapter will call attention to aspects of Marx's concept of the future society of communism that are of particular interest when his socialism is regarded from the standpoint of social science. A good deal that is relevant in this connection has been discussed in earlier chapters. Some reference will be made here to what has gone before, but I will bring in materials not yet considered, drawing chiefly on his later writings, including the *Grundrisse* manuscripts of 1857-58.

SOCIALISM AS A RETURN TO SIMPLICITY

In the philosophical manuscripts of 1844, Marx had indicated some of the primary aspects of what can be called his evolutionary, dialectical sociology. It was clear that he was regarding the dialectical movement of history as a problem solving process. Various forms of social division that had developed naturally in the post-primitive economic systems of the pre-capitalist era and which had characterized capitalist society also, would gradually disappear in the socialist era. In addition, the movement that would carry humanity beyond capitalism would eliminate the problems that had arisen in philosophical consciousness. There was to be a return toward an earlier condition of unity which resembled the process of "return" described by Hegel. In his *Philosophy of Nature,* Hegel had referred to the involutionary aspect of the evolutionary process in nature. Involution took place when the initial deadness of inorganic matter was nullified by being absorbed into the higher organic life forms (1). Hegel had referred also, in other writings, to the return of Spirit, at an enriched, fully actualized level, to the unity of the Idea. The involutionary phase of the natural social evolutionary process begins, in Marx's system, with the abolition of the capitalist economy. The movement of communism, properly defined, ". . . knows itself as the reintegration or return of man to himself, as the overcoming of human self-alienation. . ." (2).

1. *Op. cit.,* Introduction, section 252, p. 26.
2. "Private Property and Communism" (1844), translated by Easton and Guddat, *op. cit.*

It was a movement away from complexity, disunity and conflict toward a condition of higher simplicity, unity and freedom from conflict. Marx had also said that post-capitalist society would not be ". . . an impoverished return to unnatural, primitive simplicity. Rather, they [atheism and communism] are primarily the actual emergence and actual developed realization of man's nature as something actual" (3).

The term "actual" in this passage can be understood in relation to Aristotle's philosophy of being and becoming. Actualization is the movement from a condition of potentiality to a condition of realization or fulfillment through a temporal unfolding of potentialities inherent in the beginning. In his reference to "unnatural primitive simplicity," Marx was concurring with Hegel in rejecting what they both considered were reactionary cults of artificial modern primitivism.

A good many years later, in a letter to Engels (March 25, 1868) he indicated that he had not abandoned this idea of return. He expected that the progressive movement of history would end by replicating, at a higher level of culture, the unity of self with society that had existed at the beginning of national life, in the remote past:

> The first reaction against the French Revolution and the Enlightenment bound up with it was naturally to see everything as medieval, romantic; even people like Grimm are not free from this. The second reaction is to look beyond the Middle Ages into the primitive age of every nation, and that corresponds to the socialist tendency, although these learned men have no idea that they have any connection with it. Then they are surprised to find what is newest in what is oldest. . .

The future society of communism was to have a good deal in common with Aristotle's conception of political society, even though Marx did not describe his own outlook in this way. Marx's negative attitude toward the solipsist (the supreme individualist and anarchist) who believed himself to be independent of society, was markedly similar to the views of Aristotle concerning the "self-sufficient" individual who places himself outside of the State. The relation of the individual to the whole in the society of communism was to resemble the right relation of the individual to the political community as described by Aristotle.

Unlike Hegel, Aristotle had not defined the State as a divine institution, directly linked with God or Idea outside of nature. The Aristotelian State and the political society of the State had developed within nature, as part of a total realizing movement which included humanity. Aristotle had defined men as "political" and also as "social" animals. Society had at first been pre-political. The Aristotelian State had developed out of a more primitive, barbaric condition. The State that had so emerged was regarded in a transcendental light as a perfect (Platonic) form, actualized in history by the telic power

3. "Critique of Hegelian Philosophy" (1844), Easton and Guddat, *op. cit.*

of creational nature. The State of Aristotle was so closely identified with the society with which it was connected that the two were almost indistinguishable. To be outside of soiety was also to be outside of the State. It was to exist in a moral and psychological limbo, in a state of "self-sufficiency" and detachment incompatible with the life of the political community. The individual who was born into the fully developed political society could achieve the highest possible personal condition of self-realization only insofar as he was morally dependent on the order maintained in that society. His personal life could be completed only through his relation to this "self-sufficient" community. Justice in such a community was defined by Aristotle as "the principle of order." That order corresponded to a principle of perfection (and of circular motion) that had been established in the sphere of the heavens, in the motion of the heavenly bodies. The individual who belongs to the Greek political community must conform to the norms of his society and to the laws of the State: ". . . he who is unable to live in society, or who has no need because he is sufficient for himself, must either be a beast or a god; he is no part of the state. He who by nature and not by mere accident is without a state, is either a bad man or above humanity; he is like the 'Tribeless, lawless, heartless one' whom Homer denounces – the natural outcast is forthwith a lover of war; he may be compared to an isolated piece of draughts" (4).

"War" in this context seems to mean only the aggressive and destructive anti-social actions of an isolated individual outside of the State, beyond its moral control. A transcendental sanction is given, by implication, to collective enterprises of war undertaken by a rightly ordered State society. "Heartlessness" is an attribute of an isolated individual, presumbaly not shared by those who are united with the order upheld by the state: ". . . man, when perfected, is the best of animals, but, when separated from law and justice, he is the worst of all. . . "

Like many other social thinkers of the Judeo-Christian era, Marx eliminated a major contradiction that was so evident in Aristotle, namely the contradiction between the biological and medical frame of reference and the moral and political frame of reference. Only a limited portion of the human species could be included within the political State form, experiencing a personal self-realization based on such membership. The State co-existed with less developed forms of society and also with inferior types of individuals. The slaves that were economically subordinated, excluded from the political life of the free citizens, were said, by Aristotle, to be "naturally" inferior. As a biologist Aristotle studied mankind as a single species, but he abandoned this scientific universalism in his social outlook. The existing hierarchies and ranks of humanity were regarded as manifestations of a beneficient natural and cosmological order.

Aristotle did not deny that the State society maintained relations with group outside its own boundaries, and also with non-citizen and slave groups who were within the political territory, but it appears as though the State

4. *Politics,* Book I, Jowett translation.

cannot err with respect to these relations. In Marx's society of the future, membership in the community will no longer be restricted. It will be open to all who are members of the human species. However, the moral simplicity of the life that was lived within the boundaries of Aristotle's political citizen society would be restored. All social relations would be internal, occurring within a single category of persons possessing an equal, and equally acceptable status as human beings. The return of man from alienation and estrangement would be a return to life in a society which would no longer have to cope with moral and practical problems of external relations, nor of relations with groups socially designated as "inferior." A potentially troublesome category of individuals who are self-excluded, who remain apart from community life and outside of the order of society, would pose no serious problem, since these would always be a small minority, if indeed they existed at all.

Marx's relation to Aristotle was mediated by Hegel's *Phenomenology of Spirit* (Geist), where the focus was on the development of a personally detached self-consciousness. This was a necessary pre-condition for the advance to a higher form of unity in which the individual would be morally at one with society, while at the same time preserving intact his personal individuality. The society of communism could not be established until the kind of personal individuality that Marx associated with the emergence of ancient and modern forms of "private property" had first appeared. Primitive communism of the "Asiatic" type was by no means to be duplicated, since individuality could not have developed in these non-Western, tradition-bound systems. The Asiatic folk societies of India were primitive communes, since agricultural land was owned by the community, not by individuals. They were said to be regulated impersonally by fixed tradition, the functional equivalent of unconscious instinct. The social and economic order was maintained and perpetuated in an automatic way, without the need for conscious-level forms of political, moral or social authority. Marx declared, in *Capital:*

> . . . the law that regulates the division of labour in the community acts with the irresistible authority of a law of Nature, at the same time that each individual artificer, the smith, the carpenter, and so on, conducts in his workshop all the operations of his handicraft, but independently, and without recognizing any authority over him (5).

The relation of the individual to the community was a primitive kind:

> Cooperation, such as we find it at the dawn of human development, among races who live by the chase, or, say, in the agricultural Indian communities, is based, on the one hand, on ownership in common of the means of production, and on the other hand, on the fact that in those cases, each individual has no more torn himself off from the navel-string of his tribe or community,

5. Volume I, chapter 15, p. 358.

> than each bee has freed himself from connexion with the hive. Such cooperation is distinguished from capitalistic cooperation by both of the above characteristics (6).

In the earlier *Grundrisse* manuscripts, he had said that "... man is only individualized through the process of history" (7). Referring to the agricultural communities of India, he said that "The *community* is here... the first pre-condition... that substance, of which the individuals are mere accidents (Aksidenzen) or of which they form mere spontaneously natural parts..." (8).

In societies which were post-primitive, the individual had gone beyond the "substantial," i.e., the almost pre-natal, womb-like condition which had existed at first. The original tribal ownership of property in land and in other means of production had been superseded by individual proprietorship. This meant that individuation had taken place. The individual was no longer joined with a pre-individualized "substance." In the developing and changing societies of the West, a specific way of life could not be reproduced indefinitely, or reconstituted in a process of almost instinctual, automatic self-renewal, as the Asiatic (Indian) village communities were said to have been able to do before they had succumbed to the final Western invasion.

Marx looked back in the direction of the city-state civilization of classical antiquity, which had been superior in some ways to the civilization of capitalism. The best features of this early form of civilization were to be restored in the age of socialism. The limitations of that earlier time were to be surpassed. Production, in the societies of classical antiquity, had not been merely economic. It had been the production, and the attempted reproduction, of an entire way of life, It had included aims that could not be reduced to individualistic economic and social status aims. Production activity in socialist society would be similarly inclusive, reinstating what had been most admirable and worthy of emulation in the earlier civilization:

> Among the ancients... enquiry is always about what kind of property creates the best citizens...
>
> Thus the ancient conception, in which man always appears (in however narrowly national, religious or political a definition) as the aim of production, seems very much more exalted than the modern world, in which production is the aim of man and wealth the aim of production (9).

The community of the future was to be supra-national rather than international. Ethnic, cultural and regional localism would not disappear, but the differences would not be divisive, and the nation as a significant moral entity would no longer exist. Henri Lefebvre, in *The Sociology of Marx*, has

6. *Ibid.*, chapter 14, p. 334.
7. *Pre-Capitalist Economic Formations, op. cit.*, p. 96.
8. *Ibid.*, p. 71.
9. *Ibid.*, p. 84.

tentatively concluded from his reading of *The Communist Manifesto* and of *The Critique of the Gotha Programme,* which he calls Marx's "last political will and testament," that ". . . the proletarian will do away with national boundaries, completing a process begun under capitalism." He adds, however, that Marx was ambiguous about the future status of the nation: "Why not admit frankly that to some extent these famous texts are puzzling to us today?" (10)

At least some of the confusion arises from a failure on the part of interpreters of Marx to distinguish between the first stages of political socialism, as conceived by Marx, and the later classless phase. In his writings on the proletarian dictatorship he emphasized the importance of maintaining and strengthening national unity and national power in those countries where the workers had come to power and were seeking to establish socialism within their own limited political territory. National boundaries would gradually lose their importance in the process by which the transitional political phase of working class rule was supplanted by a classless form of social and public power. The unity of the classless future was to resemble the unity maintained in those pre-commercial, agriculturally based societies of antiquity which had contributed to the later Western advance. The return to a post-primitive simplicity presupposed the elimination of the need for certain functions that had been carried on in these earlier, territorially limited political societies.

In the *Grundrisse* manuscripts, Marx had written, with respect to the city-state "communes" of Western antiquity, that

> The continuation of the commune. . . is safeguarded by the surplus labour of its members in the form of military service, etc. The member of the community reproduces himself not through cooperation in wealth-producing labour, but in cooperation in labour for the (real or imaginary) communal interests aimed at sustaining the union against external and internal stress (11).

He included the ancient Judaic community among those societies in which the economic arrangements were regarded as a means for promoting and maintaining a total way of life, and the development of individuals as community members. He quoted with approval a passage from a history of Rome by Niebuhr, a German historian, who had said that

> . . . the first preoccupation of the pious monarch was not the worship of the gods, but a human one. He distributed the land conquered in war and left to be occupied: he founded the worship of Terminus (the god of boundary-stones). All the ancient lawgivers, and above all Moses, founded the success of their arrangements for virtue, justice and good morals (*Sitte*) upon landed property, or at least on secure hereditary possession of land, for the greatest possible number of citizens.

10. Chapter 5, pp. 173-174, Pantheon Books, New York, 1968.
11. *Pre-Capitalist Economic Formations, op. cit.,* p. 74.

Marx said that under such circumstances

> The individual is placed in such a condition of gaining his life as to make not the acquiring of wealth his object, but self-sustenance; his own reproduction as a member of the community; the reproduction of himself as a proprietor of the parcel of ground and, in that quality, as a member of the commune (12).

The territorial ground of the world economy is the global land territory that supports human life. Political boundaries will have no future moral significance. They have already been rendered obsolete on a material level, through the system of world-wide economic interdependency and commercial exchange which came into existence during the age of capitalist expansion. In the new age, individuals will sustain and develop the material and spiritual life of humanity, and their own personal life, through production activity.

Under the new conditions of production ". . . man does not reproduce himself in any determined form, but produces his totality. . . he does not seek to remain something formed by the past, but is in the absolute movement of becoming." Marx projects a cosmos that is open-ended, never completed. The creative potentialities of humanity, disclosed in the alienated age of capitalism, are unlimited. These powers will be liberated in post-alienated time:

> In bourgeois political economy – and in the epoch of production to which it corresponds – this complete elaboration of what lies within man, appears as the total alienation, and the destruction of all fixed, one-sided purposes as the sacrifice of the end in itself to a wholly external compulsion. Hence in one way the childlike world of the ancients appears to be superior; and this is so, insofar as we seek for closed shape, form, and established limitation. The ancients provide a narrow satisfaction, whereas the modern world leaves us unsatisfied, or, where it appears to be satisfied with itself, is *vulgar* and *mean* (13).

HUMANITY AS A DOMINANT CASTE COMMUNITY

When Marx wrote to Engels that socialism looks back in the direction of the beginning of each modern nation, he seems to have been referring to a time preceding the development of slavery. In the future society there will be no more domination and enslavement of human beings by other members of the same species. The dependency of humanity on nature, as mediated by modern science and technology, was to replace the former dependence of the classical civilizations on slavery. Humanity would be organically dependent on the subordinated realm of nature, just as earlier slave societies had been

---

12. *Ibid.*,
13. *Pre-Capitalist Economic Formations, op. cit.*, pp. 84-85.

organically dependent on human slave labor. The future organic economy includes an essential but subordinate realm of non-social nature. It will also possess an inner moral duality, resembling the duality that had developed in the earlier caste-divided economic systems of the pre-capitalist slave societies. Humanity as species would become a new kind of dominant caste community, conscious of its separateness from, and superiority to, the subordinate realm of outer nature, to which it was organically linked and on which it will remain forever dependent.

In his philosophical writings of 1844, Marx had said that the essential nature of man was social, and that sub-social "nature" was a quasi-organic "outer body" of man. In these essays, he had blurred the distinction between "organic" and "inorganic" phenomena. In the later *Grundrisse* writings, this tendency is expressed in a somewhat different way. When he describes the agriculturally based slave-holding societies, he becomes something of a psychosociologist. He makes inferences about the subjectivity of those individuals who belong to what he calls the "producing community." In this context, this category excludes slaves and serfs attached to the land. It consists of those who belong to the dominant political-economic strata. He says that the slaves and serfs are perceived by the dominant community members as part of a natural environment which includes animals and other "organic" and "inorganic" properties of the land:

> In the relationship of slavery and serfdom. . . what happens is that one part of society is treated by another as a mere *organic and natural* condition of its own reproduction. . . It is. . . *labour* itself, both in the form of the slave as of the serf, which is placed among other living things (Naturwesen) as inorganic condition of production, alongside the cattle as an appendage of the soil. In other words, the original conditions of production appear as natural prerequisites, *natural conditions of existence of the producers*. . . (14).

Marx implies also that members of the dominant society feel "naturally' entitled to make use of whatever substratum resources, human or non-human, have become available to them as a result of their dominating position, or as a result of their active economic and political initiative as a community engaged in external conquest and in the "labour of war":

> In general, property in land includes property in its organic products. Where man himself is captured as an organic accessory of the land and together with it, he is captured as one of the conditions of production. . . (15).

14. *Ibid.*, p, 87.
15. *Ibid.*, p. 89.

The individual in the subjugating group holds property by virtue of his status as a group member. The external population deprived of this property and the power which goes along with it is not part of the humanly significant social world:

> The fundamental condition of property based on tribalism (which is originally formed out of the community) is to be a member of the tribe. Consequently a tribe conquered and subjugated by another becomes *propertyless* and part of the *inorganic* condition of the conquering tribe's reproduction, which the community regards as its own (16).

Marx implies that persons who belong to a dominant community and who accept the prevailing norms of their own moral group actually perceive and relate to persons in the subordinated categories as if the latter were nothing more than a means to support and perpetuate the way of life that they experience within their closed community. The life that is lived within the status boundaries of their own group is the only kind of life that has intrinsic meaning and value for them. Ties of common origin, language and culture bind the individuals together, even though some of them may lose their property in land and may become proletarianized. Class inequalities may develop within the upper caste society without destroying these other social and cultural ties. The Roman citizens who became proletarians lost their property, but not their status as free Roman citizens. In writing about these political societies of classical antiquity, Marx was saying that no moral problems arose in the subjective consciousness of persons in the free citizen group with regard to subordinate slave populations, and that the community as such had been unconcerned with such problems (17). He treats this kind of exclusiveness, this dissociative tendency, as a natural and normal reaction, given the limiting conditions that had existed in the pre-capitalist past. These limitations will not exist in the society of communism. All interhuman relations will then be equalitarian. They will also be "social" in the ego-transcending moral meaning which Marx attached to this word. The genuinely social, supra-egoistic relations will prevail within the boundaries of a united, nature-subordinating status group, the human species. The individuals in this universal group will have acquired a kind of personal separateness that could not have developed in the pre-individualized societies of the remote past, and in the not so remote Indian folk communities.

---

16. *Ibid.*, p. 91.

17. M.I. Finley has concluded that this kind of morally limited dominant caste consciousness did indeed prevail almost universally in the free citizen cultures of classical antiquity. His book on *Ancient Slavery and Modern Ideology* (Viking Press, 1980) includes a discussion of the moral attitudes which predominated in Greek and Roman civilization.

THE EXTERNAL ORIGIN OF INTERNAL ALIENATION

Marx had been concerned primarily with the elimination of forms of alienation and estrangement that had developed within modern industrial societies which had already demonstrated the ability of Man to dominate and subjugate the forces of external nature. Internal forms of disunity, alienation, and class-divided systems involving relations of domination and subordination between human beings in these societies had developed within a progressive capitalist civilization that had succeeded in establishing Man as the overlord of Nature. It was within this overlord civilization that the crisis of capitalism was developing.

In his later writings, Marx introduced some ideas concerning the nature and origin of modern forms of alienation and estrangement which did not appear in his earlier works. These additions did not contradict his earlier perspective, but were fused with it, adding to the complexities of his social theory. In the Introduction (September 1857) to *A Critique of Political Economy,* and also in the *Grundrisse* (1857-58) he had linked alienation with the emergence of an "isolated individual." He rejected the eighteenth century myth that this indivudal could have pre-existed society, but he had said that this myth described an objective condition of total atomization that could not have developed in the earlier civilizations of classical antiquity. The modern bourgeois form of alienation does not become ascendant until the form of individual proprietorship that had been the economic foundation of Roman political society and that consisted of property in agricultural land had been supplanted by a different kind of commercial and "alienable" property. This commercial property supported a class status based on the possession of "alienable" objects that could be transferred to another territory community. The historical process of individuation has not been completed until a stage is reached in which commercially alienable property becomes the predominant form. At this final stage, language becomes the only social tie that still links the individuals within a given national territory with one another. In the *Grundrisse* Marx was referring to the Roman political society when he wrote, regarding the individual in that society, that

> His *property,* i.e., his relation to the natural prerequisites of his production as *his own,* is mediated by his natural membership in a community. (The abstraction of a community whose members have nothing in common but language, etc., and barely even that, is plainly the product of much later historical circumstances). It is, for instance, evident that the individual is related to his language as *his own* only as a natural member of a human community. Language as the product of an individual is an absurdity. But so also is property (18).

Marx went on to say that personal individuality had emerged out of a pre-individualized condition because of economic exchanges taking place between individuals from different tribal groups, exchanges that did not

18. *Pre-Capitalist Economic Formations,* pp. 87-88.

involve property in land, but property in movable products created by human labor:

> . . . man is only individualized through the process of history. He originally appears as a *generic being,* a *tribal being,* a herd animal – though by no means as a "political animal" in the political sense. Exchange itself is a major agent of this individualization. It makes the herd animal superfluous and dissolves it. Once the situation is such, that man as an isolated person has relation only to himself, the means of establishing himself as an isolated individual have become what gives him his general communal character. In such a community the objective existence of the individual as a proprietor, say a landed proprietor, is presupposed, though he is a proprietor under certain conditions which chain him to the community, or rather constitute a link in his chain (19).

In *Capital* the theory of individuation through the exchange of alienable objections was stated more simply:

> The first step made by an object of utility toward acquiring exchange value is when it forms a non-use-value for its owner, and that happens when it forms a superfluous portion of some article required for his immediate wants. Objects in themselves are external to man, and consequently alienable by him (20).

Economic exchange transactions, even in the form of barter, cannot take place until individuals treat one another as "independent" individuals and as "private owners":

> In order that this alienation may be reciprocal, it is only necessary for men, by a tacit understanding, to treat each other as private owners of these alienable objects, and by implication as independent individuals (21).

The reciprocal exchange system, and the interdependency so established, develops apart from any other social tie. The community of origin of each of the private owners may be the same, or they may come from separate communities. Their specific identity is irrelevant to the exchange process. In capitalist society, reciprocal interdependence is both internal and external, intra-national and international:

---

19. *Ibid.,* p. 96. There is a good deal of obscurity in this passage, and indeed in almost all those anthropological writings of Marx which deal with the evolution of modern humanity and society out of earlier conditions. In the passage cited above, he says that persons become private owners of landed property only after intertribal object-alienating changes have taken place. The land-owning individual in pre-capitalist society is also "chained" to his political society and is not as free as he will one day become in the society of communism, where he will be a member of an owning community, and will no longer be bound by the chains of the past. Land itself must first be fully commercialized, bought and sold like other "alienable" objects, before the universal earth territory can be repossessed by a future social association of freely combining individuals.

20. Volume I, chapter 2, p. 87.

21. *Ibid.*

> . . . such a state of reciprocal independence has no existence in a primitive society based on property in common, whether such a society takes the form of a patriarchal family, an ancient Indian community, or a Peruvian Inca State. The exchange of commodities, therefore, first begins on the boundaries of communities, or with members of the latter. So soon, however, as products once become commodities in the external relations of a community, they also, by reaction, become so in its internal intercourse. The proportions in which they are exchangeable are at first quite a matter of chance. What makes them exchangeable is the mutual desire of their owners to alienate them. Meantime the need for foreign objects of utility gradually establishes itself (22).

When external exchange becomes internal, it appears that the relations between the transacting persons in the home community become atomic and "abstract." Persons become as aliens – as strangers – to one another, even though they inhabit the same political territory and speak the same language. Capitalist society is above all a trading society, where ". . . the behavior of men in the social process of production is purely atomic" (23).

THE PROBLEM OF WORKING CLASS DISUNITY

Marx had expected that the political unity of the working class in the modern industrial nations would develop as the workers learned to identify the social, political and economic causes of their class-shared misery and oppression. They could carry through a successful political revolution agsinst capitalism in their own country only if they achieved a class solidarity that would transcend all division of race, creed, and nationality. The working class association, in other words, would have to be a universal association. It would embody and defend the unity of the nation, but the power of the nation, in the time of the proletarian dictatorship, was essentially the power of universal society, unlimited by particular, restrictive group boundaries.

In his earlier writings on the condition of the modern working class (24) Marx had recognized that class political unity might be hard to achieve. He attributed the difficulty to individualistic competition within the class. Impoverished workers, forced off the land into cities, would at first compete with one another for a chance to work and to survive under the onerous conditions imposed by capitalist manufacturers. The political class unity that could overcome the power of capital had to be inter-regional and international as well as local. While the unity of the capitalist class was both national and international, the capitalists were to a large extent dependent on the power of the national State to maintain their hegemony. The workers had no such national resource. Marx, however, seems to have treated the mass grouping of the

22. *Ibid.,* p. 87-88.
23. *Ibid.,* p. 92.
24. This discussion must be read in connection with what has been said in chapter 5 of this book, "The Social Condition of the Modern Working Class."

workers into the large manufacturing industries as a source of class unity offsetting the localized national political class unity of the bourgeoisie. The direct social experience of cooperation in the work task would give workers a confidence in their collective power, and a realization that without their social labor, modern society could not maintain itself.

When he regarded the workers as a universal class, Marx minimized and almost entirely overlooked the social and psychological obstacles to working class unity which might impede the development of working class political consciousness. These difficulties became so evident, however, that Marx in his later years was compelled to take them into account. He saw that the working class was being divided and weakened by various intergroup antagonisms. He dealt with these problems in his writings on "the Irish Question." In the opinion of David Fernbach "Marx's writings on the relationship between England and Ireland mark a significant new departure for his political theory" (25). This statement is open to question. These writings demonstrate his capacity for making brilliantly acute sociological observations, but he did not revise his political theory to any significant extent. He was able to interpret these problems in a way that was consistent with his abstract historical dialectic. He implied that problems of disunity within the working class could be attributed, in the final analysis, to incomplete modernization.

During the 1860s and 70s he had become increasingly pessimistic about the English working class movement. In the first part of the nineteenth century, when the radical chartist movement was still influential, it had seemed that the English workers would lead the way. This was no longer so. There were internal difficulties that only external influences and events could overcome. Up until the end of 1869, Marx had hoped that the International would be able to persuade the English workers that their hostility to the Irish workers whom they regarded as competitors was an irrational reaction, contrary to their own class interest.

> I have become more and more convinced – and the only question is to drive this conviction home to the English working clsss – that it can never do anything decisive here in England until it separates its policy with regard to Ireland most definitely from the policy of the ruling classes. . . And this must be done, not as a matter of sympathy with Ireland, but as a demand made in the interests of the English proletariat. If not, the English people will remain tied to the leading strings of the ruling classes, because it will have to join with them in a common front against Ireland. Every one of the movements in England itself is crippled by the strife with the Irish, who form a very important section of the working class in England. . . (26).

25. *Karl Marx: Political Writings,* Volume III, edited and Introduced by David Fernbach, Introduction, p. 28, The Marx Library, Vintage Books, Random House, New York, 1974.
26. Letter to Kugelman, November 29, 1869.

By the following year, Marx began to doubt that efforts of the International to influence the English workers by direct argument could succeed. The situation was not hopeless, however. The English impasse could be broken by political action from the outside, i.e., by the victory of the Irish national emancipation movement. The prejudices of the English workers against the Irish workers in England were deeply ingrained. In a letter to Meyer and Vogt (April 9, 1870) he discussed the problem at some length, saying among other things that

> Every industrial and commercial centre in England now possesses a working class *divided* into two *hostile* camps, English proletarians and Irish proletarians. The ordinary English worker hates the Irish worker as a competitor who lowers his standard of life. In relation to the Irish worker he feels himself a member of the *ruling* nation and so turns himself into a tool of the aristocrats and capitalists of his country *against Ireland,* thus strengthening their domination *over himself.* He cherishes religious, social and national prejudices against the Irish worker. His attitude toward him is much the same as that of the "poor whites" to the "niggers" in the former slave states of the U.S.A. . . .

He had said much the same thing in a confidential communication (March 28, 1870) to the General Council of the First International:

> The average English worker hates the Irish worker as a competitor who lowers wages and the *standard of life.* He regards him somewhat like the poor whites of the Southern States of North America regard their black slaves (27).

Marx attributed the various irrational, class-divisive reactions which he had described to the persistence of outmoded feudalistic institutions and customs in England. The English workers were not yet sufficiently uprooted and detached from the general culture of their nation. The nation itself, as a political power in the world of nations, was likewise somewhat handicapped. England was governed by a class coalition, not by a single bourgeois class. The state power was not completely bourgoeis. The landlord interests and the clerical influence of the Anglican Church still had some national importance. Feudal power could not be overthrown either by the English workers or by the English ruling classes. However, the success of the Irish revolution against British landlord interests in Ireland might speed up the pace of progressive modernizing and revolutionizing developments in England. In a letter to Kugelman, April 6, 1868, Marx had said that

> . . . the *English* Established *Church in Ireland,* or what they call here the Irish Church – is the religious bulwark of English landlordism in Ireland, and at the same time the outpost of the

27. *Selected Works of Marx and Engels, op. cit.,* Volume II.

> Established Church in England itself. (I am speaking here of the Established Church as a *landowner.*) The overthrow of the Established Church in Ireland will mean its downfall in England and the two will be followed by the doom of landlordism – first in Ireland and then in England. I have, however, been convinced from the first that the social revolution must begin *seriously* from the bottom, that is, from landownership.

The Irish struggle for national emancipation was regarded by Marx as a struggle of the united people of Ireland against external landlord class oppression, which in this case was also oppression by an external nation. In these circumstances, national sentiments in Ireland would have a progressive effect. The united people of that country would become politically sovereign in their own land after defeating the English. In another letter to Kugelman (November 29, 1869) Marx wrote that

> . . . once the affairs are in the hands of the Irish people itself, once it is made its own legislator and ruler, once it becomes autonomous, the abolition of the landed aristocracy (to a large extent the *same persons* as the English landlords) will be infinitely easier than here [in England], because in Ireland it is not merely a simple economic question but at the same time a *national* question, since the landlords there are not, like those in England, the traditional dignitaries and representatives of the nation, but its mortally hated oppressors.

The abolition of English landlord rule in Ireland would have a favorable effect not only on the English workers, but also on ruling class policies in England:

> *The prime condition* of the emancipation here – the overthrow of the English landed oligarchy – remains impossible because its position cannot be stormed so long as it maintains its strongly entrenched outposts in Ireland. . . And not only does Englands's internal social development remain crippled by her recent relations with Ireland; her foreign policy, and particularly her policy with regard to Russia and the United States of America, suffers the same fate.

It appears that the persistence of a pre-modern culture is being considered as the primary cause of various particularistic group reactions and political responses that are dividing the working class into hostile segments in countries which have not completely thrown off the yoke of the past. This means that Marx's view of the psychopolitical situation in the fully modernized countries was not in line with the social realities. The pessimism he expressed about the English working class movement was in contrast to his optimism about the potentialities of the movement in the United States, where he thought that there was no problem comparable to the Irish-English antagonism. The "poor white" hostility to the black population was confined to the southern area of the United States, where the landlords and slave owners were the ruling economic class. In spite of their proletarian status, the southern white workers, even after the civil war, continued to regard the blacks as "slaves," i.e., as vastly inferior, as well as potential competitors. He implied that workers outside the south were unaffected by the agrarain caste situation. His optimism about the United States working class movement outside of the south was demonstrated in his decision to transfer the seat of the General Council of the First International to the United States. In a speech of September 8, 1872 before the Hague Congress of the First International he announced a decision for which he and his supporters had been responsible:

> . . . the Hague Congress has transferred the seat of the General Council to New York. Many people, even among our friends, seem to be surprised by that decision. Are they forgetting, then, that America is becoming a world chiefly of working people, that half a million persons – working people – emigrate to that continent every year, and that the International must take strong root in soil dominated by the working man? (28)

Marx said that the reaction of English workers was irrational, inasmuch as they could not see that their antagonism to the Irish workers in their midst was contrary to their own interest as members of an oppressed class. He also said that the English workers failed to understand that their national State could not represent their own interests. I interpret Marx's statements regarding English working class disunity as follows: The most essential psychological pre-condition for the development of a unifying political clsss consciousness among the worker was their ability to perceive their own political government as a totally alien, oppressive power. The English workers were being kept down by their tendency to be impressed by the formal rituals and trappings of the State, i.e., by the appearance that masked the reality. Upper class persons in political positions were invested, by their office, with a dignity and a status that Marx associated with feudal hierarchy and also with ecclesiatical ceremonialism. These trappings were symbols of national power and prestige. The feudalistic component of nationalism was apparently responsible for the tendency of the English worker to feel himself "a member of the *ruling* nation," a nation dominant over other national groups. He had been impressed by national symbols, signifying national greatness, participating in a sense of common national identity and dominant national status. This identification diminished his class consciousness, his awareness of belonging to a socially inferior, powerless stratum within the nation. Deluded by the national symbols, the worker was unable to act against the State and against the national ruling classes that occupied State office.

The situation in the United States was very different. Conditions of life

28. This address is reprinted in Fernbach, *op. cit.*

in the New World promoted attitudes of social equality and democratic informality in social relations. Hierarchical status distinctions, sustained by traditionalized customs, conventions and manners in England, did not survive in the freer American environment. There was no marked sense of social distance dividing the free, enfranchised citizens from persons in positions of national governing power. The workers, unimpressed by the trappings of State, were able to regard the political representatives of the nation in a disenchanted light. The farther the culture of a nation is removed from feudalism, the less it is encumbered by a landed aristocracy and by traditions developed in pre-capitalist society, the more favorable the pyschological conditions for popular working class revolt. Economic conditions in the United States would inevitably deteriorate, because that country was involved in the general crisis of capitalism, along with other capitalist nations. When conditions became intolerable the people of the United States would not be inclined to support a government which was obviously incapable of taking steps to reverse the process of deterioration and of acting in the interests of the people.

Marx had included France in the category of the most advanced, fully modernized, post-feudal nations. In his writings on the political situation in France, he seemed to think that the majority of the people in that country had been liberated by the"gigantic broom" of the French Revolution, which had swept away ". . . all manner of medieval rubbish, seignorial rights, local privileges, municipal and guild monopolies and provincial constitutions." The French working classes, and also the French middle classes, upheld the enlightened, progressive culture of modernity. Politically, the Paris Commune government had been ". . . the true representative of all the healthy elements in French society, and therefore the truly national government." It was ". . . at the same time, as a working men's government, as the bold champion of labour, emphatically international" (29).

MARX AS A SOCIOLOGICAL THEORIST

Marx is recognized as having been, to a conspicuous degree, a sociological thinker. The sociological elements are linked with his philosophical materialism, and with his philosophy of Man in relation to Nature. Henri Lefebvre, in *The Sociology of Marx,* hesitates to class him as a sociologist, because he is so much else besides:

> Are we to view Marx as a sociologist? Such an interpretation would be just as inadequate as the others. . . *Marx is not a sociologist, but there is a sociology in Marx.* . . Marxian thought is simply too broad to fit into the narrow (and ever narrower) cate-

29. "The Civil War in France," *Selected Works of Marx and Engels, op. cit.,* Volume II.

gories of latter-day philosophy, political economy, history and sociology. Nor is it correct to refer to it as "interdisciplinary," a conception recently advanced (not without risk of confusion) – to remedy the disadvantages of a latter-day division of labor in the social sciences (30).

There are three chief aspects of Marx's social and historical theory which justify the contention that a sociology is contained within his synthesis. 1) He focuses on group processes that cannot be reduced to processes going on at the "individual" psychological level; 2) he conceives of the "social life process of society" and the major events of economic and political history, as "naturally determined," expressing inclinations, motives, forms of will and of energy that arise naturally under certain conditions. All manifestations of human culture, and all forms of political and ideological consciousness, are included in this naturalistic perspective; 3) social processes, systems, and structures are treated as primary, culture is secondary. Only those aspects of culture that reinforce naturally arising primary tendencies and social processes are historically significant, and have an appreciable effect on the course of history.

Marx's theory of social change was to a considerable extent an historical sociology. Lenin, writing in 1894, believed that Marx's interpretation of history fell entirely within the category of social science. Marx, he said, had been the only social theorist ". . . to elevate sociology to the level of a science." He had been able to apply, more consistently than any other sociologist, the basic method of sociology, which was to focus on group actions and group relations taking place within organic systems of production relations and conditions. As a theorist Marx had ". . . evolved the concept of *the economic formation of society*" and had been able to make important generalizations about the process of systematic historical change, ruling out as irrelevant those aspects of individual action that did not lend themselves to systematization. Actions of "living individuals" had been ". . . generalized and reduced to the action of individuals differing from each other in the role they played in the system of production relations. . . " He was able to formulate laws of social change by cutting below the confusions, complexities, and variabilities, separating what was important from what was not, discerning the uniformities and the recurrent phenomena of social life, which he then used as the basis for scientific prediction. He ". . . applied to social science that objective, general criterion of repetition which the subjectivists declared could not be applied to sociology" (31).

Bottomore and Rubel, as contemporary sociologists, approach Marx from the perspective of a post-Marxist conception of a universal sociology that is not tied to any particular philosophical system. They believe that important aspects of Marx's theory have been incorporated into modern sociology:

---

30. *Op. cit.,* chapter 1, pp. 21-23.
31. From an article on "The Economic Content of Narodism," reprinted in *V.I. Lenin: Selected Works,* Volume XI, International Publishers, New York, 1943.

> The outcome of the prolonged "debate with Marx" has become clearer with the maturity of sociology itself. A great deal of Marx's work is a permanent acquisition of sociological thought; the definition of the field of study, the analysis of the economic structure and its relations with other parts of the social structure, the theory of social clssses, and the theory of ideology. But this incorporation of Marx's ideas entails the disappearance of a "Marxist" sociology. Modern sociology is not the sociology of Marx, any more than it is the sociology of Durkhiem, or Weber, or Hobhouse. It is a science which has advanced some way toward freeing itself from the various philosophical systems in which it originated, and with which its founders were still embroiled (32).

Certainly the sociologist of today has access to new perspectives and insights, and to more adequate anthropological information, than was available to Marx. But there has not yet developed, during the century following the death of Marx, a unified sociological theory which has incorporated one universally accepted general view, one preferred kind of methodology, and one philosophy of science. There have been certain predominant trends, however, which are academically entrenched and shared by a good many sociologists who may differ from one another considerably in their beliefs and in their views about the viability of capitalism. Marx's sociology contains a good deal that is compatible with these now predominant trends. He seems to have anticipated certain modern developments. The influence of Hegelian philosophy has made itself felt in the United States in ways that by-passed the theories of Marx. Partly on this account, Marx's social theory includes forms of determinism as well as a special moral focus that converged to some extent with the approach of American sociologists.

While not denying that Marx was more than a sociologist, C. Wright MIlls classed him as one of the thinkers who belong to "the classic tradition" of sociological thought. He went so far as to say that "Within the classic tradition of sociology, he provides us with the most basic single framework for political and cultural reflection. Marx was not the sole source of this framework, and he did not complete a system that now stands closed and finished." Mills noted a resemblance between Marx's early writings and the psycho-sociology that rose to prominence in the United States more than a century after these early manuscripts were written:

> Just as Adam Smith's *Theory of the Moral Sentiments* reminds us of George Herbert Mead's "social behaviorism," so Marx's 1844 manuscripts and other earlier works remind us of the most contemporary social psychology (33).

---

32. *Karl Marx: Selected Writings in Sociology and Social Philosophy, op. cit.,* Introduction, p. 48.
33. *The Marxists,* chapter 2, pp. 34 and 35, Dell Publishing Co., 1962.

The early writings to which Mills refers include an abstract discussion of the "individual" in relation to "society." which has no direct connection with class struggle theory. Marx sets up a dichotomy which appears also in most standard American textbooks in introductory sociology. Some kind of radical tension is implied between the two units. Marx's social theory, insofar as it is dialectical, anticipates a condition of unity that will be realized in the future, and includes a program for eliminating this tension. Non-Marxist sociologists are not as firmly rooted in the future. But they refer to a normal, ideal-type of individual who is continually being "socialized," who is always open to peer-group influences and pressures, passively receptive and morally dependent, accepting whatever norms and moral attitudes develop in the course of social interactivity in the various groups and social situations which form the immediate social environment. Sociology in the United States has been much concerned, also, with conflict between the various groups that are included within the nation. The nation is characteristically regarded as the primary social unit. The social system, social order and social structure to which sociologists refer is nationally enclosed. As a social systems theorist, Marx was more inclusive. He stressed those aspects of the economy and social structure that were common to all capitalist societies. But in spite of this broader scope, he looked forward to a future universal society that would be in a psychological and a moral sense, the equivalent of a single nationally enclosed community. His treatment of problems of the moral life and of moral culture stayed within the limits of the "in-group" method which Ralph Linton defined as the only acceptable sociological approach:

> *It must be stressed that the significant units are societies,* not individuals. . . not only is the society the unit. . . but *ethical systems function only in terms of in-groups.* . . Most groups at the tribal level limit the application of ethics to dealings with tribe members, with animals or objects which are intimately associated with the tribe, such as totems. . . Ethical behavior is prescribed toward and expected from all members of such an in-group. Toward anything outside it, people included, ethical rules in most cases simply do not apply. . . (34).

Marx was well aware of the existence of "rules of society." When he referred to capitalist society in some of his later political writings, he also noted the contradiction between external and internal moral conduct which appeared at the national political level. This duality was regarded as one manifestation of a more general duplicity and hypocrisy that characterized bourgeois life. The contradiction between internal and external moral conduct would of course disappear in universal society. The proletarians, representing that society, were already beyond the duality. In Marx's social theory,

---

34. Essay on "Universal Ethical Principles: An Anthropological View," published in *Moral Principles of Action,* compendium edited by Ruth Nanda Anshen, Harper and Bros., 1952.

this kind of transcendence would be accompanied by the elimination of need for "rules of society" relating to moral conduct.

Specific, transitory customs and forms of custom-morality appeared and disappeared as part of the natural life process of society that continued on through all phases and transformations of social life. This is what seems indicated in Marx's scattered writings. Customs developed in the material *base* of society, in the socio-economic system, but could also appear in the political superstructure in societies that had developed beyond the primitive condition. Some customs were incorporated into legal statutes in ancient and modern societies. In developing his concept of a future post-capitalist world order, Marx came to expect that the power of custom would persist in two forms. In *Capital* and in other writings on economy, he focusses on the universal economic customs that would be much the same in all countries, since all countries would have the same kind of producing system. This universal custom morality would not take the form of "rules of society." Socially developed standards of living, consumer norms, operating with compelling effect, would play a large part in determining the kinds and amounts of material goods that would have to be produced in the socialized economy by "socially necessary" labor. Localized customs, institutions and traditions might also persist, but not in a way that would interfere with the development of the universal economic norms.

A.J. Shumpeter, in an essay on "Marx the Sociologist" regards Marx's interpretation of history as a sociology of history, and as an outstanding achievement in this field: ". . . the so-called Economic Interpretation of History is doubtless one of the greatest individual achievements of sociology to this day." He notes that this sociology was called by Marx as well as by others a "materialist" interpretation, but he thinks that the adjective, in this context, is "entirely meaningless."

> Marx's philosophy is no more materialistic than is Hegel's and his theory of history is not more materialistic than is any other attempt to account for the historic process by means at the command of empirical science. It should be clear that this is logically compatible with any metaphysical or religious belief – exactly as any physical picture of the world would be (35).

It is true that human beings in both the Hegelian and Marxist systems belong to the world of nature and that they could not exist as persons apart from the biological base. As social theorists, however, they both make use of abstractions to construct self-system theories which overcome "contradictions" in a way that is metaphysical and suprascientific. They are both concerned with the moral condition and situation of a universal "individual"

---

35. Reprinted in *Karl Marx,* a collection of essays on Marx, edited by T.B. Bottomore, for the "Makers of Modern Social Science" series of Prentice Hall, Inc., 1975.

who is involved in three primary relationships: 1) a relation to self; 2) a relation to others in the same self-status group; 3) a relation to a total society that includes all these persons. In both systems, the individual is subjectively insulated from moral concern about persons who are outside of his particular community of "identity." In both systems, it is also important that the individual not belong to an *excluded* group.

Hegel had described the "essential nature of consciousness" as the awareness of a socially acceptable personal identity which could be secured only by persons who had acquired "private property" which other people would acknowledge as inviolable: ". . . it is *mine,* which all others acknowledge and keep themselves away from. But just in my being acknowledged lies rather my equality, my identity, with every one – the opposite of exclusion" (36). In Marx's system, private property cannot function as the social and material condition for being "acknowledged," i.e., recognized by others as equal in status with every one else, a recognition that is "the opposite of exclusion." But in both systems, the individuals participate in a "universal" relation which implicitly excludes those who are outside of certain closed group limits. In the case of Marx, there are to be no such external groups, but this does not alter the psychological situation.

Marx's interpretation of history took account of important observable facts of human social behavior, behavior always occurring within some kind of historically developed social system. These observations provided the basis for an abstract, supra-empirical sociology of the future. There were three primary, interrelated metaphysical premises which made this construction possible. The first was his belief that the economic behavior of individuals toward one another in capitalist society was purely "atomic," and that this indicated a solipsistic condition in which the individual was related "only to himself." He was thereby abstracting individuals from external psychological and moral influences arising on the group level. He was regarding classes in modern society as groups united by common egoistic interests but not also by class-particular forms of culture and convention. He then proceeds to carry out a second abstractive operation by treating a generalized sociality as the antithesis of atomism. A third step is required in order to bring about a condition in which membership in society will become, for the individual self, a means to a complete kind of security, a security which will not contradict freedom but will be its essential condition. He detaches the atomic persons from their specific localities and cultures and also from their location in *present* time, relocating them in a time beyond. They will then again be open, psychologically, to group influences arising on the inter-subjective level. This restoration of sociality will re-unite persons universally, in an indivisible union.

The workers presently engaged in the struggle against capital, and who are not yet in the time beyond, are totally in the present, in a psychological sense. They have escaped from the past more completely than have their class

36. *The Phenomenology of Mind,* Part B, section C, pp. 448-449.

antagonists. They have no need to refer back to the past for moral reinforcement, comparing favorably in this respect with their predecessors, the bourgeois revolutionaries who had once fought heroically against the feudal system. In the opening section of his 1853 address on "The Eighteenth Brumaire of Louis Bonaparte," Marx said that these earlier revolutionaries had not fully broken their bondage to tradition and to the past: "The tradition of all the dead generations weighs like a nightmare on the brain of the living." Even though they had seemed to be engaged ". . . in revolutionizing themselves and things, in creating something that never yet existed," they were prone, in the period of revolutionary crisis, to ". . . anxiously conjure up the spirits of the past to their service and borrow from them names, battle cries and costumes in order to present the new scene of world history in this time-honoured disguise and this borrowed language." Marx conceded that this conjuring of the past had aided the revolutionaries in their struggle, but it was always a form of self-deception. The participants had to ". . . conceal from themselves the bourgeois limitations of the content of their struggles and keep their enthusiasm on the high plane of the great historical tragedy" (37). The proletarian revolutionaries, on the other hand, are *actually* revolutionizing themselves and things. They are not initiating a project that will fall short of the aims of revolutionary action.

Marx's philosophy of the future includes a transcendental sociology. He is basing the societal unity of the future on "naturally arising" social sentiments which have, in the past, often served to unify individuals into particular, limited identity groups – class, ethnic, national, and religious, and also to divide persons in such groups from others outside the group boundaries. The boundaries are being eliminated from the future social universe by a process of transcendental abstraction. When the ideally atomic persons freely combine in a universal, cooperative producing association there will be association, but not dissociation, inclusion but not exclusion. There will be no problem of intergroup relations, either within a nation, or between separate nations. No one would be perceived or treated by others as an outsider or as a stranger, singled out as different, or as a target for moral hostility. All persons will be equal in status, belonging to the same universal identity group. What is equally fundamental to Marx's liberationism is the elimination of punitive, morally declassing kinds of ostracism and expulsion, directed against individuals who had originally been located within and not outside of the equal status membership and identity group. As noted in previous chapters, Marx conceived that in the future society, the single individual would be helped by others to overcome his own tendencies to self-rejection and self-exclusion. What this meant is that he was also, but without explicitly saying so, eliminating dangers that this same person might face from other people, from personal and also from group reactions originating outside of himself, which he did not share. The individual of the future will be dependent on others in a way which is totally non-threatening and which provides him with permanent security. He is being

37. *Selected Works of Marx and Engels,* Volume I, pp. 398-399.

delivered not only from dangers arising from within, but also from social dangers arising from without, and from which he might not, as a single self, be able to cope. The reassuring aspects of human, social "nature" are being preserved. Other, more fearsome aspects of sociality, are being dialectically negated in the passage to the future.

Afterword

Marx's optimistic outlook on the future is expressed in terms of a logical dialectical synthesis which tells us a good deal about the real life problems of the historical present. Through that same synthesis, he is also able to skip over, by a process of abstraction and of exclusion, other aspects of that same situation. Misunderstandings about the nature of his predictions arise when the relation of his theory of socialist revolution to his overall dialectical synthesis is not taken sufficiently into account. This relation, discussed at greater length in the forgoing text, is being summarized briefly here.

Hegel had said, in his first, introductory lecture to a series he gave on the history of philosophy: "Philosophy is that which is most antagonistic to abstraction and it leads back to the concrete" (1). In the concrete situation, the philosopher is able, as a political citizen, to perceive his own political and economic society as one in which the meaning of history and the relation of humanity to a cosmic process outside of history, has been made manifest. The concrete is a reconciled condition which eliminates the need for the mind of philosophy to take refuge ". . . in a clear space of thought to create for itself a kingdom of thought in opposition to the world of actuality" (2).

In Marx's philosophy, the present capitalist society is abstract. Concreteness as a condition of society and of mind in society will be reached through a transformation which begins in the first stage of political-economic socialism. This is a process of world unification, resulting in the formation of a new social order, a world order. In the absolute, concrete phase of history, the phase of ultimate classless communism, all peoples of the earth will have been included within a supra-national world economy and a universal society, in a condition beyond war and beyond preparations for war.

The decisive break with capitalism occurs when the State-supported institution of private property in land and in the humanly created, historically developed means of production has been replaced by social property. Social property, however, is not exclusively national. Boundary lines dividing the earth territory into smaller and larger socio-economic and political units lose their moral significance in socialist economic time.

---

1. *Hegel on Art, Religion, Philosophy,* Harper and Row Torchbook edition, p. 232.
2. *Op. cit.,* pp. 257-258.

Marx's confidence that capitalism would inevitably be superseded by socialism was sustained in part by his ability to exclude problems of modern nationalism from the socialist frame of reference. Henri Lefbvre underlines this aspect of Marx's social theory: "In his writings, Marx frequently discussed specific national situations, but he treated them at the level of strategy rather than general theory. . . Nationality, he seemed to think, is already a thing of the past" (3).

This general theory is also, in a broad sense, strategic. It is directly and logically related to Marx's views about the conditions that would have to exist in capitalist civil society before the working class socialist movement could displace the power of the national state in the advanced capitalist centers. Socialism in any one of these nations could not be established to begin with unless each national working class had been socially and morally linked with the world-historical working class movement. Nationalism as it existed in conjunction with economic capitalism, and as the political support of capitalism, would indeed have become a thing of the past. The divisive, negative, limiting aspects of nationalism would have been left behind. Yet the working class struggle and mission represented an ideal unity of social spirit, will and purpose that Marx identified with the positive, integrative, and heroic aspects of nationalism. This socially unifying universal spirit would be carried forward into the future world society.

As Marx saw it, the economically advanced nations, those best equipped with the indispensable powers of technology and of science, were also those best prepared to proceed with socialist economic development, and to surpass the level of material wealth achieved in the national capitalist economies. This did not mean, however, that these favorably situated socialist nations could move ahead into the stage of classless communism, irrespective of the political conditions existing outside of their boundaries. Furthermore, from the standpoint of Marx's dialectical logic, the capitalist nations might be the last, not the first, to achieve the initial breakthrough into economic socialism.

Marx made it clear, in *Capital,* that the relative economic backwardness of some countries would not prevent them from crossing over into the socialist era. No matter how they started out, they would have immediate access to universal science and to methods of production which could not be monopolized by capitalist nations. When they abolished private property in land and in capital, they would also be re-establishing the vital organic ties of humanity to nature that had been treated as non-existent in capitalist society. The less developed socialist economies would catch up, sooner or later, to the more advanced socialist level. Sooner or later, all capitalist or pre-capitalist societies would have made the change to socialism.

Through the transcendental unification of universal society with nature, the territorial limits of the whole earth were being set aside. Economic and

3. *The Sociology of Marx,* chapter 5, p. 172, Pantheon Books, 1968.

social expansion could proceed indefinitely. The divisions between spatially separate communities do not seem to affect the operations of the world economy.

The concrete universal society would be able to maintain its moral integrity and unity without the need for abstract moral ideas. As a philosopher of history, Marx had said that ideas about what *ought to be* could play no significant part in expediting the advance toward the future. He had also said, in an address delivered in English at a London meeting in 1864, that it was the task of the politically conscious socialist vanguard to ". . . vindicate the simple laws of moral and justice, which ought to govern the relations of private individuals, as rules paramount to the intercourse of nations." This state of affairs could prevail in practice only at a time beyond the class struggle, after the distinction between international and internal, national-community relations had been obliterated, and all of humanity had been united into an indivisible world community.

Bibliography

WORKS BY MARX

I have cited both the chapter and page number of the longer works by Marx, but have omitted the page reference when citing his articles and his correspondence. All citations from his letters, unless otherwise specified in the footnotes, are taken from *The Selected Correspondence of Marx and Engels,* Progress Publishers, Moscow, second edition, 1965.

I have used various translations of Marx, preferring some to others. The footnotes indicate which translations are being used. Most citations from *Capital* (Volumes I, II, and III) are taken from the current International Publishers edition (1967), Moore and Aveling translation. I have referred also to the Eden and Cedar Paul translation of Volume I, International Publishers, New York, 1929.

In addition to *Capital* and *The Selected Correspondence,* I have used the following translations of Marx's writings:

Collected Works of Marx and Engels, Volumes I, III and IV, International Publishers, New York. 1975. These include his doctoral dissertation (1841), and the book-length work, *The Holy Family* (1844-45), as well as many shorter writings.

The Selected Works of Marx and Engels, Volumes I and II, Progress Publishers, Moscow, 1969.

The translation of Marx's high school essays, by Robert B. Fulton, in *Original Marxism – Estranged Offsrping:* A Study of Points of Contact and of Conflict between Original Marxism and Christianity, Christopher Publishing House, 1960.

Writings of the Young Marx on Philosophy and Society, edited and translated by Lloyd D. Easton and Kurt H. Guddat, Doubleday and Co., New York, 1967.

Critique of Hegel's Philosophy of Right, translated by Annette Jolin and Josoph O'Malley, edited with an Introduction and Notes by Josoph O'Malley, Cambridge University Press, 1970.

Karl Marx: On Freedom of the Press and Censorship, The Karl Marx Library, edited and translated by Saul K Padover, McGraw Hill Book Co., 1974.

Theses on Feuerbach, translated by Nathan Rotenstreich, in *Basic Problems of Marx's Philosophy,* Bobbs-Merrill Co., 1965.

The German Ideology, complete edition, Progress Publishers, Moscow, 1964.

Marx and Engels on Religion, Selected Essays, Moscow, 1957; Shocken Books edition, New York, 1964.

Karl Marx: Selected Writings in Sociology and Social Philosophy, translated by T.B. Bottomore, edited with Introduction and Notes by T.B. Bottomore and Maximilien Rubel, 1956, McGraw Hill Book Co., 1964.

The Poverty of Philosophy, International Publishers, New York, 1963.

The Communist Manifesto (Samuel Moore translation), Monthly Review Press, 1968.

The American Journalism of Marx and Engels, A selection from the New York Daily Tribune, edited by Henry M. Christman, New American Library, 1968.

Pre-Capitalist Economic Formations, selections from the *Grundrisse,* translated by Jack Cohen, with Introduction by Eric H. Hobsbawm, International Publishers, New York, 1964.

The Grundrisse (complete text), translated with Foreword by Martin Nicolaus, The Marx Library, Vintage Books, Random House, New York, 1973.

Critique of Political Economy, edited with Introduction by Maurice Dobb, International Publishers, New York, 1970.

Karl Marx: Political Writings, Volumes I and III, edited and Introduction by David Fernbach, The Marx Library, Vintage Books, Random House, New York, 1973 and 1975.

Theories of Surplus Value, Part I, Progress Publishers, Moscow, 1963 and 1975.

Critique of the Gotha Programme, with appendices by Marx, Engels, and Lenin. International Publishers, NY, 1938.

OTHER WORKS CITED IN THIS BOOK

Adams, James Luther: *On Being Human Religiously,* Selected essays on Religion and Society, Beacon Press, Boston, 1976.

Aristotle: *Politics,* Book I, Jowett translation.

Aristotle: *The Works of Aristotle,* Volume V, Clarendon Press, Oxford University, reprinted 1972.

Aristotle: *Aristotle's Metaphysics,* edited and translated by John Warrington, J.M. Dent and Sons, London; E.P. Dutton and Co., New York, 1956.

Avineri, Shlomo: *The Social and Political Thought of Karl Marx,* Cambridge University Press, 1968.

Berland, Oscar: "Radical Chains: The Marxian Concept of Proletarian Mission," *Studies on the Left,* September-October 1966, *6:*27-81.

Bottomore, T.B.: "Karl Marx: Sociologist or Marxist," *Science and Society,* Winter 1966, *30:*11-21, and also in essays by Bottomore, *Sociology and Social Criticism,* Morrow, New York, 1974.

Davis, Horace B.: *Nationalism and Socialism:* Marxist and Labor Theories of Nationalism to 1917. Monthly Review Press, 1967.

Deane, Herbert A.: *The Political and Social Ideas of St. Augustine,* Columbia University Press, 1963.

Fernbach, David: Introduction to *Marx's Political Writings,* Volume III, The Marx Library, Vintage Books, Random House, New York, 1975.

Feuerbach, Ludwig: *The Essence of Christianity,* translated by Geroge Eliot, Harper and Row, 1957.

Feuerbach, Ludwig: *Principles of the Philosophy of the Future,* translated, with Introduction by Manfred E. Vogel, Bobbs-Merrill Co., 1966.

Findley, J.N.: *Hegel: A Re-Examination,* Collier Books, New York, 1962.

Finley, M.I.: *Ancient Slavery and Modern Ideology,* Viking Press, 1980.

Fromm, Erich: *Marx's Concept of Man,* Frederick Ungar, New York, 1961.

Girardi, Giulio: *Marxism and Christianity,* MacMillan Co., 1968.
Harris, Catherine R.: "Religion and the Socialist Movement in the United States," in symposium on *Marxism and Christianity,* Humanities Press, 1968.
Hegel: *The Phenomenology of Mind,* translated by J.B. Baillie, Harper and Row, 1957.
Hegel: *Hegel's Philosophy of Right* [Law], translated by T.M. Knox, Clarendon Press, Oxford, 1952.
Hegel: *Hegel on Art, Religion, and Philosophy* (introductory lectures to the history of art, religion and philosophy), edited with Introduction by J. Glenn Gray, Harper and Row, 1970.
Hegel: *Hegel's Logic,* Part I of the Encyclopedia of the Philosophical Sciences, translated by William Wallace, Clarendon Press, Oxford, 1975.
Hegel: *Hegel's Philosophy of Nature,* Part II of the Encyclopedia of the Philosophical Sciences, translated by A.V. Miller, Clarendon Press, Oxford, 1970.
Hegel: *Hegel's Philosophy of Mind,* Part III of the Encyclopedia of the Philosophical Sciences, translated by William Wallace and A.V. Miller, Clarendon Press, Oxford, 1971.
Hegel: *The Philosophy of History,* translated by J. Sibree, Dover Publications, Inc., 1956.
Hobbes, Thomas: *De Cive* or *The Citizen,* edited with an Introduction by Sterling P. Lamprecht, Appleton-Century-Crofts, New York, 1949.
Hobbes, Thomas: *Leviathan,* or The Matter, Forme and Power of a *Commonwealth,* Ecclesiastical and Civil, edited by Michael Oakeshott, Introduction by Richard S. Peters, Collier Books, New York, 1962.
James, William: *The Varieties of Religious Experience,* The Gifford Lectures on Natural Religion delivered at Edinburgh in 1901 and 1902, Random House, New York.
Kant, Immanuel: *Groundwork of the Metaphysics of Morals,* translated by H.J. Paton, Harper and Row, 1964.
Kant Immanuel: *Critique of Judgement,* translated by H.H. Bernard, Hafner Publishing Co., New York and London, 1968.
Kant, Immanuel: *Kant's Political Writings,* translated by H.B. Nisbet, edited with Introduction and Notes by Hans Reiss, Cambridge University Press, 1971.
Kant, Immanuel: *Critique of Practical Reason,* translated with an Introduction by Lewis White Beck, Bobbs-Merrill Co., 1956.
Kant, Immanuel: *Religion Within the Limits of Reason Alone,* translated with an Introduction and Notes by Theodore M. Greene and Hoyt H. Hudson, Harper and Row, 1960.
Kant, Immanuel: *The Metaphysical Principles of Virtue,* Part II of *The Metaphysics of Morals,* translated by James Ellington, with an Introduction by Warner Wick, Bobbs-Merrill Co., 1964.
Lefebvre, Henri: *The Sociology of Marx,* translated from the French by Norbert Guterman, Pantheon Books, Random House, New York, 1968.
Linton, Ralph: Essay on "Universal Ethical Principles: An Anthropological View," in *Moral Principles of Action,* edited by Ruth Nanda Anshen, Harper and Bros., 1952.
Lowith, Karl: *Meaning in History,* University of Chicago, 1949.
Lucretius: *The Nature of the Universe,* translated with an Introduction by R.E. Latham, Penguin Classics, 1951.
McLellan, David: *Marx Before Marxism,* Harper and Row, 1970.
McMurtry, John: *The Structure of Marx's World-View,* Princeton University Press, 1978.
Miliband, Ralph: *Marxism and Politics,* Oxford University Press, 1977.

Mills, C. Wright: *The Marxists,* Dell Publishing Co., 1962.

Morris, William: *News from Nowhere,* in Centenary Edition of Morris's Stories in prose, stories in verse, shorter poems, lectures and essays, edited by G.D.H. Cole for the Nonesuch Press, London, 1948; Random House, New York.

Pascal R.: Editorial notes to incomplete edition of *The German Ideology,* International Publishers, New York, 1947.

Rotenstreich, Nathan: *The Recurring Pattern:* Studies in Anti-Judaism in Modern Thought, Horizon Press, New York, 1964.

Rotenstreich, Nathan: *Basic Problems in Marx's Philosophy,* Bobbs-Merrill Co., 1965.

Schumpeter, J.A.: Essay on "Marx the Sociologist," reprinted in *Karl Marx,* a collection of essays on Marx, edited by T.B. Bottomore, Prentice Hall, 1975.

Stephen, Leslie: *Hobbes,* University of Michigan Press, reprint 1961.

Stirner, Max: *The Ego and his Own,* translated by S.T. Byington, 1907, selected and Introduced by John Carroll, Harper and Row, 1971.

Strauss, Leo: *The Political Philosophy of Hobbes,* (1936), University of Chicago, 1952.

Tawney, R.H.: *Religion and the Rise of Capitalism,* Harcourt, Brace and World, Mentor Book reprint 1963.

Tucker, Robert C.: *Philosophy and Myth in Karl Marx,* Cambridge University Press, 1961.

Van Leeuwen, Arend Th.: *Critique of Heaven,* Gifford lectures, 1970, on Marx's philosophy in relation to Christianity, Scribner's, 1972.

Analytical Index

(Unless otherwise specified, reference is to the views of Marx)

* Includes index of names.